FORGOTTEN
EAGLE

OTHER WORKS BY THESE AUTHORS

BRYAN B. STERLING

The Will Rogers Scrapbook
The Best of Will Rogers
Will Rogers, USA (play historian, editor)
Will Rogers, USA (CBS Television)
Bully! (Theodore Roosevelt documentary)
Eleanor (Eleanor Roosevelt documentary)
Appomattox (play)

BRYAN B. STERLING AND FRANCES N. STERLING

A Will Rogers Treasury (1983 Western Heritage Award)
Will Rogers in Hollywood
Will Rogers' World
Will Rogers & Wiley Post: Death at Barrow
Will Rogers Speaks
Will Rogers, A Photo Biography

FORGOTTEN
EAGLE

WILEY POST, AMERICA'S

HEROIC AVIATION

PIONEER

BRYAN B. STERLING & FRANCES N. STERLING

CARROLL & GRAF PUBLISHERS
NEW YORK

FORGOTTEN EAGLE: WILEY POST, AMERICA'S HEROIC AVIATION PIONEER

Carroll & Graf Publishers
An Imprint of Avalon Publishing Group Inc.
161 William St., 16th Floor
New York, NY 10038

First Carroll & Graf edition 2001

Library of Congress Cataloging-in-Publication Data is available.

ISBN: 0-7867-0894-8

Printed in the United States of America
Distributed by Publishers Group West

John Ford owned a yacht, *The Araner,* which he had docked at Santa Monica, just down the road from Will Rogers' ranch. Late in July 1935, he gave a party and invited Will Rogers and Wiley Post. He had just completed directing his third film starring Will, and kept trying to persuade his star that rather than go to Alaska, they should make another film together—perhaps in Hawaii. He was heading there right after their current film was "in the can."

John Ford tried to persuade Will to come along on the yacht. Will was tempted, then he made a decision: "You keep your duck and go on the water, I'll take my eagle and fly."*

This is the story of that "eagle," now almost forgotten.

John Ford by Andrew Sinclair, © 1979, Dial Press, p. 62

CONTENTS

If you will observe, it doesn't take
A man of giant mould to make
A giant shadow on the wall
And he who in our daily sight
Seems but a figure mean and small,
Outlined in Fame's illusive light,
May stalk, a silhouette sublime,
Across the canvass of his time.

—John Townsend Trowbridge,
Author's Night 1827–1916

PROLOGUE

O N AUGUST 26, 1930, an elite group of aviators started on a flight from Los Angeles in an air race that was to be nonstop and end in Chicago. The winner of this, the grand derby of air competitions, would not only win a purse of $7,500, but would be considered by his peers as having a rightful place among the foremost pilots in America. Almost all the entrants were not only well known to each other, but their exploits were so frequently reported in the newspapers that their names, if not their faces, were familiar to the public. They were the current heroes of the country's youth and admired by those who viewed the air as the next, if not the final, frontier.

There was betting and guessing on just who would be the winner, and the relatively few radios then in use would intermittently report on the progress of the race. The newest boy on the block in this group of pilots, at least as far as the public was aware, was some little, chunky fellow named . . . what was it again? Oh yes . . . something Post.

Almost at the outset, this fellow Post seemed to be out of the race when his only compass got stuck and refused to work. He lost forty precious minutes in the clouds retracing his route and finally had to fly strictly by eyeball and map. Still, he won the race by eleven seconds, obtaining a place in the record books and sudden national recognition.

Thus began the brief, extraordinary public career of Wiley Hardeman Post, but not his life. That had started 31 years earlier in so tiny a place, that it is not even marked on the official state map of his native Texas—a community called Corinth, in Van Zandt County—some fifty-five miles as the crow flies, east of Dallas.

CHAPTER I

TEXAS BORN AND BRED

ARTHUR HOUSTON POST, one of Wiley Post's older brothers, went home again. He had often heard it said that going home again is one thing you cannot do, but he went anyway. He knew that his remaining days could now be counted easily and that is why he undertook the sentimental journey. He traveled down the old county road to where, as a boy, more than three-quarters of a century earlier he had helped his father pick cotton and where once stood the small house in which he and four of his siblings had been born. He found no trace of the building, or the trees that had once grown beside it. All that was left was an old, worn-out sandy field, full of weeds.

Arthur Houston Post would die on October 17, 1978, and be buried near the graves of his parents and his grandparents, in the old cemetery next to the Corinth Baptist Church. It still holds in its sacred ground a goodly number of headstones, some of which have weathered so badly that names and dates can no longer be read. Other old burial sites, by farmers too poor to pay for carved tombstones, are simply indicated by fieldstones without names or dates scratched into them, while still other graves appear to have been marked solely by specially planted cedar trees.

Among the still readable headstones are those identifying the graves of the Reverend Thomas McAdams Post and his wife, Ceney, nee Howell. T. M., as the Reverend was usually called, was the son of a farmer and had been born in Shelby County, Alabama on July 11, 1843. He was raised on his family's farm and attended public schools. When T. M. was thirteen, his father moved the family to Louisiana and, as the *Herald*, the newspaper published in Canton, the seat of Van Zandt County, Texas, reported in a recollection on January 30, 1925, T. M. was "converted to the Christian Religion." It was not until 1874 that Thomas McAdams Post entered the ministry as a Baptist and became a circuit preacher. His wife, Ceney, was born on December 9, 1839, in El Dorado, Arkansas. They married on March 20, 1862, in Spearsville, Louisiana, and had eight offspring, seven of whom lived to maturity. One of their sons, William Francis "Frank" Post, was born in Spearsville on June 11, 1869. He, too, is buried at Corinth. Records show that in 1879 the budding Post family had first moved to Bowie County, Texas, around 1879, and six years later arrived at Corinth Community where the Reverend T. M. Post became pastor of the Corinth Missionary Baptist Church. The Van Zandt County tax roll of 1890 indicates that one Post, T. M., Abstract No. 418, owned 83 acres of land, valued at $415. It was in Corinth, then, that Wiley Post's future paternal grandparents had finally settled, and there that T. M.'s children grew up, although young William Francis would not stay there too long.

"Granddaddy was," Arthur Houston Post recalls in his autobiography, "the unmistakable head, not only of his family, but of the whole tribe. He was preacher, family doctor, and lawyer, but if he ever went to any school, I don't remember ever hearing of it."

Reverend T. M. Post was a spiritual man who had established a number of churches in the area, but he was by no means a single-minded religious zealot. He had a wide range of interests and a large personal library—a most unusual possession in that time and place. One of his hobbies was genealogy. He corresponded prolifically to trace his family's ancestors. When Reverend Post died, he willed his entire correspondence to his grandson Arthur. That is how young

Arthur first learned of his grandfather's short service in the Confederate Army. The most interesting discovery of an ancestor, however, was a certain John Post, "my great, great, great grandfather who had come from Amsterdam to New York and Virginia Colony in 1750 and remained in the East long enough to serve in two wars and get married."[1]

Through his correspondence, the Reverend Post had discovered that this John Post had fought in the French and Indian War, where he was wounded in the "Battle of Braddock's Defeat," and "was under Washington in the Revolution." It was said of John Post that he had died "with lead in his body." He had married one Aly Bell from Antrim, Ireland, who as a young girl had run away from a troublesome stepmother and had stowed away on a ship bound for the American Colonies. Discovered a few days out at sea, she was brought to New York and there indentured to a family to work three years to pay for her passage. Aly had worked just one year for that family when she met John Post and fell in love. The two of them worked off another year of her indenture, and were then allowed to go free and get married. "They were the starters of a southern branch of the Post family in the United States," Arthur Post believed.

The industrious Reverend Post had also discovered that long before John Post's adventure in America, earlier members of the Post family—Protestants—had fled to Holland to escape religious persecution in England. In addition, some even earlier records of the Post family name revealed that about 1066 several kin by that name had gone from Normandy to England with William the Conqueror. How the Posts got to Normandy in the first place, has so far escaped detection, though the claim has always been that the Post family's background was also Scottish.

Reverend Post was a dedicated shepherd of his flocks, but the passing years were not too kind to him and his wife. The congregations he served were small and poor, and many families drifted off to other communes. No records show why T. M., having so many descendants, slipped into poverty. What is available, however, is a column from the *Canton Herald* of Friday, February 6, 1925:

---

[1] *Around the World in 80 Years* by Arthur H. Post; Charles the Printer, 1974, p. 10

T. M. Post and Wife Express Appreciation

On last Thursday the 29th, an old preacher and his almost blind wife had a pleasant surprise. Near 12 o'clock two cars drove up to our place. We soon found out, they were from Sand Springs church. They were Brethren Selke, Anderson, Lancaster and Will Chaacy (sic) and their wives, and Sister Daniels and Sister Stringer. After they warmed, wife mentioned something about dinner. They quickly said they would attend to that and went to their cars and brought out and put on the table a dinner good enough for a king, consisting of baked meats and fried chicken, pies and cakes of all kinds.

After we all enjoyed the feast together, they cleared off the table and went to the cars and brought in two buckets of lard, one bucket of cane syrup, 15 jars of fruit jellies and preserves, four pounds of soda and a few other things. They also gave wife a nice large bed sheet and towel, and to this they added $6.00 in money.

I can't tell how much we appreciate it. Not so much from a financial standpoint, but the evidence of their love, sympathy, and respect for an old, worn out preacher whom they had known for 37 years and when I had served them as Pastor 20 years and been with them in 27 and 28 protracted meetings. We two old feeble ones now, not able to do anything to earn a living, know how to appreciate kindness. Now, late in he evening of life, I feel sure God's promises will hold good when He said: "I will never leave thee nor forsake thee."

Such happenings make me very anxious, if I was physically able, to visit all my dear friends over the county, but I have no idea this can ever be and can only pray God's blessings on all of them.

Reverend Thomas McAdams Post lived another six and a half years. He died in Edgewood, Texas, September 22, 1931. His wife, Ceney, died February 12, 1936 in Grand Saline, Texas.

Another set of tombstones in the Corinth cemetery marks the graves of T. R. Laine and his wife Pollie. T. R. was born on December 18, 1842, and died February 25, 1882. Pollie was born April 12,

1847 and outlived her husband by almost 18 years, dying on December 14, 1899. They had four children, the eldest, a daughter, May, who was born June 24, 1873. The next child was a son they named David J., born on January 13, 1877. On December 4, 1890, May Laine married Reverend T. M. Post's son William Francis, with whom she would have seven children, and her brother David Laine would marry one Katie Quindlen and father four children, the eldest being a daughter, Edna Mae, born on September 12, 1909.

When William Francis Post and May Laine were first married, they purchased a brushy, unimproved, sandy patch of 50 acres at Corinth. Even by the standards of the time, this was a very small farm, but it was probably all the young couple could afford. On this acreage, William built a very simple boxed house with just two rooms and a front porch. Arthur Post described it as being covered with home-made boards, and having a mud chimney with hearth and fireplace made of undressed rocks. Above the fireplace was a mantel that held an old striking clock, a kerosene lamp, assorted medicine bottles, and a box of matches, among sundry other items. A rickety fence enclosed the kitchen garden. In front of the house were some oak and hickory trees; a swing hung from one of them. Beyond that, at a clearing, stood some black walnut trees that in the fall provided plenty of nuts to crack and eat.

It was here that the couple's first five children, James, Arthur, Joe, Wiley, and Mary, were born. Here the family lived until 1901 except for part of one year.

That year was 1898, and while very little changed in Corinth, Texas, the world outside continued its march into what is called history, or sometimes even progress. President McKinley was in the White House and Theodore Roosevelt was his Assistant Secretary of the Navy. There was diplomatic trouble with Spain. On February 12, the U.S. battleship *Maine* on a so-called friendly visit to Cuba, lay at anchor in Havana Harbor. An unexplained explosion aboard the battleship killed some 250 men and officers, precipitating the 112-day Spanish-American War. Commodore Dewey, commanding the U.S. Pacific fleet, steamed on orders toward the Spain-held Philippine Islands. Entering Manila Bay, he faced Spanish warships. He issued the now famous order to his flagship's captain: "You may fire when you are ready, Gridley!" The result of the ensuing American bombardment was the destruction of all ten ships in the Spanish squadron. By the Treaty of Paris that December, Spain lost Cuba to independence, and ceded the Philippines to the United States for a $20-million price. It was later revealed that in this brief war more American soldiers died from consuming contaminated meat than from battle wounds.

That same year, in Geneva, Switzerland, Italian anarchist Luigi Luccheni stabbed to death while visiting Austrian Empress Elizabeth, a committed advocate of women's rights and equality. In France, novelist Emile Zola published his famous *J'accuse,* which finally forced his government to grant Army Captain Alfred Dreyfus a new trial. Though it would be established beyond the slightest doubt that the captain, accused of espionage for Germany, was the innocent victim of an anti-Semitic plot hatched by two fellow officers, Dreyfus would not be released from the penal colony on Devil's Island for another eight years. Polish-born Marja Sklodowska Curie and her French husband Pierre meanwhile isolated radium, the first radio-active element, and in Germany, an opium derivative, introduced under its own name, heroin, was openly sold as a cough suppressant by a reputable, almost fifty-year-old pharmaceutical company known as Friedrich Bayer & Co.

In the United States a new breakfast cereal, corn flakes, appeared on grocers' shelves for the first time. Trying to break into a market directed solely toward wheat breakfast cereals, they made an unfortunate debut, as they quickly turned rancid. Also in 1898, the United States manufactured almost 1,000 automobiles, and a Greater New York City, with the recent inclusion of Brooklyn, Queens, the Bronx, and Staten Island, could now claim almost three-and-a-half million inhabitants. According to sheet music sales, one of that year's most popular songs was English-American composer James Thornton's "When You Were Sweet Sixteen."

The world's total population in 1898 was estimated at 1.6 billion, most of which lived in poverty.

There is no doubt that few, if any, of those news-making accounts ever reached the American public, but William Francis Post's family had a subscription to a Dallas newspaper, and parents and children both kept fairly well abreast of world events—at least those that the newspaper thought important enough to warrant space. Arthur

Houston Post, the family chronicler, claimed that the newspaper coming to their home made him and his siblings aware that a vastly different world lay out there, and that Corinth was merely a speck in that world. Between what the older boys heard their parents discuss after reading the newspapers, and what they had learned in geography at school, they decided on a project of their own. It would show that their little farm was part of a great globe, called earth.

Alongside one edge of their section of land ran a single lane road, rarely used by carts or riders. Collecting pieces of planks and using axle grease for paint, the older boys now put up signs indicating the distances to nearby villages and towns. Not having any concept of mileage, they would ask their parents and then put down their answers. If the father said that he thought they were seventy miles from Dallas, the children would dutifully paint an arrow in the approximate direction and print "Dallas—70 miles."

The previous summer, the one of 1897, the children's horizon had been even further expanded. Feeling that the farm was in good enough shape to be left to nature, William and May had loaded a covered wagon with all sorts of camping equipment and supplies and taken the children on a two-week camping trip to Bowie County, near Texarkana, to visit relatives. There was fishing and hunting along the way and it left the family—as Arthur would later record— "so satisfied, it left us unsatisfied." Another, much longer trip was planned for the entire summer of 1898.

William Post rented his farm out to a sharecropper for the season and thus relieved of any care directed his full attention to the upcoming vacation. Another couple, Oscar and Alma Darnell, asked to join the family on this journey, which was to extend northward into the Indian Territory that nine years later would become the state of Oklahoma. The men intended to work some along the way, to earn money to cover expenses. The two families, each with children, would camp out, cook over open fires and try to live off whatever provisions they had brought along. In addition, there would be plenty of fine fishing, and unrestricted hunting for small game, deer, and wild turkeys. There was talk of selling some homemade glue along the way to raise further funds. Slowly the plans were transformed into reality, and on the set date, two covered wagons left Corinth.

With no highways or major roads or even wagon trails in the area in those days, the two wagons had to make their own tracks as they headed in a northerly direction. Bridges were also scarce, so small rivers had to be crossed at fords, and when the wagoneers confronted the wide Red River into the Indian Territory, they had to seek out a ferry.

Records available show that the two families were most congenial, that even the two sets of children had no disagreements or fights. In fact, the only reported unpleasantness on the entire trip was the children's constant encounters with chiggers while playing in the tall grass. There was a short-lived scare when, while camping along a little stream and fishing, an Indian hunting party came by. No words were exchanged. The two families breathed with relief when the Indians simply rode on without incident.

The weeks went by and eventually the Darnell family decided that it was time to get back home. At the banks of the Red River, the two families parted, with the Post group deciding to return at a more leisurely pace. May was pregnant again, but there was really no reason to rush back to Corinth.

Back in Texas, near Denison, the Posts found a most friendly farm family by the name of Hardeman. Old man Hardeman pitched up a tent for the Post family to camp on his property, and William worked for him into the fall. The rapport that developed between the two families was astounding. The Hardemans had a modern farm, with more conveniences than the Posts had seen, or could have afforded. They showered the children with presents and made the family feel as if this were their home, too. The Posts stayed there until the harvest was in and then prepared to leave. Of course William was paid for his work, and well paid, at that. However, since William was an honorable man there is no doubt that he worked hard and was well worth his pay. Arthur remembered the stay with the Hardeman family:

> The wages my Daddy made there no doubt came in quite handy.
> I was too young to think about that item. But one thing I am
> pleased to remember was the mutual good feeling which obvi-
> ously came to exist between that family and my parents. We

never saw them before, nor since, but they were long remembered by us for their kindness.[2]

The Post family traveled back to their own little farm in Corinth, where on November 22, 1898 May was delivered of her fourth boy who was named Wiley Hardeman Post. His middle name was carefully chosen to honor the family that had shown so much kindness that year. The reason or origin for the name 'Wiley' has never been explained. In Corinth, Wiley was simply one of the 'Post boys,' and nobody bothered about where a name might come from, or what it meant.

In Corinth, too, the children first learned that they were expected to help with the work around the farm, and there was plenty of it. Even the youngest was not too young to learn what a hoe was for, when crabgrass and weeds threatened to take over in the corn and cotton fields, in the potato and melon patches, or in the kitchen garden and orchards. However, all was not drudgery. The children still found time to play; especially in the long summer days after all the chores had been done. One favorite pastime was to take an axe and cut down some smooth hickory bushes to make bows and arrows, or to carve whistles or shrill flutes. There was swimming and fishing, and all the usual games that children play, or make up. The Post children had to invent their own variations, as they had no neighbor children to play or fight with.

Arthur Post recalled that not only were there no neighbor children, but also there were no neighbors for quite some distance, except for his grandfather's farm, which abutted his father's. This grandfather, the Reverend T. M. Post, had, as Arthur described it:

> . . . what it took in those days to make a farm a complete and interesting home. He had horses, mules, cows, goats, hogs, chickens, geese, guineas, and a few ducks. He had a wagon, a buggy, and a few saddles. What delighted me most was their orchard. It was on the right kind of land and they had different varieties of peaches to ripen all through the season, different varieties of

---

[2]*Around the World in 80 Years* by Arthur H. Post; Charles the Printer, 1974, p. 19

apples, red and yellow plums, and some pears. In the woods nearby were wild plums, berries, grapes, and persimmons. Also in the fall, hickory nuts and walnuts. And it was no trouble to go out in the woods and kill squirrels or quail for some wild meat.[3]

While the absence of close neighbors had numerous advantages, it failed to teach the children the social contact with families who were not their relatives. The children felt completely at a loss on those occasions when they visited someone's home in Grand Saline. They found those one-family houses and miniature back yards too restricting, the streets too narrow, and even the limited traffic of a village too heavy. Their conversations were stilted or non-existent, their vocabularies meager, and their interests defined mostly by their own day-to-day existence. The children could not wait to get out of those confining Sunday-go-to-meeting clothes they had been forced into, and return to their borderless farm in Corinth.

The family had a little longhaired red dog, named Fido by some-one, though nobody could remember who that had been. His age and breed, too, were never-solved mysteries. The children loved him and though he did not run and play with them, he followed them everywhere as if he had been hired especially to guard them. One very hot summer day, as the children were coming back from the swimming hole in the nearby creek, Fido was bringing up the rear, as if he were herding a gaggle of geese. It was the usual ritual—the children in front, the dog trotting behind them watching for strag-glers. Whether it was the excessive heat of the day, his old age, or whether he was just too fat, nobody ever knew, but Fido suddenly dropped without a whimper to the ground and died right in the middle of the sandy path. None of the kids walking ahead realized it until they had reached home. Never again in the whole, wide world, so the children wept, would there be another dog like Fido.

The children also had a little red wagon. It was bought as a play-thing, but it was often used for all sorts of practical purposes around the farm. When kindling and stove wood had to be hauled from T. M. Post's house some three hundred yards away, the little wagon

---

[3] *Around the World in 80 Years* by Arthur H. Post, Charles the Printer, 1974, p. 9

was the ideal conveyance. When it was time to go out and gather nuts, the little red wagon always brought the harvest home. When Wiley was still a baby, he had many a ride in it, with one or two of his older brothers pulling it. Once, towing little Joe in the wagon, brothers James and Arthur began to run with him down a smooth incline and the wagon turned over, spilling the boy. He was unhurt but scared and cried all the way home, getting his face dirty in the process. There May held an investigation. She let the older boys off with a reprimand and put them on probation. When Arthur Post mentioned this episode, he failed to explain just what such "probation" entailed.

On his small farm, William Francis Post planted cotton. Cotton requires a lot of work, before and after planting, and even during the long growing season. Still, it was the crop primarily chosen by area farmers, since it had a ready market. It also had a special attraction for insects, whatever the vagaries of the weather, be it late frost or no rain or too much of it. The lush foliage, the mass of blossoms all with nectaries, the long fruiting period, all act as special hosts to five hundred known varieties of destructive parasites, ranging from the notorious boll weevil to aphids. Besides, as cotton is not ready to pick until very late in the season, a farmer has to wait a long time before he can realize any cash. It becomes important, therefore, that he also raise all that he will need until his crop can be sold. He must have pigs, sheep or goats and poultry for meat, a cow or two for milk, cheese, and butter, vegetables and fruits fresh for eating in season and plenty for canning, and others, like potatoes, cabbages, and carrots for storing against the winter months. "Store-boughten" items had to be kept to a minimum and were usually obtained on credit. There were some necessities that just had to be paid for, like shoes and caps, kerosene, flour, sugar, matches, and material to sew clothing, but very few luxuries. How much a family could do without having to spend any money depended on the abilities and ingenuity of the woman of the house. Her natural talents and learned crafts could make the difference between a small farmer surviving or losing his land. If by chance or expert management a family might have some cash left over from the sale of last year's crop, it had to be held in reserve for those never-ending mortgage payments.

While raising cotton was hard work, harvesting it was the worst of all. Picking cotton was slow stoop work, hard on a sweating body bent for hours, dragging an ever heavier bag, all that while trying to breathe the dust-laden air. As was often said, "All it takes to be a good cotton picker is a strong back and a weak mind." An experienced adult cotton picker could gather about one 490-pound bale in a week. Only the hundreds of pounds they brought to the scale would translate into pay for the pickers, not the time they had spent picking it.

William Francis Post took his little troop of young sons out into the field and had them help pick his cotton. He made them an offer. If a boy had picked 100 pounds at the end of a day, he would be given a dime; if he had picked only 85 pounds, he received a nickel; a bag weighing less than 85 pounds did not count. Years later Arthur Post reminisced about those salary arrangements:

> To this day I can truthfully say that I was and still am well
> pleased with the wages, working conditions, and fringe benefits
> from those days of cotton picking. In my judgment, it was very
> valuable discipline and training. I am glad it was that way.[4]

When all the cotton had been picked, the older Post children looked forward to their annual late fall trip into Grand Saline, taking the last bales of cotton into town for sale. Those trips of less than ten miles from their farm, took place twice, or at most three times a year. (Canton, the county seat, was actually closer to Corinth, but visits there were usually just trips to pay the annual taxes. Canton made big news at the time of the Civil War. When the South seceded from the Union, the peace-loving citizens of Canton wanted to be no party to the threatening war and declared that if a state could secede from the Union, so could a county secede from a state. And that it did! Ever after, the county has been jokingly referred to as the free State of Van Zandt.) Grand Saline was the railhead to which the cotton bales were delivered for sale, so it was simpler to establish your credit there and do your selling of cotton and the buying of provisions at the same time and place.

---

[4] *Around the World in 80 Years* by Arthur H. Post, Charles the Printer, 1974, p. 11

Going to Grand Saline was always exciting. You could see things there you would never even hear of in Corinth. There was always a new shop or a bar, some new-fangled machine to supposedly make life easier. However, the most fun waited at the General Merchandise store. While their father would order the few essential provisions and settle the accumulated charges against his account, and while their mother would pick out the gingham for dresses and blouses, or flannel for their winter underwear and nightgowns, the boys were allowed to spend some of those few hard-earned nickels and dimes. Though it was the boys' money, there were restrictions on just what could and could not be bought. One thing every Post boy was permitted to buy once he was deemed old enough, was a pocketknife and maybe, just maybe, some slingshot rubber. To spend a cent for marbles was allowed, but it was more fun and challenging to win them in fair play, or get them by trading.

Though farming cotton was grueling work, the hardest worker in the Post family was always May Laine Post, the mother of the rapidly expanding family. Not only was she responsible for raising a passel of kids, being mother, doctor, nurse, and teacher, she was also expected to keep the house in order, cook the meals, can and preserve fruits and vegetables, knit socks and sweaters, do the laundry, tend the smaller animals, raise a kitchen garden, sew and mend clothes, and attend to all those other wifely duties then specifically considered to be "a woman's work."

May rarely complained. She was used to hard work. It was the story of her life. May was eight years old when her father, T. R. Laine, a poor shoemaker, died. His young widow, Pollie, was at a loss what to do next. She had little May and David, and two younger children to support. There was no way that she could earn a living in the minute Community of Corinth and raise her children. The family elders came up with what looked like a convenient solution. It was decided that it would be best if the now widowed Pollie take May and the other children and go to live with her partially paralyzed uncle, Tom Quindlen. Tom could barely get around on what passed for crutches and could not live alone. Pollie Laine and her oldest child, May—a most industrious child—so it was hoped, would take care of all the household and farm chores for the invalid man, in return for food and a home. Seemingly solving two problems, it looked like a most beneficial solution for both parties, except for two major tribulations. First, there was too much work for one woman to run a house, operate a farm, and take care of an invalid man, so that a disproportionate share of the work fell upon eight-year-old May. Second, because of his constant pain and despondency over his disability, Uncle Tom Quindlen proved a most unreasonably domineering tyrant. In his autobiography, Arthur Post reported what his mother must have told him about that period in her life:

> So, hard work and lots of it, was my mother's lot, in the field, in the house, at the wash-place down by the creek where tubs full of very dirty clothes had to be washed, around the barn and cowpen (sic)—on crutches the uncle could only boss, and he took his bossing seriously[5]

In 1890, at age 17, May Laine finally broke away from this drudgery, when she married William Francis Post. No one appeared impolite, or uncouth enough, to ever ask whether this was a match made in heaven, or simply a longed-for escape. If May thought that from now on her life would be one of greater ease, she was unfortunately mistaken. In the next ten years, she would give birth to James, Arthur, Joe, Wiley, and Mary Post, in addition to looking after a husband and helping him keep up a cotton farm. Nor would it get any easier. In the following few years, two more boys, Byron and Gordon, would complete the family with six sons and one daughter.

Life in Corinth was almost idyllic except for one major health problem: mosquitoes and the attendant malaria. Bouts of malaria attacks every summer were as regular as the sunrise. Nobody had mosquito screens on doors or windows and May filled the house with smoke at bedtime to keep mosquitoes at bay, but the mosquitoes usually won out. Even forcing the children to swallow the contents of dozens of bottles of Grove's Tasteless Chill Tonic did little to prevent or lessen their malaria's fever shakes. Of course, adults were not immune to the disease. Rather than meekly submit to what others

---

[5]*Around the World in 80 Years* by Arthur H. Post, Charles the Printer, 1974, p. 6

seemed to accept as inevitable, William and May Post finally decided to do something about it.

In addition to the daily Dallas newspaper, William Francis Post had a subscription to the *Dallas Semi-Weekly Farm News*, which had a wide circulation in the state. He was especially interested in information about health conditions in western Texas, where the climate was dry and a supposedly prevailing breeze kept infecting mosquitoes away. There were also reports that the area was being developed for farming and that land was currently cheap. It was settled. The family would move west.

The Posts made the decision to sell the small house and farm and prepare for the move in 1901. A nearby farmer, who had the money, was prepared to buy the fifty acres just as soon as the family was actually ready to leave. However, until that point was reached, farm life continued as usual for the Post family. There was still the harvest to be brought in and the last of the cotton to be picked. Then, against the advice of all his relatives and friends, William Francis Post took the train to Abilene to look for a new, appropriate farm. He had no trouble finding land on the high ground, where it was dry and windy, and where no plow had ever disturbed the soil. As Arthur remembered:

"It was eight or nine miles north of Abilene, just over in Jones County."[6]

William purchased a quarter section, 160 acres where only cattle and buffalo had grazed, made the down payment, and arranged for a mortgage on the balance. When William 'bought' a farm, as he would do many times in the future, it was always a joint ownership with various mortgage holders; he never did have enough money to buy a piece of land outright and pay for it. That is, not until years later when he finally settled permanently south of Oklahoma City, just north of Maysville, Oklahoma. With all his land deals of buying farms and then selling them over the years, William rarely made any profit on his transactions. He felt satisfied when he could get back just what equity he had so far on those properties or, at most, make a small profit.

Having bought the quarter section near Abilene, William hurried

---

[6]*Around the World in 80 Years* by Arthur H. Post, Charles the Printer, 1974, p. 22

back to Corinth to tell the family and prepare them for the move. There would, however, be a slight delay. Not only would there be one more harvest, but in August, a new member would join the family. She was named Mary. After four sons, the Post family now had its first, and as it turned out, only daughter. She was special and would always be so treated.

The children felt excited about leaving their familiar little place in Corinth and moving to the prairie of western Texas, and yet, it was like leaving a piece of their youth behind. They dreaded that their familiar lives would be changed forever, as indeed they were.

It was late in the year and winter was in the air when William chartered a Texas & Pacific Railway boxcar, stowed all the furniture, household goods, farm equipment, and animals into it and rode along in the caboose to be on hand when the animals needed water and feeding. The trip to Abilene took three days. Once William had the new farm operational, the rest of the family followed by train from Grand Saline. Provided with a big box of fried chicken, baked sweet potatoes, biscuits and butter, as well as tea cakes, May and the children went on their first train ride ever. Wiley Hardeman Post was just three years old when this migration from mortgaged farm to mortgaged farm began.

Starting out on what had been unspoiled prairie entailed far more work than had been expected. A new house had to be built. A well had to be dug. The property had to be fenced with barbed wire to keep the animals from straying. Partitions, shelters, and feeding cribs were needed for the livestock. Chickens had to have a coop to protect them at night: otherwise the prowling coyotes would have had a feast. Of all the new chores, the worst and most time consuming was to get the land ready for seeding. Arthur remembered it well:

> Most of it was covered by mesquite trees which had to be grubbed out, cut off deep enough in the ground to be out of the way of plows. Daddy hired two healthy young men to help us for two or three months. We boys had a nice long job burning brush.
>
> The bodies of the trees were dragged out of the way of cultivating the land to where they could be later cut up and sold for fire wood. Between the jobs of plowing, planting and culti-

vating a crop, Daddy cut, hauled and sold many cords of wood to Simmons College in Abilene (now Hardin-Simmons University). He sold the wood for $1 a cord. Dr. Cooper was president of the college at that time. Daddy could cut and load a cord of wood in a day and haul it to town the next day, so with wagon and team his take-home pay was fifty cents a day.[7]

William got a crop going. There was cotton, milo maize, and sorghum—for hay, not for molasses. The farm began to take shape. New families moved into the adjoining sections. They shared hardships and became good neighbors. The Post farm, having had a head start, was the shining example of what hard work could achieve, and the Posts began to receive offers to buy it. Added to this were letters from the relatives back in Corinth, suggesting that the family move back, that they were missed and that a certain piece of wooded property they had always liked was available for an appealing price. When a Mr. L. F. Bones from Illinois, a farmer and teacher, made an offer for the little equity in the new Abilene farm plus a small gain, William and May gave it serious consideration. Homesickness finally took over, and they accepted. William wrote to his relatives that he would buy the wooded property and he asked one of them to put a deposit of $10.00 on it. Once again, the family was going to pull up its roots and move. All was the same as it had been the first time. In haste they harvested the current crop, packed the furniture and loaded all the livestock. They also had another passenger. On July 12, 1903, Louis Byron Post, child number six, had joined the family.

The Posts made the trip back to Corinth, again by train. The Post family members were quickly becoming seasoned travelers. The joy of their initial, overwhelming welcome by family and friends in Corinth soon gave way to a nagging comparison of their new property and the wide-open spaces of the Abilene farm with its dry, mosquito-free air and the original reasons for leaving Corinth. The wooded lot on which William had put the deposit proved to be unsuitable for either a house or a farm and promised years of hard work and more

---

[7]*Around the World in 80 Years* by Arthur H. Post, Charles the Printer, 1974, pp. 23–25

effort than profit. Troubling thoughts began to develop about the obvious folly of the return to what once had seemed 'God's Country.' The family, needing a place to stay, rented a small house for a year, put in a crop on the land they had leased and decided to forfeit their $10 deposit on the woodland. It was a lot of money to lose in those days, and even in his autobiography, Arthur makes explicit mention of the loss: "The whole $10.00 was forfeited."

Young Wiley had meanwhile begun his schooling, intermittently and haphazardly, as there were not always schools near the farms William would buy. Even when Wiley attended one of the available schools, its terms were short, its quality of tuition irregular. School terms usually did not start until after every farmer's harvest was in, as all hands were needed to pick cotton, and then only if a teacher, a schoolhouse or room, and other students were available. Some years and in some areas they were not, and no classes were held.

A fellow student's appraisal of his classmate Wiley Post has survived. He remembers that in their early school days Wiley was often reprimanded for his dawdling progress and his hostile indifference to every one of the three R's. The classmate recalls, too, that Wiley seemed interested mostly in avoiding both farm and school work and that he was "a lively, talkative and mischievous boy." Growing up, Wiley Hardeman Post would change on all three counts.

CHAPTER II

THE PERFECT PUPIL

WILLIAM FRANCIS POST was about to buy yet another farm. Realizing that the return to Corinth had been a mistake, he once more journeyed to the Abilene area to look for farmland. The new oil fields in the Indian Territory north of the Texas border beckoned, promising riches not only to successful wildcatters, but also full employment to anyone who was willing to work hard. Farming was always a risky business. Dry farming depended solely on nature as one's essential partner to be successful. The presence or absence of rain at the right time made raising any crop an annual risky venture. Even if all the elements were in the farmer's favor, farming on a small scale did not promise riches. If a harvest was bountiful for one farmer, it was equally ample for his neighbors and a glutted market would cause prices to drop; if there had been too little rain, or too much, or any other weather catastrophe and a crop failed, prices rose—but then farmers had little, or nothing to sell. Working in the oil fields was hard work too, but at least the money at the end of a month was guaranteed. Men who had worked on the land all their lives left it for an opportunity to bring in a gusher of their own, or at least with the expectation of being on the payroll of someone that had. The temptation to quit farming was appealing to many and land became available and sold cheaper.

William Francis Post and his wife May knew nothing about oil, all they knew was farming and they would not be tempted to leave it. They would continue to work the land. This time William bought half a section, 320 acres. The land was again in the Abilene area, in Jones County, located about three miles northeast of their former farm, where Elm Creek formed the eastern border of his land.

It was now the fall of 1903. The harvest from the leased field in Corinth was in and had been sold. William and May Post and their immediate family were getting ready to move west—again. It had been decided that this time—instead of leasing a railway boxcar as before—the family would travel with their own wagon. Whether it was a choice of convenience or a necessity dictated by a shortage of cash has not been recorded. Whatever the reason, it did present many problems.

The Posts decided that it would be far wiser for their caravan to skirt Dallas and Fort Worth rather than plod through the streets of a major town. This plan would make the trip longer by days but far safer for man and beast. The uncertainties of fall weather ahead, however, did counsel against unnecessary delays. There were no highways in those days, just dirt roads and those that were graded were only in the vicinities of Dallas and Fort Worth. Rain with its mud, or worse, snow, with its blinding flakes and its drifts masking the terrain could spell additional obstacles, if not disaster. The family was fortunate; it encountered not a single rain shower on the entire trip. The distance between Corinth and the Abilene farm had been estimated at around 250 miles. If all went well, it would take some three weeks to reach their destination. That meant that they would have to travel an average of about a dozen miles a day. They would sleep out of doors, and could only travel during the fall-shortened daylight hours.

The oldest boys, Jim and Arthur—Joe was seven and Wiley was not yet four (b. Nov. 1898) years old—thought the trip a great adventure, reminiscent of those earlier pioneers they had heard about. Arthur Post, all of ten years old then, remembered the trek:

One little hitch which helped to keep our 250 mile western covered wagon trip from being a continuous picnic was that we were
taking along our three sober old milk cows (not to have milk
along the way, they were all dry). If you never tried it, normally
you can't lead a cow behind a wagon with a rope around her
neck. That is the reason, the original reason, for the existence of
cowboys. To drive cows, keep them moving along in the right
direction. And, incidentally, cows are normally slow travelers,
which, in our situation was due to make our trip easier for
Jimmy and me for we were due to playfully walk along with a
little switch behind the cows behind the wagon and keep the
cows coming along.[1]

The two young cowboys walked the entire trip, the whole 250
miles.

To pass the dragging hours of their tedious walk behind three slow
cows, Jim and Arthur thought up diversions. One that came readily
to mind was using their slingshots to hit various upright objects they
passed. Unfortunately, not too many tempting targets presented
themselves. Every so often, there would be fence posts, or better yet,
a metal sign hanging on barbed wire, which rewarded a direct hit
with a resounding clash. Then, too, there were those mailboxes. The
first rural mail delivery routes in the United States had only been
established in 1901, but such general mail deliveries had not yet
reached the wide-open prairie. Only the vicinities of major metro-
politan areas enjoyed such a service. Elsewhere, it was still the old
established practice to pick up one's mail at the post office in the
nearest towns, which sometimes lay many miles away. So Jim and
Arthur had never before seen those freestanding mailboxes they came
upon along the roadsides on the outskirts of Dallas. Those boxes on
a single support made first-rate targets for their slingshots and gave
off a beautiful sound when the boys hit the mark. Intrigued, the two
boys examined the boxes closer and found that they all had a little
flag attached to their side, which could be raised upright, or lowered
to lay flush. The idea was, of course, for the delivering mailman to

---

[1] *Around the World in 80 Years* by Arthur H. Post, Charles the Printer, 1974, p. 29

raise the flag when he placed mail inside the box, so that it could be decided from a distant farmhouse whether a trip to the roadside box was warranted; if the flag was down and not visible, there was no mail and no trip was necessary. Jim and Arthur Post knew nothing about this signaling system, but as part of passing some time, they developed a new game. Deciding it more patriotic for the flag to be up, they would raise the flag on every mailbox they passed—at least until they tired of it. In their journey past Dallas and Fort Worth, Jim and Arthur must have caused quite a number of disappointed trips to those newfangled mailboxes and elicited some meticulously selected language.

Because Jim and Arthur were following the covered wagon on foot, they wore shoes. The rest of the children—Joe, Wiley, Mary, and Byron—all barefoot, rode in the well of the wagon, sitting on the spring and cotton mattress on which they also slept. Every once in a while, when the team pulling the wagon needed a rest, May would let Joe and Wiley get out of the wagon and run around or pick the wildflowers growing along the trail. At other times, the smaller children would have to help search for firewood. As it became colder quickly in the afternoon and evening hours, they needed firewood for warmth and cooking. The children were told to gather any piece of wood they could find along the way. Even Jim and Arthur had to watch for firewood, which became increasingly hard to find since trees grew more sparsely on the prairie. Arthur recorded that on evenings when not enough wood had been found in the daytime, he and his older brother would slip onto someone's pasture at dusk and collect dried cow chips for a fire.

Mostly, though, the little children were confined to the mattress. It was an uninteresting ride for them, slow and bumpy. The so-called roads were not graded; some were rutted, and potholed, by earlier steel-rimmed wheels that had marked the earth in wet weather. If it had rained the last time a wagon had come this way, the deep furrows cut into mud dried that way and made the next traveler's journey all the more hazardous. More frequently traveled routes—such as those between larger communities—were more clearly defined, while rarely taken trails disappeared in the overgrowth quickly between uses.

Along some of the more frequently traveled roads, there might even be primitive, homemade milestone markers, indicating the approximate distance to the next town; it might say: "18 miles to Waxahachie." The children in the wagon looked out for them and had a competition to see who would be the first to catch sight of one. On one stretch, where a steep downhill incline had to be negotiated, some sardonic wit had marked a stone: "200 feet to Hell." Once, after dozens of markers had been discovered, a tired and bored Wiley, who could not yet read, but who had heard the older kids reading those signs aloud, is recorded to have complained, "I wish we could read a sign that says 'Just one mile to good Jones County.' "[2]

Finally, on the evening of the nineteenth day, Wiley's wish was granted. The family caravan arrived at the farm of one Wiley Turner, where they expected to stay until their own new house was built. In the days that followed, Turner and some other neighbors helped William build a three room, story-and-a-half house, without plumbing or paint. The children loved it. It had more space than any of their old houses, and it had a staircase to the upstairs sleeping area. The family moved into the new home as soon as both floor and roof were in place. The first outbuilding was a coop, to protect the chickens, but the Posts still lost much of their flock to coyotes. A cistern was dug to catch the rainwater as it came off the roof.

In the year since the Post family had left, the community had added some new settlers, built a cultural center, a one-room schoolhouse, and a chapel.

Though most members of the community were church-going folks, Christmas was not celebrated in any grand style.

> In our part of the country, very little attention to it was given to Christmas. A few people, mostly big boys and young fellows would buy and shoot fireworks Xmas eve night. It was common then for people in the country to have gun powder for reloading shotgun shells, blasting stumps in clearing fields or public roadways. And for celebrating Xmas or New Years they had a way of putting one anvil on top of another anvil with a space between

---

[2]*Around the World in 80 Years* by Arthur H. Post, Charles the Printer, 1974, p. 34

filled with powder and with a fuse to light to fire the powder they could touch off a blast that would rattle the windows a mile away and be heard several miles away.

Everybody knew about the anvils and would listen for them at Xmas.[3]

L. F. Bones, the man who had bought the earlier Post farm, was now the schoolteacher. Joe, Jim, Arthur, and Wiley would have to walk two miles along a trail through the pastures to attend a regular school—at least for the three years the family lived there.

As the number of farms William bought and sold increased, they were each given a name so that in conversation they could be easily identified. Thus, the first farm nearer Abilene became the 'Bones farm,' given the name of the man who had bought it. The new, larger place now became 'our home on Elm Creek.'

The land William had chosen was good land. He raised excellent crops of cotton, maize, watermelons, and potatoes. The only trouble was that coyotes loved the Post farm's watermelons. Scarecrows did not frighten them away from their nightly repasts; all-night fires only served to show them the way to the ripest watermelons in the patch, and strychnine put on chunks of raw meat as bait almost killed the latest family dog. It simply became a matter of keeping the coyotes' share of the watermelon harvest to a tolerable minimum.

The family was happy in the home on Elm Creek. The house was the most comfortable one May and the children had known, the land yielded a good return, there were no mosquitoes and no malaria attacks, there was a school and a church—yes, life was hard, but it was good. The children enjoyed the fishing and had learned to swim there. There was plenty of work even for the younger ones, but there was always some time left to explore the land and play. The family was still poor, but they were well liked in the community and had a good name for honesty and hard work. There was one thing the children wished they could change. Every other family in the community drove to church on Sundays in surreys or buggies, but the Posts had to lumber along in the wagon used in daily field work,

---

[3]*Around the World in 80 Years* by Arthur H. Post, Charles the Printer, 1974, p. 36

with half a dozen chairs in it for the kids. They had no other conveyance. It may not have bothered William or May, but it did embarrass the children.

In the late summer or early fall of 1906, after three years on the farm on Elm Creek, William decided to sell out to a family by the name of Waddell. This time, though, the Post family did not move to a place where it had to start by clearing the land. It was a move to the 'Newberry Place,' a "somewhat older and better improved farm about twelve miles south-west of Abilene,"[4] and about two miles from Caps, one of the older and more progressive communities, located in Taylor County, Texas. The town had a big white church, its own post office, a cotton gin, a number of stores, and even a four-room school. As the family arrived at its new quarters in midwinter, Jim, Arthur, Joe, and Wiley were immediately enrolled in classes. Wiley was now eight years old, but his school attendance so far had been minimal.

The New Year was 1907, the year that the Indian Territory to the north would become the State of Oklahoma. William Francis Post read all about the new opportunities in this, the latest state added to the Union. He found them tempting and he spoke about little else.

Not only a good worker, but also a good farmer, William knew how to make a farm look its most attractive to a potential customer—and there was such a buyer about. A Mr. Buchanan had been looking over the farm and had shown a more than casual interest. Between that interest and the vague promise of major opportunities in Oklahoma, William could not resist letting Mr. Buchanan prevail. The farm on Elm Creek would be the last land the Post family would own in Texas. William Francis Post was off to buy another farm, only this time in Oklahoma.

William had no trouble finding a new farm. It was the Bly place, about eight miles west of Rush Springs and about sixteen miles south of Chickasha, in Grady County. After all the formalities of the mortgage had been completed, he hurried home, and surprised his family with the purchase of a surrey with fringe around the edges of the roof. Going to church for the remainder of the family's stay in Caps would no longer be mortification for the children.

---

[4]*Around the World in 80 Years* by Arthur H. Post, Charles the Printer, 1974, p. 40

Unshaken in their conviction that their own future lay in farming, William, his wife May, and their offspring headed across the border to oil-rich Oklahoma. In the middle of the winter of 1908/1909, the Post family was once again on the move, this time via the Rock Island Railroad. William, always an optimist, was certain that the new farm would surely be the most successful yet, that the new state would change the family's fortune.

Life at Rush Springs did not start well. The Post family arrived in the middle of the night and the unlit town looked gloomy. Though all the usual sales transactions had been completed, the Bly family was still occupying the main house. William had to arrange for his own family to stay, for the time being, in a small old house. Then, though it was the middle of a frigid January, parents and all six children had to move temporarily into a tent put up in their own orchard, as the Blys refused to leave until after the birth of their latest child. Only when the Blys finally left could the Posts move into the well-built, almost-new main house.

The land was young and the yield good. The surrey William had bought to spare the children embarrassment now proved awkward. Here at Rush Springs, the Posts were the only family to own a surrey and so the family reverted to going to church like all the other folks, in the old farm wagon with chairs in the back for the children. "Joe, Wiley, and Arthur, meanwhile, got enrolled in Richland School, a little over a mile south of our place, one room, one teacher, Miss Aurelia Hubbard, an energetic, capable woman, about four-feet-six-inches tall."[5] But the family only stayed in Rush Springs for two years before William sold the farm to a family named Powers.

The Posts were on the move again. This time it was to a farm belonging to a Joe Ball, near Burns, Oklahoma, which required only a six-mile move. The relocation was made more difficult by the fact that May was expecting her first Oklahoma-born child. David Gordon Post, missing Christmas and New Years, arrived on January 4, 1910. Gordon, as the boy would be called, was the fifth boy and the last child in the family.

At the time of Gordon's birth, Wiley was already ten years old.

---

[5] *Around the World in 80 Years* by Arthur H. Post, Charles the Printer, 1974, p. 42

He was very small for his age, and his sporadic schooling had left him with an education far below his age level. Though Wiley would later claim that he had a sixth-grade education, he may have somewhat overstated his scholastic background. For years to come, for example, he could not remember whether his given name was spelled 'Wiley' or 'Wylie.' Both spellings appear in his signatures later in life. Fully aware of his stocky stature and his lack of formal education, Wiley felt ill at ease and insecure; he became introverted, withdrawn, silent, and a very poor mixer. He kept away from discussions, rarely joined in adult group activities and turned into a 'loner,' a dreamer of great deeds and international fame. For the time being, though, he was still a poor farm boy, but a boy with an unusual gift.

The instability of Wiley Hardeman Post's formative years, characterized by frequent relocations, insecurity, random education, and no lasting friendships or attachments, surely added to the boy's aversions to a farmer's life and regular schools. Furthering this dislike of the standard three R's was the boy's overriding fascination with gadgets and mechanical devices. He had an instinctive ability to understand, repair, and even improve machinery. Many times Wiley disappeared from home and seemed lost for hours, only to be found later at some neighbor's house, studying a newly arrived sewing machine, or out in some field, disassembling and then reassembling a farmer's recently purchased seeder. So exceptional was Wiley's mechanical ability that despite his youth he was continually sought out by farmers, or folks from a nearby town, who needed expert help with their mechanical appliances or farm machinery. Because nothing he was being taught in the various one-room schools furthered his primary interest, Wiley looked forward to that day when he could simply leave the farm, go out into the world, and pursue his fascination. Until that day, however, Wiley would have to trudge along at his father's side, work in the fields, or spend tedious, frustrating hours in some rural schoolhouse.

At age eleven, Wiley Hardeman Post resolutely decided that he had had enough of grade schools. He was convinced that he would never need half the lessons to which he had been subjected, and that he was learning nothing about the subjects he really wanted to know. He had no exact idea what he wanted to do and where he wanted to go, but he knew for certain that calligraphy, for example—making sure that all letters leaned the same way, or that every letter o was precisely round—was not the way to any of his goals. It mattered little to young Wiley whether a word was spelled the proper way, or whether a long division came anywhere near what the teacher considered the correct answer.

Then, too, perhaps the methods used in those rural schools were wrong for a lad like Wiley. A student's progress was rarely measured on an individual basis. The brightest and the slowest student were in one classroom, and because a teacher had to direct her or his attention to every grade equally, there was neither time nor opportunity for individual consideration. If there were several pupils of approximately the same age, they were considered to be on one level and they were treated as equals, regardless of what they had learned or failed to learn before. Transfer of records or standard curricula simply did not exist. True, schools of the day used McGuffey's Readers as their main teaching tool, but it only facilitated abuse. Will Rogers, the famous humorist, left a record of his school days. He claimed that he had studied McGuffey's *Fourth Reader*, and almost knew it by heart. When he would be sent to another school, he claimed to have just finished McGuffey's *Third Reader*, so that the teacher would instruct him to start on McGuffey's *Fourth Reader*. As Rogers knew the book, he had neither homework nor studies to interfere with his free time. According to Rogers, he did this several times, until "I knew more about McGuffey's *Fourth Reader* than McGuffey did."

To demonstrate his resolve to quit school, Wiley left home and struck out on his own. He earned money as an itinerant repairman, fixing whatever mechanical devices needed attention. Moving from farm to farm and house to house, he also sharpened knives, scythes, and reaping machines along the way. By the age of thirteen, so it has been claimed, he had saved enough money to buy the first bicycle in the county. Even though there were few, if any, paved roads in the area, it certainly made his travels from job to job somewhat easier and saved him both the time and money needed to keep a horse and buggy.

It was also at the age of thirteen years that Wiley was baptized. Surprisingly, it was not his grandfather, the Reverend T. M. Post, who performed the ceremony, but James Walter Gregston, a Baptist Minister, who owned a shoe store in Duncan, Texas.[6]

When not on the road, Wiley visited his parents' farm in Burns, Oklahoma. In the fall of 1913, the main topic around the Post dinner table was the upcoming annual fair at Lawton, Oklahoma. The county fair always was the major final event of the season, with approaching winter and its harsh weather precluding further social and public outdoor activities for the balance of the year. The fair enabled its patrons to renew acquaintances made in prior years and provided the possibility of meeting new folks. It also offered the usual exhibitions of farm products and the judging of animals, homemade baked goods, preserves, and handcrafted items. There were always exhibitions, too, of the latest models of farm machinery and labor-saving devices for the home. Of course, no fair was complete without amusement rides for children and adults, games of small or no chance, and salesmen ballyhooing miracle medicines that guaranteed cures for any known or so far medically undiscovered diseases. Established and questionable companies with demonstrations and glib salesmen introduced wonderful new products, accompanied sometimes by small free samples or printed leaflets. Younger children would compete with each other to see who could collect the most such leaflets, regardless what they advertised. A County Fair was really a diminutive replica of the world outside the county, with all that really mattered and all that was specious, all that evoked gasps of awe and all that called for prudence—yet all to be viewed in the security of each visitor's familiar home ground.

To the older folks such a fair was just like those of other years, yet it was still enjoyable. While a breeder of cattle, sheep, or swine might enter his animals in the judging for best of breed, or his wife might show off her own preserves, cakes, or pies, the Fair was really the only occasion for many to meet old friends, new arrivals, and distant relatives. At the fair they could talk over the past year, see new children, meet new spouses, and hear the latest gossip. Farming on the wide open prairie was a mostly solitary existence. Of course, there were the meetings of the nearest neighbors each Sunday at church, but any friends or relatives living at a distance of ten or so

[6]*The Daily Oklahoman–Oklahoma City Times*; March 14, 1997

miles would either worship at another church closer to home, or not attend any at all. So it was just once a year, at the county fair, that old friendships could be renewed or new ones started.

For the younger generation, the fair was an experience to be eagerly anticipated and then fully enjoyed. It gave adolescent boys and girls the chance to meet other than just the few classmates seen during the school year. At the fair, last year's pimple-faced boy might find this year's young lady, magically transformed from the last fair's pigtailed tomboy. The fair could provide the setting for the awakening of love, the beginning of courtships, or the start of an argument with a bully that would end in a fistfight and a bloodied nose.

The question the Post family discussed at their dinner table in 1913 was whether to go to the fair, or not. It would be a long trip for a horse and surrey, and might even require an overnight stay on the road. It certainly was out of the question for a girl like Mary to go, but not for a boy:

> It was . . . 1913, that Joe, Wiley and I drove the 23 miles in a
> buggy to Lawton, Oklahoma, to see Art Smith with his Pusher
> Type, the first plane to visit that part of our country. Though
> his machine was a rather crude looking affair his simple straight
> flights were successful and thrilled a lot of people . . . [7]

The trip to Lawton would shape Wiley's life. It was here that he first came face to face with two of America's life-changing innovations. The first one was an aeroplane—as they were then called and spelled. Specifically, it was an old Curtis Pusher,[8] flown by Art Smith, one of the earliest "barnstormers." Standing all by itself within a wide circle of awed admirers, the plane looked to Wiley like a bird, poised to take flight. The sight fascinated him. It might have been "a rather crude looking affair" to his brother Arthur, but to Wiley, it was a mechanical phenomenon. "I have never seen a bit of machinery for land, sea, or sky that has taken my breath away as did

---

[7]*Around the World in 80 Years* by Arthur H. Post, Charles the Printer, 1974, p. 80
[8]A Pusher airplane has the propeller behind the engine and usually behind the trailing edge of the wing. The generated thrust pushes the airplane. [*Aviation History* by Dr. Anne Milbrooke, © 1999]

that old pusher."[9] He had never seen a drawing of it. After all, not even a decade had yet passed since the Wright Brothers had first been aloft in a heavier-than-air contraption. Could a man really fly in one of these things? What made it go up? Better still, what prevented it from falling if, say, just for the argument of it, it did get up into the air? How did a man control such a weird apparatus? Wiley had another hundred questions and not a single answer. From the moment he saw the plane, as far as he was concerned, the rest of the fair was of no interest. His eyes were glued on this flying machine. "I don't know to this day what kind of harvesters and planters were on display," Wiley would write years later.[10] In addition, when he saw the pilot climb onto his seat, when he observed the engine being started, the plane rolling along the bumpy field, and finally lifting off, Wiley's imagination took flights of its own and suppressed any other thought. He saw himself at the controls, whatever they were, and doing things with this plane that no other man had ever done before. He would take such a flying machine and fly all over the world with it, better still, he would fly clear around the world in one of these. Then he would open a school and teach others to do what he had done. Yes, it would be the famous Wiley Post School of Aeronautical Science. In all those brief daydreams, he, Wiley Post, was the hero and the rest of the world would simply wonder that this simple farm boy could do all those astonishing things.

Wiley was so wrapped up in what took place before his eyes and what he imagined that he forgot the simpler realities of life. Forgotten were Joe and Arthur, the brothers who were somewhere around the fairground trying to learn more about available farm equipment to improve the farm output. Forgotten, too, was the tired horse that had brought the Post boys to the fair. "I had forgotten to feed and water the poor animal, too, and it had been a hot day. But Jim had taken care of him, so I got away with that."[11] It was long after almost everybody else had gone home or turned in, that Joe and Arthur

---

[9]*Around the World in Eight Days* by Wiley Post and Harold Gatty © 1931, Rand McNally & Co., p. 244
[10]Ibid
[11]*Around the World in Eight Days* by Wiley Post and Harold Gatty, © 1931, Rand McNally & Co., p. 245

finally found young Wiley. At the arranged hour he had not met them at the buggy for the return trip to the farm. They had split up to look for him. When they thought they had looked everywhere, they returned to where they had seen him last. There he still was, now sitting in the deserted pilot's seat of the parked airplane, off in a fantasy world all his own. Struggling, his brothers finally got him into the buggy to go back home. Though it was late, the day held yet another first for the fourteen-year-old Wiley. It was a ride in an automobile.

Exhausted from a day of traipsing around the fairground, his older brothers tried to catch some sleep, while Wiley, as the youngest of the three, was relegated to keeping alert and directing the horse to stay on the dusty, rutted road. All seemed to be going smoothly until one of those rare automobiles caught up with Wiley's buggy and tried to pass him on the narrow country road. The automobile's driver followed closely, impatiently blasting some noise-making device, waiting for his chance to overtake the much slower moving carriage. At last, Wiley was able to direct his horse onto a wider spot in the road, which permitted the irritating car driver to overtake Wiley's buggy. The automobile passed closely with its thunderous noise of frequent backfiring while trailing a cloud of exhaust fumes and road dust. Young Wiley was quite familiar with controlling horses, but the coughing, sputtering, deafening automobile engine caused Wiley's terrified horse to bolt, nearly tumbling buggy and boys into the ditch. While it had wakened the startled brothers, no damage was sustained and the horse, finally under control, continued at its steady pace. Within the hour, Wiley and the automobile met again. This time the car's engine was quiet as the car rested at a steep angle by the side of the road in the ditch.

"Would it be possible," the car's driver wanted to know, offering a silver dollar, "if the young man could attach his horse to the front end of the car and pull the car out of the sand?" The driver had made matters worse. Trying to extricate himself, he had spun the car's back wheels and only managed to dig them deeper into the soft soil.

Joe and Arthur, now fully awake, tried to help Wiley hitch the horse to the car, but the horse refused to be led anywhere near the machine that had terrified it earlier. When several attempts failed to

THE PERFECT PUPIL   33

guide the horse even close to the car, Wiley had a suggestion. He pointed out that it seemed to him that a single horse could not possibly extricate the automobile when its wheels were axle-deep in the sandy soil. He would—if that silver dollar was still being offered—drive into the nearest village, get a team of horses and come back to assist the driver. Wiley's additional fee would be that he would have to get an automobile ride home, to his parents' farm. The driver, stuck on an infrequently traveled country road, readily agreed to any plan of rescue.

The three Post boys drove to the nearest settlement where Wiley rented a team of horses and their owner for that silver dollar. Joe and Arthur continued their drive home, while Wiley and the farmer went back to assist the car driver. The two horses had little trouble pulling the car back onto the road; the farmer got a silver dollar for his minor troubles and Wiley was able to ride home in style. It was a grand finale for an important day in Wiley Post's life.

On that day in the fall of 1913, Wiley Hardeman Post found a purpose. He had to know more about those machines that could transport people in ways he had never dreamed. Who could imagine what else cars and aeroplanes could do? What was that sheer magic that somehow made gasoline poured into a tank move a car or lift a plane into the air? He knew about the strength that a man had to push, pull, or lift—but that power was limited. And he knew about horsepower, and the waterpower that ran sawmills and flour mills. But what he had seen that day of the Lawton County Fair was beyond any of them. It was the future and he wanted to be a part of it. That much Wiley was certain of. All that remained now was to find a way to it.

When Wiley heard of the Sweeney Automobile and Aviation School in Kansas City, he knew that it was the place for him. The realities of life became agonizingly apparent to the boy when he learned that tuition would be $85. There was no way he could save that much from his itinerant jobs. He approached his father with what he thought was a fair proposal. Would the elder Post lease him a ten-acre section of land on an even share basis of the yield? Wiley would plant cotton, do all the work and then do all the harvesting and divide the profit with his father. Frank Post was a realist and as a farmer would always be wedded to the land. His natural inclination was therefore to be neither supportive nor sympathetic to his son's ambition; but as a loving parent, he did not want to stand in the way of his dreams. A spoken agreement between father and son was sufficient. Both lived up to their arrangement.

A year passed before a late-harvested cotton crop produced the expected profit. The yield from ten acres was hardly enough to take care of the tuition, let alone produce an allowance for Wiley's living expenses. Wiley again demonstrated his single-minded resolution. He would not let anything stand in his way. He took on odd jobs in Kansas City, worked late into the night, and went home to study for the following day's assignments. There were frequent nights when he went to bed hungry.

Wiley's enrollment in the Kansas City school also revealed a new adolescent. Having apathetically plodded through more or less six terms of plain country schools, Wiley now developed into a star pupil. Studying subjects that fascinated him, he spent far more than the required time and attention to his lessons. He readily absorbed his mathematics lessons, a subject he had abhorred back in Texas and early Oklahoma. Physics, a subject rarely taught in grade schools, now became a favorite. He went to libraries to study books he could not afford to buy. He suddenly found joy in mathematics and even experimented on his own in chemistry. He read books not required in class, and he studied subjects allied to his studies but not taught. He was an excellent pupil and never missed a lecture. It was remarkable to see this former school dropout now leading his class in most tests. When asked whether he planned to work on machinery in the future, Wiley was reported to have answered that he did not intend to work on machines, but to have machines work for him.

To demonstrate his claim, Wiley put his newfound knowledge into operation around the family farm. He began to install gasoline engines to improve comfort and living conditions. He used one to pump water from a deep well, replacing the old rope and bucket. By a series of belts, he mechanized formerly hand-operated farm machinery, from grindstones to corn huskers, from saws to hay lift.

Wiley studied at Sweeney's school for seven months, and while it was an excellent foundation in mechanics, it answered few of his questions on aviation. That would have to wait until another day.

After graduating from Sweeney's, Wiley faced the problem of finding a paying job. The war in Europe had at last drawn the United States into it in April 1917 and men had gone overseas. Wiley's experience and natural ability made him a desirable prospect and he found employment with the Chickasha and Lawton Construction Company, a firm that had won the contract to build a government airport at Fort Sill. It was sheer coincidence, but Wiley's family had no connection with Lieutenant Henry B. Post, killed in California, for whom the field was to be named.

Sometime during the summer that year, Wiley joined the Students' Army Training Camp, housed at Norman, home of the University of Oklahoma. Here he studied radio, its use and maintenance, at a time when most radios had to utilize rechargeable wet cells. His training at Sweeney's in mathematics and chemistry now stood him in good stead. Wiley's three older brothers, who had joined the Army earlier, were sent to Europe and the newly graduated section A of the Radio School went along. Before Wiley, in Section B, could graduate, Germany had surrendered. Wiley's plan to join the rapidly growing U.S. Army Air Corps was frustrated. He was unemployed and looking for a job.

Competing with returning veterans, Wiley finally landed in Walters, Oklahoma, about twenty miles north of the Texas border, where new oil fields were opening up. His training in mechanics and his natural aptitude soon made him into a "roughneck," a general handyman who could tackle any job, from feeding and repairing boilers to climbing rigs and feeding cables. The average pay for such a jack-of-all-trades was seven dollars a day. Being a dependable worker, who did not drink or carouse with the other men, Wiley was promoted to "tool dresser" at eleven dollars a day and was well on his way to becoming a "driller" with a daily wage of twenty-five dollars. Because Wiley did not spend his money foolishly, he soon saved a respectable amount. That was when the gambling fever of the oil fields hit him. It seemed so easy when all around him were wildcatters bringing in new spouting wells and men like him were getting rich overnight. He was certain that he could increase his savings quickly if he could just find the right location. However, all he did find were so-called dry holes, and he lost what to him were two small fortunes. It was always back to the oil fields and more hard, dirty work.

Pilots returning from the war had formed into small groups and were touring the country. They gave performances of stunt flying and then gave rides to anybody who had a few dollars and the nerve to go up in one of those rickety planes. They would offer to fly you over your house or farm so you could view it from a few hundred feet in the air—and all for just a cent per pound of your bodyweight. Who could resist such a thrill at such a low price?

For further excitement and to gather a crowd, some of these groups had added parachute jumpers. It made the hearts of folks stop when they saw a man fall from a plane and just tumble toward earth and seemingly certain death until, just at the very last moment, a parachute would suddenly open and allow the man to glide safely to the ground.

At one of those flying exhibitions, Wiley paid a Captain Earl H. Zimmerman twenty-five dollars to take him up and show him all the stunts he knew. The Captain, a survivor of some aerial dogfights over France, took Wiley through all the evasive and attacking moves he had employed overseas, and showed him some aerial tricks that had little to do with warfare.

Wiley was disappointed. Somehow, he had expected more. Here was this wartime hero, and all he could do were the same maneuvers Wiley had seen others perform as a matter of routine. He did not feel that he had received his money's worth. He came away from the performance a little queasy in the stomach, but doubting that pilots were really endowed with those supernatural gifts so often alluded to in magazines he had seen. Looking for an excuse for Captain Zimmerman, Wiley rationalized that the pilot had probably done just about as much as he could dare to do with his old plane.

It was in 1920 that William Post, Wiley's father, bought yet another farm. It was located just north of Maysville, Oklahoma, about forty-five miles south of Oklahoma City. Though Wiley Post would visit his parents numerous times in the years to come, it was never his home. Despite that fact, Maysville has taken unto itself the claim of being Wiley Post's "Hometown."

CHAPTER III

JAILBIRD

Will Rogers, who was part Cherokee Indian and justifiably proud of it, was asked one time to write his memoirs. He replied that to him "memoirs" seemed to be a Cherokee word meaning that you put down the good things you ought to have done and left out the bad things you did do, and he was not about to do that.

Reading the hastily prepared ghostwritten "autobiography" published under the bylines of Wiley Post and Harold Gatty, one must wonder where the actual writer obtained the basis for so much misinformation. Perhaps Wiley Post carefully edited what is supposed to be his "Early History," wherein he does not even seem to know his own mother's correct maiden name. Of course, there are numerous other misstatements, but none so glaring as the attempt to obscure a lengthy, unexplained period in Wiley's life after he had started to work in the oil fields. He claims:

Seesawing between gambling the stake on a hole of my own and
working for other drillers, I somehow was able to get through
the next four and a half years."[1]

It is obvious that Wiley was not about to tell his ghostwriter what
he had really been doing part of those four and a half years. Of
course, he had been able "to get through" those years, but not only
by "seesawing between gambling the stake on a hole of his own and
working for other drillers." That was an intentional cover-up. It
could not have slipped his mind that he had spent some of that time
as a convict at the Reformatory in Granite, Oklahoma. Wiley Post,
however, could be fairly confident that unless it was he who blurted
out the truth about his crime record, it was most unlikely that anyone
outside a very small circle would ever hear of it. After all, why would
anybody outside Grady County, Oklahoma, even care that some
twenty-two-year-old farm boy named Wiley Post had been convicted
as a common highway robber?

The robber's stratagem that Wiley employed was basic and became
even more widely popular later, during the Great Depression days of
the thirties, when need preyed upon opportunity. A robber would
simply place some lure—be it a small suitcase, a bag of sugar, or a
new-looking tire—into the center of a quiet stretch of country road,
hide nearby and await the arrival of an inquisitive and acquisitive
victim. Seeing by serendipity a relatively costly item that apparently
had fallen off some truck, the imminent victim would stop his car to
step out and retrieve it. The robber would then pounce from his
hiding place with his gun or rifle at the ready, and demand money
and valuables. The shock of staring down the barrel of a gun or rifle
and fear for one's life usually worked—as it did for Wiley—at least
for a while.

Wiley Post's life of crime ended abruptly. The Grady County's
weekly newspaper, the *Chickasha Star* of April 2, 1921, carried the
news item on its front page:

"BANDIT CAPTURED AND LODGED IN JAIL"

---

[1]*Around the World in Eight Days* by Wiley Post and Harold Gatty, © 1931, Rand
McNally & Co., p. 251

It then went on to inform its readers "the hold-up man who had been causing so much trouble in Grady County was captured a few days earlier . . . The man's name is Wiley Post and he was at once brought by his captors to the Grady County Jail (sic)." This revelation must have shocked and mortified the entire Post family and those who thought they knew Wiley.

While the actual court records of the trial perished in a fire many years ago, it must be doubted that there were lengthy court proceedings. After all, Post had been caught in the commission of a crime and there were four respectable eyewitnesses against him. According to another newspaper report, Wiley must have confessed his entire crime spree and had thrown himself on the mercy of the court, thereby receiving the minimum sentence. On its front page, the Chickasha Daily Express of April 5, 1921, reported:

HI-JACKER GETS TEN YEARS HERE ON GUILTY PLEA

WILEY POST GIVEN MINIMUM SENTENCE FOR HIGHWAY ROBBERY.
CAUGHT BY NINNEKAH MEN NEAR CITY

Ten years in the state penitentiary was the sentence imposed on Wiley Post, young hi-jacker, who yesterday afternoon in district court entered a plea of guilty to the charge of highway robbery. Ten years is the minimum for such crime.

Post was captured several days ago by four Ninnekah men, E. R. Mercer, S. A. McClain, Tom Wood, and S. A. Null, whom (sic) he attempted to hold up. The capture was made on the Ninnekah—Chickasha road two miles south of this city.

An automobile casing was placed in the road as a decoy. When the men stopped their automobile to pick up the apparently lost casing Post rushed up to the machine and ordered the men to hold up their hands. As he stepped out of the car, Mr. Mercer grabbed the gun and told Post that if he attempted to pull the trigger, he would be killed. With these words, the young hold-up released the gun and, in compliance with orders, stepped into the car and was brought to the county jail.

He waived preliminary examination in justice court.

After arrest, Post admitted having been implicated in other

hold-ups near this city, officers say. He is a neat appearing young
man, almost 22 years of age. His parents formerly lived in this
county and, according to A. Sidney Hancock, deputy sheriff,
were highly respected citizens. They now live in the vicinity of
Wynnewood.

The prisoner will be taken to the state reformatory at Granite
some time this week.

Though the court records no longer exist, several supporting official documents have survived. Wiley's arrest sheet, his transfer from
jail to prison, and his acceptance questionnaire at the Granite,
Oklahoma, Reformatory as prisoner number 3009, go into remarkable detail, thus presenting a most accurate portrayal of Wiley Post,
the young man. They describe a "droop shouldered" man who measured five-feet-four-inches tall and weighed 131 pounds, with chest-
nut colored hair and scars on both upper arms. The document also
includes Wiley's fingerprints and such measurements as the lengths
of his feet, forearms, head, ear, and even "cheek width." When questioned he had answered that he had no religion, had six years of
schooling, did not drink, smoke or chew, was currently employed on
a job he had held for three weeks, and had only twenty-seven cents
in his pocket. When asked to sign the questionnaire to authenticate
his answers, a twenty-two-year-old school dropout misspelled his
given name as WYLIE, with the middle name not even acknowledged
by an initial.

Wiley Post's radical conversion from a Sunday-school attending,
baptized teenager just nine years earlier to a habitual criminal, is
difficult to understand or explain. In his official arrest report, he
claimed not to be a member of any religious denomination, certainly
a major surprise and blow to his grandparents and parents. He stated
to be employed, yet robbed peaceful citizens, and still only had
twenty-seven cents in his possession when apprehended.

Lack of funds, or even unemployment—if that was the real reason—was no defense or excuse for a crime. Wiley would always have
been welcomed with open arms at the home of his parents, or any
other relative. No questions would have been asked and he could
have stayed as long as he wanted. He could always have gone back
and worked with his father on the farm. He may not have liked it,

but would it not have been preferable to being a felon? Maybe not to Wiley, who might have seen it as admitting failure of his attempt at independence. Whatever the reasons, whatever the excuses, Wiley would be changed for the rest of his life, even if the world would be unaware of it. In his own mind, Wiley Post knew what he had done and what his price for it had been. Perhaps later in life he feared that eventually his secret would become common knowledge and his carefully nurtured heroic persona would be destroyed. There was no way he could ever regain total respectability, or achieve his father's reputation for honesty and decency. From now on, he would be a marked man, even if others did not know it. He knew it, and that was enough. The dread of discovery was within him and his conduct of recklessness in the years to come can be viewed either as a death wish, or as utter disdain of his own value.

The bleak reality of first jail, and then the realization of the demoralizing monotony of prison life began taking their toll immediately on Wiley. His had been a free spirit who could not bear the tedium and confinement of schools. How was he ever going to adapt to life in a cell? Once, when asked his recollection of school life in Texas, he was quoted:

> Texas is a nice place if you are outdoors, but inside a school-house, under the thumb of a strict taskmaster, if you are six years old and having trouble with geography, it gets hot and dull.

And although he was no longer six years old and learning geography was not the problem of the moment, he was now again under the thumb of strict taskmasters and the prospect was that it was going to get hot and dull for the next ten years. Wiley knew that while he might be able to tolerate it for a short while, he would never survive this routine for ten years. Despondency and total resignation set in.

Wiley began to stay away from mandatory group activities, and he withdrew from social contact with fellow prisoners, rarely speaking to others, even when spoken to. He was always courteous to guards and offered to cooperate, but quickly lost his concentration and would fail to carry out even the simplest of assigned tasks. The months dragged by, totally anesthetizing Wiley Post's mind. It was as if his brain had simply shut down and refused to take cognizance of its surroundings and obligations. Few who had known the adolescent Wiley would have recognized the now morose young adult. There was no doubt; Post was racing toward a state of total psychological failure.

That, too, was the opinion of Drs. George A. Waters and T. J. Nunnery. It is surprising to see that as early as the 1920s, there were some prison doctors who were concerned enough about the mental deterioration of an inmate in their care, that they would urge his parole on psychological grounds. Governor J. B. A. Robertson granted Post's release:

STATE OF OKLAHOMA
EXECUTIVE DEPARTMENT
PAROLE

TO ALL TO WHOM THESE PRESENTS SHALL COME,
GREETINGS:

WHEREAS, Wiley Post No. 3009, was convicted in the District Court of Grady County, on April 28, 1921, for the crime of Conjoint Robbery, and was sentenced to a term of ten years inthe (sic) State Reformatory; and,

WHEREAS, it is made to appear from letters of Dr. Geo. A. Water and a statement and recommendation from Dr. T. J. Nunnery, Prison Physician at the Reformatory; that, he is physically a porfect (sic) man, he is a submissive prisoner with an effort to be respectful to all officers of the institution and to fellow prisoners, he is making an effort to make good and obedient to every order so far as he is capable; he is not given important duties to perform on account of the fact that he does not retain the order long enough in his mind to perform it although he makes every effort to make good. His case is diagnosed as a Melancholic state which cannot be improved by change of duty or good treatment and it is steadily growing worse and on account of his mental condition of the said Wiley Post, I have decided to parole him; and

NOW THEREFORE, I, J. B. A. Robertson, Governor of the State of Oklahoma, by virtue of the authority vested in me by law, do hereby grant unto the said Wiley Post, a parole upon the following terms and conditions to-wit:-

First: "That the said Wiley Post shall abstain from the use or handling of intoxicating liquor in any form; that the said Wiley Post shall not gamble or in any way conduct a game of chance; that the said Wiley Post shall not carry firearms in violation of the statutes of this state; that he shall industriously follow some useful occupation, avoid all evil associations, improper places of amusement, all pool and billiard halls, obey the laws and in all respects conduct himself as an upright citizen; that he shall faithfully aid and support those dependent upon him;

SECOND: "It is hereby made a strict condition of this parole that the said Wiley Post shall report in writing to the Warden of the State Reformatory, once each month until otherwise ordered by the Governor and in said report he must show his whereabouts, the nature of his occupation together with full account as to what he has done with reference to caring for his dependent relatives; and failure to file said report on or before the 10th day of each month is hereby considered and understood by the said Wiley Post, sufficient grounds for the revocation of this parole;

THIRD: That the Governor shall have power at any time to revoke this parole for a violation of any of the above conditions, or for any other reason deemed sufficient and to caused the maximum sentence to be served in such prison as may be lawful and as may be determined by him; and if it shall appear subsequent to the issuance of this parole that the applicant herein has agreed, or consented, or has paid any fee or compensation, or has consented for the same to be paid to any third person in excess of that disclosed in the application or amendments hereto, such shall be deemed proper grounds for the revocation of this parole;

FOURTH: That, in the event this parole shall be revoked at any time, and the said Wiley Post shall be out of the State of Oklahoma, at the time of revocation of same, he waves all the rights and privileges allowed him under the laws and constitution of the United States, or the laws of any foreign state and expressly agrees to return to the State of Oklahoma, without the aid of requisition.

AND WHEREAS, the said Wiley Post hereby agrees to accept and comply with the said conditions, I extend unto him this parole . . ."

On June 3, 1922, Governor Robertson of Oklahoma signed Wiley Post's parole, with the Secretary of State of Oklahoma countersigning. Two days later, on June 5th, Wiley Post signed the added paragraph:

"I, Wiley Post, hereby declare that I have carefully read and do clearly understand the contents and conditions of the above parole agreement and hereby accept the same and pledge myself to honestly comply with the said terms."

Two witnessing signatures seem to read Chas. Campbell and L. A. Sugg. For the next twelve years Wiley would live more or less as the terms of his parole stipulated. He may have violated the limitation on firearms, but Wiley was often out of the state of Oklahoma and the parole terms did not interfere with Wiley's frequent hunting trips, be they for deer or wolves. There is no record of any parole violation being noted, but there is also no record of his having made his reports regularly, or on time. His history of the robberies, conviction, and incarceration remained a secret.

The nightmare of incarceration might have been over with Wiley's release from Granite Reformatory in June of 1922, but the emotional wound seemed never to have fully healed. Wiley Post knew that a parole was not absolution, or purification; it was still part of punishment.

Since his earliest youth had indicated that Wiley was a nonconformist and with a mind of his own, the strangeness of the rest of his life can easily be understood. Still, the thirteen months stay at the Granite Reformatory must have added much to his character. It certainly increased his determination to succeed at some important endeavor at almost any cost, no matter what the consequence. This drive was so urgent that his own life was often the stake in his ventures, and Wiley gladly took the gamble. He must have silently believed that he had lost his value as a person somewhere along the way—perhaps in prison, perhaps earlier. Was he really nothing but an ex convict, found guilty of crimes against his neighbors. Why was he not like his brothers, or, better yet, why was he not like his father?

From the few details we do know, not counting the problematic autobiography, Wiley obviously suffered an inferiority complex. Was it his small stature? Was it his lack of education? Was it the fact that he was a convict out of prison only at the sufferance of the legal system? We shall never know, for at that moment in Wiley Post's life, nobody cared to ask and record it.

One must also wonder whether it takes a special person, like Wiley Post, willing to take risks that others will not, to achieve the progress that others, however, will gladly share with him later. Wiley may not have had an explanation, though he had the drive and the need to raise his self-esteem, to prove his own worth. He could tell that he was different, and even if he did not at first recognize the difference, he would be meeting many along the way that would tell him so— not a few of them to his face.

Not until December 27, 1934, would then Governor William "Alfalfa Bill" Murray grant Wiley Post a full pardon. By that time, he would be already famous around the world, and admired by many. It has been said that when the mailed official notification of the pardon came to Wiley's home, he did not open the envelope but simply had it forwarded to his parents in Maysville, Oklahoma. It was a son's final apology to his parents for having brought them pain and embarrassment.

However, when released from prison in June 1922, home was the last place Wiley wanted to go. He could not face his parents or siblings. There was only one place he knew where he could find acceptance without questions being asked, where his talents as a mechanical wizard were needed and appreciated—the oil fields. Wiley Hardeman Post went to work.

In 1924 Wiley showed up in—of all places—Chickasha, some thirty-five miles from his parents' home in Maysville. He could not seem to leave the familiar neighborhood. He went to see his former boss, W. L. Klingman, who was now drilling for Powell Briscoe. Klingman remembered the time he had first hired Wiley straight from the farm some years earlier. He had warned him then: "Be careful!"

> Wiley looked at me sorter funny, and said he knew how to take care of himself. It wasn't long before I realized he could. He was always a careful fellow and never talked much. He never got drunk and raised Cain like some of the boys in the field. After about a year and a half, Wiley drifted with the 'oil gang' to other fields. He went to Graham, Healdton, and the other fields of Carter and Stephens County. He was always a roughneck in those days; it was a job carrying little responsibility, but a lot of hard work.[2]

Klingman had always liked the way Post worked and he rehired him immediately to keep pumps and engines running. The boss was an old-timer and a keen judge of men. He had observed Wiley in the past: "He looked to me like he was just working to make enough money to do something else."

Oil-field workers were a hard-working, tough-talking lot, given more to drinking than to reading newspapers. Besides, most of them had rushed to the latest Oklahoma oil strikes from other areas and knew nothing about Wiley's prison record. Had they known, it would only have served to enhance the little man's reputation.

Wiley did not join his fellow workers in any of their favorite pastimes. His parole condition insisted on a clean, law-abiding life style and Wiley had had enough trouble with the law. He was going to keep to the letter of the parole—at least at the beginning. His bosses liked the young man, so serious, so knowledgeable about machines and motors, so seemingly dedicated to his work. Only one thing could distract Wiley's attention from his tasks, and that was the occasional sound of an airplane flying by. Wiley would drop whatever he was doing and rush from any cover to gain an unobstructed view

---

[2]Interview with W. L. Klingman

of the sky and plane. He would stand there, face upturned, and watch until both airplane and sound had faded away. That old ache to be a great pilot was still gnawing at him.

It happened suddenly, according to Wiley Post. While on a drilling job near Holdenville, in the eastern section of Oklahoma, a passing plane decided Wiley to quit the oil business and follow his heart. From now on, so he resolved, he would "embark on my aviation career."

He remembered having seen an advertisement announcing Burrell Tibbs' Flying Circus for the following weekend at Wewoka. He headed for the small town some ten miles to the west, and there found the three men who ran the group. They looked over the tough-looking youth. At first they wanted no part of him. What would a Flying Circus want to do with a man who had no flying experience except a short flight as a passenger? But there was an opening. Peter Lewis, the featured attraction parachute jumper, had sustained an injury during the previous afternoon's show, and would be unavailable for that day's widely advertised and paid for performance. This presented a major problem since most spectators had come not so much to see planes flying upside down or looping but to see a man hurling through space toward certain death—to be rescued only if a flimsy parachute opened.

"Had Wiley ever used a parachute before?" Tibbs wanted to know. Wiley had to admit that he never had. But, so he assured them, he was willing to jump if they would explain what he had to do. Downplaying the inherent danger, they told him that there was really nothing much to it, and that all he had to do was simply put on the parachute and jump. They would watch how well he did and if they liked his performance, he would be hired and could have a job with the Circus at fifty dollars for each jump.

The money sounded more than tempting. The simple description of the job did not make it appear to be too difficult; and best of all he would be close to airplanes and could learn to fly. Wiley agreed to jump. Before that Sunday's performance, Peter Lewis took Wiley aside and carefully went over the mechanics of the jump in detail.

The parachutes used in those days were of the Hardin exhibition type. The 'chute was packed in a bag which was tied to one of the interplane struts in the bay of the right wing. There was a little cord attached to the release which let the 'chute out of the bag, and a rope, strong enough to hold the end of the canopy but intended to break with a man's weight, pulled the 'chute open in the wind. They were queer contraptions, those old-type parachutes, but I had good instructions before I went up.[3]

This job description sounds quite a bit more complicated and dangerous than the one Wiley had received at the job interview. Still, he was determined to go through with the jump.

When the plane took off and gained altitude, Wiley had forgotten all he had been told about the jump. At two thousand feet, Tibbs cut the throttle to lessen the power of the slipstream. The blast from the propeller could easily tear the jumper prematurely off the wing. Wiley did not move from his seat. It was as if he was paralyzed. Tibbs raised his hand and pointed down toward the ground. Still Wiley did not move. He later claimed that it was not fear but ignorance of what to do next that caused him to freeze. Then, as if in a trance, Wiley swung his legs onto the wing and slowly inched his way toward the bag with the parachute. On the ground it had been an easy thing to practice attaching the chute to the harness he wore. Here, at two thousand feet, with the cut-down propeller blast almost knocking him off his feet and with one hand holding onto anything that seemed to promise support while connecting the chute with the other hand, it was an entirely different undertaking. Finally, all seemed in place and Tibbs began yelling at Wiley to jump. Wiley released his handhold and fell—just far enough off the wing to dangle in space. He swung there for a moment that seemed like eternity until he remembered to pull the release cord. Once free from the plane, he dropped before the parachute opened with a sharp yank. From then on it was a sensation of floating which Wiley still remembered years later as "one of the biggest thrills of my life."[4]

---

[3]Pp. 252; *Around the World in Eight Days* by Wiley Post and Harold Gatty, © 1931, Rand McNally & Co., p. 252

[4]*Around the World in Eight Days* by Wiley Post and Harold Gatty, © 1931, Rand McNally & Co., p. 254

During the time Wiley worked with the Flying Circus, he used assumed names. It has never been established whether that was because he feared a connection with the recent robbery conviction, or whether it was to give the impression that there were several jumpers instead of just one. Whatever the name, he received fifty dollars a jump. When he thought that he was worth more and demanded one hundred dollars per jump, he found Tibbs unwilling to meet his asking price. Wiley was not upset. He had learned enough to venture into business for himself. During the early part of each week, he would visit various towns and persuade the mayors and town councils to pay him for a planned parachute-jumping spectacle on the weekend. He would point out to the town elders that it would draw attention to their towns, bring visitors and be good for business. Once he had a financial supporter, Wiley would find a local pilot and pay him twenty-five dollars for a flight. Then he would hire a plane, and he was in business. All that was left was to make sure the pilot knew how to take off and fly the plane to the desired height. Wiley kidded that he didn't care how poor a pilot he had chosen to take him up, since he never intended to land with him anyhow. Any pilot felt he had made an easy payday, and Wiley pocketed the balance of the town's fee. Some days he made as much as $200—a small fortune at a time when an average American with a family was happy to earn fifty dollars a week.

Wiley liked the job. He had developed his own philosophy about a crowd's reaction to the feats of a parachute jumper. He realized early that an audience found little thrill in watching a routine performance of a man simply floating to earth. He experimented with adding his own stunts like delaying the opening of the chute to the last prudent moment, when the spectators thought that it was too late. Or jumping with two parachutes, opening one and discarding it, then falling chuteless to give the impression that he had accidentally been separated from his one and only life saving device before deploying the second chute to everyone's surprise and relief. On other jumps, he would tumble from the plane as if he had lost control: he could almost hear the crowd gasp. He changed from a simple jumper to a performer, and the crowds loved it.

I was studying crowd psychology. My desire to thwart the spectator's hope of witnessing my untimely end was so strong that at times I grew so reckless as to scare myself.[5]

In all, Wiley made over one hundred parachute jumps and had but a single accident. It happened near Hugo, in the southeastern corner of Oklahoma, near the Texas border. On the morning of the jump, Wiley had inspected the meadow where he intended to land. It was a nice, clear piece of land, free of trees or other hazards. He expected no trouble. In the afternoon, the plane took him to two thousand feet, his preferred height for a jump. As he fell from the plane, he saw, to his horror, that the meadow he had selected in the forenoon had changed. A mule was grazing right in the middle of it, with no concern over what was about to descend on him from the sky. Wiley tried to steer his fall as far away from the mule as he could, but just as he was about to plant his feet for the contact with the ground, a gust of wind took the shroud of his chute and blew it over the animal's head. Terrified, the mule took off, unable to see where it was running, it dragged an unfortunate Wiley all over the meadow. Wiley managed finally to release himself from the chute and escaped with bruises only to his dignity.

The one jump Wiley remembered best was the one at Maysville, his parents' current hometown. Because of these family ties, he thought it would help business if he used his own name and charged the local Chamber of Commerce a special low price of seventy-five dollars. When he unexpectedly walked in on his parents wearing his flier's outfit and carrying a parachute under his arm, they were stunned. When he told them that he was going to perform a parachute jump on the coming weekend, they were even more shocked. Since he had used a variety of made-up names before, they had not known that Wiley was making a good living as a parachute jumper. William Post then tried to persuade his son to change his mind about ever jumping again, and the two men began a serious argument. Wiley's mother, as he told the story later, was just so glad to see her

---

[5] *Around the World in Eight Days* by Wiley Post and Harold Gatty, © 1931, Rand McNally & Co., p. 263

long-absent boy that she acted as the temporary peacemaker between a worried father and his daredevil son.

Sunday, the day of the jump, found Wiley frantically searching for his parachute. He remembered distinctly where he had stowed it the day he arrived, but now it was gone. Nobody seemed to know what had happened to it. When the time came for Wiley's jump, it had still not been found. The person least concerned about the missing parachute seemed to be Wiley's father. Since he had been so opposed to his son risking his life on such a stunt, it appeared logical that he might have wanted to prevent him from jumping in the only way he could. Parachutes were not standard equipment in those days and certainly not in villages like Maysville, Oklahoma. Wiley, to his humiliation, had to inform his sponsors and the assembled spectators that there would be no performance that day. He promised them a special treat the following Sunday, however.

Wiley took the train to Oklahoma City the following day, Monday morning. There he borrowed a parachute from a flying friend, but did not go back to Maysville. He was not going to take another chance on 'somebody' hiding his equipment. He hired a young pilot and only went back to Maysville early on the following Sunday. This time everything went just as Wiley planned it. The pilot performed some stunts and when it was time for the great climax, Wiley performed his advertised "death defying" jump. Even his father had to admit that he was impressed.

Between barnstorming and parachute-jumping, Wiley spent the next two years taking an occasional flying lesson wherever he could find the opportunity. It was not always the same type of plane, nor was there any consistency of teachers. Mostly he would watch pilots as he took off for a jump. Other times he would ask the pilot to let him take off then turn the controls over as he prepared to jump. When he first thought about soloing, he realized that while he had practiced taking off, he had rarely, if ever, landed a plane. But Wiley did not really need teachers so much as opportunities to practice and experiment by himself. He still dreamed of owning his own plane some day, even though the chances had not improved over the years.

In 1926, a somewhat overconfident Wiley felt that he was ready to solo. According to Wiley's own calculations, he had no more than four hours of properly tutored airtime. The airplane he rented for the auspicious occasion from his friend Sam Bartel, was a Canuck—a Curtiss JN-4, built in Canada. Affectionally called the "Jenny" because of its initials, this was the plane in which many pilots were trained during the war. "After the war, the 'Jenny' was the plane of choice for the barnstormers and flying clubs."[6] Post chose that plane because he had flown in it more often than any other, and he was certain that he could handle it well. Wiley may have had confidence in his own ability, but the plane's owner did not. Though Sam Bartel was an old acquaintance—or maybe just because he knew Wiley Post well—he had serious doubts about Wiley's readiness. While the market value of a 'Jenny' was no more than $150, Wiley was required to leave a cash deposit of $200 before he was allowed to leave the ground.

Wiley confessed after the solo flight that he really was not ready to fly alone, and that at least twice he nearly lost control of the plane. However, the solo flight ended without a mishap and Wiley became rather fond of the veteran plane. So much so, that many times, and to anyone who was within earshot, he would announce that he was saving his money and that some day he would buy just such a "Jenny". The thought behind this fervent wish was that Wiley wanted to get into commercial aviation and for that he needed far more flight experience. If he would have to pay for flying lessons Wiley would never be able to amass enough flight hours. It was essential that he have a plane of his own. However, where to get the money to buy one, was the question. The answer came sooner than Wiley Post had anticipated, and certainly not in a way he could have foreseen.

Wiley hated to admit defeat, but he had seen the end of his barnstorming days. Airplanes had become more commonplace, people barely looked up when one flew overhead, and the revenue at some exhibitions barely paid for gas and oil. Much as Wiley disliked it, he would have to return to the oil fields where a man could find a job. He vowed to himself that he would stay in the oil fields only as long as it would take to save the two or three hundred dollars to purchase his own *Jenny*—and that should not take too long.

---

[6]*Aviation History* by Dr. Anne Millbrooke, © 1999, Jeppesen Sanderson, Inc.

Wiley could not foresee just how short his employment with Drop-pleman & Cuniff, an oil-drilling company, would turn out to be. On October 1, 1926, he started his new job on their rig near the town of Seminole, located some 55 miles southeast of Oklahoma City. The pay was to be seven dollars a day. Available reports of events on that first day at work have two very different beginnings, but unfortunately the same tragic consequence. Talking as of December 1925 (sic) Wiley Post recounts in his and Harold Gatty's so-called autobiographical book:

> My first day [October 1, 1926—Ed.] on the drilling rig a rough-neck was driving a bolt through the derrick. I was directing the work. The sledge came down hard on the head of an iron bolt. Under the terrific blow of the hammer a chip flew off and struck my left eyeball before I had a chance to close the lid. Infection set in, and the doctors found it necessary to take my eye out."[7]

This account puts the culpability for the tragic accident on someone else, some unidentified lowly worker at the bottom of the social strata of oil-field society. It makes Wiley Post the victim of another's action, and makes the hero of the account ever more epic and impressive. The fact is that it might have happened just that way, and that in retrospect Wiley could have so easily understated that tragic accident.

Opposed to Wiley's account is the eyewitness article in the Tulsa (Oklahoma) Tribune of May 20, 1936, carrying the headline:

HOW WILEY POST LOST HIS EYE RELATED BY FORMER EMPLOYER

The story carries an interview with Raleigh P. Coats, who in 1936 was drilling superintendent for the Olson Drilling Co., for the state of New Mexico. His account of the accident differs on the most pivotal point of responsibility:

---

[7]*Around the World in Eight Days* by Wiley Post and Harold Gatty, © 1931, Rand McNally & Co., p. 264

> Wiley was working derricks for me in Seminole back in 1926.
> We were working for John Dropperman (sic), a drilling con-
> tractor.
>
> A rotary chain broke and Wiley took a ball pean hammer with
> a punch and knocked a pin out of the chain. A piece of steel
> flew into his eye.
>
> I drove him to Wewoka and a doctor worked on his eye with
> a needle but it didn't do any good. I finally took him to
> Oklahoma City to a specialist. By that time steel poisoning had
> set in and he lost his eye.

One can easily explain the error in the name of his employer as a
reporter's mistake in noting a spoken name, or a typo, a printer's
fault, or even Mr. Coats's lapse. The point here is that there is no
hesitation in blaming Wiley Post for the accident. There are no records indicating that the wearing of safety glasses was mandatory, or
was even contemplated in those days. In any case, if Wiley himself
was responsible for the loss of his eye, he would surely have won
less compassion for his affliction than if he had been a victim.

Whether the "needle" used by the first doctor—probably an effort
to extract the steel chip—or indeed, "poisoning," resulted in the loss
of the eye will never be determined. What is obvious is that an infection of the injured eye did occur and that the drugs of the time
were unable to control it. Attempts not only to save the affected eye,
but to keep the infection from spreading to the right eye, failed. To
prevent the possible loss of that healthy eye through a spreading
condition called sympathetic ophthalmia, the removal of the infected
eye was a tragic, but standard procedure.

The first thought for Wiley's acquaintances must have been the
dismay that the potential loss of his vision spelled termination to the
one dream that had kept him going; he would never be a pilot with
just one eye. But if that was in their minds, they did not know Wiley
Post. Years later, after the briefest of acquaintanceships, Will Rogers
summed up his opinion on that point: "That Post is just full of determination. I would hate to tell him he could not do anything."[8]

---

[8]Will Rogers Weekly Article, July 26, 1931.

On advice of counsel, Wiley immediately submitted his claim for compensation to the State Industrial Commission of the State of Oklahoma. The agency responded surprisingly quickly:

BEFORE THE STATE INDUSTRIAL COMMISSION OF THE STATE OF OKLAHOMA

W. H. POST . . . . CLAIMANT)   CLAIM
                    VS   #
                                                91165

DROPPLEMAN & CUNIFF . . RESPONDENT)
MARYLAND CASUALTY COMPANY . . INS. CARRIER

ORDER

Now on this 30th day of October, 1926, the State Industrial Commission being regularly in session, this cause comes on to be considered in its regular order on application of claimant for a lump sum settlement; and the Commission, having considered the records on file herein and being well advised in the premises, finds the following facts:

-I-

That the claimant herein was in the employment of the respondent and was engaged in a hazardous occupation covered by and subject to the provisions of the Workmen's Compensation Law and that while in the course of such employment and arising out of the same the claimant sustained an accidental injury on the 1st day of October 1926;

-II-

That as a result of said accident the claimant sustained the loss of the left eye;

-III-

That the claimant's average wage at the time of his injury was $7.00 per day.

THE COMMISSION IS OF THE OPINION: By reason of the aforesaid facts, that the claimant herein is entitled under the law to compensation at the rate of $18.00 per week for a period of 100 weeks computed from October 6th, 1926, less any sums heretofore paid as compensation.

AND IT APPEARING: That 3 weeks' compensation should have been paid to October 27th, 1926, and that it would be to the interest of the claimant and in the furtherance of justice to commute to a lump sum the remaining 97 weeks' compensation at the rate of $18.00 per week, amounting to $1746.00, the present worth of which, after deducting 3 per cent compound discount to $1698.25;

IT IS ORDERED: That within ten days from this date the respondent herein, Droppleman & Cuniff, pay to the claimant in one lump sum $1698.25, being the present worth of 97 weeks' compensation due beyond October 27th, 1926, and also pay to said claimant any compensation that may be due to October 27th, 1926, in full and final settlement under this award.

IT IS FURTHER ORDERED: That within thirty days from this date the respondent or insurance carrier herein file with the Commission proper receipt or other report evidencing compliance with the terms of this order.

(dated) October 30, 1926.   (signed) A. E. BOND
Secretary, State Industrial Board

To recuperate from the operation, Wiley went to stay with an uncle in the Davis Mountains of western Texas, close to the Mexican border. Two wounds had to heal—his body and his mind. Not surprisingly, Wiley's strong determination made his mind heal first. He quickly accepted the irrevocability of his mutilation and vowed that he would overcome it. He knew, of course, that with the loss of one eye his depth perception, and thus his assessment of distance and height, would be dangerously impeded. In the 1920s, still the days of early aviation, all flying was done strictly by sight. Flying by instruments, or blind flying as it was usually called, was yet to be learned and trusted.

Every day, for many hours at a time, Wiley would walk into the woods, guess at the height of trees, then measure them to see how close or far his estimates were from the facts. He would guess at distances of rocks, then boulders, then mountains, and walk miles to become skilled at accurately estimating heights and distances. It took the better part of two months and a great deal of determination and patience to reach precision. Later, Wiley would challenge anyone to beat him at guessing measurements of height or distance. Invariably he would best anyone.

To make those long walks in the Texas mountains more tolerable and doubly productive, Wiley took along a rifle to help decimate the resident coyote population. His uncle had mentioned the considerable damage they were causing the local ranchers and farmers. The more proficient Wiley became in overcoming his serious new handicap and in killing coyotes, the more confident he became that he would still become a pilot. The secret aspiration of a Wiley Post School of Aeronautical Science was still very much alive.

With Christmas approaching and with both his physical well-being and mind vastly improved, Wiley decided to visit his parents. The calmness of his parents' home life with his mother's familiar cooking would be just the right thing to celebrate the holidays and then welcome the New Year.

When he arrived at his parents' home, Wiley was surprised to discover that another visitor had preceded him—his first cousin Edna Mae Laine. She was the seventeen-year-old daughter of his mother's younger brother David Laine, and had come from her parents' farm at Sweetwater, Texas, to visit her aunt and uncle.[9]

---

[9]Edna Mae Post interview, *Daily Oklahoman*, December 10, 1950

CHAPTER IV

MAE AND *WINNIE MAE*

E DNA MAE LAINE, called simply Mae, knew little about her much older cousin Wiley before she had arrived at Maysville. When she met him, he talked little, but when he did speak, his topic was inevitably this new thing, aviation. It fascinated her. She kept asking questions about it and he found such interest in a young girl surprising and flattering. The two of them talked a lot during their stay at the Post farm that Christmas, and not all of it was about flying. After Mae returned to her home at Sweetwater, Wiley could not stay away.

Using some of the lump sum of money awarded him by the State Industrial Commission of the State of Oklahoma, Wiley bought a Canuck, the Curtiss JN-4 Canadian-built "Jenny," with an OX-5 motor, the plane of his long-nurtured dreams. He paid $240 to two young men who had crash-landed it, doing slight damage. As the men did not have the funds necessary to pay for the ordered repairs, they had put the plane up for sale. Wiley spent an additional $300 to have it rebuilt throughout. Unfamiliar with the controls, he asked one of the previous owners to fly him to

58

Holdenville. There he paid his old friend Sam Bartel for two hours of flying lessons, then practiced an additional three hours on his own. After that, he was open for business. He began to give flying lessons, and hired himself out to oil prospectors and lease buyers, to hunters and fishermen, to private citizens who wanted to get somewhere in a hurry. Anybody who had the money could hire Wiley and his plane—especially if they wanted to fly anywhere near Sweetwater, Texas.

Always being part daredevil and part responsible pilot, Wiley became known for his ability to land in troublesome places most other fliers would gladly avoid. The remote areas of Oklahoma and Texas that were most often the destinations of the oilmen or sportsmen Wiley transported had neither airports nor paved roads. Flying to the locations was the easy part; landing there and later taking off from the same sites, was not. There were hills and gullies, soft soil and hidden rocks, deep erosions and challenging outcroppings. Wiley could land a plane by seemingly dropping it into a tight spot and then, when he had to leave, pick it up and take off almost vertically. Wiley's uncanny ability to find a landing spot where others might not, became his trademark, and he practically made this part of the two states his private domain. One of his students put it best: "Wiley Post did not just fly a plane, he wore it."

Wiley's old friend Jack Baskin, a classmate from the Sweeney's Auto and Aviation School days, would later explain where Wiley first learned—what he called—the shotgun takeoff.

> One noon I was working on my ship at the Ponca City airport, and heard a plane drone. The motor cut out, and I saw it land in a field of wheat. I drove to where it had landed, and out stepped Wiley. "Well, here I am in a wheat field, knee high to a tall Indian," he said. "broke my oil line."
>
> We taped the pipe and I cranked the motor for him, but in three or four runs across the field he could not lift from the wheat. Just then I saw Wiley stand up in the cockpit, shouting, "Look, Jack, at the farmer with the long shotgun!" And there was a big Polack farmer coming with a whale of a gun. Wiley gave the bus the gun and I lifted the wings above the wheat to

catch the air. That farmer let go a couple of shells but was too far off. That's where Wiley learned to lift a ship from the ground with a short run. I left pretty quick myself, for that farmer was still shooting at Wiley.[1]

Wiley Post's know-how of taking off on short runs may have been an asset in those days of prospecting and hunting trips, but it would one day prove to be a fatal problem when his life was at stake.

Even Edna Mae would later witness Wiley's—by then her husband's—landing and takeoff capability on a trip she took with him. She observed that, "He [Will Rogers] would want Wiley to land in the most difficult places. Sometimes I think he thought Wiley could have made a landing on a mountain top and then take off again."[2]

Only one thing distracted Wiley from his budding one-plane airline and flying school, his sole source of revenue, and that was courtship. He began dropping in on Mae and her folks unannounced at the oddest times, just because "he had been in the neighborhood." David Laine and his wife, May, could see what was happening between their daughter and their nephew, and they were not supportive. They had their own good reasons for taking issue with this rapidly developing romance. For one, they were entirely opposed to a union between two first cousins; for another, there was the great difference in their ages. Mae was only 17 years old— a child—while her beau was a mature 28. Worst of all, Wiley was not exactly first-rate son-in-law material, neither being a steady provider nor offering a secure future. His passenger service was hardly a full time occupation, and the fact that he would join Flying Circuses as a parachute jumper on weekends portended an earlier demise rather than a promising future. No, there was no support in the Laine family for a marriage between these two—definitely not!

Some claim that the marriage of Wiley Post to his cousin Edna Mae Laine took place on the day it did only because of a forced landing after a harmless Sunday afternoon outing by plane. Wiley,

---

[1]*Ponca City News*, article by Jack Baskin, August 18, 1935.
[2]Edna Mae Post interview, *Daily Oklahoman*, December 10, 1950.

however, refers to it as a carefully planned elopement. He does not tell just what the couple had planned, whether there was a preacher waiting somewhere to join them in matrimony, or where they had arranged to spend their honeymoon—nothing. All that Wiley says of the wedding day is:

> So on June 27, 1927, after the business of the day was over, the soon-to-be Mrs. Post and I piled into the ship. She had a small bag with her and I had a license in my pocket. Her father, Dave Laine, a rancher on a small scale, was not favorably disposed to our marriage, so we decided to take the matter into our own hands. Together we fled the town.[3]

All did not go quite smoothly on this elopement. In the time since Wiley had purchased the plane, when he had it completely over-hauled, the Canuck had flown some 800 hours without showing any signs of problems. Over Graham, Oklahoma, just thirty miles due south of Maysville and Wiley's parental home, the Canuck's engine quit. Looking for a place to set the plane down, the prospective groom spotted a recently harvested field and landed somewhat unevenly but safely. Checking the engine, he found that the rotor in the magneto distributor had ground itself to dust and needed to be replaced. Even a cursory pre-flight inspection would have detected this relatively obvious developing problem. A quick replacement at that time would have avoided the need for an emergency landing, which could have been disastrous. As Wiley had no spare rotor on board, this being a part rarely needing replacement, he had no chance of getting the plane off the ground that day. Nor was it likely that he would find the rotor in any of the small towns of the area. So the respectable thing, with a young lady aboard, was to find a local preacher first, to perform the wedding ceremony. Mae divulged years later that the newlyweds spent their wedding night out in the open on a nearby oil derrick's wooden base.[4]

---

[3]*Around the World in Eight Days* by Wiley Post and Harold Gatty, © 1931, Rand McNally & Co., p. 267
[4]Edna Mae Post interview, *Daily Oklahoman*, December 10, 1950.

Their honeymoon started with a two-day stay out on the open prairie, while Wiley overhauled the distributor and found a replacement rotor. Being married to a flier was hardly the routine and stable life to which a farm girl like Mae was accustomed, but Wiley had found a great partner who shared with him whatever life presented. Mae gladly would fly with her husband, work with him, help him load and unload the plane, and even manage to keep house and cook—when they had a semi-permanent address. It was a bohemian life, but Mae never complained. The only thing she wished that Wiley would stop was one of the few jokes in his repertoire. Referring to the eleven-year difference in their ages, Wiley would claim that it was he who really had raised his child bride. Even more annoying to Mae was that many people actually believed it.

Wiley still had some students and his plane was still for hire, but now that he was married, he gave up the dangerous weekend parachute jumping. He had to be more concerned about caring for a second person, although the loss of income from his daredevil stunts cut severely into their budget.

Running his simple little airline, Wiley not only met a variety of people, but also really learned his trade. As he flew in all sorts of weather, over all types of landscape, he was able to perfect his gift of setting a plane down on all kinds of uneven terrain. It was a great school, and best of all, he was being paid for it.

One time, though, in Wyoming, Wiley had a lesson he had not anticipated. The subject was 'atmospheric pressure.' Having made a landing on a meadow at an altitude of six thousand feet, he was approached by two ranchers who wanted to fly to Cheyenne. The agreed fee was $200. Their voluminous luggage was packed and in the midday sun, Wiley tried to take off. The engine started and the plane rolled quickly on the more or less level grass. To his bewilderment, Wiley could not lift the plane off. Even with the throttle wide open, the plane seemed too heavy. The load was lightened. Some fuel was drained. Still, the hot, thin air of the high altitude would not support the heavy plane. Not until the late afternoon, when the sun began to set and the mountain air had cooled and become denser, was Wiley able to lift off.

When the chilly fall temperatures of Oklahoma began to hover around discomfort levels, Sunday crowds at air shows thinned considerably. People, understandably, refused to stand shivering in open fields to gawk at planes overhead, or even at a descending parachute. The passenger business, too, slowed dramatically. Would-be pilot students became more unwilling to take lessons in an open-cockpit plane where the rushing air increased the numbing harshness of the cold. When a ground loop damaged his beloved Canuck, Wiley barely had enough money left to pay for the repairs. It was time to sell the "Jenny" and start looking for a permanent job. Times became ever harder for the young couple. Years later Mae Post readily admitted it: "We had a struggle in those first years. We lived out of a suitcase, so to speak. There were times when we traded milk bottles for potatoes. Sometimes we'd go to the home of Wiley's parents to live."[5]

The economy worsened as oil prices plummeted further. Smaller producers found it unprofitable to continue drilling or pumping; there were ever fewer jobs and far more unemployed roughnecks vying for them. It was then that Wiley heard of a couple of enterprising oilmen in Chickasha who might have an opening for a pilot. Their names were Powell Briscoe and F. C. Hall. The F stood for "Florence," which Hall found too girlish for his taste or use, so he was always just "F. C. Hall."

Briscoe and Hall had long ago learned the lesson that speed was essential in their business: Be among the first on a drilling site and the first to get an oil lease signed and registered! They had used airplanes before, but had lost several deals when no plane or pilot was available at the time they needed them most. They had come to realize that if they wanted to advance in this highly competitive business, they had to have their own exclusive plane and pilot ready to go anywhere at any time.

A number of applicants competed with Wiley for what promised to be a good job, but he proved to be the most persistent. Wiley hounded Briscoe and Hall's office continuously, and, with a patch over the left eye socket, he was hired at a salary of around two hundred dollars, and with the understanding that he would be able

---

[5]Edna Mae Post interview, *Daily Oklahoman*, December 10, 1950

to use the company's plane when the partners did not foresee needing it. As it turned out, Wiley also acted as the pair's chauffeur and Briscoe's hunting companion. Briscoe remembered that when Wiley was paid his first month's salary, he immediately went out and purchased a hunting rifle he had seen advertised, when it was obvious that he needed a new suit far worse.

The plane the partners decided to buy was a new, 1928 three-passenger, open-cockpit Travel Air biplane, manufactured in Wichita, Kansas. It was a fine plane—for what it was—and did serve well. Wiley had no problems with it.

Wiley did have other problems, however, when he took the job with Hall and Briscoe. Not only had he been breaking a new law, but he had also been running dangerously afoul of his parole conditions, since he had been flying without a pilot's license from the U. S. Department of Commerce, Aeronautics Branch. Established in 1926, that department had instituted specific standards for all who operated aircraft. Fearing that his loss of one eye would prevent him from meeting the basic requirements, Wiley had carefully avoided landing at major airports, seeking instead those where government inspectors would not watch and check licenses. If it became unavoidable that he had to fly into an airport staffed with permanent inspectors, he would schedule his arrival for the hour just before dusk and plan his departure for very early in the morning. He knew from experience that he would thus avoid those inspectors who kept bankers' hours—arriving late for their jobs and going home early.

Now that he was fully employed as a pilot it became essential that he have a license. The requirements were explicit: Section 66 of Chapter 4, "Licensing of pilots and Aircraft, of the U.S. Air Commerce Regulations, effective December 31, 1926, spelled them out:

> Industrial pilots must have an absence of any organic disease or defect which would interfere with the safe handling of an airplane; visual acuity of not less than 20/30 in each eye, although in certain instances less than 20/30 may be accepted if the applicant wears a correction to 20/30 in his goggles and has good judgment without correction; good judgment of distance; no diplopia [double vision] in any field; normal visual fields and color

vision; absence of organic disease of the eye, ear, nose and throat.[6]

This regulation did not bode well for Wiley, nor did the law make any allowance for Wiley's natural talents and special training. However, through F. C. Hall's intervention,[7] a waiver of certain requirements could be arranged under specific circumstances, such as in the case of experienced pilots. The Secretary of Commerce could grant these waivers for physical insufficiencies, if in his opinion the experience of the pilot made up for the shortcomings.

Wiley took a written test given by the Aeronautics Branch that he passed without difficulty. Because he had never kept a log of his flying hours, and therefore could not prove that he had many hundred hours of experience, it was determined that he would be required to fly a probationary period of 700 hours before he could be granted a license. He accumulated the required number of hours within eight months and on September 16, 1928, he was given transport license number 3259. A major step forward had been taken and another obstacle had been hurdled.

The trio of Hall, Briscoe, and Post worked like a well-trained team. On a personal level, they were most congenial. Hall came to look on Post almost as a father would on his first-born son, and Briscoe could not have found a more knowledgeable hunting companion. The two oilmen had the utmost confidence in Post and felt secure with their one-eyed pilot. To anyone who would ask, Briscoe would say: "Wiley doesn't have a nerve in his body. When other people were scared, Wiley would just grin." Briscoe might have been referring to a day in the Texas Panhandle. The three of them were flying to Amarillo, Texas, near Shamrock, when their small plane unexpectedly encountered a violent rainstorm. The strong winds caught and tossed the light plane until it was bouncing like a floating cork in a hurricane. Flying in an open cockpit exposed to the raging elements might have recalled to Wiley the mockery of one of his

---

[6]Wiley Post, *His Winnie Mae*, and the World's First Pressure Suit. by S. R. Mohler and B. H. Johnson, Smithsonian Institution Press, 1971
[7]*Around the World in Eight Days* by Wiley Post and Harold Gatty, © 1931, Rand McNally & Co., p. 273

instructors: "When you are flying in a storm, the best place to be is on the ground." He tried to make out the ground, looking for a place to set the plane down. Hall and Briscoe became increasingly nervous and airsick. At last, Wiley spotted a recently seeded field. As carefully as poor visibility, strong winds, and the soggy, rough ground would allow, Wiley set the plane down. It proved not to be one of the smoothest landings in Wiley's career, and the bumpy contact with the ground resulted in a broken strut, but the two oilmen could not have been more relieved. They had reached the safety of the ground without a mishap, and they were uninjured. That was all that mattered.

They were also very wet; they had gotten drenched in the open plane. After the rain stopped, the three men examined the damaged aircraft. The oilmen were certain that they had missed the deal in Amarillo, and would have to return to Oklahoma by train. Not so their resourceful pilot. Wiley found a piece of two-by-four timber and some wire, which he used to patch up the broken strut, and the trio, soaked to the skin, continued their trip to Amarillo. It probably was the memory of this and similar experiences that prompted Hall to attend a Lockheed-sponsored display of their latest cabin plane, the Vega. Lockheed, a subsidiary of Detroit Aircraft Corporation, had an excellent reputation as a leader in its field. This $20,240 plane was the latest word in Lockheed's catalogue. It was their fastest and most comfortable plane, with a Pratt & Whitney Wasp engine, cruising between 150 and 190 miles per hour.

After taking a short demonstration flight, Hall was convinced that this was the plane for their purpose and he placed an order for his first Lockheed plane. Wiley was told to fly the company's current Travel Air plane to the Lockheed plant in Burbank, California, where it was to be traded in on the brand new Vega. Wiley was now in his element. After having so far only flown relatively short distances of— at best—a few hundred miles, he was now off on a trip across half the North American continent. Not only would there be a lot to see, but also a lot to learn. For the first time he would be flying an open cockpit plane over scorching deserts and then in icy altitudes, through high mountain passes and over towering peaks. Used to flying by sight, he would now have to study detailed topographical maps before ever starting the engine. Yes, this was going to be quite a learning experience, but that was exactly what Wiley Post wanted and needed. From Los Angeles, Wiley wrote home:

Dear Honey

Late as usual Ill write a little, arrived here 13 oclock day after I left E. P. nothing had been done on a plane for F. C. H. [F. C. Hall, Ed.] so I started trying rush thing along a little I thought they might get one finished in about 10 days but of course that would be impossible here it could have been done but the extra things I get took time to get here and they used that as an excuse that there was no use in hurrying on any of it now everything is here and a thousand things that could have been done has to be done yet

Im sure fixing this thing up putting in a Radio beacon and weather receiver of course it would take to long tell how much that will be worth am having Earth inducter compass as well as one like I used on the Ford tour and other things too numerous to mention it is upholstered with purple mohair plush that cost $12.00 a yard trimmed with white leather, outside is white trimmed with purple, as the fellows in the paint shop liked me pretty well I got the swellest paint job ever turned out here It will be very passionate should completely rejuvinate old man H.

There's so much I could write but I'm completely worn out, yesterday being Sat we were expecting some radio shielding for the motor in by air mail so they could put that on and install the motor today of course it had to get lost in the mail terminal at L. A. I went down to Burbank Postoffice just before it closed and started raising a *big one*. Postmaster decided to back me to the limit on a search for the out fit and after getting thrown out of the L.A. terminal twice I located it there twelve thirty last night then being registered and consigned to Burbank the fun really started. Well I had practically everybody except President Hoover out of bed after midnight last night believe me the training I got taking a car into Mexico and then selling it there sure was worth a lot. It's just as easy to do something unusual like that in Mexico as it is here I arrived at the Lockheed plant with the box on my shoulder at 6:40 this morning rounded up 3 mechanics got authority from Squires for them to work on it today and it is all . . . [illegible] . . . and the motor on the ship tonight I hope it is worth the trouble

Am staying at Valencia Apts. Mrs what's her name seemed extremely glad to rent me an apt. and take care of it for me. It only costs $1.20 a day which Mr. H. will appreciate maybe. Moving in here kind to have turned out disasterously that being the address the Capt got on that ticket I got takes too long to tell but it turned out nice and funny.

If you positively have to have a suit case buy a good one cheep as you can would rather you box that junk and ship it express to O K City [Oklahoma City, OK—Ed.] when you leave and Ill get a wardrobe trunk when I get to O K City. He last move I made with my suit case I had to carry it under my arm first because the handle was pulled off and next, the other fastener was off and I had to keep it closed someway Im going to have to buy somekind of out fit myself and as we should be located in Okla. quite a while, I hope we wont need much baggage but just as you like—by the way don't write any checks—I got a draft from Mex. For that hundred Pesos I missed when I left carried it to that lousy bank and they wanted to charge—.50¢ for collection on it. I just picked up a check book signed my name and told them I wanted what I had in the bank in cash. Got a cashiers check at the other bank and have it in the safe at Lockheed will send it to Okla by registered mail when I leave I think Ill be at Sweetwater Sat but of course don't know will wire later

I got offer of another job that tempted me quite a little, The Insurance man that was around so much here gave me such a boost up at Oakland to Boeing that the operation manager came down and offered me a job flying the *mail* here to Oakland. Well I haven't made a step that later didn't get me a little higher and I hope this job I'm taking will be the hum-dinger it ought to be

> Will see you soon I hope
> Mucho Gusto y adios
> Wiley

On the return trip, Wiley flew the new plane, one that marked a radical departure from the standard designs of the late 1920s with the exposed struts and cables on their wing supports, and a fabric-covered fuselage. The trend-setting Vega presented a sleek, streamlined plywood body with wing support and control cables hidden. Wiley must have been amazed by how far airplane designs had advanced since the days of his first love, the "Jenny," even as he watched Hall's Vega come off the assembly line with the serial number 24. On the wing ends and fuselage of the white plane with purple trim were painted the federal registration number NC 7954. F. C. Hall named the plane the "*Winnie Mae*," after his daughter. Oddly enough, this new leader in the field of aviation had everything— everything, that is, except a U.S. Aeronautics Branch Type Certificate of Airworthiness.

F. C. Hall and his partner Powell Briscoe used the plane often and Wiley grew very familiar with its capabilities and idiosyncrasies. The months rolled by, almost routinely. With his monthly paycheck coming in regularly, Wiley and Mae Post now lived a most ordered existence. All seemed well with their world and the young couple had few worries. Wiley still had his dreams, of course, but he was in no hurry. Having just turned thirty years of age, he was still a young man. Some dreams just take a little longer to come to fruition— especially when they are confronted with a Depression.

The stock market crash of 1929 and the onset of the Great Depression had a massive impact on the oil business. This seemed surprising, since the United States was already heavily dependent on oil and its by-products. However, because of the Depression, new car sales plunged. Ford Motor Company's Model A's sales dropped from 2 million in 1929, to 1 million in 1930, but statistics show that the country had already one passenger car for every 5.5 citizens. And even though the sales of new cars dropped, used cars continued to have one rebirth after another. Therefore, with 23 million motorcars on its seven hundred thousand miles of paved, and 2.3 million miles of unpaved roads, gasoline would have appeared to be essential. Americans simply were not willing to give up their new love affair with the motorcar. It prompted Will Rogers, the United States' resident wit and philosopher, to note: "We are the only nation in the history of the world that will go to the poorhouse in an automobile."

The budding airlines industry, too, found itself seriously affected by the Depression. Many small local air carriers merged to reduce overhead and to survive, forming future giants. Thus, in 1930, a merger of Boeing Transport and National Air Transport created United Airlines. Transcontinental and Western Air (TWA), American Airlines, National Airlines, and Braniff Airways all saw their emergence, while PAN-AM expanded with flights to South America. By the end of 1930, there were three transcontinental carriers in operation with more or less regular passenger flights.

Wealthy in investments but strapped for cash, Hall and Briscoe had ever less need for a plane. Wiley was rarely flying the *Winnie Mae*, but her expenses continued. Wiley could see the inevitable coming—the plane, and with it the pilot—would soon have to go.

During the early stages of aviation, young, daring pilots actively sought publicity. They lived flamboyantly; they kept exotic animals as pets, which made the rotogravure sections of Sunday papers; they hobnobbed with celebrities in trendy speakeasies, thus gaining publicity for all three; and they tried to establish long-distance-flight records. In these youthful days of air transport, almost any long-distance flight between two unrelated places was hailed as a new record. Sometimes huge prizes were offered, for what then seemed extremely hazardous, if not impossible, distances. The press coverage of any major "hop"—as these trips were called—constituted the publicity sought by the sponsors of such flights. One such "spectacular act" was Charles A. Lindbergh's flight to Paris in a plane named "Spirit of St. Louis" to acknowledge its sponsorship by that city's businesses. A modified Ryan M-1 Brougham with a 223 horsepower Wright J-5c Whirlwind radial engine, the plane was not commissioned to further aviation by testing a radically advanced design, a new type of engine, or even special instruments, but simply to win the Orteig Prize of $25,000 for the first solo crossing between New York and Paris, in either direction. At the same time, of course, it advertised a city, a plane manufacturer, and the Wright engine, not to mention Mr. Lindbergh. While this trans-Atlantic flight demanded a heroic effort by a man surely risking his life, it advanced Charles A. Lindbergh farther than it advanced aviation. Along with the lure of a prize of $25,000, which constituted a small fortune in the 1920s, came honor and international acclaim.

In the attempts to garner the prize before Lindbergh's flight, lives had been lost. But Colonel Lindbergh succeeded where they had failed. His brave solo flight stands as a testimony to man's and machine's endurance.

In the 1920s and even in the early Depression years, the American public cried out for deeds that shocked and entertained and appealed to a spirit of adventure that was bound to a stove, a desk, or a routine. Those were the days when the newspapers reported on college students who established new records by demonstrating that a single-occupancy telephone booth could hold a dozen healthy undergraduates, or more. Records captured the public's imagination, and contestants would vie with each other to see who could sit on a flagpole, dance, or kiss the longest; eat the most hot dogs, swallow the most goldfish, or drink the most bottles of beer; or who could accomplish any feat better, higher, faster, or simply different from anybody else. It was an era when women "bobbed" their hair, made every effort to appear flat chested, smoked cigars in public, and first wore trousers, simply because they wanted to show their freedom and individuality by imitating the other gender. As the Depression took hold and deepened, a whole multitude of habits and practices changed.

The year is 1930. The occupant of the White House is Herbert Clark Hoover, his Vice-President is Charles Curtis, a man whose name few know and even fewer will remember. The world's population is estimated at 2 billion, 123 million of which are American citizens. The so-called civilized world is learning the meaning of Depression and the western United States is beginning to experience the deprivation of an era that will become known as the Dust Bowl years. The world's oil-price structure collapses after a wildcatter named Columbus M. Joiner, aged 71, discovers a huge new oil field and brings in a gusher in Rusk county in eastern Texas.

Although most industries suffer, tobacco companies in 1930 will produce 123 billion cigarettes, as compared with 9 billion just twenty years earlier. An infant radio industry, meanwhile, will sell more than 13 million radio sets; $60 million will be spent on commercials. William Randolph Hearst already owns thirty-three newspapers, and Aristotle Socrates Onassis will buy six freighters for the ridiculous price of $20,000 each. These ships, which had cost the Canadian Pacific

Railway $2 million each to build, will form the nucleus of a future shipping empire. In contrast, to prove that the rich get richer and the poor stay that way, American farms show an average annual income of a pitiful $400 per family, while staggering under a total mortgage of $9.2 billion.

Hollywood, having found a voice for its films, produces such 1930 classics as *All Quiet on the Western Front*, starring Lew Ayres, and *Lightnin'*, with Will Rogers and Joel McCrea. Dashiell Hammett writes *The Maltese Falcon*, and Grant Wood paints the famous *American Gothic*, using his own sister and his dentist as models for the dour pair.

One of the most far-reaching innovations of the year 1930 in the U.S. is the introduction of sliced bread. At first, there is strong reluctance to accept the fast drying slices, but its advantage is soon recognized and gives currency to the phrase, "This is the best thing since sliced bread."

In aviation, for the first time, an airline stewardess walks up the aisle, serving cold meals, beverages, chewing gum, and candy. Discriminatorily, the industry requires that all such servers be no older than twenty-five years of age, stand no taller than five foot four inches, and weigh no more than 115 pounds. They all must have pleasant personalities and help passengers in case of airsickness. With their squads of eye-appealing stewardesses, the airlines launch their campaign to allay the public's fear of flying.

As the weeks went by and the Depression forecast only more hard times, Briscoe and Hall faced economic facts. Fearing a dramatic reduction in their oil business, and in a hasty attempt to cut their expenses before they created a financial problem, the two oilmen laid off their pilot and sold the *Winnie Mae*. Her new owners, Nevada Airlines, deleted the name and in short order sold the plane, which would find several other owners, including such famous pilots of the time as Roscoe Turner, Art Goebel, and Laura Ingalls. Perhaps not too strangely, Wiley Post would meet his former plane one more time.

Once again, Wiley was unemployed, with no prospect of getting into the embryonic airline industry. Looking for a job around Oklahoma City's airport one day, Wiley met the man who was to become his guardian angel, Joe Crosson. Neither Wiley nor Crosson could possibly have envisioned the roles they were going to play in each other's lives. As it turned out, Wiley would be the sole beneficiary, for Joe would always be the one offering aid and giving advice, helping his friend in times of trouble or need, just the way a guardian angel is supposed to be.

Joe Crosson, a well-known pilot working for PAN AM, had come to Oklahoma City simply to pick up a plane, which he was to fly back to Los Angeles. The two men started a conversation and liked what they saw in each other. It was Joe who suggested to Wiley that he should think about leaving Oklahoma City, where job opportunities were limited, and try California instead. When Wiley worried about how he'd cover traveling and living expenses until he could connect with a firm in the west, Joe invited him to fly to California aboard the plane he was ferrying there. This free ride was a courtesy often extended by one pilot to another. As for the cost of living in California, Joe offered Wiley the possibility of staying at his parents' home in San Diego. He assured Post that his parents were most hospitable and had played host to pilots before. Joe also promised that he would try to get Wiley a job at PAN-AM. The prospect looked far brighter than anything Wiley had encountered in Oklahoma City, and he accepted the logic in Crosson's proposition.

Joe did not let Wiley down. The Crossons welcomed Wiley as if he were their own long-absent son, and made him feel at home. Joe also tried to get Wiley situated at PAN-AM, but finding a position for a one-eyed pilot proved to be difficult, especially when so many unemployed two-eyed pilots were available.

Then one day, Wiley Post disappeared from the Crossons' home in San Diego. He left without a note, without a thank you, with no good-bye. He next appeared in Burbank, California, the home of Lockheed Aircraft Corporation. Wiley had been there the year before, when he had picked up Hall and Briscoe's Vega. Now he hired on as a contract test pilot, an important, but certainly not the most enviable job. Being on contract meant that he was not on the payroll; instead he was paid for the single jobs assigned to him. A test pilot's function was to determine if a new design, appearing safe on the drawing board, could stand the rigors of actual flight. No engineer or machine could determine how a new plane would react to a power dive, for example, or worse, to pulling out of one. Dozens of checks had to be made and assessed by pilots in the cockpit, by men willing to risk the serious accidents that were the price of progress.

When no planes, whether new or repaired, had to be tested, and newly ordered planes had to be taken to customers, Wiley was often called on to fly those deliveries. It was a wonderful opportunity to fly the latest models and a variety of planes. He logged many hours of airtime while working for Lockheed, where he met the foremost fliers of the time. When Amelia Earhart planned to participate in what Will Rogers was to dub "The Powder Puff Derby," the women's airplane race from Los Angeles to Cleveland, she brought her aging Lockheed Vega, Model 1, to the factory to have it checked out. Calling her plane "a third-rate clunk," she asked Wiley to test-fly it to see whether it could be overhauled, or at least improved for the race. After just a few minutes in the air, Wiley determined that Earhart's descriptive name for the plane was an understatement and suggested that Lockheed—just to protect its good name—lend her a far superior demonstrator Vega model they had on hand. Earhart did not win the race, but then she was never considered an outstanding pilot like Jackie Cochran, Laura Ingalls, Fay Gillis, or Marvel Crosson. The winner was Louise Thaden; Earhart came in third.

While in California, Wiley also met Harold Gatty, a native of Tasmania, Australia, who had spent three years at the Royal Australian Naval College in preparation for a career as a navigator. He now taught astral navigation to aviators who had to act as their own navigators in a time before reliable radio-beacon air routes or dependable weather forecasts. Dreaming about some day entering the Bendix Air Race, Wiley had asked the much-esteemed Gatty to lay out the most advantageous route from Los Angeles to Chicago. Gatty promised to give it some serious thought. There was no sense to even talk to Gatty about a flight around the world yet, Wiley must have thought—one thing at a time.

When Briscoe and Hall realized that they had sold their Vega too hastily, they contacted Wiley in California. Was he available, they wanted to know? And if so, would he consider coming back to his old job? When he answered in the affirmative to both questions, they asked him to pick out the most up-to-date Lockheed Vega and fly it back to Oklahoma.

Wiley was present every step along the assembly of the plane that was to become known the world over as the *Winnie Mae*, even though she was not the first to bear that name. Wiley claimed that during the various stages of production, he suggested several changes in the basic design to improve the plane's performance. That may be quite possible, as he had picked up some engineering fundamentals while working as a test pilot.

When the new *Winnie Mae* came off the assembly line, Wiley took her up for a spin and put her through every test he knew. She passed them all. He then helped his wife, who had joined him in California when he began flying at Lockheed, pack their few belongings and together they flew back to Oklahoma.

Hall and Briscoe were pleased with their new plane. She was indeed a beauty. All white, with purple trim, and roomy enough for seven passengers, she attracted attention wherever she flew. Best of all, F. C. Hall now suggested that if Wiley was still thinking about entering some of those air races he had always talked about, now was the time to do it. Wiley did not have to hear such an offer twice. He immediately wrote to Gatty, reminding him of his promise and their conversation. Gatty replied, sending along a routing that he thought would be the shortest, yet would avoid high altitudes and the effects of locally prevailing elements.

The Bendix Trophy race took place on August 26, 1930. It attracted the best pilots in the country, who sought not only the prestige attached to winning a race among an imposing group of aviators, but also the substantial cash prize of $7,500. The planes left at set intervals from Los Angeles; their aim, to reach Chicago nonstop. Elapsed time between takeoff and landing was the criterion for the race, not the order of arrival. Shortly after takeoff, Wiley's compass became stuck and he lost an irreplaceable half hour at the onset of the race. Still, he won the race, beating the second place plane by eleven seconds. Astonishingly, the plane awarded second-place honors turned out to be a familiar friend. Piloted by the famous Art Goebel, the former holder of the transcontinental speed record, and repainted a different color, it was unmistakably the first *Winnie Mae*. Especially surprising was the disclosure that Harold Gatty had laid out the course for Art Goebel as well as for Wiley. The fact that two Lockheed Vegas took top spots at the race gave birth to the catchy advertising slogan: "It takes a Lockheed to beat a Lockheed."

On August 11, 1941, piloted by Laura Ingalls, Vega # NC/NR 7954, the first *Winnie Mae*, came to a heroic end at Albuquerque, New Mexico, when she was totally destroyed in a crash. Ms. Ingalls escaped uninjured.

CHAPTER V

ONCE AROUND THE WORLD

WILEY POST LEFT Chicago a famous and richer man, having won the $7,500 first prize. It was the first time in his life that he had that much money at one time. The newspapers had interviewed him, photographers had insisted on taking just one more picture, and perfect strangers had stared at him and/or wanted his autograph—for their son, of course. It was all a bit too heady for a country lad not to attach some importance to any of it. Wiley was not a colorful individual; it was only what he accomplished that was impressive. He did not know what to say to reporters that would sound significant or make him look sophisticated. There can be little doubt about Wiley's insecurity, or his inferiority complex. They were based on his lack of formal education, his diminutive size, and his dread that at any moment somebody might find out about his criminal past. Instinctively, he had built a protective wall around himself. The only way Wiley Post knew how to keep at a distance people that he thought could harm him, was to not appear friendly. Thus he seemed mostly curt and rude; a poor mixer. He would bully people he deemed subservient, like mechanics or waitresses, who could

not retaliate. It made him feel superior. Of course, the sudden attention was definitely flattering and should have given Wiley self-
assurance, but he did not know how to handle it. An insecure man,
he would never learn how to accept his fame with grace, or give back
what fame demanded of him.

> I went back to Oklahoma and my duties as a pilot to the Hall
> family. I got a slight taste of being the returning hero when I
> landed in Chickasha, but I hope it didn't go to my head. Mr.
> Hall was so overjoyed at the performance of his new plane that
> he ordered me to go ahead with my around-the-world plan as
> soon as possible.[1]

Hall was indeed pleased by the success his plane and his personal
pilot had garnered in Chicago. He basked in the reflected glory as if
he had in some way participated in the feat. In interviews, he would
claim at times that Wiley had sold him on the idea of a flight around
the world as a sporting proposition, while later, he would claim that
the idea had been his late wife's.[2] He enjoyed having his picture in
the papers, being mentioned as the owner of the *Winnie Mae*, as the
man who had financed Post's victory, and he wanted more, much
more publicity. Hall made only two simple demands of Post: He
insisted that Mrs. Post approve of such a flight. His thought must
have been that he did not want it said in case of an accident that it
had all been arranged behind Mae Post's back. The other demand
was that there were to be no commercial interests involved in any
attempt involving his plane. This meant that Wiley could not raise
funds by selling advertising space on the fuselage, or—as others had
done—rename the plane to advertise some company, product, or
city. Powell Briscoe, Hall's partner, refused to have anything to do
with his partner's scheme, fearing that Post might be killed and that
he could be held responsible, either by the law, or by his own con-
science. Hall had to foot the bill for most expenses, and he was
explicit when he told Post: "Whatever profits, if any, result from the

[1]*Around the World in Eight Days* by Wiley Post and Harold Gatty, © 1931, Rand
McNally & Co., p. 281
[2]F. C. Hall in an interview, *Daily Oklahoman*, April 15, 1931.

flight will be used to defray the expenses, and you will have to hope for a surplus for remuneration."[3]

Being optimistic, Hall foresaw substantial riches from the round-the-world trip for both Post and Gatty. The latter had been guaranteed $5,000 plus 25% of profits, while Hall predicted that Post would make at least $75,000 from the flight alone, not counting at least $125,000 from endorsements and another $100,000 from barnstorming tours.[4] As a little sideline, Post and Gatty planned to carry along several hundred autographed envelopes, which they would have postmarked in every country they visited and then would sell as souvenirs.

Wiley knew the dream that had been with him since the day he saw his first airplane had suddenly come within his grasp. However, if he was not allowed to advertise products, how was he going to make any of that big money that Hall foresaw? After all, he had spent a few thousand dollars of his own on this upcoming flight, and he deserved to realize some return on his investment. Post and Hall finally agreed that Wiley would be allowed to solicit assistance from aviation-related firms, provided they did not realize profits directly from the flight. Further, Wiley would be allowed to file progress reports under his byline with newspapers as the flight progressed. Until after the flight was completed, Wiley and Gatty were not to endorse any equipment or merchandise. After their safe return and after their agreement with Hall had been fulfilled, they were at liberty to do what they deemed right and proper, and if possible, lucrative.

If Wiley Post had thought that making preparations for a racing hop from Los Angeles to Chicago was difficult and time consuming, he was now to find out just how much more was involved in an attempt to fly across unforgiving oceans or over foreign lands. The number-one item on his list was to persuade the man he believed to be indispensable, Harold Gatty, to map the route and then to agree to come along and keep the plane on course. Wiley did not know that the Australian had only months earlier accompanied the pilot of the 1930 long-distance flight to Japan and his experience had been

---

[3]*Around the World in Eight Days* by Wiley Post and Harold Gatty, © 1931, Rand McNally & Co., p. 23
[4]*Daily Oklahoman*, June 28, 1931.

none too happy. On that flight the weather refused to cooperate after the plane was well on its way. The storm became so severe that they decided to turn around and the plane barely made it back to its home base on American soil. The flight attempt was subsequently abandoned. This experience was only one reason for Gatty not to jump at the invitation. Mapping the course might be one thing, but to take time off again from his wife and three sons, close his school and cancel classes, which were his only source of income, were something else. What if there were some malfunction and the plane had to make an emergency landing? How long would it be before a replacement part could be rushed to, say, the Soviet Union? He might be away for many weeks. Against those arguments he could weigh that a successful flight would bring students swarming to his navigation classes. What better advertising could there be than to set a new record flight around the world? Of course, there was that $5,000 guarantee, win, lose, or draw. Whatever did affect his decision was not recorded, but he finally agreed to map the course and come along on the trip.

Having secured Harold Gatty, Wiley knew that this part of the great trip was in most competent hands and he would not have to concern himself further with that phase—from now on the plane needed his attention.

There had been only three successful earlier "Round-the-World Flights," though more attempts had been made. In 1924 alone, fliers from Britain, France, Italy, Germany, and the United States attempted to circle the earth by "aeroplane." In that year, too, on April 6, the U.S. Army Air Service sent out four aircraft, Douglas "World Cruisers," from Sand Point, Seattle, Washington. Five months and twenty-two days later, on September 28, just two surviving planes limped back after more than sixty repair and/or refueling stops and a few dozen replaced engines. Those two American Army planes, each with a crew of one pilot and one mechanic, were the only ones to accomplish their task. For just five years, those four men could enjoy their unique distinction. In 1929, the German dirigible Graf Zeppelin broke their record by taking a mere 21 days, 7 hours, and 34 minutes to circle the globe successfully.

Wiley was convinced that barring a serious engine malfunction along the way, he could easily break that record. He told acquaintances that he could fly around the world in fewer than ten days. Being dedicated to airplanes, he felt certain also that the future of air travel lay with airplanes, rather than with dirigibles. In time, passengers would definitely opt for speed over safety. He reasoned that even though dirigibles could so far claim a safety record superior to that of airplanes, America's motto would always be "time is money." So far, despite the planes' oft-proven greater speed, the public was still apprehensive about air travel, for as there were more planes than dirigibles, there were more sensational plane crashes than dirigible accidents. If Wiley could now demonstrate that airplanes were not only fast, but also safer than any other form of transportation, he would make converts to the modern way of travel.

Leaving their Chickasha, Oklahoma, apartment, Wiley and his wife flew the *Winnie Mae* to Burbank, California. There, Lockheed was to make a variety of alterations to the plane and thoroughly check it out in preparation for the long flight. Wiley was on familiar ground in California. He had spent time at the factory and knew most of the folks who would now work on his plane.

The changes to the plane were dictated by specific needs. To lessen the number of landings required to refuel and then to gain precious time, a substantially larger fuel capacity had to be installed. A gallon of airplane fuel weighs six pounds, and Wiley wanted the *Winnie Mae* to carry at least 500 gallons of gasoline, so the rest of the cargo, including the two men, had to be restricted to the barest minimum. An electric starting motor, for example, was immediately dismantled just to conserve weight. From now on, the *Winnie Mae*'s engine would have to be started by hand.

It was Wiley's belief that the packing and stowing of equipment and luggage was critical. He was convinced that some plane accidents were actually caused by the ill-planned arrangement of freight aboard small planes:

> Then came the problem of loading the fuselage . . .
> So many things can happen to airplanes that are badly loaded. A tail heavy plane, flying through the air with its elevator and stabilizer set at maximum nose-down position, more or less has the tendency to 'mush' along with undue lifting forces exerted on the wing and tail surfaces. . . . The reverse situation—a nose-

heavy plane—while better than tail heaviness, still wears the pilot
out, and sets up undue strains on the top side of the horizontal
tail empennage . . .

It was up to me as pilot of the *Winnie Mae* to get the last
ounce of efficiency out of her. I figured on loading up so that I
would not dare put on an extra five pounds. My calculations
had to be accurate, for I was not going to run any advance tests.[5]

It seems strange reading this passage now in a book supposedly written by Wiley Post. Did he really have such strong beliefs in 1931 and
forget all about them by 1935, when he was flying around Alaska
in an unbalanced nose-heavy plane?

The constantly diminishing weight of the fuel in the course of the
flight would play no role if all of it was loaded in the plane's center
of gravity, but Wiley was not storing all his fuel in one place. He
had fuel tanks in the wings, as well as some new ones filling the
fuselage. As a result, pilot and navigator were cut off from each
other; they could neither see each other, nor speak directly. To com-
municate, at Gatty's suggestion, they utilized a tube through which
their voices could be heard. This tube worked fine when the plane
was on the ground and the engine was not running. In the air it
proved impractical as a speaking tube, though it did provide a con-
duit for passing hand-written messages back and forth.

To further solve the problem of having a potentially unbalanced
plane in which to fly around the world, Wiley devised a system by
which the tanks could be shifted forward and aft to retain the plane's
equilibrium. Even Harold Gatty's seat and work area could be moved
in flight to correct imbalance.

Two structural alterations to the plane were required—the installation of a hatch in the top of the fuselage, and the addition of a
hatch at the navigator's feet. The overhead hatch, equipped with a
windshield, would allow the navigator, Gatty, to make frequent ce-
lestial readings, while the lower opening in the fuselage would accommodate the instruments with which he could calculate the drift
and air speed of the plane. The government inspectors thought these

---

[5]*Around the World in Eight Days* by Wiley Post and Harold Gatty, © 1931, Rand
McNally & Co., pp. 34–35

additions significant enough to change the plane's classification from NC 105W—the "C" standing for "Commercial," to NR 105W—the "R" standing for "Restricted." Displayed prominently on the wings and on the rudder, the new classification in essence meant that the plane could no longer serve as a passenger transport, and could carry only the personnel necessary to perform specific tasks. This type of restriction would come again to plague Wiley some other day and some other place.

As Wiley's projected round-the-world flight was no secret, he received important advice from experienced fliers like Jimmy Doolittle, the first pilot to perform the dangerous task of taking off and landing "blind," which meant that in a completely blacked-out cockpit, unable to see either the ground or his surroundings, Doolittle had to depended solely on his instruments. Doolittle advised Wiley to group the "bank-and-turn" indicator, the "rate-of-climb" instrument, and the "artificial gyroscopic horizon" for easier and faster scanning during times of enforced blind flying, in total darkness or through clouds. Doolitte also suggested that certain instruments like an airspeed indicator and a compass be installed for both pilot and navigator. In addition to all the standard instruments carried by planes of the time, the *Winnie Mae* also had radio equipment. Intended primarily for use in emergencies, such as communication to direct rescuers in the event of a crash, it proved a total liability and strictly dead weight.

Gatty planned the route primarily to keep refueling stops at a minimum, though at the same time he had to consider the possibility of an emergency. What if a malfunction occurred, for instance, and they had to set down for assistance, be it mechanical or medical. A conscientious planner, Gatty had to keep in mind the possibility that at any moment they might need alternative landing sites. In western Europe, where numerous towns and cities marked the landscape, choosing a site in an emergency would be less problematic. If they had bucked headwinds or had flown through stormy weather and used fuel at an excessive rate, for instance, they could simply select the nearest city to refuel. Or if they experienced serious problems with the motor in western European cities or towns, they would generally be able to find a mechanic, even if only an automobile mechanic. Also, since Wiley had studied motors and engines, he could handle most minor problems, and at least offer advice on major ones.

In the Soviet Union, however, even simple refueling and the matter of repairs promised to be critical problems. Since the United States had so far not recognized the Soviet government as legitimate, on the basis that it had come into power by force, diplomatic relations between the U.S. and Russia had not been established. Communication therefore was difficult, and indeed for some time it even appeared that the Soviets would not grant permission to enter their airspace. In the case of an emergency, like a fuel crisis, or a mechanical failure, the Soviet Union offered far fewer centers of habitation, especially in the long stretch across Siberia. And would any town that did exist be able to supply proper aviation fuel? (Wiley would carry with him typed information in Russian regarding the airplane fuel in order to eliminate the language barrier.) Then, too, whether or not the Soviet Union would allow an American plane, whatever its crucial needs, to land anywhere it chose, posed a life-threatening question.

On advice, Wiley followed protocol, and on March 14, 1931, outlining the flight's aim and the need for assurances and information, he appealed to Henry L. Stimson, U.S. Secretary of State. Listing himself as pilot and Harold Gatty as crew, Wiley indicated that the flight was to start in Oklahoma City, with projected landings and refueling at Cleveland, Ohio; Harbour Grace, Newfoundland; Berlin, Germany; Moscow, Irkutsk, Yokutsk, USSR; Nome, Alaska; and finally at Portland, Oregon, before his return to Oklahoma City. The letter noted that the projected length of the flight was nine days; that equipment would include one small still camera, one 16 m/m movie camera, a radio under construction but not yet licensed, a thirty-six-meter transmitter with a range of approximately 1,000 miles, and a receiver, range 1,500 to 1,600 miles; and that the plane would carry no firearms.

On March 30, 1931, Wiley H. Post received an official envelope, c/o F. C. Hall, with the sender identified as the U.S. Department of State. Wiley, expecting a response to his request for over-flight permissions, eagerly tore open the envelope. Enclosed was a bill for two long distance telephone calls that the State Department had made in the matter of Wiley's proposed flight, namely, one to the U.S. Embassy in Paris and the other to the U.S. Legation in Ottawa, Canada. The total charge was $13.17. The bill was paid.

The long awaited answer from the State Department did not arrive until six weeks later, on May 12, 1931, indicating only that the authorities of the Netherlands and Germany had issued over-flight permissions. As expected, there was no word about the Soviet Union. However, enclosed was an official application blank requesting permission to have cameras aboard while traversing Belgian territory. As Belgium had not been mentioned as a projected landing site, and figured as only a possible over-flight country, one would have to wonder how the U.S. Department of State, or for that matter, Belgium, envisaged that the Belgian authorities would check whether Mr. Post or Mr. Gatty indeed had official permission to carry or use cameras while aloft.

As the U.S. State Department was obviously unable, or unwilling, to involve itself in the matter as far as the Soviet Union was concerned, Wiley approached Patrick Hurley, President Hoover's Secretary of War, and an Oklahoman, and asked him to intercede. Hurley, a realist, felt that the U.S. government was not the proper intermediary and suggested that Wiley approach Senator William E. Borah of Idaho, who had a special interest in foreign policy and over time had negotiated with the Soviet Union as an unofficial U.S. government spokesman. Wiley followed Hurley's advice and contacted Senator Borah.

Questions arose about which countries would provide assistance if it were required; what documents besides passports and visas would be required; and which countries would supply detailed maps of the terrain to be traversed. Wiley contacted each country they might fly over or in which they may be forced to land.

The important choice, whether to fly west or east was debated. Not an insignificant issue to Wiley; he held out for a flight in an easterly direction. His argument was irrefutable: Because flying the North Atlantic demanded the most concentration and attention, it should come at the beginning of the protracted flight, when bodies and minds were freshest, not at the end when they were exhausted. As for the argument that they would be flying into ever-earlier dusks, Wiley and Harold pointed out that whatever time they would lose by an earlier evening each day, they would gain the next morning.

Post had a special request. Instead of the usual hard, stiff-backed pilot seat, he wanted a comfortable, upholstered chair installed; he felt that sitting in one of those standard bucket seats for up to twenty hours was more than he should have to endure.

Wiley also put himself through a rigorous personal training program before the flight. Anticipating that a rapid change of time zones—they would come faster than anyone had ever experienced heretofore—would throw his biological timetable out of its acquired rhythm, Wiley developed his own program to alter his habits. He ate no meals at the same time every day. Breakfast might be in the evening, while supper might become a midday snack. He also trained his system to sleep at irregular times of day or night, and only for short periods. He reduced his food intake so drastically that Mae thought he was on a reducing diet to lighten the plane's load.

In addition to the hundreds of details that had to be checked and the numerous problems that could be anticipated, there was one most important factor that nobody could accurately foretell, or alter: the weather. Dr. James K. Kimball, known as the guardian angel of transatlantic fliers, was the U.S. Weather Bureau's meteorologist in New York. Ever since 1927 he had advised every pilot attempting to cross the North Atlantic, including Charles Lindbergh, whose flight to Paris Kimball had delayed for four days because his forecast predicted a storm over the ocean. The same Dr. Kimball was now asked to assume his angelic duties for Post and Gatty.

In the year 1931, radio was still in its infancy, and weather reports were not only sketchy but also mostly inaccurate. In the case of the North Atlantic, forecasts depended entirely on radio reports from ships plowing the lanes between the North American continent and Europe. Based on those reports Dr. Kimball would draw up his weather map and strive to divine the kind of weather pilots headed for Europe might encounter. Not always convinced of the accuracy of his own forecast, Kimball always tried to err on the side of prudence, yet despite his caution in the case of Lindbergh, he sent the Spirit of St. Louis into rain.

Dr. Kimball came aboard and the team seemed complete, but some pieces still had to fall into place before the big journey could begin. The Soviet Union had yet to agree to play her part. Wiley and Harold decided to fly to New York and await developments there. On their way they stopped in Washington to see whether they could do a little lobbying for their project. Wiley wrote to his wife:

Dear Mae

Am run to death but will write a few lines. Arrived at Washington last Fri after leaving OK City the day before and found we had been given permission to fly over Russia, it having been wire (sic) to us about thirty minutes after we left OK City, Well I was quite relieved and I now feel more so than ever that things always turn out for the best. Nothing could have happened that would have put us in the position we are in now but just what did. We will have no competition and we gained quite a lot of interest and attention at Washington as well as at other places.

We just about have everything set to go could go Fri morning if the weather would get all right. Kimball thinks will be June 1, before weather gets real good. I don't care if it does because I would have time get all set then have time get all rested before going.

Leslie, Weenie and Mr. Hall are here and I guess will stay till I get back or 'sumpen.' I sure wish you were here and you would be if we had the dough. Anyway when I arrive at Nome you take the first train or airplane and be sure to get here before I do even though you have to sell the car or guns

I am well, pleased the way our flight is being taken by the ones in the business that know how it should be done. All of them admire our equipment, preperations (sic) and everything which is just another reason we will have to bring home the bacon.

When we get all set will write more news while Im resting.

Say I had to let that guy I sold the parachute to deposit the money in the bank so it was deposited in our old account so you can just check it out that way, don't go over 90 or 95 dollar so they will keep the account open.

Will stop for now. Lots of Love and I sure feel like we will make it

Wiley

Senator Borah's efforts behind the scenes had proven fruitful. On May 21, Secretary B. E. Skvirsky, of the USSR Information Buro, one of those unofficial, yet official Soviet organizations in Washington, DC, sent Wiley Post a telegram and a letter. Both were sent to Wiley Post, care of F. C. Hall, Oklahoma City.

Dear Mr. Post:

This is to confirm the following wire, which has been sent by me to you today:

INFORMED BY FOREIGN OFFICE PERMISSION YOUR FLIGHT GRANTED STOP ROUTE TO BE FOLLOWED FROM SOVIET WESTERN FRONTIER TO MOSCOW IS THAT OF DERULUFT SOCIETY FURTHER TO IRKUTSK KHABAROVSK ROUTE OF DOBROLET SOCIETY STOP AM MAILING YOU DETAILED ITINERARY DERULUFT SOCIETY TO MOSCOW STOP ITINERARY FOR REST OF TRIP YOU MAY OBTAIN IN MOSCOW STOP IT IS UNDERSTOOD THAT NO CINEMA APPARATUS IS TO BE HAD ON BOARD OF AEROPLANE STOP TAKE UP MATTER OF GAS LUBRICANTS WITH AMTORG STOP WIRE ME DATE OF FLIGHT AS MOSCOW AUTHORITIES HAVE TO BE INFORMED BEFOREHAND PLEASE CONFIRM RECEIPT

The announced letter contained the following Itinerary:

ITINERARY

To be followed by the airplanes of the DERULUFT SOCIETY and airplanes following the same route from the Western frontier of the U.S.S.R and further to Moscow.

(Scale of map—10 versts—1 inch)

/ *1 verst = 3,500 feet* /

Flights across the border of the USSR between the Stations of Bigosovo and Balbinovo may take place only during the day and at a height of not over 500 meters. Airplanes will then follow a direct line passing through the points: Rositza (20 kil. NW of Drisa), Mikulino (12 kil. SW of Osovel), Leshnya (20 kil. SW of Kliastitzi), Station Tolmachevskaya (on the Polotzk-Idritza railroad), Station Polota (on the Polotzk-Novel railroad, 20 kil NE of the city of Polotzk), Kabak (10 kil. North of Sirotin), Buyani (15 kil, North of the city of Vitebsk). From the point Leshnya to the point Kabak the airplane may digress from the route indicated only in a Northward direction, and for a distance of not more than from 7 to 7 1/2 kilometers. Any digression Southward from the route indicated is strictly forbidden.

From the point Kabak to the point Buyani and further along the route to Moscow the airplane may follow a corridor fifteen miles wide, the central line of which cuts through the following points: Zabezhni (10 kil. South of Yanovichi), Barkova (10 kil. North of Rudil), Morozovo (20 kil. North of the city of Smolensk).

Flights in the region of the city of Smolensk are limited to the zone: Lake Kuprino, Olsha, Volyntzi, Koroleva, Ilinka, Station Dukhovskaya, Staniuchki, Katyno. When there is a North wind the landing at the Smolensk Aerodrome must be made by circling to the right and on approaching the aerodrome within a radius of one kilometer on all sides, the height of the plane must not exceed one hundred meters.

On leaving Smolensk the airplane may continue its flight along the fifteen mile corridor passing over the towns in the center of the corridor, and has the right to digress from it to the North or the South by no more than 7 to 7 1/2 kilometers.

Seltzo (10 kil. South of the city of Yrtzevo), Leonovo (20 kil. North of the city of Dorgobuzh), Rozhdestvo (20 kil. North of the city of Viazma, Sloboda (10 kil. SE from the city of Gzhatsk), Simakovka (25 kil. East of the city of Gzhatsk). From there the airplane must follow the direct line toward the railroad Station Kolog, from there Southeast to the Station Baranovo, from there Northeast to Station Shelkovka, or from Station Kolog it must turn Northeast and follow to the station Ratchina, from there Southeast to the station Shelkovka, and then follow along the Belorussko-Baltisky (White Russian Baltic) railroad, bearing to its north side, until this line crosses the Moscow Okrug railroad. From there, the plane must fly Northwest to the beginning of the Oktiabrski Lager and from there in a Northeastern direction by the shortest route to the Moscow aerodrome.

The same route should be followed in the opposite direction
from the Moscow aerodrome to the Western border of the
U.S.S.R., crossing the border between the points Biogrosovo-
Balbinovo.

The above Itinerary, reported here in toto, reached only as far as
Moscow, from where similar narrow channels were stipulated to the
easternmost point of Siberia. Gatty was not to see the new maps and
borders of the path across Asia until their actual take-off from Moscow. It would appear to be almost impossible to keep a plane flying
at speeds of three miles every sixty seconds and at the same time
adhere to the conditions stated in the itinerary. How could a pilot
know that he was only twenty kilometers from a city he was not
allowed to approach? The reverse is equally puzzling: How would a
Soviet military officer know whether a pilot was twenty kilometers
from a key city, when he might only be nineteen kilometers distant?
There is no indication that either Post or Gatty paid any attention
to the Soviet instructions.

With the arrival of the Soviet permit, the keystone fell into place.
By then the point of departure was changed from Oklahoma City to
New York City. The rationale was sound. Now, when the weather
across the North Atlantic was favorable, the plane and crew would
be ready to leave at once, not have to fly first across half a continent.

On their way east, in the *Winnie Mae*, Post and Gatty stopped in
Washington, D.C. They called in person on the diplomatic representatives of Great Britain, Poland, China, and Japan, asking and receiving permission to fly over their countries, or land in case of
emergency. Although they planned no landings in all but one of those
countries, they felt it was wiser in the event of the unforeseen to
make arrangements beforehand.

The *Winnie Mae* arrived at Roosevelt Field, on New York's Long
Island on May 23, 1931. While Post and Gatty moved into Manhattan's Biltmore Hotel, the plane was washed and scrubbed clean
and stood ready to leave. All that kept it on the ground now was
Dr. Kimball and his weather charts.

The days went by and the meteorologist refused his blessings. With
inactivity came boredom. This soon translated into impatience and
under ordinary circumstances might have led to a foolhardy depar-

ture. Dr. Kimball remained adamant. What kept him from sanctioning a departure was a 500-mile band of thick fog across the flight path to Europe. Wiley would have to fly through it, very blind, without a chance to shoot stars or sun to check location. An additional danger lay in the formation of ice on the wing, which would not only change the lifting qualities of the wing, but also add enormously to the total weight of the plane. Already heavily laden, the plane would then not have enough power to keep it flying. As Wiley Post wrote: "Any error under conditions where the formation of ice is possible usually proves disastrous."[6]

Still the pilot and his navigator waited. If it was not cold Arctic air hitting the Gulf Stream off Newfoundland and creating thick fog, it was fog shrouding Harbour Grace, their first landing and refueling stop, so they would be unable to land.

By Tuesday, June 23, Post and Gatty had been in New York a month to the day. The weather continued to be the stumbling block. Rain had been coming down in sheets, ahead of a cold front from Hudson Bay. How long would it last? There was no way of telling. On inspection, Wiley had discovered that some of the rain had seeped into the plane's tail section; it was drained. Then the decision was made. The rain was tolerable, they would take off at daybreak!

As the white plane sped down the runway on Roosevelt Field No. 1, Harold Gatty, ever the perfectionist, started his log: "Tuesday, June 23." Under the heading of "G.c.t. (Greenwich civil time) he made the entry "8:55:21" and in the last column, under "REMARKS," he wrote: "Took off 4:55 daylight-saving time, set course 65°, visibility poor."

Six hours and forty-seven minutes later, Wiley Post set the *Winnie Mae* down on the primitive landing field at Harbour Grace, Newfoundland. Their average speed from New York had been 168.3 miles per hour. To his annoyance, Gatty realized that he had left his billfold at the New York hotel and all he found in his pocket was a single dollar bill. It was immediately spent on food. Wiley had thirty-four dollars on him, which now would have to serve both men until they returned. Fortunately, F. C. Hall had prepaid reasonable ex-

---

[6]*Around the World in Eight Days* by Wiley Post and Harold Gatty, © 1931, Rand McNally & Co., p. 43

penses at the various anticipated stops, thus fuel, food, and lodgings would be no financial drain on their combined assets.

A mechanic sent ahead by Pratt & Whitney, the builders of the *Winnie Mae*'s engine, carefully checked every inch of the plane. Everything was in perfect order and the refueling went on. The entire stay had taken three hours and forty-three minutes. As soon as the fuel tanks had been topped, Wiley himself inspected the plane. Then the two men climbed back into the plane and Wiley spent the next ten minutes just warming up the engine. Again they took off. The next landmark, England, lay 1900 miles away.

If it was good weather they had been waiting for, their wait had surely been in vain. The setting sun revealed banks of dark clouds ahead and once the sun had set, the rain cloud and fog enveloped the plane. Shooting the moon or any stars was an impossibility, and Wiley was forced to fly blind, something he had done only three or four times—and then for no longer than about twenty minutes while crossing a band of storm clouds. Now he was flying blind hour after hour. Gatty could help only by attempting to determine their wind drift and correcting their previously determined direction.

Here, over the North Atlantic, Gatty first experienced one of Post's precautionary practices. Like most long-distance fliers, Wiley drained the last drop of fuel from one gasoline tank before switching to another. This procedure was perfectly logical to the pilots, who saw no sense in leaving some small indeterminable quantity in any tank only to be found short near the end of a trip without knowing the exact fuel reserve. If a tank was completely drained, the pilot knew it was totally empty and that one's reserve comprised whatever fuel remained in untapped tanks, not a gallon here and a couple of gallons somewhere else. However, when a pilot emptied a tank completely, for a few moments the engine would sputter and cough and nearly stall, until the pilot switched to the next tank. To the uninitiated ear, it sounded as if the engine was failing and disaster was threatening. For that reason airline pilots were not allowed to practice that particular type of fuel economy; passengers unfamiliar with the sound would fear the worst. In fact, airlines would fire pilots who landed with any totally empty tanks. Though Gatty became familiar with the sound, and understood Post's reasoning, it never failed to alarm him.

To escape the oppressing fog, Wiley climbed as high as twelve thousand feet, but it did not help. He then tried to fly due south for an hour in search of a weather break so that he and Gatty could at least get a fix on the moon, or the stars. Nothing helped, so they resumed the original northwest direction. At last, calculating the elapsed hours and their average speed, they felt that by then they must have reached land—any land—maybe Ireland, maybe Wales, maybe even Scotland—whatever it was, let it be land. So they began to descend. Lower and lower through the thickness the plane dropped, until Gatty, wedged behind the fuel tanks and having only side and rear vision saw only water, while Post, looking frontward, shouted: "Land!"[7]

Within minutes, Wiley spotted an airfield. He did not care whose it was, he was going to land and find out just where they were. He looked at his watch, the time read 7:42, New York time. For the moment, he did not know whether that meant night or morning New York time, and frankly, he did not care. He and Harold had crossed the Atlantic in 16 hours and 17 minutes.

As the wheels set down, Wiely saw four men running toward him and noted from a distance that they all wore uniforms. They identified themselves as Royal Air Force men, stationed at Sealand Airdrome just outside Liverpool, England. When Wiley tried to talk to the men, he could neither hear his own voice, nor their answers. He had temporarily become deaf.

While the arrival of the *Winnie Mae* was a welcome event, it was not exactly a total surprise. The small town of Bangor in Wales had heard the plane overhead some time earlier and had alerted England's west coast. The whole western world was aware of the Post-Gatty attempt to set a record round-the-world flight, since airports had been alerted to expect the fliers.

Post and Gatty were anxious to set off for Berlin, their next scheduled stop, but the RAF insisted on sharing lunch with them, and on servicing their plane. Wiley declined the offer of free gasoline, as he did not want to add too much weight to the plane. The British me-

---

[7]*Around the World in Eight Days* by Wiley Post and Harold Gatty, © 1931, Rand McNally & Co., p. 114

chanics figured out the gas consumption of their own planes on flights to Berlin and fueled the *Winnie Mae* accordingly. After lunch and a short farewell, the white Vega took off for Germany. The stay at Sealand Airdrome had taken one hour and twenty minutes.

Having received detailed RAF maps of their course to Berlin, Gatty did not need to determine their position, and Post could simply follow the map. They crossed the North Sea into Holland, kept straight on, and landed at Hannover, Germany, to inquire about the exact location and the proper approach of Tempelhof airfield in Berlin. Both men were extremely tired by now and Wiley later admitted that he had great difficulty concentrating. He just wanted to reach Berlin—and sleep. He had, however, neglected to check the fuel supply before the takeoff from Sealand, assuming that the RAF lads had calculated and added enough to reach Berlin. Well, they had, but not for as big an engine as the *Winnie Mae*'s.

After takeoff from Hannover, Wiley realized that the fuel tanks were practically empty and without more fuel they could not make it to Berlin. The smart thing to do was to turn around and gas up at the airfield they had just left. Their return so soon caused the Germans some surprise. As Wiley mused, they must have wondered just how organized those American fliers were. The return to Hannover cost an additional loss of forty-five minutes.

It was eight-thirty local time when the *Winnie Mae* set down in Berlin. Both men looked forward to a shower and a comfortable bed, maybe even in reverse order, but the hospitable Germans had other plans. They practically pulled the two fliers out of the plane, hoisted them onto friendly shoulders, and marched them ceremoniously to the airport restaurant where a festive meal had been arranged. Reporters fired questions at Wiley, who, speaking no German, did not understand a word and tried to speak in English, which the reporters did not understand. They left him alone after a few unproductive attempts at an exchange of questions and answers. Wiley liked it better that way. He would have rather flown another one hundred miles than experience this kind of adulation. Having now gone without sleep for almost thirty-six hours, the two dead-tired men were told that a transatlantic radio hookup wanted to interview them for an American radio network. Wiley managed to say "Hello, Germany and America," while Harold stammered: "I was very glad to have landed in Germany."[8] Even Post felt that they had not exactly performed eloquently.

So the carefully planned dinner progressed lavishly. Wiley and Gatty met local dignitaries and politicians, who toasted them with champagne. Course after course arrived with a different wine and/or beer. Wiley, however, upset the hovering Maitre d' by asking for a glass of ice water, and the gathering stared in disbelief that anyone would prefer water to such a fine selection of wine and beer.

When, finally, Wiley did get to his room, he had to tell his story in English and in full to a reporter for the syndicate that had bought his story. Several times, he had to be prodded back when he fell asleep in the middle of a sentence. At eleven o'clock Berlin time, Wiley was at last allowed to slip into bed. He left a wake-up call for 5:30 the following morning.

Post and Gatty woke the next morning to the news that they had broken the record for an Atlantic crossing, established by Alcock and Brown twelve years earlier. Well, that was yesterday's news; today they had to reach Moscow, a thousand miles away.

Breakfast was served at the airport restaurant, where only hours ago Post and Gatty had been feted. While the two men were not interested in more food, they did check with the airport's meteorological station, which had information flowing in from all over Europe. The inclement weather that they had passed on their way to Berlin now lay ahead of them. According to all reports, rain, fog, and low visibility were waiting to plague them all the way to Moscow.

In near ceiling-zero conditions Wiley was forced to practically hedgehop across Eastern Europe into the Soviet Union—at times flying at an altitude of just 400 feet in order to keep in sight of the ground. Racing along at a speed of close to 150 miles an hour, he had to pull up sharply many times to avoid hitting smoke stacks.

At one point, suddenly and without warning, the *Winnie Mae* ran into the heaviest cloudburst Wiley had ever experienced:

---

[8] *Around the World in Eight Days* by Wiley Post and Harold Gatty, © 1931, Rand McNally & Co., p. 125

Worse than all else, I couldn't see. Not seeing here was much
worse than it was over the ocean. There we had plenty of altitude
and nothing to hit, but hedgehopping through Russia with about
200 yards visibility and 100 or more miles an hour speed is
enough to make your hair stand on end every time you cross a
fence."[9]

Weather conditions were so poor that it had to be near impossible
to follow those detailed instructions issued by the USSR for the only
permitted "legal" approach to Moscow's October Airdrome. It is
safe to assume that the same conditions frustrating Post and Gatty
also impeded the Russians in tracking the *Winnie Mae*. From the
report still available, it seems that Post and Gatty never even attempted to abide by those rigid instructions and merely sought the
fastest way to Moscow.

To the two fliers' surprise, only a handful of people formed the
reception committee at the Moscow airport. Post and Gatty were
happy not to repeat the Berlin excitement the night before. But they
rejoiced too soon. Post and Gatty were barely out of the plane, when
members of Ossoviakhim—the Society for Aviation and Chemical
Defense, and Voks—the Society for Cultural Relations with Foreign
Countries, took them in tow. The first stop was the office of the
commandant of the flying field where their reception was "frigidly
formal and efficient."[10] Passports and papers were carefully examined and studied. With everything apparently in order, Wiley left
instructions for the servicing of the plane. Then they were off to the
Hotel Savoy. To Wiley and Harold's surprise, they were riding with
representatives of two solid Soviet organizations in an American
Packard automobile.

If either flier had thought that they were going to make an early
night of it, that notion was quickly dispelled. They had to clean up
and get ready for a nine-course dinner held in their honor by Ossoviakhim. Toast followed toast, but the guests of honor stuck

---

[9]*Around the World in Eight Days* by Wiley Post and Harold Gatty, © 1931, Rand
McNally & Co., p. 141
[10]*Around the World in Eight Days* by Wiley Post and Harold Gatty, © 1931, Rand
McNally & Co., p. 144

strictly to water, lest a hangover compromise their concentration or intestines. The dinner lasted until eleven o'clock. The sun rose in Moscow at 2 a.m at that time of the year, so Wiley left a wake-up call for 1 a.m., allowing for just two hours of sleep—hardly enough time to dream of flying to Irkutsk the following day.

Neither man was awakened in a good and friendly mood. Neither wanted breakfast and so they headed off to the airport, where another problem awaited them. This one was Wiley's fault. Having left exact instructions as to how many gallons of fuel he wanted in the tanks, he overlooked the fact that the Russian Imperial gallon of 277 cubic inches exceeded the American gallon of 231 by 46 cubic inches. With the Vega so heavily laden, Wiley knew that he could never lift her off the short runway at Moscow's airport. There was only one thing to do: reduce the load. Wiley suggested opening the cocks at the base of the tanks and allowing some fuel to run out into canisters. Fearing the possibility of fire, the Russians insisted on siphoning the fuel directly into cans. Hoses had to be brought, then cans, then mechanics, until finally the liquid began to flow. By this time, it was three o'clock. Repeatedly the mechanics lost the vacuum and had to start over by sucking out the air by lungpower. When another hour passed by, Wiley treated the spectators to one of his periodic losses of temper. Unfeelingly insulting, he displayed the richness of his four-letter-word vocabulary, which made the interpreter—a young woman who had studied in New York—blush, and censor her translation. Fortunately, none of the mechanics spoke English, but Post's tone of voice left little doubt as to his opinion. Finally, Post and Gatty took over the work and simply finished the job themselves.

At 4:35 a.m., Post climbed into the gleaming Vega and gave Gatty the signal. Harold started the propeller by hand and the engine caught immediately. For the next ten to fifteen minutes, Wiley allowed the engine to warm up, while Harold climbed aboard and readied his equipment for takeoff. As this was the first Russian fuel they had purchased, Wiley wanted to make sure that the Pratt & Whitney Wasp engine needed no adjustments. It didn't, and so Wiley signaled the ground crew to remove the blocks halting the wheels. The *Winnie Mae* began to roll down the runway on her way to Irkutsk.

However, she only got as far as Novosibirsk. The delayed start, the lack of sleep, the long banquets, all added up to fatigue and slowed reactions. Harold suggested, and Wiley agreed, that they spend the night in Novosibirsk and then, fully rested, make up the extra mileage the next day. Wiley, surprisingly, made excellent time racing toward what he thought would be a full night's sleep. They landed in Novosibirsk about ninety minutes ahead of their planned arrival, and only a few people had assembled to greet the two fliers. Wiley had just given instructions on the servicing and exact fueling of the plane when members of the Flying Club arrived in an old Ford, a "Tin Lizzie." They escorted Wiley and Harold into town and to a so-called hotel, which provided a room on the fifth floor—a perfectly acceptable room, except for the fact that there was no elevator. Tired, as the men were, they slowly climbed the stairs. It was then that they discovered that there was also no shower, no bath, and neither hot nor cold running water. Wiley flopped on his bed. He was nearly asleep when someone knocked on the door and politely informed him and Harold that a banquet had been arranged in their honor. Wiley was fully prepared to forego the meal in favor of a few hours' sleep, but he was told that his refusal would be considered impolite, if not an insult. As the hotel had no dining room—which probably was a blessing—they had to walk to a nearby restaurant. While all they had so far seen of Novosibirsk had been most disappointing, the quality of the meal turned out to be first class and favorably comparable to top western restaurants.

At last, near ten o'clock, the final toast had been made and for the final time Post and Gatty had raised their glasses filled with water imitating Vodka, and made appropriate noises. Everyone stood and cheered, and then accompanied the two bone-tired fliers back to the ramshackle hotel. Once more, Post and Gatty dragged themselves up the stairs to their fifth floor room. They had left a wake-up call for 1 a.m., so only three hours' sleep lay between them and their twenty-hour flight to Khabarovsk. Wiley, fully dressed, flopped on what felt like a concrete mattress and was asleep before he could even pull up the single blanket. Harold took a few seconds. He had to turn out the light.

Less than an hour later, Gatty awoke, scratching himself furiously. He felt welts on his face and immediately knew the cause. By the light of a pencil flashlight, he began a merciless hunt and succeeded in substantially reducing Novosibirsk's bedbug population. Untouched and undisturbed, Wiley Post slept in the next bed until an excited Russian woman knocked on their door. To their annoyance, they realized that it was not one o'clock, as ordered, but rather two o'clock. Obviously, their wake-up instructions had suffered in the translation.

On their way down the unlit stairway, Wiley missed the last step on the second floor and barely caught himself from falling. He did, however, sprain his ankle. As a pilot used his feet to control the rudder, Wiley suffered a throbbing ankle for a couple of days before he could walk without a limp. He never mentioned it to Harold, because he didn't want to give Gatty the opportunity to gloat, the way Wiley had done when he first heard about the bedbug episode. According to the diary of the trip, Wiley kept score of the misadventures that befell him and Gatty, as if to prove in this journal contest that he, Wiley Post, was the better man. Wiley may have resented that Gatty could sit at his little makeshift desk in the back of the *Winnie Mae* and give the orders to turn X degrees left, or right, while he, as pilot, had to take those orders and do exactly as he was told. Somehow, Gatty did not help matters by making an occasional joke about "pilots' intelligence."[11] An insecure man takes umbrage easily.

The takeoff from Novosibirsk was as uneventful as the six-hour flight to Irkutsk. In fact, following rail lines through rain became so monotonous that Wiley suggested that Harold, after his bedbug-hunting night, should catch up on his sleep. Gatty actually caught several ten-minute snatches of shut-eye. Just as Irkutsk came into view, Wiley shook the plane to wake his navigator. He needed him to shift his weight into the tail section to balance the *Winnie Mae* for the landing.

At Irkutsk the reception committee was the largest since the crowd in Berlin, but no one among them, it seemed, could speak English. Gatty tried his French on several Russians, though with little success, he reported later, at communication. While the Russians understood his French, he could not understand theirs. Eventually Annie Polikof turned up. A sixteen-year-old who spoke a mixture of Cockney and

---

[11]*Around the World in Eight Days* by Wiley Post and Harold Gatty, © 1931, Rand McNally & Co., p. 167

pidgin English, she had been born in London, but had moved to the USSR when she was six years old. With young Annie's help, with sign language, and by using fingers for numbers, Wiley managed to give the local mechanics their instructions. The Soviet gas worked fine, only their oil seemed thin and heated too fast. Wiley had them drain the plane's oil and replace the lot.

It was Gatty who cut the visit in Irkutsk short. He pointed out that they still had long to travel if they were going to reach Blagoveshchensk before dark. Once in the air, Wiley wanted to reset his dashboard clock to local time, only to learn that the time difference with New York was exactly twelve hours, so they were now half way home. Wiley's reaction was not surprising:

> "I felt like climbing around the outside of the ship and hitting him for not having told me sooner. But I satisfied myself with bawling him out."[12]

The contest between Wiley and his navigator continued. Still, no matter how late, the news was welcome to Post. They were on the home stretch now, even if a lot of the most difficult terrain still lay ahead, for they would have to cross all of Manchuria without the benefit of weather reports, knowledge of the landscape, and information regarding primary or emergency landing sites. They had been given maps in Moscow, but Gatty had long ago found them to contain minor and major inaccuracies. He found the small pocket atlas that he had brought from America, which he frequently consulted to back up his measurements, more useful, though he wished for a larger display. The two fliers attributed the imprecisions in the USSR map to the newness of the Socialist regime, the shortness of time to map so vast a country, and possibly the lack of trained engineers to conduct the survey. The real reason never occurred to either of them: that the errors were intentional. Not until decades later, after the fall of the Communistic structure, would the Soviets acknowledge that they had deliberately falsified their maps.

Always suspicious of the intent of nations the USSR considered

---

[12]*Around the World in Eight Days* by Wiley Post and Harold Gatty, © 1931, Rand McNally & Co., p. 179

inimical, the Communist regime did not plan to assist its enemies by providing them with accurate information. The Soviet regime could not possibly have anticipated that the anomalies in their maps would not escape detection by the experienced navigator Gatty and expert pilot Post.

The *Winnie Mae* had left Irkutsk at 2:09 p.m. local time, which made it 2:09 a.m. in New York City. It was rapidly growing dark as the plane approached Blagoveshchensk. Wiley circled the town several times, trying to locate the airport. He had been promised that flares would outline the landing strip, but the lights were hard to spot. It had rained all day, and what was supposed to be—and later proved to be—the airport looked more like a small lake than solid ground. Wiley circled several more times, but he still could not find dry ground on which to put the plane down. He knew this was going to be a difficult landing. Soviet landing strips, outdated and in disrepair, the pavement uneven with soil exposed in some areas, had made landings bumpy and bone-shaking under the best of weather conditions. Now, though, all Wiley could see in front of him was water, and who knew what lay under it. At last, he spotted a small, dry area and headed for it. Through the tube connecting him to Harold he yelled:

> "Get as far back as you can! Hold your instruments so they won't break! Set yourself for a jolt and hang on like hell!"[13]

As cautiously as he could, Wiley tried to set the plane down. Mud sprayed over his windshield, and he could see even less in the semi-dark. He could feel the wheels sinking into the ooze; then he could feel the mud grab the wheels and hold them. He was landing at a speed of about eighty miles an hour and he rolled barely 400 feet. He was positive that with less than 400 miles of Siberia left to cross, he was now destined to be stuck in that mire, never to move again. The ten-day trip around the world was over. When reported in the American press, the *Los Angeles Times* noted: "It was the first mishap of the flight."

---

[13]*Around the World in Eight Days* by Wiley Post and Harold Gatty, © 1931, Rand McNally & Co., p. 183

Harold jumped from the ship. He had landed in two inches of water over a six-inch layer of ooze. His feet made strange noises when he tried to extricate them and take a step. Like Wiley, he was convinced that the adventure was over. They would never be able to move the plane. Even if the falling light rain would stop that instant, the ground would take a long time to dry. And as the ground solidified, who would dig the *Winnie Mae* out of the muck that threatened to swallow her up?

A Ford car slowly sloshed toward the plane. It carried some Ossoviakhim men and two Danish telegraph operators, Jacobsen and Nelsen, who spoke English. (Their company maintained a line through Russia and Siberia to the Orient.) Several attempts to pull the *Winnie Mae* out of the mud with the Ford failed, even when assisted by the plane's motor. The futility of it all became obvious. The Russians and Danes launched into lengthy discussions in Russian that sounded more like arguments. The Danes translated. They had formulated a plan. Post and Gatty would go to the Danes' homes, where they could eat and sleep, and meanwhile a tractor would make the three-hour trip to the airport so that the *Winnie Mae* could be rescued in the morning. The prospect of a shower and a good meal followed by a comfortable bed immediately appealed to Gatty, but Post demurred. Harold should go and bring him back something to eat, but he, Wiley, was going to stay with the plane to be sure that it got hitched up properly to the tractor and got correctly refueled. That way, they might not lose too much time, after all.

While Harold enjoyed the hospitality of the Danes, Wiley crawled into the plane and slept for four hours. The tractor—supposedly—was still on the way. When Harold returned with a gift basket of Danish delicacies for his partner, the rain had long stopped and the ground had begun to dry. It certainly was hard enough to drive on, but still the tractor had not arrived. A team of horses was hitched to the plane. When Wiley started the engine to assist, the animals nearly bolted, but they did not move the plane an inch. Their hooves, unable to get an adequate foothold, kept slipping. Another five hours elapsed before the ground dried enough for the horses to pull and men to push the *Winnie Mae* out of her muddy hole. The tractor was still "on its way."

By the time the two fliers said their good-byes, twelve hours and twenty-one minutes had elapsed since their unfortunate landing. The flight ahead to Khabarovsk, a distance of 363 miles, took two hours and thirty-five minutes and was routine. It required little navigating, as all Wiley had to do was follow the rail line.

On this day, June 29, 1931, back on the North American continent, Will Rogers mentioned Post and Gatty for the first time in his column, which appeared in some 600 United States and Canadian newspapers. Post and Gatty had only recently become familiar names to most Americans, but Will Rogers was unquestionably the most popular personality in the country. At a time when the entire population of America—men, women, and children—was only 120 million, 40 million of them were reading Rogers's newspaper articles seven days a week. Will Rogers was the number-one male box-office star, leading Clark Gable, James Cagney, and Fred Astaire. Part Indian, part cowboy, he was also one of America's most politically astute radio news commentators, and millions who would miss church on Sunday morning would never miss his broadcasts on Sunday afternoon. He was a humorist, a philosopher, a philanthropist who gave away a fortune, and was known to hand out his last dollar bill only to have to borrow carfare home. Rogers seemed to speak for all those who had no pulpit. Had he desired to hold public office, he could have been elected to any he chose—perhaps even the presidency. He was, as someone said of him, the typical American as Americans imagined the typical American to be. One of the earliest advocates of a strong United States Air Force as well as a vocal and enthusiastic supporter of civil aviation, he flew wherever early airlines allowed.

In his squib for that date, Will Rogers wrote:

> No news today as big as this Post and Gatty who are making this world of ours look like the size of a watermelon.
>
> This pilot Post is an old one-eyed Oklahoma boy. He has just got that good eye glued on the horizon and he is going to find that horizon if it meets the earth anywhere, and Gatty, this reformed Australian 'brumby and wombat'[14] (you boys

---

[14]"Brumby," feral horse, descendant from stock introduced in 1788; "wombat," burrowing marsupial, native to Australia and Tasmania.

that didn't go to Oxford are lost in another maze of intellect)
well, this Gatty, just give him a compass and one peek at the
Giant Dipper and he can tell you where you are even if you
ain't there.

This is one ship I would have loved to been a stowaway on.

Sincerely,
Will Rogers.

Post and Gatty might have relished making news back home,
but at the moment they had other things on their minds. Before
them lay ahead the long stretch of the trip. It would be to Solomon, Alaska: 2,441 miles over open sea, through dense fog and
over high mountains. They would need more than luck to make it
safely, and the lack of weather information didn't help. Fortunately, Gatty was able to pick up a translated Japanese forecast;
unfortunately, it promised stormy rain, and fog. When a strong
crosswind blasting across the runway at Khabarovsk made the
takeoff with a full load of fuel impossible, the two men decided to
get a few more hours of sleep before determining their flight plan.
Four hours later, the wind had shifted and they faced the question
as to which route to take. Although the originally scheduled next
refueling stop was Petropavlovsk, on the southeastern tip of the
Kamchatka peninsula, Post and Gatty chose instead to cut across
on the Great Circle Route to Solomon and shorten their flight by
two hundred miles.

The storm forecast in the Japanese weather report hit and brought
with it hail. Wiley took the plane to a lower altitude, where a warmer
temperature would prevent icing. It was safe enough to fly low, almost skimming the surface of the water, over the Sea of Okhotsk
until the wind began to buffet the light plane and threatened to toss
it sideways into the heavy seas. Wiley climbed to an altitude of three
thousand feet—and Gatty again discovered the inaccuracy in the
Soviet-supplied maps. The Russian maps showed no mountains in
their path higher than 2,500 feet, but right in front of them loomed
a snow-covered peak, which measured at least 4,000 feet. Gatty wondered: "Say! That isn't on the map at all. Either these elevations are

all wrong, or our altimeter is haywire."[15] Wiley had no time to wonder, he had to get out of the way. Soon enough no mountain obstructed his view or his flight path. Fortunately, daylight was on its way and Soviet territory was for the most part behind them. "My mistake was," Wiley admitted later, "I thought a map was a map." From then on he referred to a Soviet-supplied map as "the-maybe-its-right-map."[16]

Daylight arrived, and Harold was able to get a sun- and moon-line fix. To his surprise, he learned that they had made better time than they had anticipated. They made a correction in their headings and felt almost certain that they would have enough fuel to make it to Solomon. Heading out over the Bering Sea, they set course for St. Lawrence Island, which would be their first and welcome sight of American territory. Somewhere off Cape Navarin the *Winnie Mae* passed from 11 a.m. Tuesday, June 30, 1931, to 11 a.m. Monday, June 29th, 1931, by crossing the International Dateline on the 180th meridian.

During the next three hours the *Winnie Mae* passed through fog, rain, fog, and more rain. Consulting the gauges, Wiley noted that he had two more hours of fuel. In less time than that, at 2:45 in the afternoon, Alaska time, they set down on the beach at Solomon. The sand was soft and made a good break. As it was still early in the day, the two fliers decided only to refuel and journey on to Fairbanks, where oil, fuel, and other supplies would be more readily available. Although Nome was nearer, the runway there was too short for a heavily laden plane. So they simply purchased 100 gallons of fuel, more than enough to make it to their next stop, Fairbanks.

Wiley backed around to taxi for the takeoff. He felt the loose sand shift under the wheels and "banged the throttle open" to keep the ship from sinking further. He succeeded, however, only in lifting the tail and thus digging the propeller blades into the sand. He quickly cut the engine to keep the plane from standing on its nose—an eventuality that would have killed any chance to complete the flight.

Checking the damage Wiley found that both propeller blade tips

---

[15]*Around the World in Eight Days* by Wiley Post and Harold Gatty, © 1931, Rand and McNally & Co., p. 207
[16]Ibid p. 209

had been bent, but not to an extent that made temporary repair impossible. With a broken-handled hammer, a wrench, and a round stone he found on the beach as tools, he was able to align the blades enough so that they would fan in the right direction.

The plane had to be started by hand and Gatty again assumed his position at the propeller. He had performed this hazardous duty several times before. Taking hold of one of the two propeller blades, he pulled sharply downward—a maneuver comparable to starting an old-time automobile with a crank—when the hot engine backfired. The propeller blade flew out of his hand and spun round, the flat side of the blade just missing Gatty's head but hitting him on the shoulder, and knocking him to the ground. Had the blade spun the other way round, the cutting edge would have hit him and he could have been killed. As it was, Gatty suffered a bad bruise and a wrenched back. Gamely, Gatty picked himself up, started the engine, and then climbed back into his work area.

Wiley made it safely to Fairbanks where, to his surprise, his guardian angel was waiting to do whatever guardian angels are supposed to do. Joe Crosson, the famous flier who had helped Wiley so much earlier in his career, was now the guiding spirit at Pan Alaska Airways (PAA). Under Joe's supervision, their expert mechanics took control of the plane, while the two fliers slept the sleep of the deserving just. About four hours later, returning to their plane, they found it wiped down, refueled and oiled, and—to their amazement—refurbished with a shiny, new propeller. Success seemed to be assured. Surely, they could now manage to fly from Fairbanks to New York—a trip that entailed only a straight flight of 1,500 miles to Edmonton, Alberta, Canada, and from there an easy eighteen hundred miles, or so, to their final destination. Yet, to Gatty, those seemed the longest segments of the whole adventure.

In perfect weather the shiny white Vega left Fairbanks and made great time until heavy rain began falling in the Canadian Rockies. All was not going to be ideal. Still, once Wiley picked up the tracks of the Canadian National Railway branch that connected Edmonton with Prince Rupert, British Columbia, he was able to simply follow it east, and Gatty was spared the need to make sightings and give directions. The rain, though, stayed with them all the way into Edmonton.

One look at the rain-soaked landing field in Edmonton brought Blagoveshchensk immediately back to the two men's minds. The whole airfield lay hidden under a liquid blanket of mud. Looking at it, Wiley wished that the *Winnie Mae* were on pontoons. Gatty braced himself as Post half skidded and half flew the plane across the surface. It came to rest on the apron leading to a hangar.

Despite the rain and the condition of the ground, a large crowd awaited the two fliers and the moment the propeller stopped spinning, the crowd broke the police lines and surrounded the plane. Post and Gatty did not alight until after order had been restored. Once they had planted their feet on terra firma, newspaper reporters and radio and film crews, all of them yelling questions and none of them listening for answers, were descending on the pilot and the navigator. One reporter thrust a microphone in front of Post; the national and international listening public learned that he was tired of sitting down.

The formalities at the airport began with official greetings from the mayor of Edmonton and the acting premier of the province as well as customs and immigration officials. The one consolation was that at least this ceremony did not require an interpreter. An hour went by with no one exhibiting sympathetic concern for two tired and hungry men. Wiley and Harold had planned to have the plane serviced immediately and then take off for the last leg of their trip. That, however, now seemed out of the question. The rain had stopped, but it had left the airfield soggy and a dry runway could be many days distant,

A suggestion from one of the airmail pilots present saved the day. He pointed out that Portage Avenue, the road leading straight up to the airport, offered a 2-mile straight, paved runway, without interruptions and wide enough to accommodate the *Winnie Mae*. Only the electric wires strung along the roadsides could possibly interfere with a clean takeoff. Post and Gatty were told not to worry and were assured that everything for their take off would be ready by morning. In the meantime, they could rest at the hotel reserved for them.

The next morning, 3:30 a.m. local time, when Post and Gatty arrived at the airport; they discovered that the entire town had turned out to see them off. Furthermore, during the night, crews of electricians had carefully removed all the electrical wiring on both sides of the Avenue, and street cleaners had swept the roadway to ensure a safe takeoff. The *Winnie Mae*, spotlessly clean and fueled, stood at the end of Portage Avenue, poised to roll down the street.

Revving the engine one more time before releasing the brakes, Wiley checked his gauges. Then the Vega headed down the street. At seventy-five miles an hour it raced past lampposts and spectators. It was an eerie sensation, for Post and Gatty, as neither man had ever taken a street at that speed before. The white bird lifted off easily and flew toward Cleveland, the last stop for fuel before proceeding to Roosevelt Field, the place they had left just eight days before. In Cleveland it took exactly forty-five minutes to gas up. There was no need to delay further. The *Winnie Mae* took off for the final hop of the trip around the world.

Wiley Hardeman Post, pilot, and Harold Gatty, navigator, flying a single engine propeller Lockheed plane, model Vega, powered by a Pratt & Whitney Wasp-C engine landed at New York's Roosevelt Field on Wednesday, July 1, 1931, at 8:47 p.m. They had been gone eight days fifteen hours and fifty-one minutes.

When the two men climbed out of the plane, pandemonium broke loose. The police were no match for the throng that had gathered despite the late hour and the admission of 25 cents—a lot of money during the Depression. The signed and notarized statement accounting for the gate receipts at Roosevelt Field reports that after the deduction of expenses for gatemen, ticket salesmen, etc., the event took in $835.25, an amount that Roosevelt Field, Post, and Gatty shared. Of course, there were many hundreds more who simply stole over fences and walked nearly a mile to avoid paying admission.

Mrs. Post had been anxiously waiting at the Field for almost an hour. She had arrived at the airport soon after she had learned that the fliers had left Cleveland. In a roped-off section of the field she joined an invited group of celebrities, which included Colonel Charles Lindbergh and his wife Anne. Mrs. Lindbergh had been one of Harold Gatty's pupils, taking his navigation course. Mrs. Gatty had left California in plenty of time, but inclement weather had forced her plane down in Pittsburgh. She did not reach New York until the following day.

If Wiley Post did actually have a hand in writing the published account of his flight around the world with Harold Gatty, its last paragraph would no doubt come back to haunt him:

> In our flight around the world, I had satisfied my life's ambition. But it was Harold who was the guiding hand of the '*Winnie Mae*.' All I did was to follow his instructions in steering, and to keep the ship from spinning out of the thick 'pea soup,' of which we encountered so much in our trip *AROUND THE WORLD IN EIGHT DAYS*.[17]

---

[17]*Around the World in Eight Days*, by Wiley Post and Harold Gatty, © 1931, Rand McNally & Co., p. 236

CHAPTER VI

A NEW, STILL UNBROKEN RECORD

W HEN WILEY POST was wakened in his hotel room in New York City on July 2, 1931, the day after the *Winnie Mae*'s return to New York City, he had only one wish: to sleep undisturbed for the next three days! It was not an unreasonable wish, but like many another wish—reasonable or not—it failed to be translated into reality. New obligations accompanied Wiley's newfound fame— a fame that was emblazoned in the front-page banner headlines of practically every newspaper in the United States that day, and just possibly in most major cities of the western world. And that was as it should have been. He had, after all, performed a feat never before accomplished by anyone. He had flown 15,474 miles in the span of 107 hours and 2 minutes actual flying time. This meant that the *Winnie Mae* averaged 144.57 miles per hour while consuming 3,455 U.S. gallons of fuel. The averages showed that the Pratt & Whitney engine, a Wasp, traveled 4.479 miles per U.S. gallon, and used 32.28 U.S. gallons per hour in flight.

Flying a plane is not like driving a car or a truck. A pilot cannot pull over to the side of the road for a short nap or visit a gas station to fill up the tank. A pilot cannot stop for a cup of coffee or a quick lunch. Piloting a plane in 1931 was a 60-minutes-an-hour job, with no copilot to ease the tension. Harold Gatty may have to sit in the fuselage behind fuel tanks, and work at doing his computations, often without pressure, or he may have to stare into a rising sun or try to make out landmarks through a curtain of rain or hail; or attempt to penetrate total darkness while flying blind; but he could steal time now and again for a short nap. Wiley Post, however, had to be totally alert to his task every second of the flight. He had to listen to the rhythm of the engine, so acutely that he could hear the slightest deviation from the norm. He had to watch the instruments, scan the horizon for any changes in the weather or wind ahead, remember any possible landing sites he had just passed in case of emergency, and, of course, he had to control the plane. During the entire trip of eight days, Wiley Post slept less than a total of 15 hours.

With the round-the-world flight behind him, Wiley had accomplished what he had dreamed of in his youth. Now he found that all was not quite as he had envisioned it. Fame introduced him to two types in the human family he had not encountered before: promoters who wanted to latch on to his achievements, claim a part of them and bask in his glory on the one hand, and on the other, detractors. The former included politicians who pretended to shower honors upon him, but in reality just sought the benefit of his limelight. Similarly, organizations and businesses of all kinds wanted Wiley to endorse them and their services, although they had no connection with him, the plane, or the trip. Advertisers, too, solicited the use of his picture, to increase the salability of their clients' products. Conversely, Wiley's detractors, unable to match his success, tried to diminish it by criticism. "Well," they would say, "he didn't really fly around the world at its equator where it is widest, he merely flew around a small circle in the northern hemisphere, where it is only 15,000 miles." They attempted to trivialize the fact that Wiley and Harold had flown across the North Atlantic, across all of Europe, across the European and Asian Soviet Union, and across the entire North American continent—and all that in a single-engine propeller plane in record time. Or they belittled Wiley's accomplishment by inflating Gatty's role. "Wiley Post merely steered, he was the chauffeur!" they would say. "It was Harold Gatty who was the brains behind the effort. Wiley simply took orders! Isn't that what Post had said in his book?" they would ask.

Flying around the world was easy compared to dealing with schemers and detractors, Wiley might have thought. But he was not allowed such idle musings. He had commitments to honor. A formal invitation from President Herbert C. Hoover, brought him and Gatty to the White House for a visit—an exciting distinction, whether you are a farm boy from Oklahoma or a transplanted Tasmanian. Moreover, a Joint Resolution of Congress granted Wiley the Distinguished Flying Cross. The City of New York honored him with a tickertape parade up Broadway, yet neither he nor Gatty had ever lived there. Wiley might have wondered where all these well-wishing folks were when Mr. Hall had been looking for investors to finance this trip. Now they could not do enough to try to get in on the glory. The tonnage of tickertape easily rivaled that of Charles Lindbergh's parade, although in 1927 the tape had carried higher figures. Since then the stock market crash of 1929 had altered the fortunes of Wall Street investors and speculators and had affected countless innocent men, women, and children. On the day of Post and Gatty's parade, thousands upon thousands of people lined the street from Bowling Green to City Hall. Mayor Jimmy Walker welcomed the fliers officially, then presented them with medals and a key to the city. He quipped that the plane "had been the *Winnie Mae* before the flight started, the Winnie Must while in progress, and was now the Winnie Did!" Pictures were taken on the City Hall steps, and the ceremony was over.

Not so the interviews. Reporters from every news service, from every foreign, national, and local newspaper represented in New York, and from all the nearby states, swamped the two celebrities. Radio stations wanted to record their voices, newsreel cameras rolled, and photographers flashed innumerable pictures. They took photos of Post and Gatty looking left and looking right and looking straight into the camera; pictures of the fliers alone and with their wives; shots of the two men looking at each other, looking at maps— there was no end to it. Wiley was heard to mumble something about just what they planned to do with all the photos that were taken.

And, Good Lord, there were those tiresome questions. Just when

Post and Gatty thought that surely not another question remained to be asked, some reporter, who had arrived late, would ask them to cover all the same ground yet again. Post and Gatty thought it agony. Both men hated all this publicity. Not so F. C. Hall, or at least not quite so much. He always seemed to have another news-worthy tidbit to add. He surprised reporters and their readers, for instance, when he told them that he had sent his *Winnie Mae* around the world without a cent of insurance. "It would have been very costly, so I decided to take a chance," he said. "I gambled on the boys' success. Anyone who'd gamble on oil wells coming in would gamble on anything."

And Hall did receive special recognition from Will Rogers. It was Rogers's squib of July 3, 1931, that brought Will Rogers into the circle of Post, Gatty, and Hall:

> The Governor of Australia (Gatty's home) cabled "Australia is proud of Gatty and I am sure Gatty is proud of Post." Now beat that for beautiful and diplomatic wording, and say, let's give a great big hand to Hall that financed and made the thing possible. Never has a promoter remained so much in the background. If some other men had backed that trip, they would have had Gatty and Post riding in the jump seat parading in New York.
>
> It was a great combination, a great flier, a great navigator and modest backer.

F. C. Hall, ever the gentleman, but with an eye to promotion, knew what to do. He did not let the compliment go without acknowledgment. Neither did Will Rogers:

> I got my first thanks this morning for ever saying a nice thing about some man, and I do lots of times brag on our prominent men but always take it as a matter of fact. But the old Oklahoma oil man that backed the flight come through.
>
> Many thanks for your kind notice, and the best I can do in return is to take Post and Gatty to visit Claremore, Okla. Advise if you want us.
>
> Now, here is a chance for these two boys to really make good.

If Gatty can navigate enough to really find a field there, I'll say
he is a Columbus, and if Post can land on the field, I'll say he is
a magician. I have always had to use a parachute.[1]

Claremore, Oklahoma, approximately twenty-five miles northeast
of Tulsa, had claimed itself Will Rogers's birthplace, although he was
actually born on a ranch near Oologah, some twelve miles distant.
Located at the intersection of two major rail lines, Claremore had so
far not found it necessary to agonize over where to build an airport.
But now, having been mentioned so prominently in Will Rogers's
column and offered a chance to make national news, the town
launched itself frantically into a search for a landing strip. Within
days an eighty-acre oat field northeast of town and adjacent to famous Route 66 had been purchased and converted into what became
known as Will Rogers Airport. Fittingly, the town invited Will Rogers to come and dedicate the airfield. He left his home in Pacific
Palisades on the morning of Monday, July 13, and flew to Tulsa after
a stop in Amarillo, Texas. That evening he met with Hall, Post, and
Gatty at a special dinner in honor of the fliers.

The next day, they all piled into the cramped quarters of the *Winnie Mae* and flew the twenty-five miles to the brand new airport at
Claremore. Only Wiley knew that they were breaking the law, as the
plane's license specifically excluded any passengers. Had anyone chosen to be vindictive or exacting, Wiley could have been fined and
thus lost his parole.

The festive luncheon in Claremore was held in the Silver Room of
the Hotel Will Rogers. After a brief airport dedication ceremony that
followed, Post and Gatty took off for Indianapolis, while Rogers went
to nearby Chelsea, Oklahoma, for an overnight visit with his older sister Sallie. On July 14, 1931, Will Rogers's daily column, datelined
Claremore, Okla., described the events of those twenty-four hours:

> Well this was a great day for Gatty and Post. It was just an
> ordinary day for Claremore, but it was a big thing for those boys.
> They never saw a town like ours.
>
> We built a real airport in four days just to welcome 'em. I

---

[1]Will Rogers's Daily Telegram # 1544, July 5, 1931.

was with 'em in Tulsa last night and flew over here in the *Winnie Mae* with them today. It's the combination of those two that make 'em so great. I'd bet on 'em going around the world endways and cross both poles.

In all the excitement and rushing around, you know when they sleep? At the banquets. They said if it wasn't for banquets they wouldn't have any time to sleep at all. Smart fellows.

F. C. Hall, ever the optimistic gambler, had predicted that Wiley would strike it rich after a successful flight around the world. Hall estimated that the flight alone would bring Post at least $75,000, while endorsements would garner at least $125,000, and barnstorming tours another $100,000. What Hall had not taken into account was the ever-deepening Depression.

The public relations firm of A. Bruno—R.R. Blythe had been hired to arrange a lecture tour for Post and Gatty, under the sponsorship of Aviation Mobilgas Ethyl and Mobiloil Aero Oils. Scheduled to begin July 18 and last until September 7, it covered some twenty-five cities from coast to coast. The fee was anticipated to be in excess of $20,000.

DATE		FEE	AMOUNT COLLECTED	AMOUNT UNCOLLECTED
July 18	Schenectady, NY	$ 500.00	$ 500.00	—
19	Walden, NY	393.72	393.72	—
21	Boston, Mass	1,500.00		1,500.00
23	Springfield, Mass	0		
25/26	Chicago, Ill	2,400.00		2,400.00
27	Milwaukee, Wis	500.00		500.00
28	Toledo, O	500.00		500.00
29	Pittsburgh, Pa	500.00		500.00
30	Newark, N.J.	500.00		500.00
31	Auburn, Me	1,000.00	1,000.00	
Aug 1	Charleston, W.Va.	500.00	500.00	
2	Cincinnati, O	1,200.00	1,200.00	
3	Wheeling, W.Va.	500.00	500.00	
4	Davenport, Ia	1,200.00	1,200.00	
6	Janesville, Wis	750.000	750.00	
7	Madison, Wis	400.00	400.00	
8	Sioux City, Ia	1,200.00	1,200.00	
13	Old Orchard B. Me	1,000.00	1,000.00	

DATE		FEE	AMOUNT COLLECTED	AMOUNT UNCOLLECTED
16	Burlington, Vt	1,000.00	1,000.00	
18	Ionia, Mich	1,000.00	1,000.00	
25/26	San Francisco, Cal	1,500.00		1,500.00
27	Los Angeles, Cal	500.00		500.00
Sep. 3	Spokane, Wash	1,200.00	1,200.00	
6	Detroit, Mich	1,000.00	1,000.00	
7	Bridgeport, Conn	174.00	174.00	
	Total	$20,917.72	13,017.72	7,900.00

Total amount collected   13,017.72
Post & Gatty Share 80% $10,414.18
NBC[2] Share 20%   2,603,54
                       $13,017.72

Post & Gatty Share   10,414.18
Less Amount due NBC for share of expenses to date   470.99
Amount payable to Post & Gatty   9,943.19

A "FINAL STATEMENT" submitted on September 11, 1931, reduced the collected amount even further to $6,091.98, with an additional 10% deduction for agency commission, leaving a mere $5,482.78 for division between Post and Gatty. According to the terms of the contract, Post and Gatty shared the guaranteed $15,000, which was more than the tour took in.

The telegraphed columns written by Wiley during the flight, and syndicated through the the *New York Times*, also proved less than successful. The final statement, dated July 15, 1931, indicated that the *New York Times* paid $6,856.25. The accompanying letter expresses regrets and an explanation:

> I am sorry this could not have been more, but the papers in this country and Canada were very thoroughly canvassed and I do not think an opportunity was missed to make a sale. The papers are just simply not buying anything more in the way of features than they absolutely need, and even the editors who thought the flight was a brilliant achievement refused to purchase the by-line story.

---

[2]NBC—The National Broadcasting Company was a sponsor of the tour.

ALL the latest news by wire every day from the United Press Association.

CHICKASHA D

Volume Twenty-Two   Chickasha, Oklahoma, T

Local newspaper account of Post's conviction.

EARLY VOTING IS ONE FEATURE OF ELECTION TODAY

Both Parties and Candidates for Mayor are Confident of Victory As End of Fight at Polls Draws Near

HI-JACKER GETS TEN YEARS HERE ON GUILTY PLEA

Wiley Post Given Minimum Sentence for Highway Robbery; Caught by Ninnekah —Men Near City

HARDING SOUNDS DOOM OF TREATY CONCERNING U. S.

States He's Convinced No Practical Way Amerika Can Consider Ratifying Pact; Denies Approval Knox

◆◆◆◆◆◆◆◆
WEATHE
For
◆ Tonight re
◆ nesday fair, ◆
◆ lahoma.
Local T
Maximum 72
Rain 1.11.
◆◆◆◆◆◆◆◆

BROOM C

START

COUNT MAY REACH 2,500 MARK, SAID

Campaign Will End With Close of Polls This Evening at 7 o'-Clock; Returns to be Available at 8

◆◆◆◆◆◆◆◆◆◆◆◆
◆ "I am confident of victory ◆
◆ and believe that I will win the ◆
◆ race by a majority of from 100 ◆
◆ to 200" G. Coffman, demo- ◆
◆ cratic candidate for mayor. ◆
◆ "I do not fear the outcome; ◆
◆ the outlook is bright." Orin ◆
◆ Ashton, republican candidate ◆
◆ for mayor. ◆
◆◆◆◆◆◆◆◆◆◆◆◆

Early Voting Feature

Early voting was one of the out-standing features of the city general election being held here today. At o'clock this afternoon, it was estimated that approximately 1,500 votes had been cast and it was predicted around the polls that the total vote would reach the 2500 mark. Votes of both parties, as well as both candidates for mayor, this morning were confident of victory. Election of a full democratic ticket is "assured," said Thomas H. Shepard, one of the city democratic campaign committee. "We expect to win the city by a majority of approximately 1000."

Republicans have faint hopes that an entire republican ticket will be elected, said W. S. Richards, chairman of the city republican campaign committee. "We are confident that a republican entry for mayor will be a sure majority."

The campaign will end with the closing of the polls this evening at

Ten years in the state penitentiary was the sentence imposed on Wiley Post young hi-jacker, who yesterday afternoon in district court entered a plea of guilty to the charge of highway robbery. Ten years is the minimum punishment for such crime.

Post was captured several days ago by four Ninnekah men, E. H. Mercer, H. A. McClain, Tom Wood and H. A. Hall, whom he attempted to hold up. The capture was made on the Ninnekah-Chickasha road two miles south of this city.

An automobile casing was placed in the road as a decoy. When the men stopped their automobile to pick up the apparently lost casing, Post rushed up to the machine and ordered the men to hold up their hands. As he stepped out of the car, Mr. Mercer grabbed the gun and told Post that if he attempted to pull the trigger, he would be killed. With these words, the young holdup released the gun and, in compliance with orders, stepped into the car and was brought to the county jail.

He waived preliminary examination in justice court.

After arrest, Post admitted having been implicated in other holdups near this city. He is a neat appearing young man, about 23 years of age. His parents formerly lived in the county and, according to A. Sidney Hancock, deputy sheriff, are highly respected citizens. They now live in the vicinity of Wynnewood.

The prisoner will be taken to the state reformatory at Granite some time this week.

City Street Crew

By T
W
on th
prese
day,
to at
that
made
the—
whic
rativ
Pi
that
that

By Ii
Par
presi
infor
next
Ameri
count
cording
Vivian
Lausanne, cabling his newspaper to Matin here, said that Senator Knox had informed him that his reparations that will leave that question to be settled by the various governments.

The resolution will be couched in terms that are favorable to France, the cablegram stated.

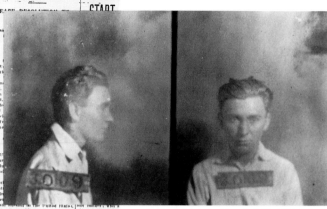

Post, convicted of robbery April 28, 1921 in Grady County, Oklahoma. COURTESY: ARCHIVES & MANUSCRIPT DIVISION OF THE OKLAHOMA HISTORICAL SOCIETY.

pan robbery, who u of town to attend business of the co concluded Wednesd mainder of Wednes over to entertainm

Big Barbecue
Tomorrow at 12
barbecue will be se
home of the Thomp
ton and knitting in
eastern edge of the
run is open to the

Oklahoma State Reformatory, Granite, OK, c. 1920. COURTESY: ARCHIVES & MANUSCRIPT DIVISION OF THE OKLAHOMA HISTORICAL SOCIETY.

Mr. and Mrs. William Francis Post, Wiley Post's father and mother. 1935.
COURTESY: ARCHIVES & MANUSCRIPT DIVISION OF THE OKLAHOMA HISTORICAL SOCIETY.

Wiley Post and his wife, Mae

Simple sign north of Maysville, Oklahoma, home of Post's parents, but Wiley only visited here.

Wiley checks out rebuilt plane, still on wheels. COURTESY: ARCHIVE UNITED TECHNOLOGY CORP. HARTFORD, CT, 06101.

Wiley's crash landing at Flat, Alaska, June 26, 1933.
COURTESY: ARCHIVES & MANUSCRIPT DIVISION OF THE OKLAHOMA
HISTORICAL SOCIETY.

Ill-conceived telegram sent by Post to
Fay Gillis, who spoke Russian, inviting
her to accompany him from Novosibirsk
to Khabarovsk to oversee refueling.

Wiley Post and Harold Gatty beside the *Winnie Mae*.
COURTESY: ARCHIVES & MANUSCRIPT DIVISION OF THE OKLAHOMA
HISTORICAL SOCIETY.

Breakfast with Fay Gillis, at which the Alaska-Siberia-Europe trip is born.

Official welcome at New York's City Hall, 1931; front row left to right: Vera Gatty, Wiley, Mayor Jimmy Walker, Harold, Mae Post. COURTESY: ARCHIVES & MANUSCRIPT DIVISION OF THE OKLAHOMA HISTORICAL SOCIETY.

st and Gatty land after a suc-ssful flight around the world in ew York. July 1, 1931. COURTESY: CHIVES & MANUSCRIPT DIVISION OF E OKLAHOMA HISTORICAL SOCIETY.

Official reception at Chickasha, Oklahoma. Left to right: F. C. Hall, Post, Governor William (Alfalfa Bill) H. Murray, and Gatty. 1931. COURTESY: ARCHIVES & MANUSCRIPT DIVISION OF THE OKLAHOMA HISTORICAL SOCIETY.

After his solo flight, with President Franklin D. Roosevelt, 193[
COURTESY: ARCHIVE UNITED TECHNOLOGY CORP. HARTFORD, CT, 06101.

Wiley Post's flight achievements. COURTESY: ARCHIVES & MANUSCRIPT DIVISION OF
THE OKLAHOMA HISTORICAL SOCIETY.

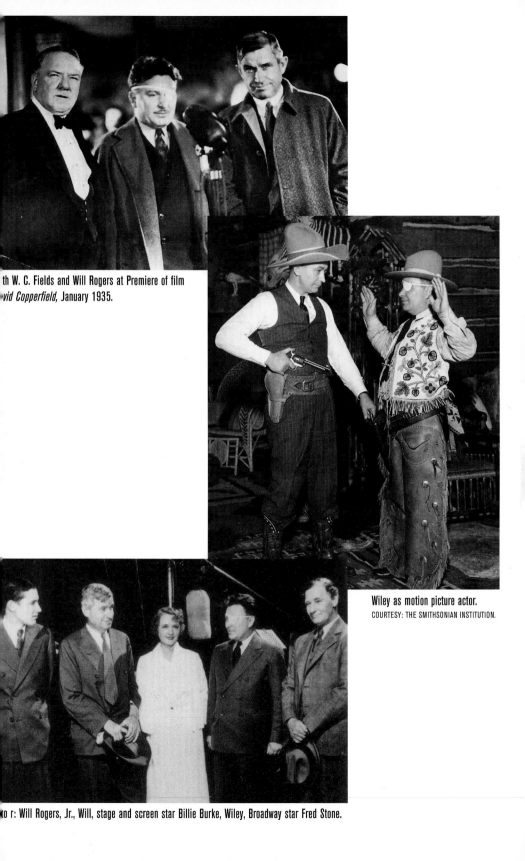

th W. C. Fields and Will Rogers at Premiere of film
vid Copperfield, January 1935.

Wiley as motion picture actor.
COURTESY: THE SMITHSONIAN INSTITUTION.

o r: Will Rogers, Jr., Will, stage and screen star Billie Burke, Wiley, Broadway star Fred Stone.

Wiley Post—without eye patch—and Harold Gatty honored by New York's tickertape parade, July 2, 1931. In his parade two years later, Post having circled the world alone, accumu-

The records show Wiley's earnings from his personal endorsements of goods and services, though they were probably modest at best. Other minor testimonials paid him between $500 and $1,000. If "guest columns" and articles were written in Wiley's name, his approval was sought pro forma, and a fee was paid to him.

Then there was the book, *Around the World in Eight Days*. The contract between Wiley Post and Harold Gatty, the authors, and Rand McNally & Company, the publishers, was signed on July 22, 1931. The contract gave the publisher the manuscript with:

> . . . all rights titles and interest in and to the same including all rights of translation, abridgement, dramatization, selection and all silent motion picture, serial and other rights of every kind and nature now or hereafter during the term of this agreement recognized as the property of the Author in said work or in any parts thereof got the United States of America and all other countries together with any existing copyrights thereof.

The contract also stipulated that "a manuscript prepared for the compositors" be delivered "on or before July 25, 1931," in other words within three days. The contract was signed for the "authors" by H. A. Bruno, for H. A. Bruno—R. R. Blythe Associates.

The schedule of the Post and Gatty speaking tour indicated that during the period of July 22 to 25, 1931, the two authors were somewhere between Boston and Chicago, and no doubt too busy to write the 304-page book that was indeed published and copyrighted later that year. According to the contract, the cover price was "no less than two dollars and fifty cents," and royalties were set at fifteen percent on the first ten thousand copies sold in the United States and twenty per cent thereafter. It had long been assumed that Mr. Leo Kieran, a writer, was hired to follow Wiley and Harold on their lecture tour, to bombard them with questions regarding all the essential facts of the flight, and then to add to the material he had collected the necessary descriptive minutiae. In fact, though, it was Mrs. Dorothy Wayman, later an ace reporter for the Boston Globe, who actually ghostwrote the book. The common practice in 1931 was never to identify ghostwriters, so as to create the impression that the famous person named on the book's jacket had indeed written every word. According to Wiley, the book fell far short of a great financial success, and instead of the riches F. C. Hall foresaw for him after the Round-the-World Flight, Post claimed to have cleared only about $500. The claim is not entirely credible, especially in light of the temporary affluence Post displayed shortly thereafter.

Most people in adversity and obscurity can easily forge bonds that last a lifetime. Those same people, however, will often find it difficult to maintain a friendship when fortune elevates them to the heights of success. Wiley Post and F. C. Hall had thought only the best of each other. They had trusted each other, they had relied on each other, and neither had had any cause to doubt the other's word or good will—that is, until Wiley became world famous. On July 8, 1931, just a week after his safe return from the round-the-world flight, at a public function, Wiley forced F.C's hand in a confrontation over the sale of the *Winnie Mae*. In the presence of a number of people, Wiley not only insisted that Hall sell him the *Winnie Mae*, but also that right then and there, Hall draw up a record of sale and letter of agreement, written in hand on hotel notepaper. The only contingency to the agreement was *Winnie Mae* Fain's approval of the use of her name on the plane. Wiley paid $3,000 in cash and the rest on an $18,200 note. The bill of sale and the note were dated July 8, 1931. The promissory note bears two dates: July 8 and 8—8—1931 at the bottom. Across the face of the note is written "Paid in full Sept. 15, 1931 (signed) F. C. Hall. If Wiley indeed made only a few hundred dollars from his trip, as he claimed at various times, the question arises as to just where Wiley obtained more than $20,000 to buy a plane. Another minor mystery lies among Wiley Post's papers in a bill of sale that indicates the *Winnie Mae* is sold by *Winnie Mae* Fain, claiming to be the lawful owner, to Wiley Post for "the sum of Ten Dollars (10) and other considerations to her in hand." This second "sale" raises more questions: If F. C. Hall had already sold the plane—as the paid and signed promissory note clearly shows—how could *Winnie Mae* Fain, his married daughter, sell it again? Furthermore her father had sold the plane on July 8, 1931, while this later bill of sale, executed by *Winnie Mae* Fain, was dated and notarized almost two years later, on February 4, 1933. It has been suggested that Post, unable to keep up payments, had sold the plane back to the Hall family, but no proof has yet been found to support that possibility.

In the almost two years between the two "sales" Wiley used the plane as he chose and left no doubt that it was now his own. He had ordered structural changes and prepared the plane for what was to be another dash around the world, only this time he would fly alone. In light of the advances in the intervening two years since his last flight, Wiley decided he would need no navigator. The Sperry Autopilot, now vastly improved, could take over much of the work by holding a set course. To check the efficiency of such a "Mechanical Mike," as Wiley came to call the installation, Wiley flew the *Winnie Mae* from Oklahoma City to Mexico, and found the Sperry instrument reliable. Not wishing to trust his own judgment alone, Wiley asked his friend, Luther E. "Red" Gray, an experienced pilot with Braniff Airways, to check his findings. He also invited Oklahoma businessman Harry G. Frederickson—a likely patron— and another passenger to come along. The flight, scheduled to be a short one, could have taken Post's life.

Though always reputed to be a cautious man, Post could be faulted for impatience and a short temper, which sometimes prompted him to take shortcuts, ignore rules and regulations, and break laws for his own gain. April 21, 1933, was a day on which Wiley wanted everything to go well, and he wanted to impress Frederickson. He had purchased fuel for the plane the evening before their flight, and when the *Winnie Mae* stood ready the four men climbed aboard. Wiley had asked Red to pilot the plane, and Gray immediately noticed—and pointed out to Wiley—that the fuel gauge needle indicated the tank to be practically empty. Probably embarrassed to have been found ill prepared, Wiley insisted that the gauge had to be wrong since he had purchased fuel just the evening before. Although trained never to second-guess instruments, Gray finally bowed to Wiley's insistence, and started the engine. What neither man knew, was that some boys had entered the hangar during the evening hours and siphoned most of the gas out of the plane and into their car tank.

The engine warmed up, and Gray sped down the runway. The Vega took off, but at an altitude of about 50 feet, the engine quit, all the fuel spent. Gray, familiar with Lockheed Vegas, managed to gain some control. He hit the earth hard and ground-looped just short of a peach tree orchard. The fuselage split open, damaging the propeller and engine, cracking two of Frederickson's ribs and cutting Wiley's finger. Gray and the passenger escaped unharmed.

The wreckage was taken to Braniff Airways at Curtiss-Wright Field for repair. The bill came to $1,763.92, an amount almost $600 short of the cash Wiley had in his account. Braniff Airways refused to release the plane until the entire bill was settled. Wiley was in danger of losing his plane on a mechanic's lien, which would have given Braniff the right to sell the plane to settle the account. Several of Wiley's friends—operating manager Tom Braniff, pilots Red Gray and Claude Seaton, head mechanic Sterling E. Perry,[3] and several other Braniff employees, including chief overhauler, George Brauer, donated their off-hours to work on the famous plane. The September 1933 issue of *Aviation* magazine reported on page 294 that Wiley later saw to it personally that each man was paid double for the hours he spent on the *Winnie Mae*.

Wiley had the repaired and reconditioned plane equipped with some extra fuel tanks in order to extend its cruising range. For his solo flight, Wiley was planning fewer refueling stops—just Berlin, Novosibirsk, Khabarovsk, Fairbanks, and Edmonton—than on the first trip, although the route would be essentially the same. With just a little luck and none of those time-consuming mud delays, Wiley knew he could easily better his record—and this time he would show those critics that Wiley Post was both brain and pilot on a world record flight.

The need for more money was constant. With the Great Depression showing no sign of abating, aviation did not stand uppermost on most people's minds, and F. C. Hall was no longer available. Harry G. Frederickson, befriended by Post for some time, was willing to help but only by cutting himself in for a ten percent commission on any amount he raised. Wiley really had no choice but to go with Frederickson. However, he made one stipulation: all the money would have to come from Oklahomans interested in aviation. Frederickson went to work. He approached Stanley Draper, the director

---

[3]*Oklahoma City Times*, July 31, 1933.

of Oklahoma City's Chamber of Commerce. Intent on making Oklahoma the center of the budding aviation industry, Draper embraced the project immediately and made the first contribution toward a goal of $40,000. At a Chamber-sponsored luncheon with the state's foremost industrialists, Frederickson found a lot of enthusiasm, but little cash. Then he met John Kroutil. Although John had no connection with aviation—he was a miller from Yukon, a town near Oklahoma City—he did want to boost his hometown. Whenever Post needed some extra money, John Kroutil came up with it. It is believed that he alone contributed around $5,000.

The campaign to raise funds took a more positive path when Walter Harrison, the managing editor of the Oklahoma City *Times* embraced the project, both personally and in print. In all, more than forty sponsors eventually donated enough money to make the flight a reality. Among the contributors were men who had already made names for themselves in some circles in Oklahoma, and who would become American household names in the years to follow, men like the future senator, A. S. "Mike" Monroney; Frank Phillips of Phillips 66 Oil; Tom Braniff of Braniff Airways; and Gomer Smith, the Congressman.

Wiley then thought of asking the major aircraft manufacturers and parts suppliers to donate needed components. Pratt & Whitney not only supplied all necessary parts to update their engine, but also offered the full-time services of technical specialist Lionel B. Clark, who stayed with the plane up to the moment it left for Berlin.[4] The Sperry Gyroscope Company was less altruistic. The latest model of its autopilot, which used the most up-to-date technology, had been tested only on short hops within the United States. A flight around the world would provide the ultimate test and advertisement for Sperry's product. The U.S. Army Air Force, too, was anxious to put this automatic pilot through rigorous tests and supported Wiley Post's effort. Wiley may have been assigned the task of testing the "Sperry Robot Pilot" for the United States Army, as many believe, since it was the Army (there was no separate Air Force in 1933) that installed the Sperry Gyroscope in his plane. Conventional opinion holds that the Army had also supplied the mechanism. That belief is

---

[4]Sterlings' Interview with Lionel B. Clark

now proven false by an invoice from the Sperry Gyroscope Company, Inc., dated February 15, 1933, which states:

> Sold to: Mr. Wiley Post: 1 Automatic Airplane Pilot Pt.640169, Ser. 14 $5,000.00 Terms: $3,000.00 upon signing of Contract. Balance within 30 days.

Also there is Wiley's own letter to the Internal Revenue Service in which he claims to have paid $3,000.00 for the Robot Pilot:

Collector Internal Revenue,
Los Angeles, Calif.   December 20, 1934

Dear Sir:

The list of deductions on Income Tax Return filed for 1933 is as follows:

Sperry Robot Pilot (Brooklyn, N.Y.)	$ 3,000.00
Installation of Pilot, Tests	1,500.00
Expenses Sam G. Grihi, Advanceman to Russia and Siberia	1,600.00
Miscellaneous personal Transportation	1,500.00
Rebuilding Airplane and Engine Braniff Airways in Okla. City	2,100.00
Repay of loan advanced on expenses	1,125.00
Fuel Tanks (Lockheed Aircraft Corp.)	600.00
Fuel Tanks (Mr. Whitney, New York)	75.00
Russian Government	750.00
State Department (Washington, D.C.)	100.00
Lee Tranholm, 22 East 40th, New York Salary and expenses	3,000.00
Harry Frederickson, Oklahoma City Salary and Expenses	2,655.00
Doctor, Nurse and Hospital, Quincy, Ill.	350.00
Car wreck Oklahoma, (Hickman Smith)	40.00
Cables, Telegram, Oil, Gas, Misc (sic) Mechanic, Hotel	2,100.00
Total	$ 20,495.00

Another mechanical device that needed thorough testing was a new "radio-compass." This system, an Automatic Direction Finder (ADF), which simply followed existing radio beams, could be used anywhere radio stations existed. The Army asked Wiley to test this system as well and installed it at Wright Field, near Dayton, Ohio. The public was not too familiar with the details of either the ADF or the Robot Pilot, but it was clear that navigating a plane had become a lot simpler since 1931. *The New York Times of July* 16, 1933 remarked on page 3:

> He [Post] will ride around the world on radio waves while the robot flies the plane.

In addition, a rather ingenious, home-built device was installed to enable Wiley to lubricate and grease the plane's rocker boxes during flight. Not only did this device reduce the possibility of an in-flight emergency, it also eliminated the need for on-the-ground lubrication, and thus saved valuable time.

When Socony-Vacuum came aboard by offering fuel, oils, and greases, the last major hurdle had been cleared—until at almost the last minute the Soviet Union demanded a security payment of $1,000 in cash, to cover any unforeseen expenses incurred by Post and his plane. As usual, Post had no such cash in reserve, but through the efforts of Texaco Oil the Russians settled for a Letter of Credit calling for $1,500, so no actual funds had to be tied up overseas.

Once again, Wiley went through the personal toughening-up process. He slept in short spurts, ate small meals at irregular hours, cleared his mind so he could concentrate on a single purpose, studied maps and memorized names and distances. He took long walks, exercising the body, although he would be sitting practically motionless for seemingly endless hours. He had done it all before, but the regimen was no easier the second time. Besides, this time he had neither Harold Gatty nor F. C. Hall to lighten the burden of organizing details. Wiley himself had to deal with the faulty wiring, with fuselage gas tanks that were too large and would not fit, with parts that disappeared in transit, with wrong instruments—there seemed to be no end to the variety of problems that arose. With so much on his mind, it was not surprising that he occasionally made mental errors.

One of America's outstanding women pilots—and the first woman to enter the rolls of the Caterpillar Club, all of whose members had had their lives saved by a parachute—was Fay Gillis. During one of her earliest flying lessons, over Valley Stream, New York, the plane's tail surfaces had separated from the rest of the fuselage in midair and eliminated any possibility of a landing, so both Fay and her instructor had had to "hit the silk." Since then Fay had developed into one of America's best pilots. In 1933, however, she was living with her family in Moscow, where her father had been asked to build two electrolytic zinc plants for the Soviet government. So impressed were the Russians with Fay's flying skills that she was the only foreigner given permission to solo over Moscow. A charming, intelligent, and outgoing young lady, Fay had learned to speak Russian fluently and moved comfortably in her new milieu. Wiley had again agreed to wire a daily report on his progress to a news service, and if the offer from a rival syndicate for Fay to telegraph from Moscow reports on the Post flight at first bemused her, she was taken aback when she unexpectedly received a slightly garbled wire from Wiley:

NLT FAY GILLIS ANANEVSKY ᴘER DOM 5 APT 26 MSK   LIKE YOU
ARRIVE NOVOSIBIRSK BY JULY FIRST ARRANGE GAS PLANE IN TWO
HOURS WHILLE (SIC) I SLEEP THEN FLY WITH ME KHABAROVSK TO DI-
RECT SERVICE THERE GET ME BEST MAPS NOVOSIBIRSK KHABAROVSK
WILL PAY YOUR EXPENSES REGARDS
                                                    WILLEY (SIC) POST

Fay could only wonder whatever had possessed Wiley to suggest that she come aboard his plane, since that would immediately negate his claim of a solo flight. Whether Wiley realized the error in his thinking later is not known, but he wired Fay no further information or correction, or at least Fay never received a second telegram.[5] She did, however, obtain the maps Wiley had requested and made plans to be in Khabarovsk by the time he was expected to arrive there.

Post was determined to leave New York as close to July 1 as possible. The lengthy delay before the first flight had demonstrated to him only how inaccurate the so-called science of weather prognostication could be, since the flight had been plagued by inclemency almost along the entire way. With that departure date in mind, Wiley left Oklahoma City in the *Winnie Mae* on June 14. On board with him was Harry Frederickson, his friend and fundraiser. They stopped over in Washington, D.C., and the next day landed at Floyd Bennett

<hr>

[5]Sterlings' Interview with Fay Gillis Wells.

Field on Long Island, New York. Shortly thereafter, danger loomed suddenly from a totally unexpected source.

On June 27, 1933, the *Daily Oklahoman* reporter Bennie Turner revealed that Wiley Post, quartered in a free (usually thirty-five dollars a day) suite at the Roosevelt Hotel at the corner of Madison Avenue and forty-fifth Street, had received life-threatening letters. The City of New York immediately stationed police at the *Winnie Mae* and assigned special guards to Post personally. At Floyd Bennett Field mechanics had succeeded in foiling one attempt to tamper with the plane's engine, and had discovered another attempt to damage the plane's carburetor. In addition to the police, soldiers were also guarding the plane because the ADF, which had been installed by the U.S. Army, was considered not only government property, but also a still-secret development.

That Bennie Turner broke this story is not surprising. It was said that he knew Wiley probably better than anybody, as was evident when he wrote:

> We called him Weeley and he often had some personal name for his friend . . . None ever knew Wiley. He was completely self-contained, so much so that few knew he was subject to moods that could change from blue to rose in a flash.
>
> It's little traits of personality that make a man, a man for friends to enjoy. Little traits like his habit of waking in the middle of the night with a desire to go for a walk, and dressing in the dark so as not to disturb his companions; or his half-anger when anybody worried about him; or his dislike of liquor, yet always eager to mix drinks for others; his love for flying, yet his devotion to automobiles.
>
> There was nothing sentimental about Post, except his love for children. He would never pass a ragged newsboy without buying a paper. He would swear until the rafters rang and memorize the name of a person mentioned in print in any child abuse stories: "Some day I may meet him. I like to beat the hell out of guys like that!" he would say.
>
> He would sit on the floor for hours and play with a child. I can remember when he left his clothes behind and used the space

in his old plane to bring a doll from California for the daughter of old friends.

One of Post's amusements was caring for his watches. He had 42 of them that had been given him by civic clubs and admirers. Often, when idle, he would take them all out, wind each and set it to the split second. Then he would keep them going until he went off on some trip.

His guns were another passion, but unlike his watches, whenever he got a good gun, he wanted to give it away to a friend.

Post had another passion only his friends knew—it was for baths. Four or five baths a day were not unusual.

Post disliked parades as much as he disliked to talk; but in parades he would often stop to tell police that they were not to chase the usual following of kids away from his car. "Leave 'em alone, someone should get some fun out of this," he would say.

By July 6, Wiley was informed that the *Winnie Mae* had again been given experimental plane status and was now listed as being owned by the Fain and Post Drilling Company.

As in 1931, Dr. Kimball was the meteorological prognosticator, and his forecasts were no more optimistic than they had been two years earlier. Four weeks went by and Dr. Kimball still saw no clearing. Some days the moment they had been waiting for appeared to have arrived when sudden atmospheric changes would abort the takeoff. Wiley waited less impatiently than he had before, perhaps because this time he had Mae with him. He could also move around New York City more freely and unrecognized by inserting his glass eye instead of wearing the famous white eye patch. When flying, Post had to wear the eye patch because the glass eye became very cold and caused him headaches.

Late on July 14, Dr. Kimball decided that the following morning would offer conditions suitable for take off. Just before the first hint of dawn on the fifteenth, a small group assembled by the *Winnie Mae*: Wiley and Mae, Harry Frederickson, Bennie Turner, and Lee Trenholm, Wiley's business manager. Wiley dashed off a telegram to editor Walter Harrison, thanking him and his fellow Oklahomans for all the help they had so generously given him. Then, in a most unusual public display of affection, he kissed Mae and told her: "See you in six days—or else . . ." That said, he climbed up on the plane and dropped into the cockpit.

At 5:10 a.m. on July 15, 1933, Wiley Post, having warmed up his engine, released the brakes and began to roll down the runway. After gathering speed of nineteen hundred feet in twenty-nine seconds he slowly lifted the heavy, fuel-laden plane off the ground and headed into the sun just rising in the east. Only five minutes later he ran straight into a solid barrier of fog. He turned on his Sperry autopilot. Less than half an hour later, barely out of the fog, he caught up with the thick rain clouds that had kept him prisoner in New York City.

The hours passed slowly for Wiley, alone now with his thoughts. Secure in the knowledge that only the sea was below him, he could skim along at low altitude. Then, somewhere past the halfway point across the Atlantic, he heard a British voice on the radio: "This is a special broadcast for Wiley Post . . ." It was station G2LO in Manchester. Wiley immediately adjusted his ADF radio compass to the signal and followed it. As he neared England and then the continent, the various radio signals proved a priceless aid to his navigation.

Twenty-five hours and forty-five minutes after take-off in New York City, Wiley set the *Winnie Mae* down at Berlin's Tempelhof Aerodrome, where the local time was 11:55 a.m. A goodly crowd had assembled, since the plane had been sighted along the way and its arrival was expected. Here Reichsminister Hermann Göring, only recently appointed to his post by Germany's new Chancellor, Adolf Hitler, greeted Wiley.

Two hours and fifteen minutes later, the plane had been serviced and refueled and was racing down the runway. The next scheduled stop was Novosibirsk, but Wiley again discovered how the best-laid plans can be upset by the smallest of lapses. With Tempelhof barely behind him, Wiley realized that he had left his maps at the airport. He could have gone back, but rather than look highly incompetent, he pushed on. Problems with the Sperry autopilot caused him to make the first unscheduled stop, at Königsberg, East Prussia. The local mechanics, however, had no means to diagnose or correct the problem with the autopilot. Wiley's left eye socket had meanwhile become inflamed. A local doctor simply prescribed a boric acid solution to soothe the inflammation. As night approached, Wiley made the most of the enforced delay and slept for the next six hours.

At dawn, Wiley set out for Moscow, to see what could be done about the leak in the Sperry autopilot. His eye socket had profited greatly by the night's rest. Wiley was also flying slightly lighter; he had forgotten his suitcase. What was far more worrisome than a wardrobe reduced to the clothes he currently wore was the fact that Wiley had fallen almost a day behind his schedule and that he was flying without proper maps and with a malfunctioning autopilot.

Wiley made his second unscheduled landing at Moscow. Because he had not been expected, no reception committees awaited him with planned festivities, fortunately. The mechanics had little trouble stopping the loss of fluids in the autopilot and the maps were promptly replaced. Thirteen hours and fifteen minutes later Wiley landed at Novosibirsk. Fay Gillis greeted him. She had been waiting for three weeks and had spent the time making arrangements for Wiley's arrival. She had made sure that the grass on the runway was cut short every other day, that a room awaited Wiley so he could rest while the plane was being serviced; that a variety of meals offered him alternatives—Wiley only had a light snack, in keeping with his routine. He was happy to receive the maps Fay had brought him, and he explained to her the mental error he had made in the telegram, when he asked her to accompany him, though he was certain she understood the infeasibility of the proposal.

Wiley did not know that Fay was the Soviet correspondent for the *New York Herald Tribune*, covering aviation, while he himself was wiring first hand reports to the *New York Times*. In fact, while he rested in the room Fay had arranged for him, Wiley dictated his report to the *Times* to her. Fay felt herself obligated to file Wiley's column before sending her own account to the *Times'* number one competitor. As she described it: "I had to scoop myself!"[6]

Post took off from Novosibirsk with all systems working, but problems with the Sperry gyroscope autopilot continued to plague him. Acting up again, it necessitated another unscheduled landing, this time at Irkutsk. And still another at Ruhklovo. Here, Wiley also discovered that his drinking water supply had not been refurbished at one of his recent landings and he was becoming dehydrated. Try though he did, he could not make himself properly understood to

[6]Sterlings' interview with Fay Gillis Wells.

the men at the airport. Sign language seemed only to confuse the request, because the Russians interpreted Wiley's gesturings as a request for alcohol and tried to dissuade him. Finally, one soldier took pity on the American, and traveled into town, and returned with two bottles of vodka. Wiley never got his drink of water until he landed on American soil, eighteen hundred miles away. When Will Rogers learned of the incident, he remarked that had he been Wiley, he would have poured one bottle into the engine and the other into himself—and been back in New York City by sundown.

The next lap of Wiley's journey was perhaps the most difficult, for he had to fly "blind" for seven hours. Mountains—some as high as fifteen thousand feet—lay hidden in heavy cloudbanks. Even if the autopilot was working perfectly, it would have been most risky for Wiley to depend on a preset course, especially as he was following unreliable maps. Furthermore, flying high over the peaks deprived Wiley of vital oxygen. Yet flying through the passes in unknown territory would be suicidal. Piloting a plane for eighteen hundred miles taxes a rested man and Wiley was near exhaustion, but he was fortunate in that the Pratt & Whitney engine worked without a flaw. Wiley therefore focused all his attention on directing the plane, instead of having to concentrate on the sound and rhythm of the motor. Wiley kept his eye trained on the control dials, as the *Winnie Mae* gulped down mile after mile, sometimes reaching a speed of 170 miles per hour. He did receive some help in his trial by flight from the radio stations of WAMCATS [the Washington–Alaska Military Cable and Telegraph System] in Nome, Teller, and Hot Springs, Alaska.

Starting in the north of Alaska, from Barrow (call letters WXB) where the U.S. Signal Corps' Sergeant Stanley Morgan kept watch, a number of official and private wireless stations dotted the entire territory. These radio stations did not broadcast entertainment; some of them were WAMCATS in service of the U.S. Army and primarily dispensed military news and information. As WAMCATS was also the only communication network in Alaska, it concerned itself also with civil government and the population of the Territory. Most of these WAMCATS stations were manned and operated only during daylight business hours. Some had prescribed broadcast times; others were on the air twice daily for only brief periods, to transmit by Morse code weather reports or requests for medical information or help, or simply to pass on information deemed of interest or importance to Fairbanks and Anchorage. Other than at broadcast times, most of these stations were neither staffed nor on the air, so they could not be contacted unless they had been alerted beforehand to stand by for continuous communication. Such unbroken contact with ground bases might be needed in a rescue-and-search operation, if a pilot was down or if a trapper was missing and feared lost. When special rescue missions were in operation—or attempts to set world records were being made—stations along the expected route might stand by on a twenty-four-hour basis. When Wiley Post was expected to approach Alaska on his solo round-the-world flight, WAMCATS stations at Nome, Flat, Teller, and Hot Springs were alerted. They proved to be of inestimable help, for without their assistance, Wiley would not have set a record, and most assuredly never completed the flight.

Naturally, Alaska also had a large number of private radio sending and receiving sets, which were the sole contact with the outside world for settlers, trappers, and Eskimos. Most of those sets were "on" around the clock, even though there was no broadcast, much like today's scanners. Help was needed when the nearest WAMCATS station stood unmanned, in which case a private station would pick up the call and relay it "down the line," thus saving time and often lives. Of course, actually flying in help always remained subject to weather conditions, which could often delay rescue for days, and in severe winters, for weeks.

Alerted to Wiley Post's flight, WAMCATS stations along the expected flight path went on alert after the *Winnie Mae* was reported to have left Khabarovsk. They continued on alert until after she passed Nome. Hot Springs stayed on the air for a solid twelve hours, until their batteries ran down.

Despite their readiness to help, as it turned out, there was absolutely nothing these stations, or even the radio station in Fairbanks, could do. What none of them—nor indeed Wiley himself—knew was that suddenly, without warning, the ADF, the Automatic Direction Finder, so vital to his navigation, had stopped working. He was now up in a plane not only where he could not see the ground, but also where he could not be heard or contacted by anyone on the ground. In an article bearing his byline, Wiley described this period as the worst in his flight from Siberia to Fairbanks:

When mountains began to appear again above the clouds, I knew I had crossed Bering Strait and was above Alaska. I had crossed without even a fleeting glimpse of the surface. I flew to the north side of the mountains, where the wind had blown the clouds away, dropped down low and flew back to the coast. I followed it around Cape Prince of Wales to Nome, where I circled the radio station and the airport, then headed for Fairbanks,

The clouds were low and the visibility poor, and so I decided to climb back on top and, unable to pick up radio signals from Fairbanks which I expected would be broadcast for me, began what turned out to be a 1,200 mile wandering about the central part of Alaska. For seven hours, I dodged mountains, including 20,000-foot Mt. McKinley, and followed rivers to no avail. I was completely lost. I therefore headed back toward the coast of Nome, and on the way I spied what I later found was Flat. I landed at the airport there seven hours after I had circled the Nome radio station.

Noel Wien, famous Alaskan pilot, and his wife Ada were flying a Bellanca aircraft headed for Fairbanks, when they suddenly spotted the *Winnie Mae* circling. It struck them as a most peculiar sight. The Wiens knew that Wiley Post was on a record-breaking flight around the world, yet here he was, lazily circling over Alaska. The thought that he might be lost occurred to them, and they attempted, unsuccessfully, to contact him with directions to Fairbanks. Their much slower Bellanca was no match for Wiley's Vega, so they continued their own trip, expecting to find Wiley's plane on the ground when they arrived. When they discovered he had not yet landed, the Wiens concluded that most likely Wiley had put his plane intentionally into a circling course and was trying to catch up on his sleep. The Wiens had no sense of alarm since all had appeared well when they had last seen the plane.

But all was not well. After seven hours of meandering, Wiley returned to the place where he had last seen the ground—Flat, Alaska. He inspected the tiny airport from the air. It was really just a short field, no more than 700 feet in length, with a ditch at the far end— hardly long enough for the *Winnie Mae*. Wiley circled the field one more time, then headed into the wind. His wheels touched the ground close to the start of the field. They were bouncing over the uneven surface, when suddenly the right landing gear support collapsed. The engine cowling dug into the ground, causing the propeller blades to be twisted beyond repair and the right wing tip to hit the ground. Wiley was unhurt. The landing was almost identical to Wiley's accident on Solomon Beach, except it caused far greater damage. He could not possibly solve this problem with just a hammer and a stone as repair tools. This was the second time Wiley had come to Alaska, and the second time that he had started with an accident.

Wiley must have looked with reality at his position. He knew that he was almost thirty-one hours ahead of his 1931 flight schedule. That would give him some time to effect repairs—if he could find a repair shop that had a replacement propeller and could take care of his broken landing gear. But here he was stranded in a tiny mining village that did not even have a proper airfield. There was no sense fretting; Wiley went to sleep.

The resident WAMCATS operator had reported both Wiley's arrival and his accident to Fairbanks. There the news reached Wiley's personal guardian angel, Joe Crosson. After ascertaining via the wireless network a detailed description of the damage, Joe assembled a new propeller and tools to temporarily repair the landing gear. He alerted Loren Fernold, Pan Alaska Airway's chief mechanic, and his assistant Larry Davis to prepare for the trip to Flat. Needing a radio operator, Joe asked Robert Gleason, PAA's communication superintendent and his best friend, to come along. Estimating the total weight of parts and tools, adding to that the weight of the men and considering the short field at Flat, Crosson decided that he would have to rid the plane of some of its cargo. He definitely needed the mechanics, but if he kept in-flight communication to a minimum, he could act as his own radio operator. So Robert Gleason remained at the radio setup in Fairbanks, where he could then pass on any news from Crosson to the WAMCATS operator in Flat.

When Joe Crosson and his crew arrived at Flat, he found that the local men had already built a simple derrick to righten the plane. Crosson and Post decided which repairs would have to be made on the spot in order to allow the plane to fly to Fairbanks, and which could wait for the better facilities at Fairbanks. While the mechanics went to work, Post decided to catch up on his sleep.

At dawn, the *Winnie Mae* was considered able to limp into Fairbanks. Wiley followed Crosson's plane. Once both planes had landed safely on the ground at Weeks Field, Fairbanks's airport, Crosson recruited the best mechanics in town, whether they worked for PAA or some other airline. Jim Hutchison was called on to rebuild the right landing gear, while Robert Gleason was asked to check, and possibly repair, the Automatic Direction Finder. He quickly diagnosed that the left/right indicator was malfunctioning, a matter simply corrected by the replacement of a defective tube. Wiley had no further trouble with this equipment.

Eight hours were lost in Fairbanks alone, but Wiley was well rested now. He would have to be because he had some long distances yet to cover—almost 1,500 miles to Edmonton, and beyond that, another two thousand miles to New York City. In addition, further problems arose, though none with the plane. After leaving Fairbanks, adverse weather conditions like fog and rain clouds, in conjunction with the high mountains, forced Wiley to fly for brief periods at an altitude of 20,000 feet—almost twice the altitude considered safe for humans without oxygen support. He landed at Edmonton after only nine hours and twenty-two minutes. This time the field was dry and the refueling took only ninety minutes.

The final two thousand miles to New York City were flown under excellent weather conditions. The engine was purring happily and with both the autopilot and ADF working, the only danger was that Wiley might doze off.

> I'll bet I fell asleep two hundred times before I reached New York City. Each time I actually got to sleep my muscles relaxed and my hand loosened its grasp on the stick and as the hand dropped, I would be awakened.

Actually, the last part of the trip was not only the easiest, but in some ways the most enjoyable. As he neared cities, Wiley tuned in to various radio broadcasts that amused him with their various predictions as to when he would be arriving in New York.

On July 22, 1933, precisely seven days, eighteen hours and forty-nine minutes after taking off from Floyd Bennett Field, a single man had completed a flight around the globe he called home. He had bettered the time he and navigator Harold Gatty had set just two years earlier by more than twenty-one hours.

In the process of that record-breaking solo flight, Wiley Post had learned something no one else knew. When he told anyone about it, though, no one would believe him. Indeed, it would take the United States government another decade—until after World War II—to recognize his wisdom and acknowledge his foresight.

But by that time, Wiley Post would be dead.

CHAPTER VII

UP AND DOWN, GETTING NOWHERE

T HE MOMENT THE *Winnie Mae*'s wheels touched down at Floyd Bennett Field, New York, that July night in 1933, Wiley Post's honored place in the annals of aviation should have been assured. He had just completed an extraordinary effort, which, though attempted since, has never been equaled under the same conditions. He had made a complete circle around the earth in a single engine propeller plane in just 115 hours and 36 1/2 minutes of actual flying time.

Distance In miles	From	To	Time
3,942	New York	Berlin	25:45
340	Berlin	Königsberg	4:30
651	Königsberg	Moscow	5:15
1,579	Moscow	Novosibirsk	13:15
1,055	Novosibirsk	Irkutsk	6:33
750	Irkutsk	Rukhlovo	7:32
650	Rukhlovo	Khabarovsk	4:20
2,800	Khabarovsk	Flat	22:32
375	Flat	Fairbanks	3:14

Distance In miles	From	To	Time
1,450	Fairbanks	Edmonton	9:22
2,004	Edmonton	New York	13:18:30
15,596	New York	New York	115:36:30

Wiley Post was not only the first man to fly around the earth twice, but also the first man to do it alone. It is true that he had two electronic assistants aboard—the Sperry Autopilot and ADF, the Automatic Direction Finder—but both were in experimental stages and Wiley was testing them as much as he was using them. Wiley had to monitor both devices closely at all times, and often they malfunctioned during the trip. Although they saved him some work, they created numerous problems of their own and caused the loss of valuable time. They also required constant human supervision so that performance of their tasks could be identified, verified, or corrected. When a faulty vacuum tube caused the total failure of the ADF, Wiley got lost for seven hours over Alaska, and as a result crashed at Flat. The erratic performance of the Sperry Gyroscope Autopilot forced Wiley to make several unscheduled landings to attempt repairs, and Wiley could never rely on it fully. The autopilot proved to be useless over uneven terrain, unless it was set to over-fly the highest expected peaks in its path, information that—as in the case of the Soviet Union— was not always possible to ascertain. Weather conditions and visibility also interfered with the use of the autopilot. Flying, for example, over unfamiliar territory necessitated that Wiley follow certain rivers or railroads, paths that could not be programmed ahead of time.

When the *Winnie Mae*'s wheels touched down at Floyd Bennett Field, not only had history been made, but aviation had certified its progress from infancy. One man had dramatically demonstrated the fact that long-distance flying was no longer a possibility of the future, but the reality of the present. If a small plane with but a single engine could safely fly from New York nonstop to Berlin in just over a day, surely, so could businessmen in two-engine planes. Why spend five days on a ship just sailing to reach Europe, when in the same five days one could be flying to Europe, attend to business, and be safely back in America?

When the *Winnie Mae*'s wheels touched down at Floyd Bennett Field, Wiley Post had firmly established himself as America's newest hero, and there was no one like him. The six hundred policemen assigned to control the expected crowd could not contain the fifty thousand spectators at Floyd Bennett Field, who had come to see Wiley land. Men and women broke through the barriers and swarmed onto the field, forcing the police into an ever-smaller circle to protect the plane. It was feared that the crowd would tear the *Winnie Mae* to shreds to carry away some part of the plane as a souvenir of having witnessed history being made.

Confusion reigned at the Field and it was some time before Wiley could even leave the plane. Having forgotten his suitcase in Königsberg, East Prussia, he had had no chance to change his clothes. His shirt and trousers looked as if he had slept in them—which he probably had. His trademark white eye patch, carefully sewn by Mae, had become so soiled that he had to borrow someone's clean handkerchief to tie around his head and cover the empty eye socket. It took some time before Mae Post could struggle her way through the shoving crowd to embrace her husband.

In the days that followed, New York honored Post with another tickertape parade up Broadway to City Hall where the new mayor, John P. O'Brien, welcomed him with a speech and a medal. Wiley and Mae took the train to Washington, D.C. to honor the invitation by President Franklin D. Roosevelt to come to the White House. Parades celebrated Wiley in numerous cities across the country. On the parade drive between Schenectady and Albany, New York, Wiley sent word to the accompanying state troopers to slow down and not speed unsafely over 30 miles an hour. When a motion-picture producer asked him to fly low over Manhattan, Wiley refused. He did not think it safe. As before, he was being inundated by offers that would supposedly make him rich, while in reality he would be making money for the promoters.

For his historic feat, Wiley received the Gold Medal of the Fédération Aéronautique Internationale, one of aviation's highest awards, which was presented annually to the greatest contributor to aviation. At the time it was only the second such medal ever accorded an American flier, Charles Lindbergh having received it for his historic 1927 solo flight from New York to Paris. The League of International Aviators awarded Wiley the coveted Harmon International Trophy for 1933. While Wiley certainly had earned and well deserved these public recognitions, Wiley could not convert these and other honors into large coins of the realm.

Sperry Gyroscope wanted to boast nationally about its contribution to the successful circumnavigation of the globe. Its publicity department wrote a self-congratulatory article about the efficiency of its invention, intimating that without it the trip could not possibly have succeeded. Indeed, Sperry tried to take most of the credit for the success of the flight. Whether the article appeared in print is not known for certain, but it is fairly safe to assume that Wiley did attest to its veracity and that Sperry sought to have it published under Wiley Post's byline.

SPERRY GYROSCOPE COMPANY INC.,
Manhattan Bridge Plaza
Brooklyn, New York

Reference 13.5   August 23, 1934.

Mr. Wiley Post
C/o Standard Oil Company of New York
112 State Street
Albany, New York

Dear Wiley:-
Attached herewith is your story of the world flight. I hope you will like it. Please criticize it in any way you like and return it as soon as possible.

Jobby tells me that he thought you took five or six snapshots on the trip. If it is agreeable with you, we would like to publish them along with the article, providing that they are suitable. With best wishes for happy landings,

Sincerely yours,
SPERRY GYROSCOPE COMPANY, INC.
J. A. Fitz, Manager, Publicity Department

The attached article referred to in this letter has also been preserved. It is five-and-one-third typed pages long and the very first paragraph already gives a full idea of its tone and intent:

MY WORLD FLIGHT

by Wiley Post

I could almost call it flying blind around the world. There were hours on end during all but one or two laps when I was forced to fly absolutely blind, or above the clouds out of sight of the ground. The weather was so consistently bad that I was able to take only half a dozen pictures from the air throughout the whole trip. It was called a solo flight. And so it was, strictly speaking, but I never could have made the record without the efficient little co-pilot—the Sperry Pilot—which made the journey with me. Without the Sperry Pilot the strain of flying through the extremely bad weather, some of it the worst I have ever flown through, would have been too great to permit flying some laps when I did. . . .

No document exists anywhere to indicate whether any money did, or did not, change hands involving the publication of this purely self-serving article. Chances are that money was involved, as Sperry surely wanted this most powerful endorsement. Since the autopilot had been installed by the U.S. Army, which would certainly want a report on its effectiveness, it would have been interesting to read what Wiley had to say when neither publicity nor money was forthcoming.

There were other endorsements, few if any to be taken seriously. Wiley, a non-smoker, signed with Camel cigarettes for a single magazine advertisement in a series of famous "smokers." The ad pretended to quote Post: "It takes healthy nerves to fly around the world alone. Smoking Camels as I have for so long, I never worry about healthy nerves." To keep up appearances, Wiley sometimes would pull out a pack of Camels in public and light one, just for show, then take only a few puffs.

Another source of revenue for Post came from the Socony-Vacuum Corporation. Their contract stipulated that starting on August 14, 1933, Wiley Post was to spend the following sixty days traveling exclusively for Socony on a public relations tour. This trip was cut short after thirty days. Yet, on February 14, 1934, a new contract was signed, offering $15,000 for the continuation of the publicity junket for the balance of the original contract term of sixty days.

While on the first part of his lecture tour, on September 19, Wiley spoke at a fraternal dinner in Quincy, Illinois. The following morning, taking the *Winnie Mae* to his next engagement, Wiley took off, as usual. Reaching less than one hundred feet in altitude, the engine suddenly sputtered to a stall and the plane fell into a wooded area surrounding the airport. The plane was badly damaged and Wiley was briefly hospitalized with bruises and abrasions. The mechanics at Braniff in Oklahoma, where the plane was under repair, showed that someone had added five-and-a-half gallons of water to the fuel tank. Was it a careless accident, or an intentional attempt on Wiley's life? If it was the latter, it would definitely not be the last.

Buick provided Wiley with a brand new automobile in return for a sycophantic endorsement. Show business, too, tried to capitalize on Wiley's celebrity with an appearance on the Radio City Music Hall stage in New York City's Rockefeller Center, which was in the process of being built. In one of the preparatory excavations close to the theater, the promoter exhibited the *Winnie Mae*, which drew large crowds. Wiley's stage performances consisted of his personal account of the flight accompanied by newsreel footage that showed him leaving and arriving in various cities. Post had hoped to realize some $40,000 from this venture, but actually earned only about $7,000. Magazine articles, usually ghostwritten, also brought Wiley some money.

Overall, Wiley made more money from his solo flight than from the one with Gatty. But he received no demand for his services from private industry, which would have provided a regular income. No budding airline invited him onto their Board, or recruited him for their planning or development department. Surely Post had enough experience and knowledge to contribute to any airline's expansion plans: he had traveled widely, he had flown through every kind of weather, he had tested aircraft, he had flown passengers and freight, and he had flown alone around the world in a race against time. He had unparalleled experience and yet nobody wanted him. Charles Lindbergh had had no such problems. Now one of PAN AM's executives, he had suggested that he would lay out a route to Japan for them and, with his wife Anne Morrow Lindbergh as his radio operator, did just that. Nobody, however, knocked on Wiley Post's door to ask his opinion or call upon his expertise.

When the cheering stopped, Wiley went back to Oklahoma. To those who had been listening closely, Wiley had announced his next project three days after returning from his solo flight. Speaking before the Aeronautical Chamber of Commerce, he told the guests of his plans to begin studies on high-altitude flying.[1]

On both trips across Siberia, Wiley had become acutely aware of the inaccuracy of the Soviet Union–supplied maps. Although the Soviets' misinformation proved of little consequence when flying over the western part of the country, it could be seriously perilous on flights over the mountainous areas of Siberia in rain, clouds, or fog. Post and Gatty had first learned their lesson in 1931 when Wiley barely avoided plowing into a mountainside, though Gatty had directed Post to follow a path that according to the supplied maps showed no major peaks. Yet, they had encountered a mountaintop reaching thousands of feet into the clouds. Gatty rechecked his guidelines and found them correct; there had been no misdirection on his part. The same lesson was learned and confirmed several times thereafter. When the *Winnie Mae* was flying for hundreds of miles over a Siberia covered by heavy clouds, Wiley had no way to visually avoid mountains of unknown height. He could proceed only by flying high above the clouds. This, Wiley did—a tactic that afforded Gatty a regular opportunity to take his readings of the sun, or the moon, or stars. There, too, Wiley encountered a phenomenon he had never experienced before—a constant exceedingly strong tail wind. Without adding to his fuel consumption, the ground speed of the plane increased far beyond the engine manufacturer's estimated capability. On the first trip, Wiley had noted this phenomenon, but paid rela-

---

[1] *The New York Times*, July 26, 1933.

tively little attention to it. On his solo trip, crossing Siberia, he occasionally rose to heights above twenty thousand feet, partly to avoid dangerous weather and partly to recheck on the singular tail winds he had observed before. And he had experienced them again. Not aware of any official designation, he simply named the phenomenon what it was, "high winds." Since no flier before Post voluntarily flew anywhere near twenty thousand feet without oxygen, no one had discovered Wiley's constant "swift river of air."

It would be charitable to claim that Wiley's greatest contribution to the advance of aviation was a purely altruistic act, performed strictly in the pursuit of science and humanity. Charitable, but not quite true. Certainly stratospheric flying stands as Wiley Post's greatest achievement and it advanced aviation by giant steps. It was not, however, motivated primarily by altruism on Wiley's part. While the possibilities of stratospheric flying had been in Wiley's mind for some time, the driving incentive became the £10,000 prize ($50,000 by the 1934 rate of exchange) offered by Australia's Sir MacPherson Robertson. The "MacRobertson" race, as it became known, was to celebrate Melbourne's centennial. Scheduled to start at Mildenhall, Suffolk, England, on October 20, 1934, and progress via Baghdad, Allahabad, Singapore, Darwin, and Charleville, to Melbourne, the 12,500-mile race course across Europe, Asia, and Australia covered mountains and oceans. While the challenges of the race motivated Wiley, the large paycheck offered an appealing additional incentive. He was, however, aware that aviation had not stood still and that it had bypassed the now venerable *Winnie Mae*. Although he had neither the ability to modernize the Vega with a sleek metallic fuselage, nor the funds to purchase one of those newly designed speedsters, he did have one advantage. Wiley Post knew about the "high winds."

Wiley realized that the strong flow of air in the stratosphere would provide enormous help to an aircraft flying from the west to the east. There were, though, two major problems to this high-altitude flying—the lack of oxygen and the extremely low temperature. It would be impossible to fill the *Winnie Mae*'s fuselage with an oxygen-enriched mixture of air and to pressurize it, since the plane's plywood body was not airtight. Because the Vega could obviously not be pressurized, Wiley correctly reasoned that the pilot would have to be somehow encased in his or her own oxygen-controlled, pressurized environment. Late in 1933 and early in 1934, he designed details for just such a personal enclosure by borrowing heavily on a deep-sea diver's suit. What Wiley designed, was in fact the forerunner of the space suits currently worn by astronauts on their EVAs, their extra-vehicular activities. Consulting patent attorney Robert M. Pierson, Wiley had the proper drawings prepared, and applied for a U.S. patent. Discussing the feasibility of a Pressure Suit with Jimmy Doolittle, his acquaintance and often fellow competitor, he suggested that the B. F. Goodrich Company would probably be the best equipped to produce a prototype.[2]

Providing the pilot with oxygen, however, was not enough. The engine, being an internal-combustion motor, also had to be supplied with oxygen-rich air. Wiley designed those oxygen supply systems as well, and once more the *Winnie Mae* underwent significant alteration.

What Wiley had in mind was dramatically inventive, but logical. First on his list stood ascension to a height where he could experience and study at length the high wind he had detected before. Since nobody else had experience or knowledge of the winds, he himself would have to determine all details. The depth and width of the wind had to be measured, as did its speed and direction. Questions as to whether it always blew with the same force, or whether it varied its path, had to be answered. Having flown in up to twenty-thousand-foot-high altitude levels for hours at a time to escape the adverse weather conditions that were affecting the lower levels, Wiley knew that the future of aviation lay in altitudes even higher than those he had ever traveled.

The existing altitude record that any pilot had so far reached in powered flight was 47,300 feet. That record had been set for the sake of itself, by the pilot simply flying straight up to reach a certain height and then returning straight down.

No attempt had been made to explore the stratosphere or gain information. Wiley wanted not only or primarily to break a record, he was also after essential information. To get it, he had to have his new flying suit.

---

[2]Sterlings' interview 1985

While several essential changes were being made to the *Winnie Mae*, Wiley concentrated on the major bottleneck—the pressure suit. On April 6, 1934, he visited the Los Angeles plant of B. F. Goodrich. This is what he wanted:

> "A rubber suit which will enable me to operate and live in an atmosphere of approximately twelve pounds absolute (5,500 feet altitude equivalent). I expect to fly through rarefied areas where the pressure is as low as five pounds absolute (27,000 feet). The temperature will be taken care of by heating the air from the supercharger by coiling it around the exhaust manifold."[3]

The Goodrich engineers went to work immediately. They took Wiley's full measurements, cut out patterns, and designed a two-piece suit—top and bottom—joined by an airtight belt. Attached to it were pigskin gloves for the hands and rubber boots for the feet. An aluminum helmet with a small window, reminiscent of a welder's headgear, but with bulges to allow for headphones, and a small trap door over the mouth, which made it possible to eat and/or drink, completed the outfit. As the material for the body suit Goodrich chose parachute cloth and six yards of rubberized double-ply cloth. The two layers were then glued together on a bias to reduce stretch to a minimum. It is estimated that Wiley Post's first pressure suit cost close to $75.

The major difference between the Post pressure suit and a diver's suit—which it of course resembled—was that whereas air is pumped into the diver's suit, Wiley's was designed for adding vaporized liquid oxygen.

The first unmanned tests of the pressure suit showed not only a major leakage at the waist but an inability to hold pressure. Reworking this first suit seemed impractical, so Wiley and the Goodrich engineers in California decided to retain the helmet but redesign the rest according to the original body measurements. Suit number two was fabricated and shipped to B. F. Goodrich in Akron, Ohio, a location closer to Wiley's home in Oklahoma. There Post worked with project engineer Russell S. Colley. They made an excellent team,

---

[3] *Wiley Post* by Charles L. Wilson

and became friendly enough for Post to be invited frequently to Colley's home. Wiley even taught Barbara, Colley's ten-year-old daughter, how to shoot craps. Barbara proved such a skillful student that when they parted, Wiley had lost $60,000 to her and dutifully wrote out an I.O.U. Later he claimed that it was really for 60,000 kisses.

The problem with the second suit became immediately apparent. When Wiley tried it on, he was able to don it, but once inside the suit, he was unable to take it off. Nor were his body heat and the added perspiration caused by the non-breathable material the only further complications. In the months since Goodrich engineers had taken his body measurements, Wiley had gained almost twenty pounds. To extricate Wiley, the suit had to be cut from his body and destroyed.

The design and construction of a third suit began in August 1934. Russell S. Colley, now a member of the team, realized that neither of the first two suits had really conformed to Post's body. He therefore suggested two distinctly separate layers: an inner rubber suit that hugged the body contours and would contain the life-sustaining oxygen; and an outer skin made of three-ply cloth that would limit the stretching of the inner layer by holding it close to Post's body contours. Wiley knew exactly what was needed and how it would be used, while Colley, who knew the materials available and how best to deploy them, had the genius to help create it.

By this time, it had become obvious that the pressure suit could not be ready for Post to enter the MacRobertson race. As he had thought, the first three finishers were all newly designed metal-bodied twin-engine planes that averaged a speed of 171 miles per hour. It should be noted that, by comparison, on the solo flight with the *Winnie Mae*, Post over the much longer course averaged a speed of 144 miles per hour. The difference of twenty-seven miles per hour appears less substantial when considering what gains Wiley would have made had his pressure suit been ready in time. Flying above thirty thousand feet, Wiley and his aged, single engine plane would have easily outdistanced all other contenders.

The bills for the pressure suit and *Winnie Mae*'s alterations began to amass and as usual, Wiley Post's finances did not match his expenses. Contributions by Pure Oil Company and others proving to be insufficient, Wiley approached a new, rich sponsor—Frank Phillips of Phillips 66 Oil. Moved partly by his dedication to Oklahoma, the state that had made him rich, and the well-founded opinion that Wiley Post's name had great advertising value, Phillips assumed full support of Wiley's next project. With Frank Phillips as his sponsor, Wiley was relieved of the constant pressure to seek new funds. If primarily interested in promoting the name of the oil company, Phillips was also genuinely interested in aviation and Wiley Post. But he was a cautious man. Realizing the risks in all aviation experiments, he did not wish to endanger his company, or himself, by becoming involved in a high-profile lawsuit should his protégé die. He therefore had both Wiley, and Mae Post sign a legal release that would hold Phillips 66, and Frank Phillips, clear and free of any responsibility should there be an accident. When Wiley signed the release, he summed up his philosophy, saying: "I know it's dangerous, but if I get popped off, that's the way I want to go. Doing the thing I want to do."

Russell S. Colley had now taken charge of the project, and he took an entirely different approach to the design of the third pressure suit. Before Post had been measured and his body outlined while he lay flat on the ground. Colley, instead, made an exact metal form of Wiley in a comfortable sitting position, as if he were in the cockpit. Colley then had that replica covered with liquid latex, which served as the inner layer. That sitting posture is the reason that so many photographs show Wiley slightly stooped, though if necessary, he could stand up when wearing the pressure suit.

Colley also had the outer, cloth skin reinforced several times so that it would function as the restraint it was supposed to be. It was reassuring to both Colley and Post that during every static pressure test, the inner layer held at all times and never allowed any pressure to escape.

The body suit came with a helmet redesigned in light of Wiley's complaints and according to his specifications. Oxygen would now be introduced from the left side, thus entering on the same side of his head as the missing eye, while the controls for the oxygen would sit on the left knee. The new helmet also accommodated earphones for ADF and voice radio communication, as well as a microphone. To conserve oxygen during ascent, when the pilot really needed no assistance, the helmet's new window would be redesigned so that it

could be left open until the pilot reached an altitude that required
the help of oxygen. He could then begin the flow of the essential
oxygen and screw the window shut. Adjustments were made, too,
for venting the suit, so that perspiration and breath would not fog
the face glass of the helmet.

At the end of August 1934, Wiley Post and Russell Colley proceeded to Wright Field, in Dayton, Ohio, to test pressure suit number
three. Wiley was assisted into the suit and then seated in a pressure
chamber:

> 8/27/34: He 'Wiley Post' was placed in the chamber, sealed in,
> and they started the pumps to lower the pressure. At a pressure
> corresponding to 18,000 feet, Mr. Post screwed in the glass win-
> dow in the helmet and the suit took an inflated position (2 psi)
> in less than 30 seconds. At an altitude of 21,000 feet he indicated
> he wish (sic) he to descend. He was in the chamber 27 minutes.
> Tank temperature was 58° F. Failure of the oxygen generators
> to provide sufficient volume had caused him to half decompres-
> sion to a higher altitude.[4]

The next day, there was another test:

> 8/28/34: Another test was made in the altitude chamber to
> 23,000 feet. Mr. Post signaled to be brought down. The first test
> had shown the necessity of tying down the helmet. Mr. Post was
> in the chamber for 35 minutes and being completely satisfied that
> the suit was O.K. proceeded to Chicago that night.[5]

The "tying down" of the helmet noted in the report refers to an
earlier problem, which had now been eliminated. Previously, when
air and oxygen had been introduced into the pressure suit, the helmet, being the highest part, had had a tendency to rise slightly, and
pull the latex suit upward.

A few days after the last test at Wright Field, Wiley Post signed a
License Agreement with the B. F. Goodrich Company. With the pres-

---

[4]Wright Field Report I-54-458
[5]Ibid.

sure suit now a reality and the demand for such suits in the future a possibility, the two parties had to reach a clear understanding so as to avoid any later claims or amended history. The signatories to the contract were Wiley Post; for the B. F. Goodrich Company: its Vice-President, J. Connors; Witness: Russell S. Colley; Attest: Ass't. Secretary, W. D. Eakin. While the five-page agreement spells out the company's royalty commitment and legal limitations, the first few paragraphs clearly establish the spacesuit's parentage. The opening of the License Agreement reads:

> THIS AGREEMENT, made as of the 1st day of September, 1934, by and between WILEY POST, hereinafter called LICEN-SOR, and the B. F. GOODRICH COMPANY, a New York corporation, hereinafter called GOODRICH,
> WITNESSETH:
> WHEREAS LICENSOR hereby warrants and represents as a condition for the obligations of GOODRICH hereunder that he has originated and is about to file a United States patent application upon a flying suit adapted for maintaining adequate fluid pressure against the body of an airplane pilot at high altitudes and likewise warrants and represents that no license or right such as is to be in conflict with the provisions hereof has heretofore been granted or agree to be granted, and
> WHEREAS GOODRICH desires to obtain a license to make, to use, and to sell articles embodying and articles made in accordance with or by the use of the invention of the said patent application,
> NOW, THEREFORE, in consideration of the provisions hereof, the parties hereto AGREE AS FOLLOWS: (Capitalization as per original)

These opening paragraphs of the License Agreement clearly indicate that the B. F. Goodrich Company fully accepted Wiley Post as the rightful inventor of a pressure suit, enabling airplane pilots to survive and function in the hostile environment of the stratosphere. This acknowledgment on the part of Goodrich is important, for as events and bureaucracy took an unreliable course in the months ahead, the patent was never recorded.

On September 3, 1934, as part of the Chicago World's Fair, and advertised as being sponsored by the Pure Oil Company, Wiley Post made his first public test of his invention. Tom Bashaw, for the *Chicago Daily News*, filed a copyrighted article with Wiley Post's byline.

By Wiley Post
Copyrighted, 1934, by The North American Newspaper Alliance.

Chicago, Sep. 3—There is every reason for me to believe that the Lockheed Vega airplane, the *Winnie Mae*, in which I shall attempt, in a few hours to set a new plane altitude record, will fly 50,000 feet into the air, and safely. If it does that thing, it will break the present altitude record of 47,300 feet.

Although this altitude record subject is the spectacular part of such a flight from a public standpoint, my interest has much more to do with doubling the speed of the airplane, with the same horsepower. Of course, I hope to set a new altitude record for airplanes, but I shall not be disappointed at all, if I fail to do so, because I know I have increased the speed of the ship to 350 miles an hour, or more, at an altitude of 35,000 feet and could carry a load very efficiently at that altitude.

My plane was not originally developed to set a record, but to climb to the rarified air, decrease resistance and thus gain speed. Naturally, it has taken two or three times as long as I expected at first, to get the plane together . . .

It is my present intention to make the altitude flight Tuesday or Wednesday of this week. Weather requirements for such an endeavor are not similar to the requirements for a balloon flight into the higher altitudes. They are not nearly as strict in the case of my airplane, or of any other airplane, for that matter. However, I want to come back to earth at the same place where I make my start. If I were to sail through the clouds for an hour or two, in a high wind, I might not know where I was, and might not have sufficient gas to fly back to the exact point where I started.

Therefore I want a clear day for my flight, so I'll know where I am at all times. That's all I ask. On a day when there is a high barometer, and the weather is cold, I can probably fly the plane 2,000 or 3,000 feet higher than I could on a day when the weather is warm and there is a low barometer.

I shall take no food or drink with me. I expect to be up only two or three hours at the most. The especially built suit which I shall wear is lined with flexible rubber, with a reinforced canvas cover and a duraluminum helmet . . .

Inflation with compressed air will permit me to regulate the internal pressure after I have bolted the helmet onto the suit. I have made arrangements to heat the entire ship. I've been up in this plane where the temperature was 58 degrees below zero outside, up 38,000 feet in my "shirt sleeves"———street clothes throughout with no coat on.

On September 5, 1934, Wiley did take off and reached an altitude of 40,000 feet. The pressure suit worked well, but it did require some minor adjustments. Wiley wanted, for instance, a rubber strip attached to the top of the helmet as it hit the overhead top of the cockpit when the suit was inflated. Not that the hitting bothered Wiley so much, but the reverberation inside the metallic dome irritated his ears. Wiley had found, too, that the length of the plane's control stick needed to be extended, so that he could manipulate it more readily when the suit bulged with air and oxygen. Wiley also complained about the coldness of the oxygen on his face when it entered the helmet—a problem rectified by warming the oxygen. While such small complaints definitely needed attention, they in no way detracted from the fact that the world's first space suit worked.

In order to establish any aviation achievement officially, the attempt had to be supervised and/or timed by appointed representatives of the National Aeronautic Association of U.S.A., Inc., whose personnel comprised experienced aviators, with a thoroughgoing knowledge of their profession and its most up-to-date equipment. Since Wiley planned to set altitude records as part of his research into stratospheric aviation he asked the association for "sanctions," which included not only supervisory attendance at the time of the flight, but also employment of two sealed high-altitude barographs. Only if both these delicately calibrated instruments gave identical readings would the result be accepted as proof. Because the chance

always existed that an accident might destroy one or both instruments, the pilot had to pay a deposit. There were also charges for a
starter and a timer for pilots attempting to set a speed record.

On November 26, 1934, in Bartlesville, Oklahoma, the head office
of Phillips 66, Wiley Post was preparing for his next high-altitude
flight. As he had successfully tested his pressure suit, he saw no reason why he could not now reach fifty thousand feet, and thereby set
a new powered-flight altitude record. The distinction of "powered
flight" is important, since balloons had already reached even higher
altitudes, but had no controls by which to direct a flight pattern or
pre-select specific landing sites.

Up to this point, Frank Phillips had been most generous, and he
now wanted to make certain that he could use Wiley's success to
advertise Phillips 66 products, especially its aviation gasoline and
oils. He offered Wiley a contract, which was hardly generous, or even
fair.

I will attempt to break the World's altitude record from the Phillips Airport in Bartlesville, Oklahoma with the understanding
that should I officially break the record in flights from the Phillips Airport that the Phillips Petroleum Company will pay me
$1,000.00.

"If I break the record I will also fly my ship, the "*Winnie
Mae*", in a tour of the Phillips territory, weather conditions permitting to principal points that may select (sic) on a personal
tour not to exceed two weeks, provided the Phillips petroleum
Company will pay me $1,000.00 for this flight. It is understood
that Phillips Petroleum Company will pay my expenses and the
expenses of my mechanic during said tour.

"I will also allow Phillips Petroleum Company to use photographs of myself and ship in their advertising of Phillips "77"
gasoline and Phillips motor oil which I will use in the ship in my
flight.

(signed) Wiley Post

ACCEPTED BY PHILLIPS PETROLEUM COMPANY
(Signed) Billy Parker [Manager, Aviation Division]

For Wiley to accept a contract at such a low salary, it must be assumed that he felt obligated to Frank Phillips. Possibly, too, no other offer lay on the table, and one or two thousand was better than no money at all. If Wiley could get to fifty thousand feet, Frank Phillips would have himself a marvelous deal.

On December 7, 1934, Wiley took off from Phillips Airport. An official from the National Aeronautic Association of U.S.A., Inc. had carefully installed two sealed high-altitude barographs in the *Winnie Mae*. After two hours and twenty-six minutes of high-altitude flight, Wiley would report

> The thermometer outside registered 70° below zero, yet I was comfortable. The flying suit worked perfectly after I had fastened the face plate of my helmet and turned on the (external) supercharger at 20,000 feet—As a result of this flight I am convinced that airplanes can travel at terrific speeds above 30,000 feet by getting into the prevailing wind channel.

While one of the barographs clearly indicated that Wiley had reached his goal of fifty thousand feet, the second barograph, due to the extreme cold, had frozen solid at thirty-five thousand feet. As both barographs failed to confirm the altitude reached, The National Aeronautics Association could not certify a record height.

Wiley had never wanted simply to pursue some meaningless record for its own sake. What he really wanted was to learn as much as he could about this strange wind he had discovered in the stratosphere, and this he had done. Why spend time and money chasing records so temporary that they could easily be broken tomorrow? The time had come to put the acquired knowledge to worthwhile use.

Wiley's doubters and detractors considered his tale of "high winds" a misapprehension or even mere fancy—the result of sitting too long in one position that impeded the blood supply to his brain. All logic argued against the existence of such a gale-like force. After all, wouldn't anybody be able to detect it up there on a clear day? Nonsense! Sheer nonsense! Cried the doubters, who ranged from the high and learned, to many a man on the street. The only way to convince them, Wiley realized, was to perform a flight in a record time that defied any reasonable explanation.

So Wiley informed the National Aeronautic Association of U.S.A., Inc. (N.A.A.) that he was planning on a cross-country record setting flight, for which he would need two timers and observers—a starter and an observer in Burbank, California, to record his takeoff, and one each in New York City, to check his arrival. To cover the basic charges for their services, he placed a sufficiently large sum, approximately six-hundred dollars, on deposit with the Association's national headquarters in Washington, D.C. In the years that he had been dealing with the staff of N.A.A., timers and observers who had covered his round-the-world flights and the current high-altitude attempts, Wiley had issued many demands, criticized their service, and expressed considerable disdain, and in general had created an unfortunately stressful atmosphere. As N.A.A.'s conduct stood above censure, the staff's personal opinions of Post were hardly complimentary.

Excerpts from an exchange of letters between N.A.A.'s Washington, D.C. head office and its field office in California indicate the open dislike Wiley had elicited with his real, or perceived, swell-headedness: "I think by this time Wiley only needs a cane to scratch his ear,"[6] wrote the Dean of Timers in California.

Responding, the Secretary of the Contest Board of the N.A.A. in Washington stated his opinion of Wiley Post:

> Wiley, as you no doubt have found out, is, we might say, a rather peculiar fellow when he gets the wrong idea of something . . . In our experience we have found Wiley Post an almost impossible person to deal with. I mean by that he never answers correspondence, etc.[7]

Possibly the harshest outburst against Wiley came in the follow-up letter:

---

[6]June 18, 1935. Letter from the Dean of Timers, Southern California Chapter. National Aeronautics Association of U.S.A., Inc., to Wm. R. Enyart, National Aeronautics Association of U.S.A., Inc., Dupont Circle, Washington, D.C.
[7]July 29, 1935 Letter from Wm R. Enyart to Joseph Nicrent

Your opinion co-incides (sic) with mine as to his big headiness. The newspaper men (sic) out here have no use at all for him. This goes for the news cameramen as well. To show you what they think, one of them told Wiley that he wasent (sic) out there to get any pictures of the take-off. Instead of that he was there in hopes that you crack up so I can get a picture of you frying on both sides, and knowing the fellow that said it I know he wasent (sic) kidding.

Well I guess we wont be bothered with him for awhile (sic) as I understand he is going to Siberia for awhile (sic)[8]

The argument began in California, when Wiley, claiming that he had money on deposit at the Washington office, refused to pay the N.A.A. fee of fifteen dollars for the starter. No local office, however, would have had that information. Then, Wiley objected to a particular starter assigned to him—a matter over which he surely should have had no control. As was so often the case, Wiley proved to be his own worst enemy, by antagonizing the very personnel who could favorably shape his fate. For example, there is little doubt that a frozen N.A.A. barograph cost Wiley his entitlement to an altitude record. Yet, rather than admitting its culpability, the N.A.A. claimed that the "results were so poor I know he [Post] would like to have blamed it on the N.A.A. barographs."[9] This statement conveniently overlooked the fact that one of the N.A.A. barographs did register a world-record height. That the other one failed to function properly and froze surely cannot be construed as Wiley's fault.

With the high-altitude pressure suit now fully operational, Wiley set out to gather more information about the "high winds." If a high-altitude record also happened to be within striking distance, setting it would only further support his claims regarding the winds. But setting a record involved a lot of time—and money—neither of which Wiley had in abundance to invest, so he pursued his primary objective: to show the world that "high wind" could speed travel in the safer environment above the vagaries and dangers of inclement weather.

---

[8] August 3, 1935. Response to above
[9] July 29, 1935 Letter from Wm R. Enyart to Joseph Nicrent

Every pilot learns early that four distinct forces work on a plane—
two of them positive and two of them negative; two of them work
for the pilot, while two work against him. The positive Lift, which
is sustained by a stream of air over and under the wing, is opposed
by the negative pull of the Law of Gravity—the one tries to keep the
plane up, the other to pull it down. Likewise, the positive Thrust
opposes the negative Drag. The former propels the aircraft forward,
while the latter slows it down as the plane flies through the air's
density. Furthermore, as Post knew, any surface provided Drag an
opportunity to slow a plane down, and also the more weight a plane
carried, the greater was the pull of gravity. Wiley therefore decided
to eliminate the landing gear, which was used only when the plane
was taking off or landing, and thereby to eliminate both weight and
surface during hours of flight. He devised a system by which the
Winnie Mae's undercarriage could be released by wires controlled
from the cockpit, and simply dropped immediately after the plane's
wheels had lifted from the runway. The underside of the fuselage
was especially reinforced to allow the pilot to bring the plane down
in a glide "on its belly," when landing. Later-model airplanes than
Wiley's Vega, would have retractable wheels, which folded flush into
"cutouts" on the underside of the wing and thus reduced the Drag
when in flight.

To further pursue his research into high winds, Wiley came to an
understanding with a budding airline, Transcontinental and Western
Airlines (TWA). In return for its financial assistance to his stratospheric flight attempts, Post would carry specially marked airmail for
them, and would display the TWA trademark prominently on the
Winnie Mae's fuselage, with the word "experimental" superimposed.
To meet the government's stringent requirements for its airmail pilots, Wiley had to pass a twenty-hour training course that included
written tests in meteorology, instrument flying, and navigation, and
had to demonstrate his radio proficiency while flying only on instruments. Wiley's instructor was James E. Reed, an inspector for the
Department of Commerce. This same inspector Reed, who was permanently assigned to the Union Air Terminal at Burbank, California,
would enter Wiley's story again just a few months later.

Wiley passed his tests, and early in February 1935, TWA would announce that Wiley Post had taken the airmail pilots' oath in Kansas City.

The B. F. Goodrich Company, ever alert for a good advertising idea, had read about Wiley's plan to drop the landing gear on his next flights and tried to get in on the publicity. On January 10, 1935, James S. Pedler of the company's Aeronautical Sales Division wrote Wiley Post a letter. Not knowing exactly where to reach Wiley, he simply addressed the envelope "Wiley Post, Oklahoma City"; it reached the addressee. The letter proposed a stunt to advertise the durability of B. F. Goodrich tires. Several years earlier an airplane had carried a Goodrich automobile tire on a regular Ford wheel to an altitude of about one thousand five hundred feet and had dropped it "over the side of the ship," wrote Mr. Pedler. "Invariably, this tire would not blow out and it was exhibited around different dealer stores with a little story." Mr. Pedler suggested that the *Winnie Mae*'s detachable landing gear, be fitted with B. F. Goodrich tires so that the company could run a similar publicity campaign. No record indicates that Wiley Post, or his representative, ever replied to Mr. Pedler's letter, although it can be assumed that nothing came of his proposal, as Wiley planned to drop the wheels from a height of just a few dozen feet, immediately after liftoff—hardly an altitude to prove the quality of any product.

The film industry, too, banked on Wiley Post's publicity. Columbia, the motion-picture company, signed Wiley to a pivotal role in the film "Air Hawks," starring Ralph Bellamy, Tala Birrell, and Douglas Dumbrille. The plot was simple: Bellamy, the owner of a struggling airline, is threatened by an evil competitor. This ruthless entrepreneur has hired a mad scientist whose invention of a murderous ray able to penetrate clouds could empty the sky of rival pilots and planes. The survival of Bellamy's airline depends on his fulfilling an airmail contract on time. Enter: Wiley Post—though not in the *Winnie Mae*! In a Northrop Gamma, he races in a stratospheric flight nonstop from Los Angeles to New York, delivers the mail on time, and saves Bellamy's company from ruin. Movie patrons were even treated to a view of Wiley's pressure suit.

Still trying to obtain complete patents on the pressure suit, Robert M. Pierson, Wiley's lawyer, felt handicapped in his arguments with the Patent Office examiner. Complaining to Post, he wrote repeatedly that he needed Wiley's expert explanations to counter the government's contentions. First, though, he had to find Post, to whom he sent copies of his letters at four different addresses in the hope that one of them would reach the elusive pilot. The government, Pierson informed Post, was citing a British Patent, and it would take weeks to obtain a copy of it from England. Only on the patenting of three innovative devices of the almost two-dozen individual patents sought did the government pose no argument. The rest—so the examiner claimed—appeared to be too similar to patents already filed on diving suits here and abroad. Pierson's responses to the government had to be filed by November 1935. By August 15, 1935, Post had not been granted the patent and Robert M. Pierson's Power of Attorney to act on Wiley's behalf expired. The lawyer's suggestion that he be reappointed, and the case pursued, received no reply from Wiley's family.

Post's first attempt to set a transcontinental speed record came on February 22, 1935. It was a much-publicized event and a welcome one at a time when the papers had only more bad news about unemployment and the failing economy to report. Any news about Wiley Post certainly promised to provide such a change. Though it mattered little to the average American whether Wiley succeeded or failed, Post's exploits always made interesting reading—if you could afford the penny to buy a newspaper.

Will Rogers, America's number one aviation booster, was at the Burbank airport:

> Was out at daybreak to see Wiley Post take off. Was in the camera plane and we flew along with him for about thirty miles. We left him at 8000 feet right over the mountains. He soon after had to land. He brought her down on her stomach. That guy don't need wheels.[10]

In fact Will Rogers was one of the people who assisted Wiley into his cumbersome flying suit and then helped him into the cockpit. At 8:07 a.m. Wiley took off from the Los Angeles area and quickly climbed to an altitude of five miles. He soon left behind planes ac-

---

[10]Will Rogers's Daily Column, February 22, 1935.

companying him. Thirty-five minutes into the flight, Wiley saw his oil gauge indicate a sharp drop. It meant serious trouble. At a 24,500-foot altitude with almost full fuel tanks, he had to shut off the engine lest he burn out every bearing. Looking for a place to set the disabled plane down, he spotted Muroc Dry Lake and dead-stick landed on the fuselage's reinforced belly. Wiley and the plane were all right, although the propeller blades—extending below the height of the fuselage—were bent.

Until he inspected the oil-pressure loss, Wiley could only assume the oil line was leaking, but at that moment the cause was a secondary concern. First, in his heavy pressurized suit, he had to get out of the cockpit unaided, and secure help. While he finally did manage to get out of the plane without assistance, he could not unfasten the screw holding down the helmet at the back—and unless he could undo the helmet, he would not get out of the pressure suit. So, in suit and helmet, Wiley walked with measured, exaggerated steps to a nearby road. There, he spotted a disabled car, with its driver head-first under the hood trying to figure out the reason his car had stalled. To gain his attention, Wiley tapped him on the rump. The man turned. As Wiley described the encounter:

> The man's knees buckled and he almost fell over. He ran around to the back of his auto and peered at me. I had a time calming him down but I finally succeeded and he helped me out of my oxygen helmet "Gosh fellow," he exclaimed when he found his voice, "I was frightened stiff. I thought you had dropped out of the moon, or somewhere."[11]

Together the two men—the automobile driver's name was H. E. Mertz—walked until they found a telephone and could call for help. The *Winnie Mae* was returned to the Union Terminal where the search for the oil line break disclosed that it had not been a break at all. Over two pounds of metal shavings and emery dust had been poured into the engine's oil. Since the plane was carrying U. S. mail, the federal government became involved in the investigation of this

---

[11]Associated Press interview, February 22, 1935.

obvious sabotage. No culprit was ever found and the mystery of this attempt on Wiley's life or his plane was never solved.

In an interview some time later, Wiley Post said, that he was no longer interested in finding the guilty party so much as he was in learning the reason for the attack.

CHAPTER VIII

WILEY'S BASTARD

T HOUGH PRIMARILY INVOLVED with the arrangements for a flight attempt to set a new transcontinental speed record by taking advantage of high winds, Wiley was also thinking ahead. He realized that while he was still flying the *Winnie Mae*, her days as a high-speed, trend-setting plane were numbered. She had stood in the forefront of aviation when first built, but the rapid progress in technology and design had since surpassed her. It was time to move on. So on February 11, 1935, Wiley went to see Charles H. Babb.

Charley, as he was called, conducted business principally at his home base in the Grand Central Air Terminal in Glendale, California, but also at branches in New York, Newark, Washington, Honolulu, Mexico City, Montreal, St. Johns, Geneva, Switzerland, and Amsterdam, Netherlands. Charley was in a brand new business. As the world's foremost airplane broker, he was not only selling whole planes, but dealing in parts as well. He claimed to have sold more Lockheed planes than Lockheed ever manufactured. This, of course, was easily possible as he could—and would over time—sell the same planes several times. He sold them to airlines, air forces of small nations, dictators, executives, and private individuals. He supplied planes to the Spanish Civil War, and managed to locate and furnish five hundred planes on a single order to China—its entire air force at the time.

On that day in February, when he walked into Charley's office, Wiley had, as usual, very little money, but he definitely knew what he wanted. On the lot, he had immediately noticed a perfect low-wing Lockheed Orion, 9-E Special, U.S. License number 12283, with TWA markings. It had arrived only three days earlier, when TWA had sold it to Charley. There was nothing wrong with the plane; it had been in service until it came to him. The Orion, considered one of the best small passenger planes ever built, had become the victim of a directive and was made obsolete for airlines overnight. A new ruling by the Civil Aeronautics Authority (CAA) had decreed that any airline carrying passengers had to have both a pilot and a copilot on every flight—an understandable precaution but impossible to effect on an Orion. The plane simply could not be altered to accommodate a second position in the cockpit. Reluctantly, TWA—like other airlines—disposed of the Orions in its fleet.

During its TWA service, this particular Orion had been involved in two minor accidents. On June 10, 1933, damage in Amarillo was so slight that the plane required no major repair and was back in service in a couple of weeks. On February 5, 1934, TWA returned the plane to Lockheed for rear spar and wingtip repairs, damages so insignificant that the plane was back in service within days. The myth has persisted that the plane had also survived a crash serious enough to force TWA to sell the plane; and further, that the damage sustained in that crash subsequently led to the plane's untimely end. Neither tale is true, but myths are not easily slain by facts.

The sales contract for the plane contained the usual clauses regarding the "where is" and "as is." In plainer words, Wiley had to pick it up from where it stood, and Babb was making no claims for its airworthiness.

The Orion would have been an ideal plane for Wiley, or anyone else, if only left alone—but Wiley had other plans. In 1935 PAN-AM was concentrating on expanding its routes to the Orient and South America, while other carriers were competing for control of the European market. Whether flying to the East or the West, however, a wide ocean had to be crossed. Because the public considered flying far more hazardous than traveling by boat in either direction, airline companies had to overcome the fear of potential passengers that they faced two dangers at one time: being forced down, and being forced down in the middle of an ocean. If a plane had to set down for whatever reason while over terra firma, a passenger could at least feel safe once the aircraft had landed, but the thought of setting down on the Atlantic or the Pacific Ocean conjured up fears of helpless and hopeless abandonment to the sea.

As Charles and Anne Lindbergh were already exploring an alternate route to Japan via Alaska, Wiley began to lay out an alternate overland route to Europe by traveling via Alaska, and then across Siberia. Except for the short, fifty-mile hop across the Bering Strait, passengers could fly assured that most of the time firm land lay beneath them, even though Siberia would hardly epitomize any degree of contentment, should they be forced to set down there. If not an ideal solution, Wiley's route west at least provided an alternative.

When Wiley first conceived of flying to Europe by heading west, he broached the idea to Fay Gillis. She would be the ideal partner on such an exploratory trip. She had an excellent reputation as a pilot with the Soviet bureaucracy, she knew the right people in the USSR, and she spoke Russian. She had also suitably impressed Wiley with her efficiency when she had arranged the refueling stops on his solo flight around the world. After listening carefully and asking relevant questions, Fay agreed to come along. Fay was to

> obtain charts, visas and special permissions to over-fly Russian territory and make a number of stops. Wiley, foreseeing some snide remarks about the team of Post and Gillis, announced to the press that he would take his wife, Mae, along. In addition, since he wanted this exploratory trip to be secret, lest someone beat him to it, he invented a cover story of wanting to hunt tigers in Siberia. He even made a big show of exhibiting his rifles, which were of course for protection and obtaining a supply of meat, should the plane be forced down in the wastes of Russia.[1]

---

[1]Sterlings' interview with Mrs. Fay Gillis Wells, November 12, 1985.

Wiley and Fay tentatively projected their new joint venture for a takeoff in mid-June. It was now up to Wiley to raise the funds and furnish the transportation. He made an appointment with PAN-AM's Lyman Peck, the executive in charge of Alaskan development. Post pitched his idea of traveling to Europe by flying west, but PAN-AM, though at first receptive, balked at his price tag. For Wiley wanted more than funding; he wanted an assurance that after he had proven the feasibility of such a route, he would be given a permanent job as one of PAN-AM's full-time pilots.

The respective positions of Wiley and Peck are easily understandable. Wiley wanted a permanent job, which nobody had so far offered him, and he felt that his plan and its subsequent execution justified his demand. After all, he was not asking for charity, and he was certainly the most famous pilot in the country. Lyman Peck, on the other hand, had enough trouble attracting paying customers to air travel in an era when pilots were considered heroes and airline passengers were admired for their courage. That PAN-AM might place an already apprehensive flying public in the hands of a one-eyed pilot celebrated for his daring ran counter to the image PAN-AM wanted to create. The company went along with Wiley and encouraged his plan in the hope that he would drop his demand for a pilot's job. When Wiley insisted, PAN-AM's answer finally was a very polite, but firm, "No deal!"

Lyman Peck attempted to soften the blow by suggesting that Wiley approach Will Rogers to see if he might pay for at least part of the trip. After all, just a few days earlier, in his March 10 weekly article to be exact, Will Rogers had written:

> I never have been to that Alaska. I am crazy to go up there some time. They do a lot of flying up there. There is some crack aviators. Wiley Post went back up there this last summer to visit one of 'em that had helped him out, and they went hunting in a plane.[2]

---

[2] Reference to PAA's Joseph H. Crosson and his vital help on Post's two round-the-world flights.

PAN-AM's written records regarding their refusal of Wiley's offer are no longer available, but Will Rogers's wife, for instance, remembers:

> [Wiley's] plan was so far advanced that he had letters from the Soviet Ambassador, maps and credentials of all sorts, and permission from the Moscow Government to travel wherever he pleased in Russia. But now, at the last minute, the great airline decided that it did not want the survey.[3]

As for Peck steering Post to Rogers.

> As related to me by Lyman Peck, Lyman felt sorry for him [Post], off-handedly mentioned that Rogers had mentioned going to Alaska. Peck never forgave himself for that ill-considered remark. Peck would nearly cry when he later related his involvement. Lyman [Peck] said he made it to get Post out of his hair.[4]

Wiley had envisioned his research trip as part work and part vacation. Since he planned to fly by way of Alaska and Siberia, where winter ice turns into shallow summer lakes, a plane with pontoons could land in a million places, where wheels would be an absolute deterrent. Since Wiley hoped to do a little fishing and hunting at the same time, he wanted to be able to land in out-of-the-way places. Should he have a problem with the engine, pontoons would also serve him better than wheels. The Orion he intended to purchase had retractable wheels; to accommodate them, the underside of its wing had the appropriate "wells" and the mechanism for lowering and raising the wheels. So the wings allowed no space to attach a solid undercarriage. What Wiley needed was a solid wing on which to attach a solid undercarriage for wheels, which, when required, could easily be exchanged for pontoons, or—as the pilots call them—floats. Once he had flown over Siberia, he would have the wheels reinstalled.

---

[3]Will Rogers, His Wife's Story, p. 302, (©) 1941
[4]Sterlings' interview with Lyman Brewster, General Reindeer Superintendent, Department of the Interior (1932-1936) headquarters at Nome, Alaska.

Lockheed also manufactured a plane model called Sirius. Its low wing matched the Orion's exactly, except that the Sirius wing was solid and it did not have retractable wheels. It was precisely what Post needed. Unfortunately, Charley Babb had no Sirius wing available. He did, however, have a Lockheed Explorer wing that had been gathering dust in the four years since the rest of its plane had been destroyed in an accident in the Canal Zone. It had quite a story to tell.

The wing had come from the third plane in the very limited production series Explorer. Lockheed had designed the prototype for the famous polar explorer Sir George Hubert Wilkins, and named it in his honor. Wilkins, though, never took possession of the plane. Like many, he had run out of money during the great Depression. In April 1930, Colonel Arthur C. Goebel, a veteran pilot of transcontinental flights, had the third plane in the series built to order for a Paris-to-New York flight he was planning. When he tested the completed plane, which had been painted blue and yellow and named Yankee Doodle, the dissatisfied Goebel refused to take delivery.

Eventually the Pure Oil Company of Chicago purchased the plane for an advertising campaign. Repainted blue with white lettering, Yankee Doodle became the Blue Flash, and Roy W. Ammel became its pilot. Almost from the beginning ill fortune followed this plane. On its maiden flight from the Lockheed factory in Burbank, California, to New York, in the summer of 1930, engine trouble forced Ammel to land at Gila Bend, Arizona, where fire seriously damaged the Blue Flash. Lockheed sent a crew to Gila Bend to disassemble the plane and ship it back to Burbank. It was September 1930 before Ammel and the plane finally reached New York.

Restless after weeks of waiting for the Blue Flash, Ammel suggested a nonstop flight from New York to Panama, a first-time-ever air journey that would surely attract a lot of publicity. On November 9, Ammel took off from Floyd Bennett Field and headed south. He claimed that he had encountered such strong head winds along the way that he had had to fly an extra one thousand miles to get back on his course. After twenty-four hours and thirty-five minutes, an exhausted Ammel set the plane down on the runway at France Field in the Canal Zone.

For the return trip to New York via Chicago, Ammel had the plane transferred to the longer, though yet unfinished runway at An-con. With its fuel tanks filled to capacity, the Blue Flash gathered speed as it raced down the uneven runway. Then the plane skidded. It lifted its tail, dug its nose into the ground, and flipped over onto its back. Fearing that some hundreds of gallons of fuel could burst into flames if they spilled onto the hot engine, the field's rescue team quickly chopped open the upside-down plane and pulled out an unconscious Ammel. As it happened, the Blue Flash did not catch fire, but the rescuers had destroyed the entire plane, except for its solid wing, which was had found its way somehow to Charley Babb's warehouse.

There was nothing wrong with the Explorer wing. Nothing, except that it was the wrong wing for an Orion. Although the Explorer wing measured almost six feet longer than the wing designed for the Orion, and although its four fifty-six-gallon fuel tanks made it far heavier, Wiley wanted to marry the TWA Orion body to the Explorer wing. Lockheed refused to perform the ceremony. Pointing out to Wiley that he was trying to wed two entirely different engineering designs—a proposal as preposterous as it was unsound—Lockheed refused to be a party to this mismatch. Months later, Lockheed would issue a statement disassociating itself from the plane:

> Officials of the Lockheed plant at Burbank yesterday said that the craft had not borne the official factory stamp of approval since it was not a product of the concern. The ship, it was said, incorporated two entirely different engineering designs and was regarded therefore, more or less, as a freak.

Undaunted, Wiley Post shipped his Orion and the Explorer wing to Jack Waterhouse's hangar at Pacific Airmotive, Ltd. at Union Air Terminal, Burbank, California. By February 15, Pacific Airmotive had checked out the plane and sent to Wiley the following list of parts they would need to complete the work required, which they also itemized:

The following equipment will be needed as soon as possible:

Wasp motor	Bypass valve
Fuel pump	Vacuum pump
Battery	Vacuum pump regulator valve

Navigation lights
Pitot tube
Ignition switch
Instruments:
Oil pressure
Fuel pressure
Oil temperatures
Altimeter
Rate of climb
Clock
Manifold pressure gauge

Venturi tubes
Propellor (sic)

Compass
Turn and bank
Gyro
Artificial horizon
Thermocouple
Airspeed

Make all shipments to the attention of, or notify Otto Santoff,
331 N. Lima St., Burbank, California

The following work to be done on fuselage:

1. Remove linen and drive down all nails, recover fuselage and paint as per your specifications or best practice.
2. Remove paint in tail surfaces and repaint, install on ship.
3. Replace plywood on wing nose leading edge, install cabin floor in wing. Place all pulleys and necessary compression tubes from Orion wing to Sirius (sic) wing for adaption on Orion fuselage.
4. Install leading edge landing lights.
5. Make necessary landing gear changes for Orion fuselage hook-up.
6. Install wheels as per your instructions as to kind of wheels.
7. Fireshield to be adaptable to new series H Wasp engine.
8. New instrument board as per your instruments and layout.
9. New Aileron hook-up.
10. New cables wherever needed.
11. Cowling to be made as per latest engineering data furnished by J. Gerschler [assistant chief engineer at Lockheed]
12. Seats to be installed as per Orion set-up as formerly used.
13. Collector ring to be used as is unless changes are authorized by you.
14. Motor mounts and controls to be used as installed by Lockheed factory.
15. All plumbing, oil and gas lines to be of annealed (sic) copper tubing.

16. If new fittings for wing are necessary, to be designed by Lockheed Engineers and made by Lockheed, parts to be furnished by you.

17. All instruments, motor and accessories to be furnished by you as per separate list.

18. Cabin to be weather proofed as much as possible.

19. Cockpit to have heater as per your suggestion.

20. Ship to NR license and be licensed by Department of Commerce.

21. Ship to be painted as per your color scheme. [Wiley's instructions were to have the plane painted "Waco Red" with silver trim]

22. All parts and accessories to be rushed as fast as possible so as not to delay ship assembly.

23. All cockpit accessories for Orion landing gear to be removed and held until shipping orders received from you as to disposition of same.

24. Any and all changes to be in writting (sic) unless you personally are in hangar at time any changes are to be made.

The two lists are astonishing, both for what they contain, and for what they omit. Here is an inspection of a Lockheed Orion that a few days earlier had been in use as an operational passenger plane by TWA. Surely as a passenger plane, all those instruments, ranging from "oil pressure" to "altimeter" and "compass," must have been in working order. What about the fuel pump? Both the Orion and the Explorer were low-wing planes. That meant that the main fuel tanks were located in the wing lower than the engine and gasoline had to be pumped up to it. In those lists, Wiley is told that most of the Orion's instruments and some vital components need to be replaced. It is known that the newly installed Explorer wing had four large fuel tanks, yet there is not even a suggestion on either list to install corresponding fuel gauges. Wiley was obviously expected to remember day after day, which tanks were full, which were empty, which contained higher octane fuel for takeoffs, how much reserve there was, and in which tank.

Bob Ames, a fine PAA mechanic, thoroughly examined the engine of Wiley's reconstructed plane in Fairbanks some weeks later. He checked the battery, added oil, and filled the gas tanks. Everything seemed to be in perfect order. One discovery, however, surprised him. Although Wiley had six gas tanks, he had only a single fuel gauge. Ames recognized it. It had come from an old Ford automobile. Wiley had it installed above the instrument panel, right in front of his face; it provided a reading for the thirty-gallon tank that was stowed under the pilot's seat. Many small planes with a single tank had no fuel gauges, as pilots would know how long they could fly on a full tank, and how much fuel their plane would consume per hour. But it seemed strange to Bob Ames, that with so many tanks, Wiley would want to rely on his powers of recall to accurately calculate not only how much gas remained in any one of those tanks, but also which tanks were empty and which were full.[5]

Fuel gauges are strangely absent from Pacific Airmotive's parts list—a list that suggests either the condition of Wiley's plane belied its history with TWA or that Pacific Airmotive, Ltd was intent on installing new parts. If so many important controls needed in fact to be replaced, the maintenance of the plane must have been neglected for a long time. No record exists to indicate what Wiley did concerning the requested parts list. He may have ordered all parts to be replaced, or only some of them, or none. One thing is certain; he did not install five more fuel gauges.

While Pacific Airmotive was working on the Orion in Burbank, Wiley was preparing himself and the *Winnie Mae* for his second attempt at the transcontinental stratospheric flight, which he took on March 5, 1935. Arrangements had been made for radio stations along the flight path to broadcast weather reports every half-hour for Wiley. Everything went smoothly until he reached Ohio. About a hundred miles east of Cleveland, Wiley ran out of oxygen, without which he could not continue flying in the stratosphere. He turned around and landed at Cleveland. He had covered a distance of two thousand miles in seven hours and nineteen minutes, for an average ground speed of 279 miles per hour—at least a hundred miles faster than the same engine could have achieved at conventional altitudes.

---

[5]Sterlings' interview with Robert Ames, July 1986.

Newspapers reported that at times Wiley had reached a ground speed of 340 miles per hour.

On April 1, 1935, Fay Gillis, Wiley's fellow pilot in the proposed western trip to Europe, eloped with famous author, foreign correspondent, and aviator S. Linton Wells. This marriage, a purely private event that occurred half the world away from Wiley Post and that affected neither him nor Will Rogers at the time, would prove yet another tile in the mosaic of what was to follow.

Having secured the help of a competent pilot and partner in Fay Gillis had been a stroke of good fortune for Wiley. There was probably no more qualified a pair in aviation at that time to undertake the planned trip, as so much of it crossed the Soviet Union. But still, obstacles remained to be overcome—money, for one. The Great Depression had shrunk the possible resources available for funding. Wiley was trying to woo a number of well-heeled sycophants, when a major setback almost scuttled the project.

Fay Gillis—now Fay Gillis Wells—had reassured Wiley that her husband, Linton, insisted she keep her commitment to fly with him on the projected trip. That was before the *New York Herald Tribune* hired Linton Wells, one of the foremost correspondents of his day, to cover the Italian-Abyssinian war from the Abyssinian side. Linton had asked his bride to accompany him. Fay thought it over briefly and then decided: "Wiley could always find another partner, but I certainly did not want my new husband to find another partner."[6] When she telephoned Wiley with her decision, she also informed him that she had completed part of her assignment. The Soviets had promised that visas and maps could be picked up after the middle of June at the Consulate in San Francisco, and that clearances for over-flights and landings were being arranged.

Already disappointed by PAN-AM's rejection of his proposal and now greatly disturbed by the loss of his copilot and translator, on whom he had so heavily been counting, Wiley had little left. He had no sponsor to pick up the expenses, no income, and no flight partner. He had only the name Lyman Peck had suggested: Will Rogers.

Usually when the names of Will Rogers and Wiley Post appear

---

[6]Sterlings' interview with Fay Gillis Wells, 1985.

simultaneously in print or speech, reference to the "old" or "great" friendship between the two Oklahomans follows. This is pure fabrication. By 1935, the two men had met on just four or five public occasions—hardly a solid foundation for an old friendship. While Rogers admired Post's remarkable feats in the air, and in print had defended Wiley's foray into show business at Radio City Music Hall, the single personal contact between them had occurred in July 1931, when Post and Gatty visited the Rogers ranch with their wives. Even the understanding that the two men eventually reached regarding their trip to Alaska, seemed by far to be more a business arrangement than a personal adventure of "two old friends going on a vacation." Will, it was agreed, would pay all the bills, and in return Wiley would provide transportation to places that he himself would never have visited on his own. As Mae Post was quoted in one of her rare newspaper interviews: "Mr. Rogers paid the bills and he called the shots." Still, Wiley Post was the pilot and all final decisions affecting the capabilities of the plane and the possible consequences of its flights were his to make.

One bit of good news did come to Wiley in April 1935. A film company invited him to sign a contract to star in his own series of "not more than fifteen episodes." Already the hero to a generation of young males, Wiley would now be playing one in Saturday matinee films. The contract with Weiss Productions, Inc. cast him as a Department of Justice agent who enforces the law with the help of the *Winnie Mae*. A clause in the contract states that should the plane be sold to the Smithsonian Institution, a similar plane, painted the same colors and named *Winnie Mae* II, or *Winnie Mae*, Jr. is to be hired "at a cost of not more than five hundred dollars per week."[7] The contract also stipulates that the fifteen episodes be filmed in a period of no more than twenty-one "shooting days," and that Wiley be paid the (less than impressive) sum of five thousand dollars for all the work. Filming was to begin "no earlier than September 1st, 1935."

Wiley, meanwhile, that spring of 1935 continued with his preparations for the transcontinental flights. The new engine for the Orion/ Explorer—a 550-horsepower Wasp engine, Model S 3H1-G—

---

[7]All quotes here are from the original contract.

arrived at Pacific Airmotive, Ltd. at the Union Air Terminal, in Burbank. Pratt & Whitney was providing Wiley with the engine on "rental terms." In fact, Pratt & Whitney had never been in the rental business; nor was it now. In its arrangement with Wiley, the company never expected either to be paid any rental fee or to collect the actual value of $3,500. Wiley Post had given the company incalculable free publicity by using a Pratt & Whitney engine in his *Winnie Mae* on both his round-the-world trips, and the company was anticipating equally substantial benefits from this "rental."

The Wasp was a very powerful engine that could develop 600 horsepower for takeoff; but it used a correspondingly large amount of fuel. For the brief period at takeoff, for example, it would guzzle eighty-six-octane gasoline at the staggering rate of sixty-eight gallons per hour, while on climb it would consume forty-three gallons. Even at a sedate cruising speed, it would gulp down an excessive 32 gallons per hour. It was important, therefore, that the new plane's tanks hold enough gasoline to sustain flight for the long distances between refueling stations. The wing contained four tanks, each capable of holding fifty-six gallons, to which Wiley added, under the pilot's seat, a special tank holding thirty gallons, as well as a smaller tank behind the pilot's head that held sixteen gallons, for a grand total of two hundred and seventy gallons. With six tanks available, a prudent pilot would fill one tank with a higher-octane gasoline that he would use exclusively for takeoffs, when full power was essential. Not until all the other tanks had been emptied would he tap the thirty-gallon one under the pilot's seat with the second-hand Ford-car fuel gauge. At this point the pilot flew warned that he had less than one hour to find an emergency landing spot.

As an American gallon of gasoline weighs 6 pounds, when fully laden the Orion/Explorer's fuel added to the plane 1,620 pounds in weight, forward of the center of gravity. Naturally, as the flight progressed and fuel was consumed, the center of gravity would shift aft. However, that was not all the additional weight the *Winnie Mae* carried. The heavier Pratt & Whitney engine added 145 pounds; the now three-bladed-propeller added 50 pounds; a deicer, 45 pounds; engine cowl, 50 pounds; battery, 65 pounds; electric starter, 35 pounds; flares and holder, 50 pounds; radio, 135 pounds; heater, 22 pounds; landing lights, 15 pounds; fire extinguisher, 8 pounds. Furthermore, the new, non-retractable landing gear that hung below the fuselage moved the center of gravity forward, thus making the plane nose-heavy.[8]

The perhaps-questionable change from a two-bladed propeller to a three-bladed one was dictated by the envisioned change from wheels to floats. On wheels, the plane's nose stood higher off the ground than it did off the water when the floats had been installed. Shorter blades therefore had to be used, and thus the change to the three-bladed propeller.

In April, Wiley attempted the first of two more transcontinental stratospheric flights in the *Winnie Mae*. On April 14, a broken supercharger forced him to land at Lafayette, Indiana. Another version of the tale behind that forced landing claims that excessive moisture inside Wiley's helmet caused its small window to keep fogging up. Unable to reach inside the helmet to wipe away the condensation, Wiley could clear it only by using the tip of his nose, which eventually he rubbed so raw that it was bleeding freely and obstructing his vision. When he no longer could read the instruments on his control panel, he was forced to land.

Wiley's mind harbored no doubts as to the fact of a "high wind." He had ridden it and it had borne the *Winnie Mae* at greatly increased speeds. Fellow believers, among them editorial writers, deemed the speeds attained in his aborted flights proof enough of their existence. But Wiley wanted the whole world to acknowledge that there was this super force. So far, his trusted, old *Winnie Mae* had done her best, and so had his brainchild, the world's first space suit. It was never the planning, never the concept, never the innovations, but rather small mechanical failures or human error that frustrated success. Wiley would make still one more try to prove to even the last cynic that the future of aviation lay above thirty-five thousand feet and that Wiley Post had pointed the way.

On June 15, 1935, Wiley left Burbank again to attempt a stratospheric transcontinental flight. Again, a mechanical failure frustrated his intent. This time a broken piston forced him to land at Wichita, Kansas, 1188 miles into the flight.

Wiley sent the *Winnie Mae* to the Braniff Airways hangars in Bar-

---

[8]Inspection certificate.

tlesville, Oklahoma, then proceeded to Burbank to oversee the work
on his new plane. Every hour possible he spent at Pacific Airmotive,
Ltd., where he began meeting Inspector James E. Reed of the Department of Commerce. Reed, who was inspecting the work in progress, and Wiley, who was directing it, shared a common passionate
interest in airplanes and flying, and over the weeks their professional
relationship assumed a more social character. Whether intentionally,
or accidentally, this familiarity bred laxity.

Wiley Post's much-publicized flights had made him the reigning
aviation hero, and he continued to be good copy for newsmen. Readers craved more information about the little, one-eyed man who
could perform almost superhuman feats. But Wiley was not a talkative man and getting him to reveal details about himself was almost
impossible. Reporters tried to get Mae Post to speak about her husband:

> "If he ever forsakes aviation," says his wife, "he's likely to turn
> to some other work out in the open—perhaps mining in Alaska.
>
> "Maybe his next aerial exploit, a reported flight from Alaska
> to Moscow, will be primarily for survey work, but almost cer-
> tainly he'll carry along one of his proudest possessions, a double-
> barreled shotgun. For his favorite recreation is hunting . . ."
>
> "Next to hunting," she says, "I think Wiley likes fishing best,
> but he's awfully proud of his guns."
>
> "Right now he is crazy about Alaska," says his wife. "He
> believes money can be made there in mining, and he might try
> it some time."
>
> "Wiley seems quite interested in Russia, although he didn't
> get to see much of it at the time." She says, "and I think he'd
> like to spend more time in some of the other countries, too."
>
> But she does find him an easy man to cook for. "He isn't a
> bit hard to please," she says. "I'm not much of a cook, but I can
> cook what Wiley likes." What does he like? "Everything."
>
> It's almost impossible to get a picture of Wiley Post, the hus-
> band. "I mainly let Wiley do the talking," says his wife—and
> Wiley talks scarcely at all."[9]

---

[9]Syndicated Associated Press column, Ponca City, July 12, 1935.

The work on Wiley's customized plane fell off schedule at Pacific Airmotive Corporation, [10] it seems. Wiley and Mae had planned to leave the Los Angeles area for Seattle on July 22, but their departure had to be delayed. The plane, so the company announced, was "not quite ready" for a long flight, and the Posts were meanwhile "in seclusion."[11]

When Pacific Airmotive, Ltd. finally had completed the union of the Explorer wing and the Orion fuselage, and made all the other changes, additions, and repairs, Wiley took the plane up for a test flight. He could not have missed the obvious nose-heaviness, yet, when Inspector Reed came around to inspect and test the plane before issuance of an airworthiness certificate, Wiley raved about the smoothness and ease of handling the hybrid plane. Wiley evidently found the lie necessary, for the truth no doubt would not have obtained the official clearance for the plane. It was solely on the strength of Wiley's glowing statements that Reed issued the certificate. Without either flying in the plane or piloting it, he declared the plane airworthy. If America's foremost aviator avowed that the plane was great and easy to handle, who was he, Inspector Reed, to contradict him? At least, that is what Reed would later say, when questioned in an inquiry.

According to General James Doolittle, any deviation from the norm in a plane's balance is of importance:

> There are forgiving airplanes, and there are unforgiving airplanes. An airplane—which, if you make a mistake—corrects that mistake, is a forgiving airplane; an airplane which amplifies a mistake, is an unforgiving airplane. Some airplanes, if you take your hands off the stick, will fly along by themselves; some have to be controlled at all times.[12]

Wiley could have had no doubt that the plane's weight distribution was wrong. With too much weight forward of the center of gravity, the plane's nose-heaviness would cause it to assume a diving attitude in flight. Still, the seasoned pilot Wiley believed that he could none

---

[10]Associated Press Dispatch, July 22, 1935.
[11]Ibid.
[12]Sterlings' interview with General 'Jimmy' Doolittle, June 22, 1977

the less fly the plane. He would just have to be exceedingly alert. A pilot can counteract the nose-heaviness of an airplane, or indeed any temporary imbalance, to a point; he simply has to compensate for the plane's inclination to deviate from the norm. Such counteraction by the pilot does, however, limit the plane's remaining maneuverability, for with the concentration of control in these circumstances comes the relinquishment of control in others. In the case of Wiley's new plane, because of its nose-heaviness, it would constantly tend to dive, and Wiley would have to put the aircraft into a climb attitude in order to compensate for that downward drive and simply to stay level. The constant employment of a portion of the plane's ability to climb just to keep the aircraft level would thus allow it less capability to climb in an emergency.

Wiley would have known, too, that should he ever lose engine power to provide an essential lift, the plane's built-in inclination to dive would be compounded by the earth's gravitational pull. Should such loss of power occur at a higher altitude, the plane would at first dive earthward, but could—after a substantial drop—be pulled out into a glide. Then a dead-stick landing might be possible. However, should power be lost at low altitude, the pilot would not have a sufficient margin in which to regain control of the diving aircraft.

Interviews and newly discovered records establish without doubt that the plane was already nose-heavy before floats were attached. Lockheed had correctly predicted adverse results: "You'll be in trouble if there's just a slight power loss on takeoff."[13] But the warning had gone unheeded. The conversion capability of Wiley's hybrid craft from airplane to seaplane only added to the problem. Post could have counterbalanced the nose-heavy plane's further lack of stability, however, had he only taken the time, money, and trouble. Instead, he intentionally kept the plane's imbalance a secret. When he applied for an aircraft license on July 23, 1935, for instance, he made several blatant misstatements of fact, placing the fuel capacity at 260 gallons, rather than the correct 270; and declaring that the Orion wing had been replaced with a Sirius wing rather than the actual much larger and heavier wing from an Explorer.

---

[13]*The Challenging Skies*, an aviation history by C. R. Roseberry; statement made by Jimmy Gerschler, then assistant chief engineer, Lockheed Aircraft Corp.

Moreover, under Point # 9 of the same application, Wiley indicates he is seeking a "Restricted" license, and states as the purpose of the aircraft: "Long Cross Country Flights and special Test Work." The "Restricted" license, as Wiley should have recalled—even though he had repeatedly violated its restrictions with the *Winnie Mae*—allowed aboard a flight only personnel who were directly involved and needed in the performance of the purpose for which the craft was licensed. In simpler words: "no passengers!" The fact that Will Rogers would later joke in print that he had been designated the man to tie up the plane at dockside on landing, would appear to indicate that he too knew he was not supposed to be aboard unless he had a job requiring his presence.

In July of 1935, Wiley and Mae Post visited with Will and Betty at the Rogers ranch in Pacific Palisades. Whether the Posts came by social invitation or by business appointment is not clear, but events would prove that Wiley and Will certainly discussed business at that meeting and arrived at some preliminary decisions.

It was summertime and the Rogers family had made its plans. Daughter Mary, under the watchful eye of her Aunt Dick, was furthering her dramatic career by playing in summer stock in Skowhegan, Maine. Betty planned to join them shortly. Will, Jr., had hired on as a stoker's assistant on a freighter bound for the Philippines, while Jimmy, the youngest, was going to drive across the United States with his cousin Jim Blake and eventually catch up with the family in Maine. Will had talked about flying to Rio de Janeiro and from there taking one of the regularly scheduled flights on the German Zeppelin to the west coast of Africa, but he had never made his reservation.

Several days after the Posts' visit to the Rogers ranch, Wiley and Mae were trying to embark their plane at the Burbank airport, but Wiley as usual was surrounded by reporters. At that point Will Rogers arrived. He purchased a magazine and a pack of chewing gum. Then, to the reporters' surprise, he climbed aboard the Posts' plane.

The trio flew to New Mexico, then Arizona and Utah, where they marveled at Zion National Park and Bryce Canyon, before stopping at Waite Phillips's ranch to visit with the co-founder of Phillips Petroleum. Whenever Wiley saw a promising stream with a meadow nearby, he would set the plane down and give the local fish a chance to bite. Rogers, who did not fish, claimed to have looked at cattle. They returned to Los Angeles via the Grand Canyon and the then new Hoover Dam.

While the Posts and Rogers certainly had chosen a most picturesque itinerary, only one reason logically explains that trip. In naval parlance, it would have been a "shake-down cruise," its purpose foremost to determine how the plane would perform; and also to see how comfortable the three people involved found the plane's interior accommodations—and each other—on a lengthy trip in confined quarters.

Why Wiley would make this test flight, and possibly endanger the lives of his wife and potential supporter, is open to conjecture. It may indeed have been a sales pitch, calculated to demonstrate to Rogers the advantages of travel in a private plane. While the limited space might have proved to be adequate for the diminutive Mae, it could only have confined Rogers. By nature a reserved person, he would have surely not viewed the prospect of sitting for many hours cramped into a small space with a strange woman as his idea of a pleasure trip. With Mae aboard, he would find it impossible to stretch out, type his column, read his newspapers, or take a little nap. The lack of privacy, his innate modesty, and the limited space together convinced Rogers that should he agree to accompany Post to Alaska, Mae would not be coming along.

After the weekend trip into the picturesque Southwest, Post and Rogers parted without firm promises. Will had never liked long-range commitments; he preferred to act on impulse. Wiley had mentioned that on the trip to Alaska he would have to stop off at Seattle in order to have the wheels replaced by pontoons in nearby Renton, Washington. Will suggested that Post call him then, from Seattle, for his decision. Will had initially expressed interest only in the Alaskan leg of the trip, although he had also been willing to consider, in light of the weekend test trip, the possibility of going with Post all the way across Siberia to Europe. In either case, Will's stipulation that only Wiley and he would be aboard that plane, was understood, but Mae did not know it yet. It would be up to Wiley to break the news to her eventually. Just as it would be up to Will to inform his wife, Betty, that he might be going to Alaska and possibly as far as the Soviet Union. He would even suggest meeting her in Europe after that. Wiley and Mae Post still needed passports. The Russians were insistent. Wiley had only an expired and cancelled passport. In his haste, he had apparently picked up the outdated passport, leaving a new one in Oklahoma City. Mae had never needed a passport before and did not own one.

On Monday, July 29, 1935, Wiley appeared before Robert Zimmerman, chief clerk of the United States District Court in Los Angeles. He was seeking renewal of his canceled passport.

"When do you want it?" Zimmerman asked.

"I'd like it right away," Post answered. "I've planned to take off tomorrow at noon on a flight to Siberia."

But the chief clerk in Los Angeles could not issue a renewal on a canceled passport. Wiley mentioned that he had another passport of later date, but that it was in a safety deposit box in Oklahoma City.

"Why don't you fly there and get it?" Zimmerman suggested.

Post vetoed the idea, impatient to be on his way. Zimmerman then wired the main passport office in San Francisco, requesting to be notified by telegram whether the Posts could pick up new passports there with a minimum of delay.[14]

Wiley and Mae obtained their passports in San Francisco. Fame had its advantage. Having been informed that Wiley Post would call, passport agent S. A. Owen kept his office open for twenty minutes after regular closing time. The case was quickly resolved.[15]

Nor did bureaucracy complicate the matter of Russian visas. Fortunately, Alexander Troyanovsky, the Soviet Union's ambassador to the United States in Washington, D.C., happened to be in San Francisco, where he was hoping to welcome three Soviet fliers en route to the United States from Moscow, nonstop via the North Pole.[16] Already quite familiar with Wiley's plans through Fay Gillis Wells's correspondence with the Soviet embassy, Ambassador Troyanovsky granted the visas immediately. He also extended his warmest wishes for a successful flight.

---

[14]*Los Angeles Times*, July 30, 1935.

[15]*Seattle Post-Intelligencer*, July 31, 1935

[16]Pilot Sigismund Levanevsky, copilot Boris Maidukoff, and navigator Victor Levchenko left Sholkovsky airport in Moscow on August 3. It was announced a few days later that a damaged oil feed line had forced the plane to turn back and land in Leningrad.

At 6:30 p.m. on August 1, 1935, Wiley and Mae Post reached Bryn Mawr field at Renton, Washington, at 6:30 p.m. The flight from San Francisco had taken five and a half hours. "A dog, a small boy, and a woman wiping her hands on her kitchen apron. That was the entire 'crowd' and reception committee,"[17] reported the Seattle newspaper, for when the plane set down on the suburban airstrip, twelve miles south of Seattle, only Marian, wife of Field Manager Ashley Bridgham, their son Jimmy and the family dog, were on hand. It was young Jimmy who first realized that Wiley Post had landed at their front door. Mrs. Bridgham would not believe him. "No," she said, "the plane's too little, Jimmy." But seconds later she had to agree. "When they got out of the plane, I invited Mrs. Post into the house. She said she was certainly thrilled about making the trip with her husband. William Lindsley and Jack Waley, attendants at the field, took charge of the plane."[18]

Seattle, however, had been expecting the Posts, but its eager crowd had gathered at Boeing Field, a dozen miles away. Wiley, though, had flown to the smaller airport so that Renton's Northwest Air Service could exchange the wheels for floats and thus complete the assault on the plane's already radically impaired balance. Once the floats had been added, the plane at last matched exactly Wiley's vision of it. But it was a grotesque hybrid, conceived in ignorance and born out of unwarranted self-confidence. All along its path, it prompted onlookers to shake their heads and click their tongues. People in polite society—alluding to these reused parts and hand-me-downs—called it "Wiley's Orphan." Far less inhibited in their use of proper English, pilots and mechanics in the airline industry scoffed at its illegitimate parentage and dubbed it with a name that stuck: "Wiley's Bastard."

Nobody seemed to like the appearance of Wiley's low-wing float-plane, yet nobody suggested to Wiley that he should not fly it—that is, nobody until Joe Crosson told him not to, in Fairbanks. However, Wiley flew it anyway, because by that time he had convinced himself that he had mastered his "Bastard."

---

[17]*Seattle Post-Intelligencer*, August 2, 1935
[18]ibid.

CHAPTER IX

ALASKA AT LAST

ONCE WILEY HAD checked into Seattle's Olympic Hotel,[1] in the late afternoon of August 1, 1935, he telephoned Will Rogers at his Pacific Palisades ranch. Not until Rogers received that call, did he definitely decide to join Wiley in Seattle when the plane was ready for takeoff, although in his heart, Will Rogers had wanted to go to Alaska all along.

Of course, Will had discussed the prospective trip to Alaska and across Siberia with his wife, Betty. She had also been present when Wiley and Mae Post had first approached Will about the project—and had been immediately troubled by the thought of her husband's flying into vast, inhospitable Siberia. The Alaskan adventure, though, she viewed with less apprehension.

Betty Rogers protected her privacy. The public knew little about her, and she willingly allowed her husband's celebrity to overshadow her and the children. She also anchored the family, so that Will could be free to be Will Rogers; so that when he decided on an impulse to

---

[1] Later, the Four Seasons Olympic Hotel.

181

fly to New York, or Washington, or to one of the world's trouble
spots, everyday life at the ranch continued smoothly. The three surviving children, Will, Jr., Mary, and Jim—Freddie had died during
the diphtheria epidemic of 1920 before he reached his second birthday—found in Will a most loving parent, but it was Betty who was
always there for them. Mary once complained that she and her brothers had to share their father with America. So it was that Betty became what Will called their balance wheel.[2] No less truth lay in Will's
description of Betty's most difficult task as: "trying to raise to maturity four children—three by birth and one by marriage."[3] She
proved to be for Will the ideal wife, not to mention a perfect hostess,
secretary, advisor, critic, friend, and lover. It was a good marriage,
a loving partnership, and Will fully meant it when—as a headline
lariat artist—he proclaimed that "the day I caught Betty, I did the
star performance of my life."

Will wanted Betty to approve his decision to fly to Alaska, even
though he knew beforehand that she had reservations. After almost
twenty-seven years of marriage, Betty could read her husband's mind
as well as he could himself, so she had intuited his decision before
he had ever voiced it. Her concern arose not so much out of pre-
monitions as from the not unreasonable fear that the plane might be
forced to set down somewhere in the wilds of Alaska or Siberia, and
be lost to searchers. Will tried to calm her. He assured her that he
had not yet decided to fly with Wiley all the way across Siberia and
would probably return home from Alaska. Then, Will came up with
a tempting new suggestion.

Should he—mind you, should he—decide to accompany Wiley
across Siberia to Europe, Will postulated, would Betty join him in
Europe where the two of them could enjoy the sights before returning
home together? Betty agreed, though she was not eager to travel
alone to Europe and she would have much preferred that Will come
back to Pacific Palisades directly from Alaska. She remembered how
just the year before, in 1934, when Will, she, and the boys crossed
Siberia by train, Will had restlessly endured the monotonous journey;

---

[2]*Daily Telegram*, November 6, 1927, Weekly Articles # 257, #265, # 268, 1928;
[3]Radio Broadcast, May 11, 1930.

how he had wanted to be up in the air, so he could survey the landscape from a plane. Wiley's Siberian escapade would give Will that opportunity, she knew, and she could only wish that the Russians had kept their word last year, and provided the plane at Novosibirsk, as they had promised.

So while Betty worried, she could not but acknowledge the joy on Will's face when he talked to her about his trip to Alaska, and maybe Siberia. He looked tired, she noticed; for the first time in his life his heavy schedule seemed to have begun to wear him down. He was looking forward to a vacation,[4] and a leisurely trip, she reasoned, in the face of her anxiety, might do him a lot of good.

Northwest Air Service, located in Renton, Washington, at the southern end of Lake Washington, was the region's only government-approved shop that specialized in airplane conversion work. Probably every plane equipped with pontoons or skis that had been flown between Seattle, Pt. Barrow, Alaska, and northwestern Canada, at some time had had work done by this company. Because Alan Blum, the major stockholder, zealously guarded the excellent reputation his company had earned at Northwest Air Service, excellent veteran mechanics worked on Wiley's plane. They replaced the wheels with used EDO J-5300 floats and rudders.[5] They also installed an overhauled generator and a new electric starter, as Wiley had reported problems with the electrical system. It was routine work for the experienced crew,[6] and Wiley was properly billed for the items as follows:

1 - M2101 Solenoid switch	$13.50
1 - Rebuild Armature	$15.00
Overhaul Generator	$26.00

Over the years more myths have developed around the floats than about any other part of Wiley's plane. The most popular story claims that the floats originally had belonged on a Fokker Trimoter and were therefore entirely unsuitable for an Orion/Explorer. Official rec-

---

[4]Ex: *Will Rogers* by Betty Rogers, p. 301; @ 1941,
[5]Sterlings' interview with Alan Blum, August 18, 1986.
[6]Sterlings' interview with Ash(ley) Bridgham, field manager at Bryn Mawr airport, employee of Northwest Air Service, July 14, 1986.

ords easily disprove this tale, however, for they show that of all Fokker airplanes built in America by that time, not a single one had been on floats.

Another legend holds that the floats were too large and thus caused the crash; but, as Alan Blum took care to explain, the EDO factory's charts prescribed the correct size and displacement of floats for specific weights, and the EDO J-5300, on Post's plane, met those requirements.

Lloyd Jarman, veteran Alaskan mechanic and airplane authority, tells an interesting tale.[7] He and bush-pilot Alex Holden were flying a Pacific Alaska Airways (PAA) Fairchild 71 from Juneau to Funter Bay, on Admiralty Island. After setting down, they were coasting the bay when the plane struck a submerged log that severely damaged the plane's left float. Both floats were shipped back to EDO Corporation, at College Point, Queens, N.Y. for repairs, and as Jarman recalls it, those same floats—now repaired—were on hand when Post brought his plane in for conversion. Joe Crosson, Wiley's friend and guardian angel, speaking for PAA, then arranged to have the floats lent to his friend Wiley. Jarman's tale receives corroboration from a story filed by a Seattle reporter who observed that "a four-inch riveted aluminum square covered a tell-tale patch on one pontoon."[8] Numerous photographs in various archives and collections also show clearly that the left float on Wiley's plane had been repaired. Still, that repair would have had no effect on the pontoons' performance.

Two other pieces of evidence further establish the veracity of Jarman's story:

1) EDO' Aircraft Corporation's Acknowledgment of Order No. 1772, dated June 26, 1935, states: "Verbal Order: "STRUTS. One complete set of struts and attaching fittings for the purpose of installing J-5300 floats on a standard Lockheed Sirius. These parts are to include revised deck plates and any other parts nec-

---

[7]*Pilot in the Float Country* by Archie Satterfield, photos by Lloyd Jarman; published by Superior Publishing, Seattle, @ 1969.
[8]Unidentified Seattle newspaper, dated August 2, 1935, on file at Museum of Flight, Seattle, WA

essary to alter floats formerly on a Fairchild 71 for use on the
Lockheed. Struts, spreader tubes, etc., are to be cadmium plated
but not otherwise finished.

REMARKS: Ship spreaders by express collect marked "Wiley
Post c/o PACIFIC ALASKA AIRWAYS, ALASKA STEAMSHIP
CO. SEATTLE, WASH. (hold for Mr. Post)" Deliver other parts
to T.W.A. (Pat Gallop at Newark Airport) marked "WILEY
POST, LOS ANGELES, CALIFORNIA." Spreaders are to be
boxed. Other parts are to be packed in paper to keep down
shipping weight.

DELIVERY QUOTED RUSH—3—4 days on spreader
tubes, 2 to 3 weeks on balance
(NET PRICE $450.00 PAID IN FULL)
2) Northwest Air Service Original Work Order #1006—dated
August 6, 1935—shows as its first item: "PICK UP FLOATS AT
ALASKA STEAMSHIP COMPANY," and as its second item:
"PICK UP ACCESSORIES FROM PACIFIC ALASKA AIR-
WAYS."

Examination of those two documents verifies that the floats on
Post's Orion/Explorer, identified here as a Lockheed Sirius, indeed
came from a PAA Fairchild 71. (The main difference between the
two Lockheed models, Orion and Sirius, was that the Orion carried the heavier weight of motor and retractable wheels, while the
Sirius bore the lesser weight of a non-retractable undercarriage,
but added drag.) The Fairchild 71 floats cannot by almost any
possibility have been too large. Should the size of floats be larger
than "recommended," the plane will simply sit higher out of the
water and encounter more drag and nose-heaviness. Should the
floats be too small, the plane will either sit too deep in the water
or sink.

The documents also clearly indicate that the two shipments picked
up by Northwest Air Service were destined for Wiley's plane. That
EDO's order unmistakably states that floats from a Fairchild 71
would fulfill Wiley Post's order belies the myth that some kind of
last-minute "emergency substitution" of unsuitable floats was made.
Instead, the arrangement regarding the floats had been completed

weeks earlier. The fact that Pacific Alaska Air received some of the tubing is explained simply by Wiley's instructions that EDO ship to PAA's address. No mystery or myth shrouds the origin or the appropriateness of the floats.

Cornered by reporters from the *Seattle Post-Intelligencer* two weeks before the flight, Wiley announced that Fay Gillis Wells, the aviatrix, would not accompany him and his wife as originally planned, but that he "may pick up" another passenger at Seattle. "I expect to hunt a little and fish a little—and look around a little, too. I hope to get a chance at a Siberian tiger." Wiley otherwise snarled at the reporters. What had upset him earlier that morning of August 2, before he had arrived at Northwest Air Service, has not been documented; his foul mood, however, has: he shouted at workmen, "switched on no-sunshine charm for the curious youngsters, airport mechanics and interviewers who saw him,"[9] reported the *Post-Intelligencer*. Wiley had always had his problems with people, and Seattle was proving to be no exception. Generally, though, the press had portrayed him as a shy, unassuming man, yet when a local newspaperman asked him when he and Mrs. Post planned to leave Seattle, Wiley turned abruptly and thundered: "I don't even know if Mrs. Post will go all the way with me. Why don't you ask her."[10]

It was surely this remark that started the rumors that would eventually find their way into the national press. The *Seattle Post-Intelligencer* headlined its story "WILEY POST, IT SEEMS, WAS JUST A LITTLE ANNOYED!" and described Wiley as "sour and glum." Wiley "gave a first-rate demonstration of annoyance this forenoon," wrote the reporter.

> "Who's in charge around here?" Post wanted to know when he learned the deck plates were set a fraction of an inch to one side of where they should have been set. Bustling mechanics gulped.
>
> "Let's get some action." Post demanded. The mechanics hurried to get some action. Angrily he strode about the hangar where the crimson mono-plane lay, picking up parts and tossing them down.

---

[9]*Seattle Post-Intelligencer*, August 2, 1935.
[10]Ibid.

Flying, not glad-handing, is Wiley Post's business, he figures. That was why he stood with hands thrust in the pockets of his unpressed suit, wisps of blond hair blowing down over his forehead, a squint in his uncovered right eye, and gave his splendid performance as a celebrity "with a mad on."[11]

When questioned about Post's display of annoyance, Alan Blum, the owner of Northwest Air Service, recalled:

I honestly believe the reporter who wrote that piece was either dreaming or was at the Renton Airport (Bryn Mawr) on an off day (either for him or for Wiley), we all have them, of course. I can't believe the reporter's statement that deck plates were off center. If they were off center they were made that way on purpose by the factory . . . And further, this was Post's first experience with floats and I doubt he would have known if such plates should or should not be centered. I discount entirely the quote "Who's in charge around here" etc., as he knew full well who was when he made the request for us to do the work and certainly none of my men would "gulp". We had a justifiable reputation of years of excellence and I don't believe anyone ever questioned our competence . . ."[12]

Meanwhile, in Pacific Palisades, California, at the Rogers ranch, Will had begun making arrangements for the trip, now that he had finally made his decision to fly with Wiley. Until almost the very last moment, finishing touches on his latest film, *Steamboat Round the Bend,* kept him too busy to deal with getting his passport validated and obtaining a Russian visa. He decided to take care of both these chores in San Francisco on Monday morning, on his way to Seattle. On Saturday morning, August 3, Will went to the Bank of America, wrote out a check on his account for $7,540 to cover a $5,000 letter of credit, $2,000 in traveler's checks, $500 in cash, and $40 for the bank charges.

That Saturday afternoon, he asked Ewing Halsell and Ed Vail, two

---

[11]Ex: *Seattle Post-Intelligencer,* August 14, 1935.
[12]Letter from Alan Blum to the Sterlings, September 14, 1986.

old and close friends who were among the Rogerses' guests at the ranch, to witness his signature on his last will and testament. The document, a one-page statement, left everything to Betty, with the stipulation that should Betty not survive her husband, his assets be divided "share and share alike," among his three children, Will, Jr., Mary, and James, or their issue, should one of the children not survive their father.

In Seattle, Wiley Post did not show up at Northwest Air Service at all that Saturday; he had gone fishing in Puget Sound with Seattle sportsman Ben Paris. Wiley was after salmon. Early in the morning he caught an eighteen-pound king salmon off Hermosa Beach, near the mouth of the Snohomish River. Actually, Wiley caught several fish that morning, but some were too small to keep, and two managed to get off the hook. Newspaper reports claim that the two 'escapees' "crowded the forty pound mark."[13] When interviewed, Wiley grinned: "I'm going out again," he said, "after the big ones that got away."

Rumors that Will Rogers might be accompanying the Posts on their flight to Alaska had somehow reached Seattle, probably through the questions regarding Wiley that the news services had sent out to their field correspondents. Keeping up the pretense, Wiley played the surprised party:

> "I don't see what basis they have for starting that story in Hollywood that Rogers will go with us," he said. "He isn't here, is he? If Rogers said he was going and I said so, there would be something to go on. I am not ready yet to make any further announcement as to who will be accompanying me."[14]

At 8 o'clock that Saturday evening, Wiley spoke at the Sportsmen's Show at Civic Auditorium, but the question foremost in the minds of reporters in Seattle concerned the possibility that Will Rogers might be coming to join Post. Everywhere Wiley went they hounded him with the same, now routine drill: Was Rogers going? When would they—the Posts and maybe Rogers—be leaving? "No!"

---

[13]*Seattle Post-Intelligencer*, August 4, 1935
[14]Ibid.

Wiley kept insisting, "And no, I won't be leaving today."[15] He also let it slip that he would be testing the plane, now that it had been equipped with floats.

Seattle is famous for its rain, and the day that Wiley had planned to test his plane and floats—Sunday—Seattle gave a most impressive demonstration of its precipitation. Most of the day had drenched the city in rain and fog. Wiley had driven a rented Oldsmobile to the little Bryn Mawr airport, where he stood dripping, forlorn in the penetrating damp and persistent rain. Hands deep in his pockets, he could only look at his plane; its engine and cockpit covered with a protective canvas, it stood tethered to the ramp sloping down toward Lake Washington. A few hardy, curious spectators had come out to see the famous man and his plane. Someone snapped a grainy picture in the semi-darkness of the gray, depressing scene.

One of the mechanics asked Wiley about flying floatplanes in the Northland. "I don't know much about Alaska," Post said, "I haven't had much experience flying planes with pontoons. I wonder how it's going to work out."[16] Talking to a reporter, Wiley said that he planned to equip the *Winnie Mae* with retractable landing gear on his return from his northern pleasure trip. He wanted to continue his exploits in the stratosphere and was tired of having to drop the wheels to reduce wind resistance, then bringing her down 'on her belly.'

In Pacific Palisades, travel plans proceeded. A United Airlines plane reservation to Seattle via San Francisco was made under the assumed name of Mr. Williams. Then, Will's two bags packed and all the chores done, he and Betty went to the Uplifters Ranch to catch the last part of a polo game. Later, back home, Will roped calves until it was suppertime. Afterward, Will, Jr., who had joined his parents for the meal, drove with them to Gilmore Stadium, where they attended a rodeo. Some of the contestants found Will and Betty in the stands and stopped by to pay their respects. After all, Will had been one of them. Though he now felt he had grown too old for it all, he still loved to watch the rough and dusty events and recall the days when he was down there performing in the arena.

---

[15]*Seattle Post-Intelligencer*, August 17, 1935.
[16]ibid.

Someone handed him a wooden trick puzzle. Will played with it for a few moments, then slipped it into his pocket.

Near midnight, Will and Betty headed for the airport. On the way they stopped to eat a sandwich at a little open air restaurant. The airport lounge was crowded. Betty and Will stayed outside until the time came to board. Will kissed Betty good-bye, then with his raincoat slung over his arm made his way to the newspaper stand where he bought several late editions. Again he waved his hand to Betty and shot her a quick boyish grin, before disappearing into the crowd of passengers.

The next day, Will telephoned Betty from San Francisco. He had had no difficulty with his passport, which, it turned out was still valid from the previous year's trip. The Russian consulate had most cooperatively issued the necessary visa immediately, so Will was able to get aboard United's 11 a.m. flight to Seattle. After a brief stop at Sacramento, the plane landed in Medford, Oregon, where Will Rogers was promptly recognized and bombarded by reporters with questions. Still trying to cover up the trip to Alaska, he stated: "I see by the papers that I am supposed to make some kind of a hop with Wiley Post, but you can say right now that I am not."[17] The reporters persisted. Will feigned confusion: "Wiley Post?" he scratched his ear, trying to look bewildered, "let's see, now. He's that flier fellow, isn't he?"[18]

But the secret was out when Rogers arrived at Seattle's Boeing Field in late afternoon and then checked into the Olympic Hotel, the Pacific Northwest's foremost luxury hotel where Wiley and Mae Post were also staying. With the last cover lifted from Will's not so carefully concealed plan to fly to Alaska, Will became the constant subject of reporters' questions. Acting as the spokesman for all three, when asked if he and the Posts would leave in the morning, Will announced: "Wiley wants to make a few minor adjustments and test out the ship again. Then the weather is not so good beyond 400 miles north of Seattle, according to the latest reports. We plan to make Juneau the first day. I've never been in Alaska and this is a good opportunity. I expect I will take a look at the Matanuska col-

---

[17]*Seattle Post-Intelligencer*, August 17, 1935.
[18]Ibid

ony while I'm up north. I want to see what the Democrats have done to the Republicans."

Interminably reporters asked questions about the plane. The strange-looking craft Wiley had compiled—this low-wing plane sitting on floats (float planes were usually high-winged craft)—had raised practically everyone's eyebrows. You could just tell there was something not right, the way she looked. Only Will Rogers seemed not to have noticed. In response to a question since lost, Will Rogers's answer is: "I don't know anything about the plane Wiley has, but if he is the pilot, I don't care. He is a marvelous flier." Will, of course, had already flown in Wiley's plane, yet in fact he knew really very little about it or its engine, or the anomalous features that made it look simply odd, especially to anyone familiar with floatplanes. Mechanics did not stand among Will's strong suits. Indeed, Betty doubted that Will even knew how to change a tire, although he did drive a car. Will himself acknowledged his shortcomings with engines and machines; he had written:

> I had to make a speech to the Automotive Engineers' Association. Can you imagine me talking to a lot of technical mechanics? . . . Out of 110 million people in America, there couldn't possibly be one that knew less about machinery. I never raised the hood of any car I ever had. If the thing stopped, I'd just get out, kick it in the shins, and wait there till one of the things came that's going to pick me up and take me somewhere.
>
> If I raised up the hood and a rabbit jumped out, I wouldent know but what it belonged in there. I drive 'em, but I sho don't try to fix 'em.[19]

Of the two men, Wiley more than Will roused the interest of pilots and mechanics, as well as the young men, and boys, who saw him as a hero—a man who had conquered space and distance, and even time. Others could only dream about what Wiley Post in this exciting, youthful age of aviation had daringly done. And he had done it twice. Twice he had flown around the globe and into the future. To the average man and woman in the street, however, Will Rogers was

---

[19]Weekly article, January 20, 1929.

the man to see, and to reporters, he offered far better copy. His quips made current news, whereas Wiley's past pioneering achievements merely made history. A performer by nature, Will welcomed and masterfully handled the reporters and crowds that put Wiley so ill at ease. As Will saw it: "Wiley is kind of a Calvin Coolidge on answers; none of 'em are going to bother you with being too long."[20]

The morning of August 5, a Monday, Wiley was up early. In Seattle, the day had broken brilliantly clear; just a few billowy white clouds floated in a sky so dazzling you'd have thought nature was begging forgiveness for the previous day's rain. The good weather brought more aviation enthusiasts than usual out to Renton airport. They milled about, gawking admiringly at Post and his strange-looking plane. After Wiley had checked over the engine, he looked around dockside, where he spotted a few, by now familiar teenagers, equipped with their cameras, among them Gordon Williams from nearby Clyde Hill, and his friend Bob McLarren (called Mac), visiting from Los Angeles. The two of them had been coming by daily to look at the conversion progress and to snap pictures. They had also besieged the famous pilot with endless questions every day, and Wiley had found himself comfortable with them. He was now about to take the new seaplane on its first test flight, but he hesitated. He conferred briefly with one of the mechanics, then Wiley turned to Gordon[21] and his friend Mac: "Hey, you kids! Want to go up for a ride? I need some ballast."[22]

The two teenagers didn't have to be invited twice. A mechanic handed them life jackets, and Post told them to position themselves as far back in the plane as possible because: "I don't have much load on board," he explained. Gordon and Mac sat on the aft two-seat bench and fastened their seat belts.[23] Gordon took the window seat. His older brother, George, took a photograph from dockside of his kid brother looking out.

Wiley climbed into the cockpit. After he slid the overhead cover

<hr>

[20]Weekly article published posthumously August 20, 1935.
[21]Gordon Sear Williams, became an internationally known aviation chronicler, public relations representative with Boeing for 42 years, died at age 69, June 25, 1985, just 6 weeks short of the fiftieth anniversary of his flight with Wiley Post.
[22]Sterlings' Interview with Gordon S. Williams, March 14, 1985.
[23]Sterlings' Interview with Gordon S. Williams, March 2, 1985.

shut, he turned around to face the teenagers: "Ready to go?" he asked. The boys assured him they were. The engine started. Wiley taxied slowly, warming the engine and experimenting with floats and rudders. Then he full-throttled, and the plane took off into the strong north wind.

For almost three-quarters of an hour Wiley flew the two kids over fifty-mile long Lake Washington. He banked, climbed, dived, and generally tested the controls. During the flight, Gordon Williams took the only existing picture of the plane's interior; it shows Wiley Post's back and the cockpit door, its pockets stuffed with maps and charts. It was a thrilling adventure for the two young aviation fans; but veteran Wiley Post should have been seriously concerned.

The work at Northwest Air Service had been completed, nothing more remained to be done—except to pay the bill and be off. As Alan Blum recalled:

> At the conclusion of the work that we did, I presented a bill to Wiley Post; the airplane was his, he had ordered the work. He wrote out a check. And a few minutes later, well . . . what caused the few minutes delay, why, Will Rogers was busy handing out $20 bills to the men that worked on the plane. And then, when he got through with that, he said [to me] did you take that man's money? I said, 'Sure!'
>
> "Here, let me have it," he said and he tore the check up. And he said: "How much is it?" And he got his check book out: "How much is it?" And I started to tell him, and he says "Oh, you know these things better than I do," and he just signed his name to the blank check and handed it to me. "You fill it out!" The bill was, oh, something like $500, which in those days was a lot of money.[24]

On August 6, the weather in Seattle was good, but weather reports from the Gulf of Alaska were discouraging enough for the Posts and Rogers to delay their departure. Will decided, though, that he would like to see how "this new ship" performed. So around noontime, Rogers drove with Mae and Wiley Post the twelve miles south to

---

[24]Sterlings' interview with Alan Blum, August 18, 1986.

Renton. The *Los Angeles Times* of August 7, 1935, reported that Mrs. Post remained in Seattle, but Will Rogers's weekly article, published August 20, but mailed from Seattle on August 6, states: "Mrs. Post and Wiley and I drive out to the field . . ." Although Will Rogers should know best, only the two men took off on the short test flight over Lake Washington. When they returned, after swooping low over the airport, Will sang Wiley's praises to the ever-present reporters: "He's sure a marvelous flier; I'll fly anywhere with him, if he'll take me along." In its report on this brief exchange, the *Los Angeles Times* of August 7, 1935 wrote that Post added: "I'll take him as far as he wants to go."

Later that Tuesday, back in Seattle, Will stopped by the Pacific Marine Supply Company, located at Western and University. There Will bought rope for a lariat, this store being one of the few in the area that sold the suitable spotted rope, as well as life-preserver equipment. He also disrupted the orderly conduct of business, as sales help and customers alike wanted to shake the famous man's hand, or get his autograph. Rogers spent the rest of the afternoon of August 6 playing polo at the Olympic Riding and Driving Club's new Polo Field,[25] where he cut a most startling figure, racing along the field, "clad in a garish red shirt and a pair of bibless overalls."[26] Will must have borrowed the remarkable ensemble at the Club; he was certainly not traveling with such items in his luggage. After the game, in the shower, Will spoke to Royal Brougham, noted sports columnist for the *Seattle Post-Intelligencer,* and that evening, as a guest at the polo dinner of the Washington Athletic Club, Will addressed several hundred members for a half hour. Rogers's presence at these events on August 6, 1935, clearly establish that he and Post, contrary to claims made at the investigation later, had not left Seattle on August 6.

Rogers and Post had, of course, taken their short test flight on the

---

[25]On August 25, 1935 the polo field was renamed Will Rogers Field. In June 1936, the club dedicated an obelisk and plaque in Rogers's honor, commemorating the place where Will had played his last polo game. The field has since given way to a housing subdivision; the monument now stands, half-hidden, in the northeast corner of the small parking lot of the Lake City Branch of the Seattle Public Library on 28th Avenue, N.E. just off 125th Street

[26]*Seattle Daily Times*, Aug. 16, 1935.

6, the same day that Will mailed his weekly article to the McNaught Syndicate. In it Will enumerated some of the items he had observed aboard the small plane:

> He has got a rubber boat and a canoe paddle, some life vests, or protectors. Oh yes and his gun case, I don't know what kind it is, I don't hunt or shoot; It's a long looking thing. I expect there is a Springfield rifle in there. Oh, yes, and his fishing rod and 80 reels. Oh yes! and two or three coils of rope, (and they are not mine). They are to tie the ship up and pull it up to the banks. That will be my job to get out first and tie the rope and then vault ashore and haul it in. I will have to have a card from the 'Longshoreman's Union.' "What no camera? No that's what we are going on this trip for to get away from cameras, then too, I don't know nothing about 'em, and can't work 'em. We may see some fine sights but you can always lie about a thing better than you can prove it. Then you always have to explain that 'this picture don't near do the scene justice.' Oh yes, and some sleeping bags, Wiley got them; said they was great to sleep in. I never was in one of 'em. You zip 'em up around you after you get in 'em some way. I always have trouble with those zippers, so I can see myself walking around in one of those things all day.[27]

After Will's brief flight with Wiley in the new plane, the first news stories that Mae Post may not be accompanying her husband and Rogers to Alaska began to appear. They hinted, too, at a rift in the Post family, as they alluded to the day that Wiley had snapped at a reporter and told him to ask Mrs. Post directly whether she would be coming along to Alaska. The *Los Angeles Herald and Express* cited a wire story that reported "friends" of the parties concerned had disclosed that Rogers had "kidded" Mrs. Post about their hunting and fishing in the Alaskan wilderness. Supposedly, Rogers had said that it was "no place for a lady," and the wire story continued: "The 'kidding' in which Post joined, finally convinced Mrs. Post not to make the trip with them."

---

[27]Weekly article, published August 20, 1935.

Will himself wrote about the change of plan. He said simply:
"Mrs. Post decided at the last minute to go up to Alaska a few days
later by boat, so it's only Wiley and I that are taking off." Indicating
no hard feelings, Rogers also noted that Mrs. Post asked him "to
take good care of Wiley." I said, "Of course you mean in the air,
after we get on the ground he is able to look after himself."

Then, in a syndicated news story by Universal Service, Mae Post
spoke about her husband and their plans:

> He's so erratic. I've always sworn that the next time I'd go with
> him, because at least we'd be together if anything happened."
> Then she explained further: "Will Rogers wanted to go to Alaska
> so badly. He'd planned it for weeks, way back to the time Fay
> Gillis thought she might come along, too. Will wanted to pay
> my passage to Alaska, after he joined us in Seattle and took my
> place in the plane with Wiley.
>
> But I couldn't let him do that.

Mae would in time offer a number of variations on the theme of
why she suddenly failed to accompany her husband, but for the moment, the official story held that Mae Post would join the two men
in Alaska. In actuality, though, plans had already been made for her
to return to Oklahoma. Wiley and Will, then, would take off alone,
but only after another unanticipated delay:

> In the early morning hours of Wednesday, August 7, everything
> was ready for Rogers and Post to begin their trip. There was
> some last minute excitement causing a delay. The evening before,
> 'Ash' Bridgham, manager of the Northwest Air Service airport,
> had pumped 6 drums of gas into the plane's fuel tanks. Each of
> those drums held 50 gallons, for a total of 300 gallons. In the
> cool of the night, when fuel contracts somewhat, it might have
> been possible to get 300 gallons of gasoline into six tanks which
> were supposed to hold only 270 gallons. Post's instructions had
> been to fill the tanks "right to the top." But in the morning, as
> the warm sun of the clear day began to heat up the plane, the
> gasoline expanded and began spilling out of the tanks. The fumes
> and smell of gas were everywhere, and the plane and the area

had to be thoroughly washed down before anybody would even
consider starting an engine.[28]

With the flight thus delayed, the usual reporters and photographers present at the scene asked the usual questions and made the
usual requests for just 'one more picture.' Wiley, though, was all
business. Rogers, on the other hand, noted that he might have to
"get a fish dinner at Ketchikan." In his banter with the newsmen, he
occasionally aimed a good-natured barb at Post, who retorted in
kind. Someone asked Rogers if he had a 'ghost-writer' to write his
many articles.

> "No," retorted Will, "I don't even own a ghost."
> Post at this point broke into the banter and showed Rogers a
> khaki-colored life jacket, to be used in case the plane was forced
> down on water. Post held the jackets up and said: "You know,
> we have to take these along."
> Will suddenly became solemn: "I don't like to think about
> that," he said, "I'm going for a good time."[29]

The moment for departure approached. Mae Post watched the
crew stow sandwiches and coffee aboard. Fourteen-year-old Earlene
Paddock, whose family lived close to Renton airport, held on to her
five-year-old brother, Franklin, as she awaited her opportunity. She
had come to take photographs with her box camera and to get autographs from the two famous men. She recalls that she thought
Wiley Post looked "just spiffy," exactly like she had seen him in the
newspapers. Will Rogers, though, disappointed her fourteen-year-old
preconceptions as to just how people ought to look. "A movie star,"
she believed, "ought to look as if he had just stepped out of a fashion
magazine." Will, in a grey suit, rumpled as if he had slept in it for
two weeks, his tie askew, and his hat crushed and stained by perspiration, simply did not meet her expectations. Nonetheless, she had
come to take pictures and get autographs, and a little disappointment
was not going to get in her way. The pad she had brought with her

---

[28]Sterlings' interview with 'Ash' Bridgham, Seattle, WA., July 14, 1986
[29]*Seattle Daily Times*, Friday, August 16, 1935.

for the autographs, came from the Renton Variety Store, and had its name and three-digit telephone number clearly printed at the top.

Wiley signed Earlene's pad; then he kissed Mae good-bye and climbed into the cockpit to start the engine. After, of course, accommodating Earlene with an autograph, Will tousled her brother's blond locks and knelt down to speak a few words with the little boy.[30] Will Rogers then boarded the plane.

The fact that Wiley Post, supposedly a cautious flier, decided to leave Seattle on a day when the Weather Bureau was still reporting inclement conditions all along the coast of northern British Columbia and southeastern Alaska is surprising. The eight o'clock Associated Press report from Ketchikan stated a light rain was falling, while a ship dispatch announced rain at Juneau. Indeed, the forecast for the entire flight route did not sound promising. The Associated Press wire story, datelined Seattle, August 7, begins: "Ignoring reports of storms on their route, Wiley Post and Will Rogers took off here today in Mr. Post's new plane for Alaska."

After the plane had taxied away from the dock, Mae Post—still sticking to the fabrication—told reporters that she expected to join her husband in Alaska in a few days. She would travel north by ship, she said, because "the flight might be too strenuous." In reality, Mae would remain in Seattle a few more days, then, fly from Boeing Field to San Francisco aboard a private plane owned by yeast magnate Max Fleischmann and piloted by Harry Ashe.

At 9:15 a.m., Wiley's little red plane lifted off Lake Washington, and headed toward Ketchikan, Alaska. Films still exist of the take off. As Will described it:

> Well, she took off like a bird, with an awful short run
>   . . . we had pretty weather for about the first 300 miles, then
> it began to kinder close in.[31]

It is interesting that Rogers noted "an awful short run," especially as floatplanes usually take off at a much lower angle of climb. The not-so-pretty weather he and Post encountered included rain and low

---

[30]Sterlings' interview with Mrs. Earlene (Paddock) Henry, Seattle, May 3, 1987.
[31]Weekly Article, published posthumously September 1, 1935.

lying clouds—hardly ideal conditions for flying over unknown terrain. When the well-known Ketchikan pilot Bob Ellis was asked
whether Post would stop there, he replied, "The weather is so bad
that even the locals are not flying." About an hour after Ellis made
that statement, Post went flying by, no more than fifty feet over the
water; he did not stop. In his weekly column Rogers commented:

> We had expected to stop in Ketchikan, our first city in Alaska,
> but Wiley I guess figured that if he stopped there he would get
> closed in and wouldent get any further up the coast. So he flew
> low over the very pretty little city right along the water's edge
> with the high mountains to the back of it.[32]

That Rogers could only "guess" at Post's intentions indicates the
absence of communication between the two men. They could not
confer on this point—or any point—during flight because, despite
the close quarters inside the plane and the small distance between
the cockpit and the last seat in the cabin, the noise of the engine
would make even shouting difficult to understand. Yet, later that
day, Rogers is quoted:

> We were flying over Ketchikan and I told Wiley I thought that
> was a nice looking place. He said he knew a better one and so
> we kept going. He's been to Alaska so often he knows his way
> around—kind of an old settler up here.[33]

Wiley obviously did not want to land at the small village of Ketchikan and be grounded there—maybe for days—so he decided on
his own to take a chance on being able to land in Juneau. Post and
Rogers landed on Juneau's Gastineau Channel at 5:30 p.m. The date
was Wednesday, August 7, 1935.

---

[32]Weekly Article, published postlumiously September 1, 1935.
[33]Associated Press, August 8, 1935.

CHAPTER X

ZERO ZERO

W HEN POST AND Rogers landed at Juneau, it was raining. The nearly thousand-mile hop had taken eight-and-a-quarter hours, but they did not arrive unexpected. Throngs lined even the adjacent docks as the plane taxied to its berth at the PAA hangar. Wiley emerged first, coming out in his shirt sleeves. Will, smiling as he surveyed Alaska for the first time from ground level, stepped from the plane with his topcoat now covering the rumpled gray suit. He shivered and said: "It was cold in the plane, but warm in the motor room." (Associated Press. August 8, 1935)

Joe Crosson was there to greet the two men. He presented Rogers with a copy of *Arctic Village*,[1] a book that he believed would provide Will with an authentic picture of good life in Alaska's remote settlements. Will thanked him and promised to read it.

Walt Woodward, Alaska's first radio newscaster and a cub re-

---

[1] *Arctic Village* by Robert Marshall, © 1933 . The book was found among the effects in the wreck and today is on display at the Will Rogers Memorial, Claremore, OK

porter covering the waterfront and new arrivals for Juneau's *The Empire*, recalled:

> I had no chance to even get close to them at the floats. I do remember, however, that many of the bush pilots, after looking at the plane, were shaking their heads in doubt—not at Wiley Post's skills, but at the plane. They apparently did not approve of it.[2]

While Woodward could not get close enough to interview either Rogers or Post at the docks, he could plainly see how tired both men looked to be and could only hope that Will Rogers would recover enough for an appearance on his 10 p.m. newscast over station KINY. The reporters at the dockside fired questions at both men. When they asked Post how long he intended to stay in Juneau, he snapped back: "We're going to stay here until we get ready to take off for somewhere!" Neither Wiley nor Will would comment on Mrs. Post's plans as to where she would meet them and how she'd be traveling. After half an hour Crosson rescued Post and Rogers from the dockside crowd and drove them to the Gastineau Hotel. They had checked in and then attended a banquet given in their honor at the Territorial Mansion, home of Governor John W. Troy. (*New York Times*, August 8, 1935)

Everybody liked Governor Troy; so did Will, noting with a favorite line: "The Governor is a nice fellow, a Democrat but a gentleman"[3]. At the governor's mansion, Walt Woodward heard Troy ask Rogers whether he was up to driving over to the local radio station for a short talk, since KINY had been announcing all day that Will Rogers would appear at 10 p.m. The governor pointed out that of course there was absolutely no obligation on Rogers's part. "Will Rogers hesitated for a long time, and then, in a very tired voice, said he'd make the broadcast."[4]

---

[2]Sterlings' letter from Walt Woodward, dated May, 4, 1987.
[3]Will Rogers's daily column August 8, 1935.
[4]Ex. Sterlings' letter from Walt Woodward, dated May, 4, 1987.

Rogers and Post arrived at the radio station on time and in the governor's car. Wiley, the first to speak, said in part:

> "I have just had a very good evening. I like Alaska, like its Governor, and like the dinner I had at the Governor's house. We ate a lot of Matanuska cantaloupes and salmon and stuff like that. Our plans are very vague. We have a lot of friends here in Alaska and I hope I will get to see all of them, but if I don't I'll be back sometime. I've always liked this country and always had a good time here, except when I broke down and got lost on my trip around the world, and even then there was a good friend to come along and pull me out of it. We plan to sort of wander around in the interior and see a lot, and hunt and fish and just sort of wander around."[5]

When Post had finished, Woodward simply and excitedly announced: " 'Here he is! Will Rogers!' Then that kindly, tired man squared his shoulders and suddenly was transformed into the brilliant humorist that he was."[6] Looking out over the visitors' gallery, packed that night with fans anxious to see the two famous men, Rogers observed:

> I have never been here before and I ought to be ashamed of myself. It ought to be in the Constitution that everybody had to come here.
>
> I am not up here on any commission. Wiley and I are like a couple of country boys in an old Ford—we don't know where we are going and we don't care.
>
> "Amelia Earhart was out to my place a couple of Sundays ago. She ought to be an authority on that sort of thing and she said she thinks Post is the greatest pilot in the world.
>
> I expect to be here a while. I will have to buy an awful lot of rain coats and rubber boots—it will take me all morning to buy all those things.

---

[5]Sterlings' letter from Walt Woodward, dated May, 4, 1987.
[6]Ibid.

I think Roosevelt will be elected by a bigger majority than before.

People wonder where I get all my jokes. I just listen to the government and report the facts. I have 96 senators working for me and all I got to do is write down what they say.

I expect we will go up to this Matanuska Valley and see where the Democrats are feeding the Republicans. think it is a good idea. I think it would be swell if they brought all the Republicans up here and put them in a valley. It wouldn't take a very big valley to hold them all.

I think Roosevelt would like to have been along on this hop. He'd rather like to get away from down there. Everyone who has any money has it in for Roosevelt. Funny thing about the Republicans; they'd rather make their money under a Republican but if they can't do that they will take what they can get.

The next morning, August 8, Rogers and Post awoke to more of the same steady rainfall, and "not a plane mushed out of Juneau," as Rogers put it. At least the Gastineau, a comfortable, fine hotel, had allowed the two men a good night. With *Arctic Village* in hand, Will went downstairs for breakfast, where he was spotted by Warren Tilman, a PAA mechanic who had flown into town from Fairbanks on one of PAA's regular flights. Noting Will's reading, Tilman bragged that he actually appeared in the book, though under a changed identity. As the two men talked, they discovered that they came from the same part of the country. Warren had been born in the Ozarks, and had even visited Claremore, Will's adopted home town. When Rogers learned that, like him, Tilman also had Indian blood, Will dubbed him Chief, a nickname that stuck.

Outside the downpour continued. To a three-quarter-inch rainfall it continued, and Will, tired of waiting it out, rushed to a nearby store and bought some rubbers as well as a couple of raincoats. He quipped, "With this weather I'll need lots of them. If I was going to stay in Juneau, I would buy at least one more outfit."

Of course, whenever either one of them, Will or Wiley, stepped outside the Gastineau Hotel, a crowd of admirers gathered, for autographs and photos. Dozens of times their Alaskan fans asked the two men to pose. Neither man could walk down the street without having a retinue of local enthusiasts follow him from a deferential distance.

The Juneau Chamber of Commerce invited Will to address their luncheon at Bailey's Cafe that day, the 8th, at noon. For 25 minutes Will ranged over a variety of subjects, from his impression of Alaska to his estimation of President Roosevelt, from aviation to politics:

> I sent a little dispatch to 650 newspapers in the United States after my arrival here. I told 'em what a swell place you got. As a last line, I added that I'd met your Governor and that he was a Democrat—but a gentleman at the same time. We—Wiley Post and I—did sorta figure on taking a hop to Skagway today. But the weather grounded us. So Wiley and Joe Crosson went down to tinker on the engine and I come up here to talk to you fellows.
>
> You know, I want to pay you people a compliment. You've got 30,000 alleged white folks up here, and 65 airplanes. That's a darn good average. But it's a national disgrace that you aren't connected with coo-coo land with an airplane route. But I guess that's coming pretty soon. Speaking of pilots, you've got a great bunch here. They have to be good. They don't need no Government tests up in these tough channels. Just send a new pilot out. If he comes back, he's okey.
>
> You know, Roosevelt is like a magician in a vaudeville show. He's arrived at the theatre, only his special properties and luggage ain't arrived yet. So he's got to borrow somebody else's magic hat. Well, he goes ahead and does his tricks. But when he reaches in the hat to draw out a rabbit, he doesn't know himself whether he is drawing out a rabbit or skunk. That's like most of these New Deal schemes. He's got to hold 'em up for public view, regardless how the idea turns out. But he's a great guy, Roosevelt is. I understand you've got a Senate with eight members, and a House with 16. All the Senators are Democrats, and so are 15 of the House members. That's all right. I'll get Farley to workin' on that other guy.
>
> President Roosevelt wants to reform business. Big business don't want him to. So the big boys are saying, "Come on, Roosevelt, just let us recover from this depression, and then we'll kinda be on the square."

I really believe that President Roosevelt is several years ahead of his time and his policies are going to be tested and found true in a few years. Well, folks, I just want to tell you how much I enjoy your Alaska and your Juneau. As a traveling committee of one, representing the Democratic Party and I'm paying my own ticket—I'll go back and report to President Roosevelt about Alaska. When he asks me, "Will, what's wrong with 'em up there?" I'll tell him, "Not a damn thing!"

Meanwhile, in Seattle, Mae Post was telling reporters a slightly different story. She was now saying that she might not join her husband in Alaska, contrary to their previously announced plans. "I haven't fully made up my mind yet, but I hardly think I will."[7]

That same day, too, the popular novelist Rex Beach arrived in Juneau by boat. On his taxi ride to the Gastineau Hotel, he learned that Wiley Post was in town, with Will Rogers, whom he had known for more than twenty years, and had last seen a year earlier, at New York City's Dinty Moore's, a Broadway restaurant famous for its chili. Rex found the two celebrities eating dinner with Joe Crosson in the cafe.

"How come you can take time out to hitch-hike up here?" the author of "The Spoilers" wanted to know.

"I have got three pictures ahead and I always wanted to see Alaska," said Will, "Wiley is crazy about it and wants to live up here."

Wiley smiled and half chidingly complained: "I want to go fishing, too, but Will won't give me a chance."

"Say, I've heard nothing but fishing since I got here," Will defended himself. "All these boys do is brag about who caught the biggest salmon. Last night an oilman brought one weighing 50 pounds into my room and wanted to put it in bed with me. Yea, the oil business is so bad that all the executives come here fishing.

"Wiley's as bad as the rest, and I can't see the use of catching salmon when they crawl out of the water to meet you. The first

---

[7]Associated Press, August 8, 1935

handshake I got when I stepped ashore was from a big cohoe. A cohoe, they tell me, is a king salmon that's on relief."[8]

A group of eager autograph collectors descended on the celebrities. Will, who disliked signing autographs, grumbled at first but then signed any piece of paper anyone held in front of him—except that he was writing not his name but names like Ben Turpin and Tom Mix. He was, of course, soon found out and persuaded to give the admirers his Will Rogers. Both Wiley Post and Joe Crosson, however, resisted the autograph seekers until Will made an announcement that made the fans only more persistent and made Post and Crosson more amenable. "This is Wiley Post," he said to the group around their table, "he flew around the world with Gatty and broke the record, then he circled the globe alone and broke it again. Both times he had trouble here in Alaska and Joe Crosson pulled him out. Their autographs are really worth having."[9] When the last fan left satisfied, the four men returned to their conversation.

"What are your plans?" Rex asked. Wiley grinned and said nothing. Will confessed:

> We haven't any. We're just on a vacation. We want to see Dawson and Fairbanks and those farmer colonists at Matanuska of course, and we would like to see the McKenzie River, too. We might even hop across to Siberia and go home that way. When Wiley was flying around the world those Russians laid out his course and told him exactly where to head in at and made him stick to it. Now they have given him permission to fly anywhere and stop anywhere as long as he wants. We have the maps and it would make a swell trip to go by way of Iceland and Greenland. The longest water jump is only 1,000 miles.[10]

The men talked until midnight, when Wiley fell asleep with his head on his forearms. "He never had a word to say," Will said. "I do the talking for the team and it works out fine." They wakened

---

[8]Ex: Column by Rex Beach, August 22, 1935.
[9]Ibid
[10]Syndicated column by Rex Beach, August 17, 1935.

Wiley when they at last decided to retire for the night. Will had taken a two-room suite, one room for Wiley and one for himself. That night Wiley shared his room with Joe Crosson.[11]

Earlier that day, Joe Crosson had left orders with the PAA crew to check the plane carefully, and to prepare it for departure. Bob Ames, a fine mechanic, thoroughly examined the engine, cleaned the plane, checked the battery, added oil and filled the gas tanks. Everything seemed to be in perfect order. It was on this occasion that Bob Ames noticed the single Ford motor car gas gauge.[12]

On August 8, the Associated Press reported a mild disagreement between Will and Wiley, over their plans for when they resumed their flight:

> Post yearned for salmon fishing with light tackle. Rogers urged a quick take-off for Nome so he could "lasso a reindeer." Inasmuch as weather forecasts were unfavorable, Rogers said he would compromise and "let Wiley do his fishing."
>
> Turning to an ever-present reporter he commented: "I guess Wiley and me'll have to flip a coin to see where we are going next. Wiley's the very best man on this trip. He fills the gas tank and then we're off."[13]

Yet the remarks that Post made to reporters indicate that takeoff and routes stood foremost in his mind, whereas his passenger, Rogers, saw the trip as an opportunity for a pleasure jaunt.

When Will came to the dock the next afternoon, the ninth, he handed out five-dollar bills to the PAA employees. The rain had stopped and a bright sun promised ideal flying conditions. The plan was to fly to Dawson City, with a couple of sightseeing stops along the way. Wrote Will Rogers: "We are going to Skagway now and see the famous Chilkoot Pass. We will do it in ten minutes and it took the pioneers two and three months."[14]

At the dock, Wiley bought an anchor so they could moor the plane

---

[11]Sterlings' Interview with Lillian (Mrs. Joe) Crosson July 11, 1986.
[12]Sterlings' interview with Robert Ames, July, 1986.
[13]Associated Press, August 8, 1935
[14]Will Rogers Daily Column, August 8, 1935

should they decide to set down either to fish, or to spend the night on a lake or river. While Post and Crosson were once more studying charts and telephoning for the latest weather reports, Rex Beach, Mayor Goldstein of Juneau, and Will loaded the personal belongings onto the plane. Will also clowned with the crowd that had once again gathered. Then, at 1:25 p.m., Post and Rogers climbed aboard. The door and hatch closed. A good-bye cheer arose from the hundreds of onlookers on the wharves at Juneau's waterfront as the red plane "took off in a smother of foam." Wiley circled over the city, then laid course up Lynn Canal toward Skagway.

Standing at the dock, Lloyd Jarman, veteran mechanic for PAA, took motion pictures of Wiley's take-off. He shook his head; he had flown thousands of miles in floatplanes, and he knew their dangers. He thought that "Wiley Post was not a good seaplane pilot, he was too abrupt on takeoff and pulled up too steep . . . it was too quick and nose high"—an experienced pilot does not take off like this and stay alive. He had known many pilots "and the few who did this type of flying were quickly eliminated."[15]

Rex Beach now regretted that he had changed his plans. The day before, he had decided he would fly along with Will and Wiley. When, however, he had telegraphed his wife in New York with his adventurous change of itinerary, she had immediately wired back, "pleading with him not to undertake any flying trip in the hazardous Alaskan country."[16] So, regretfully, he had told his friend Will and Wiley that they would have to go without him. Rex stood and watched the little red plane disappear. In his newspaper account of the takeoff, he reported that as the plane vanished into the mist down Gastineau Channel, Joe Crosson turned to him and said: "There's a ship to go anywhere with. With that engine Wiley could lift her out off a frog pond."

Three hours and five minutes later, Wiley Post put the plane down at Dawson City, Yukon Territory, Canada, 475 miles from his starting point. He had not stopped at either Skagway or Whitehorse.

When Post and Rogers climbed out of the plane at Dawson, they found that again a crowd had collected, the news of their planned

---

[15]Sterlings' letter from Lloyd R. Jarman, dated December 8, 1985.
[16]Ex: *Seattle Post-Intelligencer*, August 19, 1935.

arrival having drawn hundreds of rowdy miners into the already excited community. In Dawson, too, the autograph collectors and amateur photographers would besiege Post and Rogers and swamp them with questions and accolades.

Harriet Malstrom reported the arrival for her uncle's newspaper, the *Dawson News,* in her biggest story ever, and that evening, over dinner with Post and Rogers, she had the opportunity to interview the celebrities. At one point, Will suddenly leaned over to her and said: "No riding in any railway contraption for me. What if the thing jumped the track? I prefer an honorable death in a plane, or falling off a horse."[17] Harriet, stunned, marked down the words; she did not want to get them wrong.

The next morning Rogers rose so early to see all the local points of interest that he seemed to be the only person about, except for Miss Malstrom. "I guess I woke the miners up," he told her.

Not quite so early that same morning Wiley was stepping from one float to another, when he slipped and fell into the Yukon River. He disappeared in the ice-cold water right up to his neck. He hauled himself, soaking, out of it in a hurry, and otherwise seemed to be unaffected by the dunking.

In the afternoon, the two 'vacationers' moved on.

There was talk that Post and Rogers would fly from Dawson to Aklavik, Northwest Territories, in order to visit with Nicholas Sokoloff, the vice president of the Soviet government trading company Amtorg, Inc. Sokoloff had come to Aklavik to establish radio contact and report weather data to the Russian pilot Sigmund Levanevsky and his two Russian companions, who were still planning to fly from Moscow to San Francisco by crossing over the North Pole. They did get to Aklavik:

> Aklavik, North West Territory. Get your map out and look this up. The mouth of the McKenzie River, right on the Arctic Ocean. Eskimos are thicker then rich men at a Save-The-Constitution convention. This is sent from one of the most northerly posts of the Northwest Mounted Police. A great body of men, like the G-men.

---

[17]*Los Angeles* Times, March 16, 1936

We are headed for famous Herschel Island in the Arctic. Old
Wiley had to duck his head to keep from bumping it as we flew
under the Arctic circle. What, no night? It's all day up here."[18]

According to the *Los Angles Evening Herald and Express* of August 16, 1935, Wiley and Will were shivering with cold at Aklavik—
not because of the forty-degree temperature so much as because of
the chilling factor of relentless, penetrating winds that cut like a thousand scalpels through ordinary clothing right to the skin and numbed
it in seconds. The two men nonetheless brought warmth to All Saints
Hospital in Aklavik where they cheered up the patients. Alice Brown
led Will to the bedside of one patient in particular, a young boy who
had had his foot crushed when two boats collided with each other
in the sea. Will spent some time with the lad and when he left, he
pressed a "substantial check" into the boy's hand.[19]

While in Aklavik, Post and Rogers also visited the Anglo-Canadian
author Alan Sullivan. Sometime during their talks on Sunday, the
eleventh, and again on Monday, Will must have confided his and
Post's plans to Sullivan. Probably he felt that anything said in that
isolated northern outpost would remain secret until public events
disclosed the private plan behind them. When Sullivan arrived in
Edmonton, Alberta, on August 19, he told reporters that Rogers and
Post "wanted to see Alaska first and then both definitely intended
making the flight across Siberia. They planned to go from Nome
across the Bering Strait."[20]

As Rogers walked about the village of Aklavik, he picked up all
sorts of stories his readers in the forty-eight states would find interesting, for Alaska in the thirties was still a huge, wild, unknown, and
unexplored land mass to most Americans. On Monday, August 12,
he wrote:

"Was you ever driving around in a car and not knowing or caring where you went? Well, that's what Wiley and I are doing.
We are sure having a great time. If we hear of whales or a big

---

[18]Will Rogers's Daily Column, August 10, 1935.
[19]*New York Times*, October 18, 1935.
[20]Associated Press, August 19, 1935.

herd of caribou or reindeer, we fly over and see it. Friday and
Saturday we visited the old Klondike district, Dawson City, Bo-
nanza, El Dorado. Say, there is a horse here; the furthest north
of any horse, and he eats fish and travels on snowshoes. Maybe
Point Barrow today."[21]

Before leaving Aklavik, Post had to purchase fuel from the Canadian Airways depot. Air engineer Frank Hartley, up on the wing,
was busy filling the tanks. He turned to Rogers who was standing
close by and asked, "What's the fuel capacity of this plane?"

Will, to whom details relating to engines were a life-long mystery,
had no idea.

> "How much does that crate of yours hold, Wiley?" he yelled.
> "About 260 gallons in all seven tanks," Post yelled back. It'll
> take about 80 more to fill her up. . . ."
> Captain Farrell, of Canadian Airways, was standing next to
> Will. "And you say this gas is costing us $1.16 a gallon?" Rogers
> asked, surprised at the high price. "Well, you just go right ahead
> and fill'er up! I ain't never ridden on no $1.16 gas before and I
> want to enjoy everything you got up here in the Arctic."
> When Hartley had topped the tanks, Rogers shoved a ten dol-
> lar bill into his pocket. Hartley was reluctant to accept it and
> tried to return it. Rogers would have none of it; "You just take
> my picture and we'll call that a fee" he insisted, as he stepped
> on the wing of the plane. He posed a second, Frank Hartley took
> the picture and Rogers entered the plane, moving to his now
> accustomed seat in the very rear.[22]

The details regarding fuel capacity and gasoline tanks, as reported
in this article, are disturbingly wrong, and raise several critical questions. Why would an experienced pilot like Wiley Post say that he

---

[21]Will Rogers's daily telegram dated Aklavik, Northwest Territories, Canada, August 12, 1935
[22]Unidentified newspaper article, reprinted by the Will Rogers Memorial, Claremore,
OK., in its book *The Crash Felt 'Round the World* by Dr. Reba N. Collins © 1984
Will Rogers Heritage Press

had seven gasoline tanks holding 260 gallons when in fact he had only six tanks, which actually held 270 gallons? After flying this plane for a week, would Wiley still not have known how many tanks he carried, nor what their capacity totaled? Because only one of those tanks had a fuel gauge during flight, he would have had to be keeping track of his diminishing supply of gasoline. Besides watching the landscape and his controls, he would have had also to continually tally the time he had spent in the air, in order to calculate the fuel consumed, and which tanks at any given moment were empty and which were full. How could he correctly keep their status straight, if he did not know the size or the number of his tanks?

If Wiley believed he had only 260 gallons when in fact he had an additional ten, he might have been flying at an advantage. Those ten gallons would grant him a small margin of approximately twenty minutes added flight time, but his error regarding the number of tanks is more troubling and potentially disastrous. Post's habit of draining the last drop of fuel out of each tank, before switching to a full one, now seems even more ominous. (Every time he had done it, he had startled Gatty.) Without gauges, how could Wiley accurately and continually recall which tanks were full and which he had emptied, particularly when his flight patterns varied from day to day? Might he not, then, easily switch from one already emptied tank—when the engine began to sputter—to another already empty tank? And if his altitude was low at the time—say, only two hundred feet, he would have no chance to restart the stalled engine before the plane hit the ground; especially if the plane was hazardously nose-heavy.

Or could the reporter of this exchange with the air engineer have been mistaken—twice? Could he confuse "seven tanks" for six tanks, and "260 gallons" for 270 gallons? But even if error lies with the reporter, why did the interviewer for the Los Angeles Times report that Post told him the plane held 220 gallons? And why would Wiley, in his application for a restricted license, claim the plane's fuel capacity was 260 gallons? The fact emerges that Wiley did not know exactly how much fuel he carried, or how many fuel tanks were on the plane.

As Will Rogers knew nothing about the number of tanks aboard or their fuel capacity, this discussion at the Canadian Airways depot in no way shook his confidence in Wiley, which he had expressed in a telegram to Betty :

=AKLAVIK NWT AUG 10 800P (STAMPED) 1935 AUG 11 AM 8 14
MRS WILL ROGERS= BEVERLYHILLS CALIF
MOST MARVELOUS TRIP STOP NO DANGER WITH THIS GUY STOP WIRE
ME ALL NEWS FAIRBANKS ALASKA STOP LOVE=DAD

On August 12, at 3:40 p.m., Wiley's red plane was sighted over Fairbanks. For days it had been expected, now it was finally here. When the sound of the engine came within earshot, several hundred men and women in about seventy-five automobiles and on foot, rushed to Chet Spencer's homestead—that would later become part of Ladd Field, an Air Force Base, and is then the Army's Fort Wainwright. Chet's dock, appropriately named Spencer's Float, since it accommodated floatplanes setting down, was situated on the Chena River—referred to locally as Chena Slough[23]—some three miles from the center of town. A small stream, the Chena Slough—a tributary of the Tanana River, which in turn joins the Yukon River some 120 miles further west—wends its serpentine path through Fairbanks from east to west, dividing the city into two sections. Fairbanks, an old gold-mining town, had managed to survive when the 'yellow' ran out, but in 1935, it was still a small community of under 5,000 inhabitants. Still, Fairbanks believed that its destiny was to become the economic and cultural capital of Alaska. The city had ambitious plans, for instance, to make itself the North American hub of air traffic to Asia, and possibly Europe. Only very few of the city's dreams would materialize over the years, but in 1935, they were still generating a vitality in the community and siring a faith in the future.

Wiley made a perfect landing on the river and the plane taxied slowly up the stream, past a wooded area of birch and stunted spruce. Joe Crosson, who stood on the floating dock, directed his

---

[23] Chena Slough—pronounced "Cheena Slew."

friend Wiley with hand signals, as Wiley had no familiarity with Spencer's Float. Previously, he had flown into Fairbanks aboard the *Winnie Mae*, a land plane, and he had set down at the local airport, Weeks Field.

As Will crawled out of the plane, he spotted Crosson. "Want a rope, Joe?" he called out, then tossed a line. Once the plane got tied to the dock, Will took his first good look at the relatively narrow Chena Slough. Having just visited the wide Mackenzie River, and flown over the broad Yukon, Will drawled: "Is this all the river you got? Gotta have more river than that for an airplane."

Someone in the crowd called out: "Mr. Rogers, we're glad you're here!"

Will looked in the direction of the voice and shouted back: "Well, I'm glad I'm here too; I like these gold-mining towns. Been having a great time in Dawson talking with the old-timers."

Fairbanks' Mayor E. B. Collins was on hand to welcome the famous guests. So were Noel and Ada Wien, who had spotted the *Winnie Mae* back in 1933, when Wiley, lost, was circling for hours over Alaska on his solo trip. Noel himself had achieved aviation fame for having pioneered the Anchorage-to-Fairbanks mail flights in 1924.

In answer to the usual barrage of questions, Post tersely stated: "We flew from Aklavik by way of Herschel and Porcupine River. I don't know how long we'll be here or where we'll go from here. No, I haven't got any program." He also told the reporter for the *News-Miner*, Fairbanks's newspaper, that he would have some work done on the plane, though he did not go into specifics.

Once they had worked their way through the milling crowd, Wiley and Will loaded their little luggage into the Crossons' Chrysler, which bore the Alaskan license plate number 13, and Joe introduced Will to Lillian, his wife, and to their two children, Joe, Jr. and Don. Will, who responded warmly to children, seemed especially taken with little Joe, or Jody, as he was generally called.

As the Chrysler pulled away, an impromptu parade formed behind it. All the automobiles that had been driven out to Chet Spencer's followed the Crosson's car in one long column. The procession did not break up until Joe stopped at the Pioneer Hotel, where visitors to Fairbanks usually stayed.

The Pioneer Hotel, managed by the Gibbs family, stood proudly on Front street, facing the Chena Slough, a couple of blocks east of the only bridge; it had the distinction of being one of those rare hotels which had no lobby. As you entered, you had to turn sharply left, enter the bar, and there, with one foot up on the brass rail, you would sign the guest register. Will Rogers found it hilarious that he had to go to the bar to get his room key.[24]

Wiley spent the afternoon with his old friends, the Crossons, while Will went off on a sightseeing tour alone.

Both men were the guests of Lillian and Joe Crosson for dinner. Lillian prepared the recipe she usually served important guests—a dish she called Chicken Legs, and which Will enjoyed greatly. When he prodded Lillian about its ingredients, she admitted that the name was quite misleading, since there was no chicken in it.

> It was veal and pork and I had my butcher cut it for me so that I then could roll it in something like bread crumbs, and the only reason I recall this is because Will Rogers was teasing me about my chicken legs.
>
> I don't know what else I cooked with it—oh, yes, mashed potatoes. I had a young girl living with us; her name was Virginia Rothaker, and as part of her rent she helped out. Will wandered into the kitchen, and he assisted her by mashing those potatoes. I think I had a frozen dessert—but the chicken legs were something that he teased me about."[25]

Virginia also had a full-time job as the operator of Fairbanks's only elevator, located in the Federal Building at second and Cushman. That elevator was Virginia's pride—as if she had built it. While Will was mashing potatoes, Virginia repeatedly and more pressingly invited him to come downtown to ride in her elevator. Unable to resist her enthusiasm, Will promised faithfully to come and see it before he left town.

It was at Lillian and Joe Crosson's dinner table that the plan orig-

---

[24]Sterlings' interview with Warren Tilman, Fairbanks, July 21, 1986.
[25]Sterlings' interview with Lillian Crosson Frizell, April 29, 1987.

inated to go to Barrow. Joe had been telling Wiley and Will about the remarkable Charles Brower, the man known as the King of the Arctic, and Will decided he had to meet him. For close to half a century Brower had been operating a whaling station and trading post in Barrow, where he held the position of Commissioner, and as an officer of the U.S. government and the law performed the duties of administrator, policeman, judge and arbiter. Charley Brower had seen a world change and a history grow over the past fifty years in Alaska, and the stories Barrow had to tell Will wanted to share with his readers. "I'd rather see him than Greta Garbo," he would tell the press.

Will's curiosity knew no limits. A Fairbanks newspaper reporter asked Post when he got up, and, himself an early riser, Post admitted that Rogers arose even earlier. To illustrate the point, Post told the reporter that in Dawson City, he and Will had both gone to bed at three o'clock in the morning, but when Wiley got up three hours later, at six o'clock, Rogers was already walking around town.

Rogers then proceeded to tell the reporter that the residents of Dawson had wanted him and Post to stay longer, but he had told them that he had gained such a fine impression of the town, that he had better leave in a hurry before he changed his mind. "And they told me not to go to Aklavik because there was nothing there but Eskimos," Rogers added. "But I said, hell, that's what I want. I know what a white man will do. I want to know what an Eskimo will do. I like to have frozen at Aklavik. Water froze in the barrel the night we were there. It was the first time I had seen the Arctic Ocean, it was great."

Moving on to local topics, Will noted that he had already seen a dredge in Dawson so he saw no need to drive out and see the gold-mining operation near Fairbanks. "While in Fairbanks," Will announced, "I want to get a lot of books. That's all I can do in the plane, is read. Post won't tell you where he is going or anything. He'd have gone to Point Barrow yesterday [August 12] if he hadn't hit a head wind."

As an explanation, Will's comment about headwinds is baffling; as an excuse it strains credulity. Any pilot flies into headwinds. Already on the Arctic Ocean, all Post would have had to do to reach Point Barrow was to fly due west; instead he headed south and returned to the Alaskan interior. Of course, the weather could have been far worse than just 'headwinds,' perhaps as bad as it would be for the next few days, including the fifteenth, when Post and Rogers did set out for Barrow. But if the weather deterred Post on the twelfth, why did it not deter him three days later? Or had he reached the end of his patience by that time? The facts are that on the twelfth of August Post did not fly to Barrow because of headwinds; on the fifteenth of August, the weather bureau reported "no visibility, no ceiling," and yet Wiley went.

Around noon on August 13, Joe drove Wiley and Will out to show them his nearby Hi Yu mine, which Don Gustafson managed for the Crossons. His wife, Inez, prepared lunch and after the usual photograph-taking the three men headed back into town. Later that day, Post and Rogers also visited the experimental farm of the University of Alaska at Fairbanks. The agricultural experiments and abundant results surprised them because Alaska has a short growing season—the late spring and the early summer. They learned, though, that the northern latitudes afford the crops much longer periods of daylight than in the forty-eight states, which compensates for the shorter growing seasons.

While the two men were touring the University facilities, Warren Tilman, now back in Fairbanks, was inspecting Wiley's plane and going through "normal servicing." Actually, Tilman didn't like the plane. A low-wing plane has more lift and is speedier, and Tilman felt that putting floats on it defeated the purpose of making it faster. Nor did Tilman find Post to be his idea of a safe pilot. "I never liked his flying—he was always taking a chance."[26] When Tilman presented the bill for the maintenance work he had done, Will Rogers signed a check, without bothering to fill in the amount. Will also paid for the fuel.

Lillian Crosson had again invited Will and Wiley for dinner, but Will, reluctant to put her through a second night of kitchen work on his account, had insisted that she and Joe join him and Wiley at the Model Café. So at about 6:30 that evening the four of them were sitting in the old-fashioned booths, Will and Lillian on one side, Wiley and Joe on the other. While the two pilots on their side of the

[26]Sterlings' interview with Warren Tilman, July 21, 1986.

table discussed aviation, Will and Lillian talked—mostly about family and mostly about his family. Will showed her a picture and an article about Mary. "Will was so proud of her and her effort in the theater back in Maine—very proud of that."[27]

Pete and Alma Despot, part owners of the Model Café, were both at the restaurant when Will and his party entered. They had also rushed out to the float at Spencer's for the excitement the day before, when the two famous men landed, and with their new 16 mm motion picture camera Alma, from a raised knoll, did get excellent pictures of the arrival. Alma would long remember Will's surprise at the high Fairbanks prices. At the cash register, manned by her husband, Will put a five-dollar bill down on the counter, which in Los Angeles, or New York, would have covered the price of a meal for four. But in Fairbanks it was different. Pete Despot just looked at the five-dollar bill and laughed, "Hit it again, Will!"

Rogers looked a little puzzled; he had heard the expression used in twenty-one to call for an additional card, but never in connection with a restaurant meal. Pete Despot asked: "Do you play blackjack?"

Rogers admitted: "Well, I'm not much of a gambler but I've played it on occasion."

"Well, then hit it again!" Now Will understood; he took out a couple of silver dollars and placed them on the counter, "Here, are these any good? I just can't get used to these high prices." It was, of course, the cost of transportation that added so hugely to prices in Alaska, because virtually all goods had to travel nearly three thousand miles, in those days usually by boat from Seattle, then by train or plane. That explained, Will proceeded with Wiley and Joe to a meeting of the Q.B., the Quiet Birdmen, a pilots' organization.

Will was having a great time in Alaska, as his newspaper columns indicate. On Tuesday the thirteenth, he sent the following daily column:

> This Alaska is a great country. If they can just keep from being taken over by the U.S. they got a great future.
>
> There may be some doubt about the Louisiana Purchase being a mistake, but when Seward in '68 bought Alaska for

---

[27]Sterlings' Interview with Lillian Crosson Frizell, October 31, 1985

$7,000,000 he even made up for what we had overpaid the Indians for Manhattan Island.

The newspapers otherwise were reporting rumors of domestic differences in the Post marriage. Headlines in the Associated Press dispatched to *News-Miner*, Fairbanks, August 14, 1935 ranged from "GLOBE FLIER DENIES RIFT WITH SPOUSE" to "WILEY POST DECLARES REPORTS OF MARITAL DIFFERENCES ARE MERE RUMORS COOKED UP BY PRESS." Reporters pursued Wiley in Alaska. "Just a rumor. These damn newspapers will cook up anything," was Wiley's answer "with a laugh" as reported in the Fairbanks' *News-Miner*, on August 14, 1935. No less hounded by the press in San Francisco, Mae responded "Baloney," when she learned of the rumors, according to an Associated Press dispatch. She then explained that one of the reasons she did not accompany her husband to Alaska was her fear that the flight might prompt a recurrence of an appendicitis attack she had experienced during a recent trip.

The real reason for Mae's change of plans did not reach the newspapers until several days later. It came from Wiley Post's friend Harry Frederickson, an Oklahoma oilman who had helped finance Wiley's solo flight around the world. In an Associated Press wire story, he declared that:

> Rogers had arranged to pay all the expenses of the flight and [Post] had to fly when he wanted to and stop when and where and as long as he pleased. Frederickson declared that the fact that Rogers was paying the expenses of the flight was disclosed in a letter that Mrs. Post wrote to her parents, Mr. and Mrs. J. D. Laine of San Angelo, Tex. In this letter Mrs. Post said: "I intended to go to Alaska with my husband and Will Rogers but Mr. Rogers did not want me to go for some reason. After all, he is paying the expenses of the trip. What he said had to go."[28]

Any dispassionate analysis would conclude that under no circumstances of this Alaskan adventure could, or indeed should, Mae Post have gone along. It could be rationalized perhaps that as the wife of

---

[28]*Fairbanks New-Miner*, August 17, 1935.

the owner she was possibly excluded from the restrictions dictated by the 'R' license. But still, she could really perform no function on the planned trip. She could not send or receive Morse code messages, as Anne Lindbergh had learned to do, nor could she pilot a plane. She had no mechanical ability and spoke no foreign language. She would, however, simply add to the overall weight of the plane and thereby increase gas consumption.

Furthermore, the amenities inside Post's plane were terribly restricted. The cabin might have seemed spacious, even luxurious, to two teen-age flight enthusiasts; but not to two mature people, a fifty-five year old man and a young woman, who would have to sit for hour after hour of flight day after day for possibly weeks wedged together on a bench-like double seat. Inconvenient and confined, the cabin offered no comfortable space to relax and no toilet facilities. For a man as decorous as Will Rogers, this plane had no room for another person, whether it was Mae Post, or anyone else. Wiley Post must have realized that too.

So did Fay Gillis Wells. When she had been planning to accompany Wiley Post, she was firmly convinced that Mae Post would never come along on the trip to the Soviet Union, no matter what the newspapers were printing.[29] For whatever reason, the pretense of Mae Post accompanying her husband had been maintained. In the end, while Mae Post complained to friends about her not going to Alaska, it saved her life.

August 14 promised to be a beautiful day in Fairbanks. Up early, as usual, Will was having his breakfast at the Pioneer Hotel, where Warren Tilman joined him. It was shortly after 6:30 a.m. Nellie Norris, the waitress, was serving the two men more coffee, when suddenly the old cook burst out of the kitchen. He was at least seventy-five years old—neither he nor anyone else could remember when he was born—and a great Will Rogers fan. Having seen every one of Will's films, he could not bear to miss the opportunity to see his favorite film star in person and maybe even shaking Will's hand. "Boy," he said to Rogers, "you sure can shoot!" Will seemed puzzled. "You know, I seen you shoot in the movies."

---

[29]Sterlings' interview with Mrs. Fay Gillis Wells, November 12, 1985

"Anybody can shoot in the movies," Will tried to explain. "I probably couldn't hit the side of a barn."

"Boy," the cook insisted, "you can't tell me that. I seen you shoot in the movies, and you sure can shoot."

After breakfast, Will stopped by the post office to mail the weekly article he had typed the day before to the newspaper syndicate in New York City. It contained some newly acquired inside information about Alaska:

> An Eskimo dog from the time he is just a half-sized pup is never untied. He is always tied with a chain, and he don't bark at all, he howls. They call all Eskimos 'Huskies.' I always thought it was the dogs that were called 'Huskies' but it's the Eskimos themselves.
>
> "That's enough northern knowledge for one lesson, especially when some of it maybe ain't so."[30]

The morning report from Point Barrow's weather station on August 14 ruled out any trip in that direction for Will and Wiley or anyone else. Another day's postponement of the flight to Barrow enabled Will to visit the colony that Franklin Roosevelt's Federal Emergency Relief Administration had only recently settled in the extremely fertile valley of the Matanuska River. At the same time that the plan gave some two hundred impoverished farm families of the forty-eight states a new start, it also further developed and settled Alaska.

Rumors about governmental mismanagement of the project had, however, reached the newspapers, which were reporting that not enough housing would be ready before winter weather arrived. Will had to see for himself.

At 10:45 a.m., Joe Crosson drove Rogers, Post, and Joe Barrows, PAA's Divisional Engineer, to Weeks Field, where Warren Tilman was waiting outside a Pacific Alaska Airways Lockheed Electra. Warren said to Will: "You just sit anywhere and taking off or landing,

---

[30]Will Rogers's daily column which appeared August 15, 1935

you buckle that belt; then after you get in the air, just unbuckle it and you can walk all around."

Will settled into his seat and began to tighten the belt. "With me and Wiley it's different," he told Tilman. "In his airplane I walk around only when he's landed." Post shot Will a quick look.

As the Electra readied for takeoff, a reporter asked Joe Crosson, Operations Manager for PAA, where they were going. Crosson, who was to pilot the plane, shrugged his shoulders and smiled mischievously: "I don't know!" he claimed.

The plane arrived at Savage Camp, McKinley Park, at noon. The party stayed only five minutes on the ground before taking off and flying around the peak of Mt. McKinley, which they viewed from all sides. Then they headed toward Palmer, in the Matanuska Valley. When they arrived over the small town's still primitive airstrip, Joe Crosson circled it several times and decided the surface was too rough to land the large Electra. Anchorage lay only minutes away, but Crosson first detoured over the valley for about fifteen minutes to give his guests a perfect aerial view of the terrain and the building activity in the entire area, the panorama of mountains majestically surrounding the delta basin, where the Susitna River and a dozen streams had deposited rich topsoil for centuries.

Crosson landed at Anchorage's Merrill Field at 1:30 p.m. Anchorage had been expecting a visit by Rogers and Post, but in Wiley's red floatplane. When the big silver Electra with wheels arrived, no one connected it with them. However, the moment Rogers stepped from the plane, the news spread through the city, and residents came from all parts of town to see the two celebrities. By then Post, Rogers, Crosson, and Barrows had gone to the Anchorage Grill counter for lunch.

The four men joked and chatted with the crowd as they ate. Post said: "We are just bumming around, been to Dawson, Whitehorse, Aklavik and Fairbanks, and don't know where all we will go—but we'll visit Nome." He also explained that on his trip to Russia he would have to "hunt out" the landing places offered by communities at which he would stop because he had not been given exact information as to where the landing fields were. Asked whether he would be accompanied by Rogers on his contemplated flight to Moscow, Post said: "Go, ask him!"

Rogers did not comment on his future plans. Instead, reaching for a piece of pie, he asked, "How's the tourist business—lots of people coming this way?" Someone in the crowd told him that ships coming up the coast were crowded to capacity and that hundreds weekly were going over the Alaska Railroad. "Yes, and there will be more every year," Rogers predicted, "they will get their money's worth. Alaska's scenic charms and climate are a permanent lure and asset. Hope she works it for all its worth. It will bring fortunes to the country.   Alaska has something the others haven't."

"Will you go fishing for one of Alaska's famous rainbow trout or try to get a bear while you are here?" someone asked him.

"Nope—don't fish—don't hunt—wouldn't know what to use for bait or how to shoot or what to do with the victims. Just don't have the urge," Rogers answered.

At the airport Will made arrangements with Oscar Winchell, 'flying cowboy' of the Star Air Service, for a flight to Palmer in a small plane piloted by Chet McLean, a well known Alaskan pilot. But Wiley, the great pilot, proved to be a poor passenger. He kept looking for problems, and when he saw the landing field at Palmer, he exclaimed: "Jees! that field looks rough." Rogers, on the other hand, took a short after-lunch nap on the flight.

They arrived at 3:15 p.m. To the farmers who had settled in Palmer and the Matanuska colony, Will Rogers brought a welcome reminder of home. Although his weekly radio broadcasts, which gave America such a reassuring voice during these years of the Depression, were not aired in Alaska, they had Will Rogers, the very man, in front of them, and they all wanted to see him, hear him, talk to him, touch him.

Before Rogers could even squeeze out of the plane, the questions were bounding: "How do you feel, Mr. Rogers?"

"Why, uh, why—wait'll I get out, will you?" he drawled kindly. "I came to look around, not to report on my health. Where you boys from?" he asked, pressing into the crowd. "Anybody here from Claremore?" Everybody thought that one funny, and no one hailed from that part of Oklahoma. Wiley meanwhile watched from the sidelines, overlooked and forgotten, he stood at the edge of the crowd.

Someone shouted: "How do you think you'll like Russia?" obviously referring to the rumors that Rogers might accompany Post across Siberia. Not wanting to divulge his plans, Will parried, "Russia? Russia?" he asked, as if perplexed. "Say, I saw a Communist here a minute ago!" Then pointing at a farmer whose full red beard reached halfway down his chest, he cried out: "There he is!"

After a motor tour of several of the camps and a visit to a few of the newly built homes, with the project administrator, L. P. Hunt, an impressed Will Rogers offered this verdict: "The valley looks great, you have a mighty fine place here and the crops look good."

When they returned to the small plane and Rogers was just about to close the door, the construction gang's cook rushed up to him with a handful of brown, fat cookies. Rogers took a bite, brushed off the crumbs. "Very good!" he announced, "but I'll toss them out if we can't get off the ground!" Pilot McLean inched the plane forward. Will had left them laughing.

They were back in Fairbanks by 7:30 p.m.

On Thursday, August 15, Will was again up early, as usual. Again he ate breakfast at the Pioneer Hotel, and again Warren Tilman joined him. That morning on his walk about Fairbanks, he stopped to buy a book telling of the purchase of Alaska from Russia. With a grin, Will explained to the sales girl that he wanted "to learn how the Russians swindled us." The reporter from the *Fairbanks News-Miner*, who followed Will everywhere, wanted to know whether the two famous men would be on hand for the Gold Discovery celebration set for the next day, Friday, August 16. Will wanted to know more about it, and learned that among the events the Fairbanks baseball team would be playing against Dawson. Will promptly wrote a check for $100 that he wanted to be presented to the Fairbanks team.[31]

While Will was walking about town, Wiley Post and Joe Crosson went—of all things—house hunting. Wiley had fallen in love with Alaska, and decided that he would settle down in Fairbanks with Mae, and near his friend Joe. Like him, Wiley could prospect for gold and find his own mine; and the two of them could do things together, like wolf hunting. Wiley found just the house he wanted on Cushman Street, near the school. Without hesitation, on the morning of August 15, Wiley Post rented it.

Afterward, the two friends drove to the airport, where Crosson once more went over charts with Wiley and explained to him again the various routes, the passes, and landmarks, as he pointed out the dangers facing a pilot in the Arctic region. Shoving a selection of maps toward Wiley, Crosson said, "Here, you may need them."

Official documents state that "both Post and Rogers discussed with Crosson and others their proposed flights, and. . . . Post remarked that in their flying about Alaska, under no circumstances would he fly with Rogers "in or above any cloud or fog bank. His plan was to travel as safely as possible by so-called contact flying, turning back and landing in lake or river at any time when the weather made it dangerous to proceed."[32]

Wiley believed that he could lift off from Chena Slough with a fully laden aircraft, but Joe Crosson's wiser counsel prevailed. It was decided that Wiley and Will would take off from Fairbanks with partially filled fuel tanks, and fly to Harding Lake, some 50 miles southeast of the city. There Wiley could have the tanks topped and with an entire lake as his runway, he would have no difficulty lifting a heavy craft off the surface.

The weather in Fairbanks was perfect. At noon the thermometer had reached sixty degrees, with a gentle three-miles-an-hour breeze. But the first of two daily radio reports from Barrow was discouraging. The early morning temperature, so Sergeant Stanley Morgan of the U.S. Signal Corps manning the WAMCATS station at Barrow reported, was forty degrees and conditions were "Dense fog, nil, nil, S9," i.e., "nil" ceiling, "nil" visibility, with a southerly wind of nine miles. It was the kind of weather report every pilot dreaded, for with no view of the ground a plane could not land.

Will finished a weekly column and slipped it into an envelope. Then he sent a telegram to Mary:

FAIRBANKS, ALASKA, AUGUST 15,1935

---

[32]Official statement by "Department of Commerce, Washington D.C., released September 4, 1935

MARY ROGERS, SKOWHEGAN MAINE

GREAT TRIP. WISH YOU WERE ALONG. HOW'S YOUR ACTING? YOU AND
MAMA WIRE ME ALL THE NEWS TO NOME. GOING TO POINT BARROW
TODAY. FURTHEST POINT OF LAND ON WHOLE AMERICAN CONTINENT.
LOTS OF LOVE. DON'T WORRY. DAD

Just before 11 a.m., Lillian Crosson and her two small children
drove to the Pioneer Hotel to pick up Will and his luggage. With
young Jody, now relegated to the back seat, Will climbed into the
Chrysler next to Lillian and held one-year-old Don on his lap. Rogers
asked Lillian to stop at Lavery Bailey's grocery store at Cushman
and Second, where Will loaded up on cans of chili. He put them in
the car. Then, Will walked across to Vic Brown's Jewelry store to
pick up a gold wristwatch he had left for repair.[33]

Will Rogers did not wear a wristwatch. The watch he had had
repaired belonged to Wiley—a fact that should settle an old dispute
for all time. Investigations of the crash in the 1930s turned up certain
puzzling time inconsistencies about the day's events. These discrep-
ancies had been glossed over with the unlikely conclusion that Wiley's wristwatch was set on Oklahoma time. Why that should be so,
as Wiley had not recently been in Oklahoma, defies reason. Still it
was widely accepted as an explanation. If, however, Wiley's gold
wristwatch came directly from a Fairbanks jewelry store, it seems
reasonable to assume that Mr. Brown, like his colleagues everywhere
else, would have wound and set the watch before returning it to Will.
And he would obviously have set it to local time.

Outside the jewelry store, autograph seekers, curious passersby,
admirers and amateur photographers again awaited Will. At no time
during Will's stay, though, did the citizens of Fairbanks intrude on
his privacy; conversation and pleasantries with the people on the
street or in the shops came usually at his initiative. Back in the car,
Will asked Lillian to make one more stop. At the Federal Building,
as he had promised Virginia Rothaker, Will dutifully rode her elevator to the second floor and back down. He shook hands with Virginia and then was off to the dock.

---

[33]Sterlings' Interview with Mrs. Lillian Crosson Frizell.

When Will reached Spencer's Float, Joe and Wiley had already arrived. Joe was still trying to dissuade his friend from leaving Fairbanks in the face of the threatening morning weather report, but Wiley was intent on moving on. Joe even offered to pilot Will and Wiley to Barrow in one of PAA's Fairchild 71s—but not this day. Having none of it, Wiley said, "We might as well go, anyway." And Will supported him: "There's lots of lakes we can land on."[34] By way of compromise, Post did agree to telephone Joe from Harding Lake in order to learn the afternoon weather report, which was expected before 2 p.m.

At dockside Will handed Joe Crosson the column to be mailed and the telegram to Mary. When Betty later received the telegram, she read the phrase "YOU AND MAMA WIRE ME ALL THE NEWS TO NOME" as a clear indication that Will had made his decision: he would go on with Wiley to Russia. Now she would have to make arrangements for a flight from Maine back to California so she could prepare for the trip to Europe, perhaps even Moscow, where she would meet Will.

Will and Wiley climbed into the plane, the door closed. The time was 11:30 a.m. The engine was warm; it had been idling with the plane tied to the float. Joe Crosson unhitched the ropes. Wiley taxied away from shore.

Takeoff from the Chena River depended on the wind direction. On the morning of August 15, the wind came from the west; Wiley would take off down-river, where the Chena soon curves to the right. When PAA pilots did a down-river takeoff, they always made the turn first and then lifted off the water. The more experienced pilots had developed the technique whereby they would lift one float out of the water as they entered the curve of the river and then take off in the turn. As Wiley Post had never taken off from the Chena River, it is safe to assume that Joe Crosson had told him the usual technique employed by Alaskan pilots in takeoffs from the river.

Once in the center of the river, Post turned to face into the wind and started downriver, quickly on the step, then very quickly off the water and onto a very steep climb. In the air well before the bend in the river, he climbed steeply over the trees. Watching the takeoff,

---

[34]Ex: *Fairbanks News-Miner*, August 16, 1935.

Robert J. Gleason, Communications Superintendent for Pacific Alaska Airways, heard pilots who were standing nearby remark that "with a takeoff like that, if the engine quit, he's a goner." It was obvious that Wiley had 'over-powered' the plane, so that he had been able to literally jump the craft out of the water. Pilots and mechanics remembered how carefully, by comparison, Post had taken off two years earlier, when he was flying the *Winnie Mae* solo around the world. Then he had taken the whole field before lifting off in a very slow climb.[35]

Harding Lake was a cool, scenic refuge, away from the sometimes stifling summer heat of Fairbanks; a few year-round residents lived there, but most of the houses dotting the shore saw use only during the hot summer months. The arrival of a plane at the lake always drew a crowd of children, and even some adults. Post and Rogers had not been expected at the summer colony, so when the plane was first heard, everyone thought it was "another airplane that used to land out there every once in a while. Old Pan American had, what had originally been a tri-motor, and they just put one motor on it and ran it on floats. So whenever an airplane came over, we always ran down to the landing, that's where the airplanes came in. And that's why we were there. There were my two sisters and some other kids."[36]

The dock at Harding Lake was simple, without facilities; just some planks built on a few piles, it jutted a few feet over the edge of the shore. Joe Crosson had made arrangements for the delivery of aviation fuel from Fairbanks. Hours earlier a little blue 1931 Chevrolet pickup truck with mechanic Ron Taylor, four other men, and some drums of gasoline had rattled off the highway to Tok,[37] a trip that usually took at least an hour and a half. Warren Tilman, however, claims to have set the record for the fastest time from Harding Lake to Fairbanks. He made it in "a little over an hour, but that's the fastest ride that I ever went on." He had urgent reason: his wife had gone into labor that morning.[38]

---

[35]From Sterlings' correspondence with Robert J. Gleason, November 30, 1985
[36]Sterlings' Interview with Forbes Baker, November 16, 1986.
[37]Sterlings' interview with Gene Rogge, Fairbanks, July 21, 1986.
[38]Sterlings' interview with W. Tilman, July 21, 1986

When Wiley's plane arrived at Harding Lake, the PAA crew sent by Crosson, set to work immediately. They pulled the plane partly onto shore and then hand-pumped gasoline to top off all the tanks. They had finished shortly after 1:00 p.m. Wiley had not yet called Crosson, as he had promised to, in order to learn the afternoon Barrow weather report. There was no telephone at the lake, but two saloons in the area had telephones just a short ride away, had Wiley asked for a lift in the pickup truck to either tavern. The "18 miles Roadhouse" stood, as the name suggested, at the eighteen-mile marker outside of Fairbanks, some thirty miles back toward town, and driving only a very short distance in the opposite direction, at mile fifty-two, was the "Silver Fox Roadhouse." Wiley Post made no attempt to get to either of them, nor did he make use of Lake Harding's one-way telephone line by which he could have rung Fairbanks.

At 1:30 p.m., Fairbanks received the expected weather report from Barrow. It had changed little since the morning: BARROW ONE THIRTY PM DENSE FOG ZERO ZERO FORTY FIVE SOUTH NINE." Unmistakably, and alarmingly, there was still dense fog, and ceiling and visibility were still zero, the wind still south at nine miles per hour, and the temperature was forty-five degrees. Crosson, who had still, contrary to their arrangement, not heard from Wiley, hastily dispatched a copy of the weather report by automobile to Lake Harding.

Wiley took off from the lake close to 2:00 p.m, a half hour after the weather report had been received from Barrow. He would have had sufficient time to learn the weather conditions at his destination, if he had but telephoned. For reasons known only to him, Wiley did not pursue this vital information and by the time the automobile from Fairbanks labored up to the dock at Lake Harding, Wiley Post and Will Rogers had long left in a plane with no operational radio aboard. There was no way now to alert Wiley to the zero zero conditions that might have made him recall his pledge: "under no circumstances would he fly with Rogers in or above any cloud or fog bank."

Wiley Post had taken off, 'making his own weather.'

CHAPTER XI

TO BARROW AND BACK

WILEY POST HAD taken off from Harding Lake before 2 p.m. He must have followed Joe Crosson's instructions, because what little is known of the next few hours match the route Joe charted for what appeared to be an easy, straight-forward trip. That is, of course, if one had good weather.

By heading for Barrow without the 1:30 p.m. weather report, Wiley had not acted wisely. And he continued to make mistakes as the afternoon wore on.

A narrow finger of Alaska continues about twelve miles farther northward, ending as "Point Barrow." This is the northernmost extent of land of the North American continent. Flying more or less due north from Fairbanks, as Joe Crosson had advised Wiley, pilots reached the Beaufort Sea near Cape Halket, which lies to the southeast of Barrow. The Beaufort Sea is really just a designation for a small section of the Arctic Ocean. Once pilots arrived at the water's edge, the shoreline served as a perfect approach guide to Barrow. All a pilot had to do then was follow the shore to the northwest, or as the natives called it, the up-coast, directly to Barrow. Though a longer route than one setting a straight course for the village, flying up-coast eliminated any possible chance of missing Barrow. Aiming directly for Barrow held one major drawback. On reaching the coastline, a pilot had to determine whether to turn left or right to reach Barrow, without the benefit of clearly identifiable landmarks along either coast. This quandary could cost a pilot valuable fuel and time. Wiley had followed Crosson's advice, and flown due north to the Beaufort Sea.

Separating the North Slope area of Alaska from the rest of the state, spreading from east to west across the entire width of the land, lie the formidable Endicott Mountains, which include the Brooks Range. A rugged and barren chain of mountains, about eighty miles deep, the Endicotts reach their highest peak at 9,239 feet. Pilots flying to the north, or returning, never flew over the ranges. They flew through the lowest passes, a flight path that demanded both experience and daring, because as pilots had to negotiate unexpected turns and sudden twists between walls of towering mountainsides at speeds exceeding a hundred miles per hour. Even under ideal conditions, a flight from Fairbanks to Barrow was considered "hazardous as hell."

> From Fairbanks to Barrow—Ah! There's the rub. Only about 650 miles in an airplane, but over the precipitous Endicott Range. The saw-toothed mountains of the range leave no place in which to 'sit down' in case of mishap and no way in which to get out, even if a forced landing could be made, and a region, too, particularly subject to storm and fog.
>
> I had questioned the seemingly exorbitant rate as established, $750 for the trip, and was told that the trip is of such hazardous and uncertain character by reason of the terrain and the weather that the airways cannot risk the plane and the life of the pilot for any ordinary commercial fare, and that any contract for passage is subject to reservation: 'God willing and the weather permitting.'
>
> I now concede the reasonableness of the charge.[1]

---

[1]Ex: *New York Herald Tribune*, Aug. 17, 1935, p. 2. The account is From the Point Barrow "Settlement Quarterly," published by Dr. Henry Greist.The article was writ-

With Crosson's carefully marked maps Wiley would have had no problems flying north, until he reached the North Slope, where the basin on the north side of the Brooks Range held the fog and the low-lying clouds. While the area south of the dividing range basked in summer, the region north of it already showed harsh signs of the coming winter. New York might be sweltering in ninety-degree heat and matching humidity, but not in northern Alaska. There, the warm air meeting the Arctic ice floes created the impenetrable fog and clouds that Wiley had promised not to fly into with Rogers aboard.

Surely, Wiley must have been torn between his own mission and his duty to Will Rogers. Rogers, after all, was covering every expense and enabling Wiley to mark his route to Europe, yet Rogers was also continually delaying him with wishes that sent them detouring all over the territory. Wiley knew that the approaching winter would increase the difficulty and risk in his venture. Time was important. If he was going to wait every time he encountered a cloud or a bit of fog, he would never make it to Russia before the Siberian winter, when any malfunction would surely spell disaster for a couple of men lost in a small aircraft. If they did not fly now, Wiley must have thought, then they were facing a possible delay for another year. Ice floes drifting southward had already been reported in the Chukchi Sea off Barrow.

Wiley's gold wristwatch would have told him that in the elapsed time since he had left Fairbanks, he should have reached the north coast of Alaska a long time ago. But Wiley Post was lost, which was no cause for alarm—at least not yet. He had been lost before, many times. Like any lost pilot flying over unfamiliar territory with few or no identifying landmarks, he had procedures he could follow. He could fly a straight line until he found a river, railroad tracks, a mountain, or a town to provide a point of reference. Or, if he thought he had perhaps passed his target, he could begin flying ever larger circles until he discovered it. He could, except as Wiley would have known, this time, it was different; quite different.

Post's floatplane was circling over northern Alaska's thousands of square miles of unchanging, level tundra, dotted with a myriad of

ten in the summer of 1934 by Lewis T. Greist, of Chicago, Dr. Greist's brother, who had come to visit.

shallow lakes. During the short summer months in flat northern Alaska, ice and permafrost minimally melt to create meandering rivulets and creeks that will find each other and then combine. In twisted courses they flow slowly first one way, then another, then part to create islands, before uniting once again. Over the centuries these streams have cut into the tundra and washed away some of the loose surface soil to form shallow lakes. During the severe winter months their frozen surfaces make ideal landing places for ski-equipped planes; in the summertime, every lake becomes a harbor for a floatplane. Ordinarily Post could easily have set the plane down near a trapper's cabin or an Eskimo's hunting camp on any one of those bodies of water. On August 15, 1935, however, conditions being extraordinary, he could not see a single one of them. Below the plane, from horizon to horizon, stretched the unbroken, indefinable layer of dense fog and thick clouds forecast in the weather report Wiley had ignored.

Wiley had violated the most basic of all Alaskan flight rules: 'Never make your own weather!' Never believe the weather will be different than reported! It was an axiom based on experience and gained at the cost of many a lost life and wrecked plane. Before taking off from Fairbanks, Wiley knew the dangerous weather conditions north of the Brooks Range. The morning report from Barrow—dense fog, nil, nil; zero ceiling, zero visibility—could not have been less ambiguous or more prohibitive. In 1935, any pilot would have known that under such conditions at his destination, he could not land. But Wiley Post was not just 'any' pilot. He imagined himself indestructible, and thought he could control any situation, for he always had in the past and would always be able to do so in the future!

Should they run into a little bad weather, the resolute Wiley had quipped at the dockside at Fairbanks, they could always set down on one of the lakes, "open some of that chili and throw a party."[2]

Rogers had written that Wiley was "tough as a boot physically, and as determined as a bull."[3] If a virtue, Post's determination would have worked against him as he circled blind over the North Slope,

---

[2]Account by Rex Beach, dated Fairbanks August 22, 1935.
[3]Will Rogers's Article, September 10, 1933.

for even then he could have turned around and sought the safety of the fair weather. Although he would not have been able to see the mountain passes, he could have climbed above the highest peak and flown back some two hundred miles. He would still have had fuel enough for a retreat.

As the plane's single engine droned on steadily, Wiley was circling ever farther westward. Slowly the plane banked. No wisdom could lie in speed now; speed would only consume more fuel. Wiley could not foresee how long he could have to keep the plane aloft, so the more fuel he had, the longer he could fly, and the better would be his chances of finding a clearing. All he needed, for one brief moment, was a break in the cover, for once he could see the ground, he could land and wait for the fog to lift. Wiley's vision, however, was limited not only by the oversized engine cowl directly in front of him,[4] but also by the loss of sight in his left eye. While he stared out the right side of the cockpit, that single, life-saving opening in the overcast could slip by on his blind side and he would never know it. Even if the plane had had space for another person to look out from the left side of the cockpit, Post could not have asked Rogers to come forward from his seat in the rear section because the plane was flying nose-heavy.

On August 15, natives tending a reindeer herd on the tundra some ninety miles from Barrow heard the sound of a plane flying overhead three different times. Obviously the craft was circling, for it would approach from the east, fly off toward the west and then—later—reappear from the east.

That day, too, Gus Massick, a trader from Demarcation Point, was en route to Barrow in an open motorboat in the late afternoon. Crossing Smith's Bay, some sixty miles east of Barrow, he distinctly heard a plane overhead and once even caught sight of it. He then heard the plane head toward the tundra and after a while return, circling once again, evidently in search of some landmark. As far as Massick could tell, the plane finally went west along the up-coast. Massick, a veteran of the Arctic who had accompanied the famous

---

[4]Sterlings' Interview with Alaskan veteran mechanic James Hutchison, Fairbanks, July 22, 1986

explorer Vilhjalmur Stefansson on his northern expeditions, had been surprised to hear a plane aloft with the weather "very thick." He felt certain that the plane had missed Barrow because of the fog: "It was flying low and evidently looking for a place to settle."[5]

An Eskimo also heared the plane above Point Tangent, some fifty miles from Barrow. He reported it to Thomas P. Brower, the oldest son, by the second marriage, of Charley Brower[6]—the King of the Arctic—who authored the book *Fifty Years Below Zero*, and the man Will Rogers was flying to Barrow to meet. The men at Tom Brower's reindeer ranch some seventy air miles out of Barrow, had also heard the plane, and had spotted it circling. Since they could see the plane, they thought that the pilot must have seen them too; they were disappointed when he did not land on the nearby lake. The ranch hands further confirmed that "we had a dense fog and it came out about ten or twelve miles north of my ranch and it was right down to the bottom—you couldn't cut it with a knife to go through." Had Wiley seen them and landed, he would have found the ranch well stocked with provisions and drums of gasoline.

A radio, too, might have saved the lives of Post and Rogers. Wiley had a radio aboard the plane and had passed an examination that proved him capable of operating it. While he sat in the pilot seat, however, the radio was just 135 pounds of dead weight. A pilot fully occupied with keeping a difficult plane level and on course could not possibly deal with the radio as well.

So Wiley circled, and the engine droned on and on, its constant, monotonous noise numbing the senses. Will Rogers, unless he was napping, must have been aware of the plane's circular path. Consulting his pocket watch, he must have wondered, too, why the four-hour trip to Barrow had already taken nearly six. Although he had supreme confidence in Wiley's ability, the flight for the gregarious and talkative Rogers must have been a trying time. Once, on his 1926 flying trip into Russia, Rogers had found himself the only passenger with a Soviet pilot and his mechanic, neither of them able to speak

---

[5] Letter written December 27, 1935, by Charles D. Brower, U.S. Commissioner at Barrow.
[6] Sterlings' interview with Thomas P. Brower, July 25, 1986;

English. Rogers remarked then that what concerned him most during the long flight "was keeping my mouth shut a whole day"[7]. In addition, the cabin quarters of Wiley's float-plane afforded Rogers's five-foot-eleven-inch frame slight comfort. A restless man whose foremost pleasures lay in physical activity: riding, roping calves, playing polo—he did not sit and do nothing well. And his mind was never idle. An agile writer, he composed his weekly articles of some one thousand five hundred words entirely in his head, so that, when he sat down at the typewriter, he had only to type what he had already written mentally. Nor did he ever rewrite or make corrections. In fact, he never even re-read his finished manuscript. "I'm getting writing wages, not reading wages," was his explanation.

On August 15, in the confines of the aft section, Rogers evidently occupied himself with his next weekly article. It tells the story of Mickey, the Crosson's wire-haired fox terrier, and it had been told to Will by Don Gustafson, the manager of Joe Crosson's gold mine. One day, little Mickey sniffed out a bear that had ventured too close to camp, and with terrier courage 'attacked' him.

The third page of the article was still in the typewriter:

> . . . well, as a matter of fact Mickey went out and the bear chased him in, and Ernest had to shoot the bear to keep him from running Mickey under the bed. They say there is more fellows been caught by a bear just that way.
>
> An old pet dog jumps the bear and then they hike straight to you, and the bear after 'em, and the first thing you know you have a bear in your lap, and a dog between your feet.
>
> So there is two kinds of bear dogs; the ones that drive 'em away and the ones that bring 'em in. Little Mickey thought he had done it; As Ernest said, he chewed all the hair off the bear, after death . . .

Will stopped here at the word "death." For some reason Will had put the typewriter aside. Perhaps he planned to finish the column later, but he never would. Perhaps he had put the typewriter aside

---

[7]*There's Not a Bathing Suit in Russia & Other Bare Facts* 1927, Albert & Charles Boni, New York

and leafed through a copy of the *News-Miner*, the Fairbanks newspaper. Or maybe he continued reading *Arctic Village*, the book Joe Crosson had given him in Juneau. For hours he had nothing to look at outside the windows, except the same cottony grayness that hid both earth and sky.

To keep his circling course, Wiley would have had to check his instrument panel and done some calculations. He had started from Harding Lake, some fifty miles southeast of Fairbanks, with his fuel tanks topped. His four wing tanks held fifty-six gallons each; plus he had a thirty-gallon tank under his seat and a sixteen-gallon head tank for a total of 270 gallons of gasoline in his six fuel tanks. Wiley may have been in error by ten gallons as to the total volume of fuel, but he did know correctly that his Pratt & Whitney Wasp engine consumed thirty-two gallons an hour just to keep a steady cruising speed of 125 miles per hour. The plane was capable of a maximum speed of 180 mph. Wiley could probably have estimated that he had used close to two hundred gallons since leaving Harding Lake and that he therefore had enough fuel left to stay aloft for about two more hours—enough perhaps to fly south of the mountains and land in sunshine. He need not worry about darkness, because at this latitude the mid-August sun would not set until close to midnight—long after the last drop of fuel would have been used.

It seems reasonable to assume that Wiley was planning to use up the fuel in wing and head tanks first, before switching to the one beneath his seat, the one with the gauge. That thirty-gallon tank, his final reserve, would provide him slightly less than one hour's fuel supply. In that hour he would have to plan and execute an emergency landing.

Just after 7:30 p.m., Wiley evidently did see something below. He dropped lower and banked. He could not be sure. He dropped lower still, until he was barely twenty feet above the tundra. He now took in the hazy picture: An Eskimo summer hunting camp sat along a wide river outlet to the sea; people were moving about, a lone figure stood by the water's edge. Along most of the western Alaska shoreline on the Chukchi Sea runs a narrow beach from which an abrupt embankment rises about twenty feet to form a palisade-like barrier. Over time, the force of the water has cut through these plateaus and lowered the riverbeds to sea level. Such a river is the Walakpa. When it eventually joins the Chukchi Sea some ten miles southwest of Barrow, it first creates a sizeable lagoon. The Walakpa River, too, had cut deep into the tundra plateau and carved a break into the embankment, so that at high tide the ocean and the river became one. However, the shoreline was still elevated enough so that at low tide only the occasional wave would wash over the land barrier and the estuary basin held the river's water in a small, very shallow lagoon. Wiley circled the water and noted a long sandbank dividing the lagoon. He could see smoke wafting from the fire where dinner had been prepared. Instinctively he must have registered that it was an on-shore breeze. He circled one more time. He had to be sure of his landing site, for in seconds a submerged rock could slash open a pontoon. Wiley could see that the lagoon was quite shallow, and he planned to keep his coasting to a minimum. He lined up the plane and dropped, touching water quite close to shore. He taxied until he heard the floats scrape sand, then he cut the motor and shut off the line leading to the fuel tank. They had made it.

Wiley got out of his seat and Will Rogers walked forward; both men stepped on the wing, down onto the floats, and waded through a few feet of shallow water to the shore. The cold water did not bother them as both men wore rubber boots.[8] Will Rogers walked about; he stretched his legs, inhaled the fresh air. Approaching the plane from the Eskimo encampment came forty-four-year-old Clair Okpeaha.[9] It was his fourteen-year-old adopted son, Patrick, whom Wiley had spotted from the air, standing by the water's edge.

The Okpeaha family had been hunting on that site for a few weeks. Other families had left once August had come. With summer almost past, the Okpeaha family, too, had made arrangements to leave. They had just finished supper when they first heard the faint hum of a distant motor and rushed out of their tent. Stella, Clair's wife, who taught Sunday school at Barrow, had been cleaning up after dinner with eleven-year-old Rose, while the two younger boys—Robert, age eight, and Fred age five—played nearby. Sadie, the youngest, was still too small to take notice of events. None of them had thought that it could be a plane. "It was cold that day and it

---

[8] *Washington Herald*, August 17, 1935.
[9] Clair Okpeaha, born February 5, 1891, died January 10, 1973.

was foggy and drizzle little bit. We were waiting for the boats to come and pick us up. My uncle sent a message through somebody that he was going to come with two boats. We were waiting then."[10]

The Okpeahas were surprised when out of the fog emerged the circling plane. Finally it landed close to shore. Watching from the tent, Rose and the younger children could not hear what was said at the edge of the lagoon, where Post told Clair and Patrick that he was lost. Post then asked the direction to Barrow, and how far away it was. Clair Okpeaha, who spoke broken English, shrugged and merely pointed toward the north. "Twenty miles, maybe thirty miles," he said.[11]

'Miles,' a white man's measure, had little meaning to Clair. Patrick just stood by and studied the two men; his English was about as limited as his father's, but he understood every word. The always affable Will learned from Clair that the hunt had been very good and had provided them with walrus, seal, and caribou for their winter food supply.

When Clair indicated that Barrow lay to the north, Wiley would have realized that he had landed on the down-coast. He must have then appreciated his good fortune in spotting this camp on the very edge of the continent, for if he had continued in his search westward above the overcast, he would have been soon flying over the open sea in the direction of Siberia. Had the fog lifted shortly after that, he would have seen nothing below him but the vast Arctic Ocean, and he would not have known whether he had flown too far north off the continent, or too far to the west.

Rogers and Post walked around, about fifty feet away and back again, stretching muscles that had been cramped for more than six hours. They were the objects of close study by the rest of the Okpeaha family, but none of them approached the two strangers.

As Wiley and Will stood together in the fog, its mist wafting in

---

[10]Sterlings' Interview with Rose Okpeaha Leavitt, July 26, 1986.
[11]During the interview of July 26, 1985, Patrick Okpeaha said "it's silly, but we don't know how many miles from there." This section is entirely based on the Sterlings' interviews with: Mrs. Rose Okpeaha Leavitt (July 25, 1986); Patrick Okpeaha (July 26, 1986); Robert and Fred Okpeaha (July 27, 1986).

and out, becoming more dense one minute, then thinning somewhat the next, they must have discussed their next move. As it had taken them hours to find a break in the overcast and land here, why risk taking off again, only to be faced with the same problem further north along the coast? But, then, Wiley might have argued further, Barrow lay only "twenty or thirty miles" up the coast, or so the native had said. They could be there in a matter of minutes, now that they were on the edge of the ocean, by flying just off the coastline, and not climbing higher than, say, a couple of hundred feet, maybe less; at that height it would be difficult to lose sight of the ground.

If Post and Rogers had stayed at Walakpa Lagoon, they would have found safety, but would have lost yet another day, maybe more; one could never tell about Alaskan weather. As northern pilots said, in the face of delays: "Well, what's another day in Alaska?"[12] But Rogers and Post had a long trip ahead of them. Just off shore, they could see a mass of ice floes and had they asked, they would have discovered that this year, winter was coming earlier than usual. Clair heard the men discussing their next step. He heard of their decision: "They were in a hurry to go to Barrow." Patrick Okpeaha, too, had his thoughts. "The fog was going in and out—maybe, if my father would have asked them to wait for a clear sky, maybe they would have . . . I think my father was regretting about that."[13] But the right words were never said.

Post waded back to the plane and climbed in. Rogers thanked the Eskimos, stepped onto the float, turned and waved to Clair and Patrick on shore, and to the family by the tent; everyone waved back. Then Will, too, scrambled back into the plane. Wiley turned on the cock on the fuel line leading to the gas tank he had been using and started the engine. Will arranged himself in the very rear of the cabin. There was no need to warm up the engine. It had been shut off for barely ten or twelve minutes.[14] Wiley pulled away from shore and taxied eastward, trying to avoid the gravel bank that in places broke

---

[12]Alaskan bush pilot Jim Dodson, August 31, 1960

[13]Sterlings' Interview with Rose Okpeaha Leavitt, July 25, 1986.

[14]Report to Bureau of Air Commerce, Washington, D.C., by Phil C. Salzman, Airline Maintenance Inspector, August 23, 1935.

the surface of the water. About a quarter mile from shore, he turned the plane. He was ready to take off.

Habits, good or bad, are hard to break. Once acquired they become part of everyday behavior and are performed so routinely that they seem the norm. A veteran pilot, Wiley, too, had acquired habits. For most of his flying career he had piloted a land plane equipped with wheels, a high-wing Vega, the *Winnie Mae*. The past ten days, for the first time in his life, he was at the controls of a low-wing, pontoon-equipped plane. So far he had taken off and landed this plane only some seven or eight times, yet in that short time he had changed his takeoff technique. When taking off with the *Winnie Mae*, Wiley unfailingly lifted her up gently in a graceful slow climb. Not so with the floatplane. Provided with an extremely powerful engine, Wiley now practically forced the plane to jump out of the water in an excessively steep climb. Bush pilots called the maneuver "hanging by the propeller"; it is unsafe. The aerodynamic function of a propeller is to cause air to flow over and under the wing, to provide 'lift'. Why Post adopted this practice with the floatplane is a mystery, but the fact is that on every one of his observed takeoffs he forced the plane out of the water and climbed steeply. He did so again at Walakpa Lagoon. He also breached another of the pilots' cardinal rules: while climbing steeply, he banked sharply; dipping the right wing low and raising the left one, Wiley turned north toward Barrow.

Wiley must have turned very sharply: "I thought they were going to turn around . . ." Rose remembered. At a height of approximately two hundred feet, the Okpeahas heard the explosion of a backfire—"like the sound of a shotgun," said Patrick—and the engine stopped. For the merest fraction of a second the red plane seemed to hang in midair, its upward drive halted. Then, being in a turning motion, it began to somersault and tumbled side over side downward. It hit the shallow water head on, the impact shearing off the right wing and breaking the floats, and fell onto its back.

Clair and Patrick had walked back to their tent, barely three hundred feet away, where little Rose stood beside the tent: "we watched them in the fog, but we can see the plane there and we see my dad and my brother walking toward us, and after they took off, they were coming; right after they reach our tent. . . ." the plane crashed into the lagoon. Almost all of the plane remained visible. It had fallen into two or three feet of water.

"Was fog, was misty, foggy, and my father just started running toward the plane, he didn't want us to move from the tent; he told us not to move from there; and we stayed there and when he reached that plane—he on the shore, he said: Halloo! Halloo! many times. There was no answer. And he come back to the tent start changing his boots; he tell us not to touch it, go near it any more, no, just to watch it from there. Maybe he thought it might explode. And he told us to tell people whenever they came—tell them not to touch that plane unless the people from Barrow had seen it that way; but some of the people came—my mom told them not to—but they didn't do what my father said; they just start trying to take out the people inside the plane. After they take them—after they wrapped them up, we did go down there, we children go down there, see them there."[15]

Clair had changed his boots—"knee-high boots. He don't have rubber boots; muklucks!" Rose would remember. Then Clair took his kayak and began paddling along the coast toward Barrow. Whether it was the threat of the early ice floes, or the eastward wind, which would have forced him constantly into shore, or the dense fog, is not known, but after "half a mile, maybe quarter mile," maybe even a lot more, Clair beached the small boat and began to run along the coast toward Barrow.[16]

It was not an easy trek for the squat, wiry Clair. He had to climb the almost vertical embankment, then descend it again. He had to cross rivulets and small streams; he had to circle around deeper lakes or traverse shallow ones. He was not a powerful man, but a hardy one. Long hours of mushing behind a dog sled had hardened his muscles, and he did not find the running gait too exhausting. As he passed other hunting camps, he quickly told the story of the crash he had witnessed and a number of Eskimos, perhaps hoping to be of help, or perhaps just curious, made their way south to Walakpa Lagoon. But Clair Okpeaha continued his run to Barrow. He did not know the names of the two men who had spoken to him. There had

---

[15]Sterlings 'Interview with Rose Okpeaha Leavitt, July 25, 1986.
[16]Sterlings 'Interview with Patrick Okpeaha, Sr., July 26, 1986.

been no introductions. Even so, their names would have meant nothing to him. He had never heard of either of them.

While it was still daylight at Walakpa Lagoon, in Maine, at the Lakewood Summer Playhouse at Skowhegan, it was dark. The evening performance had ended some time ago, and the audience, mostly seasonal residents and vacationers, had gone home. Nightlife in Skowhegan was limited. The long-established Lakewood Summer Playhouse, well known in theatrical circles for having produced more future Broadway successes than any similar organization in the country, presented fine plays in stock. As actor Keenan Wynn described it: "You would forget a play, do a play and rehearse a play. You had a different play every week."[17]

On the night of August 15, the Playhouse had presented a revival of an exciting aviation drama, *Ceiling Zero*. The plot revolved around "a daredevil pilot whose reckless flying enlivens the three-act play. He becomes lost in fog en route to Newark, and from that point the action is thrillingly traced by the crackling voices on a two-way radio as he asks and receives his bearings. Suddenly the audience hears the roar of his plane over the airport and seconds later, a terrible crash off stage."[18] A young, promising actor named Humphrey Bogart played the airline's owner, a role Osgood Perkins had originated on Broadway. In addition to Mary Rogers as the ingenue and nineteen-year old Keenan Wynn as the flight controller, the cast also included Grant Mills as the gallant flier who dies in the wreck.

In Maine, Betty Rogers, her daughter Mary and Aunt Dick were sleeping as Clair Okpeaha raced along a beach in the Arctic with news that would change their lives forever. He trotted steadily on the hard, wet sand. On his right lay the coastal embankment that raised the tundra abruptly about twenty feet above the Chukchi Sea. On his left, the ocean teemed with ice floes. Clair Okpeaha could not remember another summer when so much ice had come so early. He did not know it, but even the Coast Guard cutter Northland, which had been at anchor off Barrow, had earlier that day put to sea and moved some fifty miles further south, to a point off Wain-

---

[17]Sterlings' interview with Keenan Wynn, March 31, 1982
[18]*Akron Times-Press*, August 16, 1935.

wright. Its captain, Commander W.K. Scammell, with the wind changing direction and heavy ice floes beginning to float back toward shore, did not want to risk his ship being surrounded and rendered icebound.

Clair Okpeaha stuck to the narrow shoreline. By keeping to the water's edge he knew he was headed straight into Barrow, whereas traversing the tundra with its thick, spongy miniature overgrowth like soft matting underfoot and with the heavy patchy fog wafting across the featureless plateau would be tiring and dangerous.

A man could lose his direction in minutes there, and once lost in the fog, he would have little chance of finding his course again until the fog lifted. Steadily his feet hit the sand. He ran with only the cold Siberian wind as companion—the wind and his thoughts: What would he tell them when he got to Barrow? Perhaps he should have looked into the wrecked plane, to see whether he could help? No! Nobody could have lived through that crash. But what if one of the men. . . . ?

Clair Okpeaha had little worry of being overtaken by darkness before he reached his goal. From the tenth day of May to the first of August, the sun had risen but once and not set; it made a complete circle of the sky every day and every day came near the horizon, but did not sink beneath it. Now, since the second day of August, just thirteen days ago, the sun had once again begun to dip below the sea and nights had returned to the land of the midnight sun. The first night had been only a quarter hour long; but each succeeding night lengthened by twelve to fifteen minutes until, after November 18, the sun would not come above the horizon at all for almost seventy days. The night of August 15 would last close to three hours, though between afterglow and first light it would not grow totally dark at any time.

Clair reached Barrow about 9:40 in the evening.[19] He had covered almost eleven miles of difficult terrain in about an hour and a half. That a man dressed in heavy clothing could have crossed such an exhausting topography in so short a time has strained the credibility of some experts. All sorts of mathematical gymnastics have been invented to stretch the time. One researcher theorized that Post's

---

[19]Ex: Official report RG-237, CAA, f/835, Box 373. National Archives

...ey in first model of space suit. COURTESY: ARCHIVE UNITED
...HNOLOGY CORP. HARTFORD, CT, 06101.

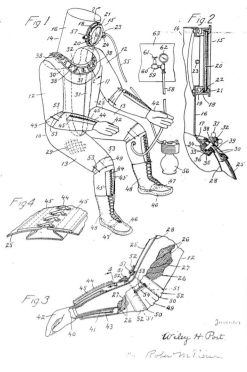

Fig.1 of application for a patent on his flight suit, by Inventor
Wiley H. Post, per his attorney.

Envelope carried on first coast-to-coast air mail
stratosphere flight via TWA, postmarked five days
after Wiley Post's death.

List of prior attempted transcontinental non-stop
stratospheric flights on which Wiley Post had carried
this envelope.

The ill-fated Lockheed *Orion* still as a first-rate **TWA** passenger plane.

The odd wing and fuselage now joined, with new engine and propeller, the *Orion/Explorer* is still on wheels. COURTESY: LOCKHEED CALIFORN CO. BURBANK, CA, 91520.

Wiley's Orphan, or *Wiley's Bastard,* now on pontoons, sees the light of day as it is rolled out of its Renton, Washington, hangar.

Joe Crosson, chief pilot of Pan-Alaskan Airline, Will Rogers, Wiley Post. PHOTO COURTESY: PAN-AM.

al farewell from Joe Crosson, and possibly one more friendly word of caution from him. Fairbanks, August 15, 1935.

The *Chicago Daily News* headline, August 16, 1935.

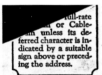

Western Union telegram informing Mae Post of Wiley's death.

Western aerial view of Walakpa River and lagoon emptying into Chukchi Sea. Tents are on the same site of the 1935 Okpeaha tent.

Clair and Stella Okpeaha.

Bodies of Wiley Post and Rogers, wrapped in sleeping bags. COURTESY: NATIONAL ARCHIVES, WASHINGTON, D.C.

WILEY POST
FATHER OF MODERN AVIATION
1898 - 1935

Simple grave marker in Edmond, Oklahoma.

Six decades after burial, this marker was erected graveside.

Wiley Post's funeral at the First Baptist Church, Oklahoma City, OK. August 22, 1935. COURTESY: ARCHIVES & MANUSCRIPT DIVISION OF THE OKLAHOMA HISTORICAL SOCIETY.

Will Rogers' funeral service at Forest Lawn Memorial Park, Glendale, California; August 22, 1935.

Mae Post at the monument to Will Rogers and Wiley Post at the crash site. COURTESY: ARCHIVES & MANUSCRIPT DIVISION OF THE OKLAHOMA HISTORICAL SOCIETY.

New memorial tribute to Post and Rogers, erected at Barrow's airport.

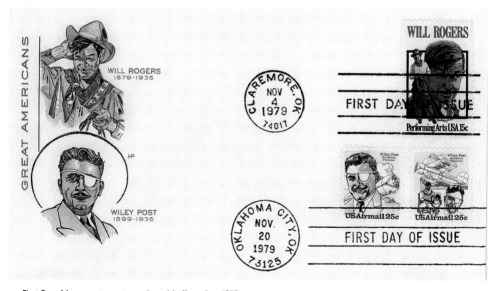

First Day of Issue postage stamps issued in November 1979.

Wiley Post

CONQUERS *new Frontier* – IN HIS RUBBER SUIT *by* GOODRICH

Reading Time 45 seconds

AROUND THE EARTH, up into the stratosphere, setting new records—Wiley Post is blazing many a trail for the aviation world to follow. He believes that future speed flying will be done in the rarefied air of the stratosphere. To demonstrate the practicability of that belief, he flies at 7-mile heights in his Goodrich-built suit which makes such flying possible.

The idea for this suit was Post's. He came to Goodrich because he found that no other rubber company had such facilities, experience and willingness to develop the unusual in new applications of rubber.

The suit is literally "air conditioned." With the special metal helmet, it completely encloses the wearer. Oxygen is forced into the suit, and a valve permits used air to escape. This suit was made by the Anode process sponsored by Goodrich—a process which results in a rubber that is light yet perfectly flexible, and with great strength.

Wiley Post's suit is only one of many spectacular uses of Goodrich rubber. In hundreds of applications, in scores of industries, Goodrich rubber is performing the unusual—adding new features to old products, making new products possible, increasing precision, reducing costs.

Goodrich rubber is on the march, to help thousands of products win new markets or hold those they have. You can have no conception of the possibilities of this amazing material until you consult The B. F. Goodrich Company, Mechanical Rubber Goods Division, Akron, Ohio.

Goodrich

ALL *products problems* IN RUBBER

Goodrich advertising attests to the fact that "The idea for the suit was Post's."

watch, which had stopped at 8:18, had been set on Oklahoma time, by which measure it would have taken Clair five hours to reach Barrow.

Clair's children, however, found nothing surprising in the fact that their father would negotiate the distance between Walakpa Lagoon and Barrow in less than two hours. "One hour forty-five minutes, no more," Patrick Okpeaha insisted.

What has added to the confusion is the mistaken belief that Wiley's gold wristwatch, its crystal broken, indicated the exact time of the crash—a crash that had had no effect on Rogers' dollar pocket watch, which was still merrily ticking and reading the correct time of 3:30 a.m. when it was found. Staff Sergeant Stanley R. Morgan of the United States Army Signal Corps, who arrived at the crash site with the first boat from Barrow, estimated that the crash occurred about 7:30 p.m., and suggested that Wiley's wrist watch did not stop until Post's arm either slipped into the water at 8:18 p.m., or that water from the incoming tide, spilling over the sandbank into the lagoon, rose to cover the watch. Sergeant Morgan's theory corroborates the Okpeaha family's claim about the time the plane landed. Rose Okpeaha Leavitt remembered: "After we have our supper, the plane arrived around seven o'clock, something like that."[20]

At Barrow, just before 10 p.m., Thomas P. Brower was docking his boat near his father's trading post. A veteran of half a century as an Arctic trader, whaler and trapper, Charley had settled at Barrow fifty years earlier and taken an Eskimo wife; when she died, he married another Eskimo. Charley had gained the natives' respect and trust because he was honest and dealt fairly. He worked hard for his new people; when he was appointed U.S. Commissioner, he represented both the Eskimos and the federal government. As chief of police and magistrate, he was the Law and he could even perform civil wedding ceremonies. He had raised his children to abide by his standards and principles.

Thomas stopped his work when he "saw a man running along on the beach and he came up to me and it was old man Clair Okpeaha, stomping down the coast." Speaking in Inupiak, the language of the local Eskimos, Clair blurted out the story: "Tom, an accident hap-

---

[20]Sterlings' Interview with Rose Okpeaha Levitt July 25, 1986.

pened down at Walakpa, there is two men landed . . . they didn't tell me their names; they taxied over to where—close to where my kid was on the lagoon side. They asked me: Which way is it to Barrow? He said, I told them up the coast. And they thanked me, went back to their plane and taxied to take off—over toward the ocean. And they were just right over the stream that emptied out to the ocean, when—roughly hundred feet, he said,—they just—-their motor conked off—and they just turned over and they dived right straight down into that stream."[21]

As Clair recounted the events to Thomas Brower, his loud, excited voice drew other Eskimos out of their homes. Eager to hear the details, ever more men pressed in on Clair and Thomas. At that point Sergeant Morgan heard the commotion and left his radio hut to join the group. Clair Okpeaha reported to him in broken English that "airplane she blew up."[22] Sergeant Morgan summed up Okpeaha's account:

> The native explained in pidgin English that the plane, flying very low, suddenly appeared from the south and, apparently sighting the tents, circled several times and finally settled down on the small river near the camp. Two men climbed out, calling the native to the water's edge and asking the direction and distance to Point Barrow. The direction given, the men then climbed back into the plane and taxied off to the far side of the river for the takeoff into the wind. After a short run the plane slowly lifted from the water to a height of about fifty feet, banking slightly to the right, when evidently the motor stalled. The plane slipped off on the right wing and nosed down into the water, turning completely over, and the native said a dull explosion occurred and most of the right wing dropped off and a film of gasoline and oil soon covered the water.[23]

Okpeaha's startling news sent Tom Brower and Sergeant Morgan rushing off to put rescue plans into action. Tom dispatched Clair to

---

[21] Sterlings' Interview with Thomas Brower, July 25, 1986.
[22] Ex: *Akron Times Press*, August 17, 1935.
[23] Ex: Sgt. Stanley R. Morgan's radioed report to the United States War Department

notify Charles Brower, the civil authority in charge. He would later recall that it was nine o'clock when "there came a sharp knock followed immediately by the headlong entrance of a panting Eskimo named Clair Okpeaha."[24]

Sergeant Morgan remembered the time as being about 10 p.m., whereas Dr. Henry Greist, head of the Barrow Presbyterian medical mission since 1921, found out about Okpeaha's arrival later, second hand, and recorded it as being 8 p.m. In light of the urgency and confusion raised by Clair's account of the tragedy, it is not surprising that nobody bothered to fix the exact time of his arrival in Barrow, and because it would be daylight at eight, nine or even ten o'clock, the various estimates are easy to explain. The ten o'clock time, which appears in all of Sergeant Morgan's communications, seems the most logical, as it fits into the overall schedule. Whether the accident itself occurred at 7:30 p.m., as Sergeant Morgan suggests, or 8:18 p.m., as Wiley's stopped wristwatch implies, Clair Okpeaha could not possibly have arrived in Barrow by 8 or 9 p.m. Morgan's time estimates also seem more dependable when one considers that his life was regulated by the clock. As the army's communicator, he had to adhere to a rigid transmission schedule, in order to make weather observations and reports at prescribed times. It seems natural that he would check his own watch frequently. To Charles Brower, on the other hand, the precise time of day would hold lesser importance. Indeed, in a letter he wrote in December, he introduced still another different time in a letter:

> That evening, the 15th, about eleven o'clock, Claire (sic) Okpeaha an Eskimo came to the village on the run and reported that a plane had crashed. . . . [25]

While Okpeaha reported to Commissioner Brower, Sergeant Morgan sent word to Frank Dougherty, the government schoolteacher and local reindeer superintendent.[26] Dougherty also worked as a

---

[24] *Fifty Years Below Zero* by Charles D. Brower, © 1942, Dodd, Meade & Co., Inc.
[25] Letter written 27 December 1935 by Charles D. Brower to Bert Bernet, St. Louis, MO
[26] Mollie Greist's *Nursing under the North Star*, © 1968

'stringer' for United Press, as did Charles Brower, but as a stringer for Associated Press. All major news services maintained contacts in remote places that ordinarily would not warrant a reporter. These contacts, or stringers, would from time to time submit accounts of local events they thought might be of interest to a nationwide readership. Only if their stories were used, would the news service pay them.

The resident doctor at Barrow, head of the Barrow Presbyterian medical mission since 1921, was Henry Greist. An elderly man, originally from Crawfordville, Indiana, he had given up a private practice to work for the church in Alaska. His second wife, Mollie, was a registered nurse. She liked her life among the Eskimos and had come to terms with Alaska—all except the summer:

> "The summer here is something awful. The weather is mostly drizzle, rain, mist, fog, fog, fog, clouds and wind and we dread it so much worse than 20 below. We all agree that 10 below is just fine."[26]

Mollie Greist and one of her helpers, Helen Surber, saw Morgan leaving for the scene of the accident. They were on

> the second floor of the hospital at the window sorting out mission boxes, when we heard the men of the village calling and we saw Mr. Morgan running and putting his coat on as he ran and his camera flying in the air from a strap around his neck. Helen said: "Oh, Mrs. Greist, something has happened." She ran down to see and I followed and we met Mr. Daugherty on the walk, running to tell us.[27]

By the time Dougherty arrived on the beach, Morgan had already chartered Bert Perrigo's fast launch, an open whaleboat powered by a small gasoline motor; he had also hired fourteen Eskimos as crew, and was ready to leave for Walakpa Lagoon to see what could be done.

---

[26]Letter dated August 20, 1922.
[27]Mollie Greist's *Nursing under the North Star,* © 1968

Tom Brower had to attend to his partially laden boat. The breeze was coming up and swinging the boat toward land, so he would have to shelter it before it beached. Afterward, he spoke to his younger brother David and his father: "Dad, you have any recollection of somebody coming up?"[28]

Of course Charles Brower knew that Post and Rogers were in Fairbanks and were planning a trip to Barrow to visit him. He was looking forward to their stay; in fact, so was the entire village. They were preparing festivities, among them a special culinary feast, featuring:

> . . . the choicest reindeer roasts to be had anywhere, infinitely more juicy and tasty than anything Fairbanks or Nome can produce. And we are by common consent permitted to shoot fat wild geese when we can, for our own consumption, since, if the game laws were observed by us we would never secure such game. And we had hoped to place before these noted travelers such a feast by way of venison and wild fowl as would prove worthy."[29]

The bad weather, however, had delayed their plans for the reception of the visitors.

> When a spell of particularly bad weather followed, with snow and sleet and no visibility whatever, we resigned ourselves to an indefinite postponement. On the morning of the fifteenth Morgan got another message. The men, still at Fairbanks, asked again for weather at Barrow. There was nothing surprising about this. You never can tell what is happening in one place from conditions in another. But it was lucky, we told ourselves, that they checked up in case they'd had any idea of taking off today. We'd seldom experienced a meaner storm. At times you couldn't see fifty yards.
>
> So Morgan sent the information warning them of what was

[28]Sterlings' Interview with Thomas Brower, July 25, 1986
[29]Dr. Henry Greist's Newsletter.

going on in the Barrow district. After which all hands dropped
back into the routine work of a nasty day.[30]

As "nasty" a day as it was, Charles knew that no experienced and
certainly no Alaskan pilots would be flying to Barrow, not with: No
visibility and no ceiling—"just dense fog that one had to shove aside
to get through it."[31]

Who, then, could those men be who crashed at Walakpa? Who
would try to come to Barrow on a day like this? In a letter Charley
Brower never thought would see the light of day, he allowed himself
a guess:

> "We did not . . . know that it was Rodgers (sic) and Post for they
> had weather reports that morning and weather there was rotten
> Rain (sic) Fog (sic) and at times snow squalls. We imagined it
> was some dam (sic) fool from the south trying to get here before
> they arrived for newspaper work."[32]

An overeager, weather-stupid reporter from the south or a famous
flier like Wiley Post, no doubt Charles Brower would hold his opinion that he was a "dam fool."

With Thomas busy sheltering his boat, and Charles making arrangements for the reception of the injured fliers—whoever they
were—it was up to David Brower to hurry south. Tom gave him
instructions:

> Dave, I said, you take a power boat, a dory—flat bottom dory—
> so you can go up that stream and from what I gather Clair re-
> marked both those men never got out. They are probably pinned
> underneath there just broken be prepared and take some of the
> utility blankets and some kind of a stretcher—canvass—if you
> have to move them out.

---

[30]*Fifty Years Below Zero* by Charles D. Brower, © 1942, Dodd, Meade & Co., Inc.
[31]Letter written by Charles D. Brower to Bert Bernet, St. Louis, MO., December 27,
1935.
[32]Charles Brower's letter to Mr. and Mrs. Clint G. Owen, Los Angeles, CA., December 3, 1935.

So they took blocks and tackles and everything, they just zoomed down these 12 to 15 miles, and went into the inlet—there were five or six of them—I have a picture of them somewhere.[33]

In their haste to reach the crash site and bring possible help to the fliers, both David Brower and Stanley Morgan overlooked the most important member of any rescue mission. They forgot to notify Dr. Greist. In a mimeographed newsletter, which Dr. Greist published "just across the ice from the North Pole, three or four times per annum . . . sometimes not at all," he allowed free rein to his displeasure at such heedless haste:

> . . . the Doctor was not even notified of the accident that he might attend with emergency kit and stretchers and other first aid apparatus. They merely wished to get there, little knowing or considering what they would or could do on arrival. The Doctor accidentally learned of the wreck after all the boats had gone, ran to the beach with first aid necessities, but could not secure a boat, not even a skiff or canoe, man or lad.

Left behind, Dr. Henry Greist and his wife, affectionately known by all as Aunt Mollie, prepared everything for emergency procedures. They sterilized instruments, laid out bandages and braces for broken limbs, scrubbed the operating table again, and prepared beds; Aunt Mollie called in all the native girls who regularly assisted at the hospital. When Aunt Mollie had first arrived at Barrow, her principal project had been to start a baby clinic and to teach both pre- and post-natal care to the Eskimo women. At her initial meeting with the prospective mothers, they shyly sat before her as she talked. After several minutes she asked them why they were sitting there, wearing their warm parkas, and suggested that they take them off, to the women's considerable embarrassment, because they had no clothing on underneath. It was then that Aunt Mollie also started sewing classes, with the first project: ladies' underwear. Thus she had begun both a women's club and a baby's club—classic missionary projects.

---

[33]Sterlings' Interview with Thomas Brower, July 25, 1986

Now Mollie and her staff made a boiler of reindeer stew, gallons of coffee and hard bread for the men when they returned. Charles Brower sent blankets, jugs of hot water and bottles of brandy to the hospital, then he himself came over to offer his service, which would indeed be much needed that night. But for the moment, there was nothing to do. Charley, Dr. Greist, Mollie, and the staff would just have to sit and wait, and talk, and eat for hours with their ears strained for the sound of the returning motors.

With his fast launch, David Brower towed an oomiak, a native skin-covered, shallow-keel wooden-frame boat that the rescuers would need to enter and exit the shoal water of Walakpa lagoon. Although he had started later, David soon overtook Morgan and reached the crash site first. But it was Morgan who first knew the full truth—that the red plane had been carrying Wiley Post and Will Rogers when it fell from the sky. He quizzed Clair Okpeaha, who rode in his boat. How did Clair know that there had been two men in the crashed plane, he asked, and Clair replied: "Me talked with mans."

"When, after they fell?" asked Morgan, and Clair answered, "No, before they fell, when they come down on water and ask me how to go to Barrow, where Barrow is, how far."

"Did they tell you their names?" Morgan kept digging. "No," Clair replied, "Mans no tell names, but big mans, two mans, one sore eye with bandage on eye, he and other man then go inside plane and man with sore eye start engine and go up, maybe ten fathoms [sixty feet] and then engine spit, start, then stop, start some more little, then plane fall just so . . . "and imitating a plane he indicated with his hands a bank, then a fall off the right wing and a nose dive into the water, with a complete somersault forward. When Morgan wanted to know whether Clair waded out to the plane after the crash, Okpeaha admitted that he had only stood on a sand spit some forty feet away and had hollered. He had received no answer and so he had hurried quickly to Barrow to summon officials.

Hampered by fog, mist, and a strong adverse current, avoiding ice floes and slowed by the semi-darkness, the powerboat trip took three hours, which may seem excessive when compared to Clair Okpeaha's run in less than two. So it was close to six hours since the accident when David Brower's boat rounded the embankment into Walakpa

Lagoon. An eerie sight greeted him. Barely a quarter mile ahead, shrouded by heavy fog, lay the tangled debris of the plane—now a haphazard heap of splintered wood and misshapen metal. The plane rested on its back; one wing, which had been torn off, lay across the wreckage pile and a pontoon stuck heavenward.

Some of the Eskimos Clair had alerted on his run to Barrow had walked south to Walakpa Lagoon. Before the boats from Barrow finally arrived, those natives had already smashed a hole into the cabin and removed Will Rogers's body, which they had carefully placed into one of the eiderdown sleeping bags found in the debris. It now rested on the edge of the lagoon. They had removed all the baggage and piled it on the beach. Will's typewriter was twisted out of shape; Wiley's rifle was broken, his fishing rods snapped. In fact, almost everything in the plane had been smashed or splintered, except for small items. Some of the women began to salvage the papers, charts, and personal effects scattered about the site. There were several Russian dictionaries and translations,[34] and the book that Will must have been reading just before the landing at the lagoon, for tucked inside it, as a bookmark, were Will's reading glasses, miraculously unbroken. Soggy from floating in the brackish water, these personal effects now lay in neat stacks on the shore.

The major problem was the removal of Wiley Post's body from the plane. The Eskimos had already tried, but without success. David Brower took a flashlight and entered the cabin. The plane's nose had struck with such impact, that it had forced the engine well back into the cabin, and pinned Post's body solidly against the back of his seat, with the weight of one of the pontoons holding the body firmly in place. There was only one solution: they would have to break the plane apart in order to wrench free the body.

First David attached the tackle to the pontoon and had it pulled off the plane. By this time about thirty Eskimo men had assembled, all eager to assist—and all fortified by Stella Walook Okpeaha's cooking. (Rose Okpeaha Leavitt remembers how she was "helping my mom cooking for people to eat, getting ready for them to eat. Those people who were working on the thing."[35]) David Brower next

---

[34] *Washington Herald*, August 17, 1935,
[35] Sterlings' interview with Rose Okpeaha Leavitt, July 26, 1986

attached the rope to the side of the plane to tear it open. The rope
broke. He reattached it and the men on shore pulled. This time the
plane, already cracked, split open. With great difficulty, David was
able to free Wiley's body and pass it to his helpers. Post, too, was
put into an eiderdown sleeping bag.

Sergeant Stanley Morgan took a series of photographs in the half
light of the new day. He photographed the wreck from all sides and
took close-ups of the engine hanging from the debris. His is the only
picture showing both the lagoon with the split plane, and, in the
foreground, the carefully wrapped bodies of the two fliers. Morgan,
an accomplished photographer, owned a Graflex camera with all the
latest equipment; he was also especially proud of his modern dark-
room, where he did all his own processing.

David, too, must have taken photographs, which Charles Brower
later sent to Seattle. Though sitting on the biggest American news
story of the year,[36] Charles felt troubled by the thought of benefiting
from so sad a time. As he explained his feelings: "To make it worse
for me Rodgers (sic) was on his way to pay me a visit and that rather
broke me up for a while."[37] He would send those photographs to
the Associated Press, but he refused any further participation.

When all the personal belongings had been salvaged and stowed
in boats, both bodies were placed into the oomiak. Slowly the caravan left the lagoon and began its trek back to Barrow. There was
no need for speed now. As the boats turned toward Barrow, Morgan
could see fragments of the shattered plane floating seaward.

The Eskimos had no idea who the two victims were, but Brower's
and Morgan's attitude indicated to them that these two strangers
were important men. They, too, felt the loss and a profound connection to the two victims they had just helped to recover. Death can
summon a universal bereavement that transcends the limitations set
by race or nationality. As the boats began their slow way northward,
"one of the Eskimo boys began to sing a hymn in Eskimo and soon

---

[36]American Newspaper Editors judged the Rogers-Post crash the most dramatic
news story of 1935, superseded on a worldwide basis only by Mussolini's invasion
of Ethiopia.
[37]From a letter written by Charles D. Brower to Bert Bernet, St. Louis, MO., December 27. 1935.

all the voices joined in his singing until our arrival at Barrow."[38] Mollie Greist, too, remembered the Eskimo's sad chant; she called it their funeral dirge.

At the Presbyterian hospital in Barrow, the Greists and Charles Brower could hear the cruising hum of the motors a long way off as the little convoy made its way along the down-coast. The fact that the engines were not approaching at full power announced the sad news a long time before the words were actually spoken. Were they bearing injured men, Charles Brower knew, his son would have raced at full throttle to get them to needed attention. Henry and Mollie Greist knew, too, but they could not foresee how they would spend the coming hours.

As the Eskimos struggled to beach the heavy whaleboat at Barrow, a piece of paper fell from Rogers's pocket. It was a newspaper clipping with a picture of his daughter, Mary, and a story about *Ceiling Zero*—the aviation play in which she was appearing at the Lakewood, Maine, summer theater.

It was about 3 a.m. Alaska time when the Eskimos carried the bodies into the hospital, where Dr. Greist, Mollie, Charles Brower, and the hospital staff took over. With the bodies now in the proper hands, Sergeant Morgan hurried home to check whether his superiors had been notified. When the news of a crash had first reached Barrow, Sergeant Morgan had immediately attempted to raise any station down the line which might be on the air, in the hope that the message would then be passed on. The late hour, however, had found nobody listening and he had had to leave for the site of the accident.

During their years in Barrow, Stanley Morgan had taught his wife, Beverly, who officially held the job of government meteorologist, how to operate a Morse code key.[39] So thoroughly had Stanley taught his wife that she had acquired many of his idiosyncrasies, and most listeners could not tell by the usually recognizable sender's "hand" whether it was Stanley, or Beverly, sending a message. During the hours Sergeant Morgan had been away, Beverly had been

---

[38]Sgt. Stanley R. Morgan's radioed report to the United States War Department, August 16, 1935

[39]Clipping dated 12/9/1935, from Air Force Central Museum, Wright-Patterson Air Force Base

sitting at the key in the stark radio shack, trying to raise just one responsive voice on land or at sea, but the southern United States Signal Corps stations had not responded. Now that Sergeant Stanley Morgan was back at Barrow, he took his seat at the key. And now it was up to him to tell the world that two of its best known citizens lay dead at the top of the world.

At the Presbyterian hospital, Dr. Henry Greist and his wife, Mollie, began their gruesome task. They placed the bodies on the operating tables, and Dr. Greist began to cut their clothes off. When the small plane had crashed into the shallow lagoon and broken apart, the impact had forced sand and gravel into the clothing of the two fliers with great pressure. The Greists put aside the sodden, bloodstained, silt-laden clothes for the moment. Later they would be washed and returned to the widows—everything except the cut rubber boots, which were thrown away.

Carefully emptying the pockets, the Greists found that Will Rogers had about $770 in cash, $2,040 in travelers' checks, and a trick puzzle in his pocket. Will also had a pocketknife—"the kind a Boy Scout might have for trading purposes," Dr. Greist noted—a reading glass and two watches, one an inexpensive Pocket Ben-Westclox watch attached by a string to his vest, the other, a much larger watch, a St. Regis, which he used as an alarm clock when he traveled.[40] "In all it was a strange assortment," Dr. Greist observed.

Curiously, none of the accounts of the accident recorded the contents of Wiley Post's pockets, although an Associated Press report in the *Seattle Times* of August 17, 1935, refers to an item in Will's pocket Greist did not mention. It was a Washington sales tax token given Will in Seattle as a good luck charm by Ralph Rogers, a man who had identified himself as a "third cousin." (None of the detailed family trees available recognize any relative by that name.)

With the clothes and boots now removed, Dr. Greist could start his examination of the bodies. The injuries were massive. In the abrupt nosedive and subsequent impact of the plane, Will Rogers, who evidently was not strapped into his seat, had been badly tossed about, and struck sharp projections in the cabin. He had suffered a fracture of the frontal bone over the nasal region; his scalp had been

---

[40]Homer Croy interview with Dr. Henry Greist.

detached and was hanging forward over his face, and one ear hung by a thread. There was a star wound in his right cheek. The nose, one eyebrow, and one lip had been cut to the bone as though dissected by a surgeon. His chest was crushed and a chunk of flesh as big as a man's fist was missing from one hip.[41] His left arm was broken. Despite the fact that Will Rogers had worn rubber boots, both legs were broken,[42] and the tibia, the bone of the lower right leg, had sustained a compound fracture, with a section of it thrust several inches through trouser-leg and boot. It was "a ghastly sight even to one who has seen many terrible sights."[43]

Dr. Greist, with Mollie assisting him, worked feverishly on Will Rogers. Since there was no electricity, Helen Surber had to hold a flashlight so that the Greists could proceed. Dr. Greist made undersutures, repaired all surface cuts, replaced a six-inch section of the tibia, and restored the body as best he could.

Wiley Post had sustained a massive abdominal wound, compound fractures of both legs and arms,[44] and lacerations to the trunk and face. With Frank Daugherty holding the flashlight for hours, Charles Brower sewed up the many cuts on Post's body, but Dr. Greist had to close the gaping one "where some part of the plane had punctured his lower abdomen and emptied it of all intestines."[45]

For five hours Dr. Greist, Mollie, Charles Brower, Helen Surber, and Frank Daugherty worked on the two bodies. Then they "rouged and fixed the faces as best we could."[46] All that remained was to re-clothe the bodies. The few white men at Barrow, though, had no spare suits to donate, as they wore Eskimo clothing. The solution was the missionary barrel—clothes collected and sent by charitable organizations from the States for distribution by missionaries. Mrs. Greist found two old-fashioned long nightgowns in which the bodies of Rogers and Post were carefully dressed before being "wrapped in white, freshly laundered sheets, taken to the new warehouse and put on the floor under lock and key. There are no morticians on this

---

[41]*Nursing under the North Star* Mollie Greist, © 1968
[42]*Washington Herald*, Aug. 17, 1935.
[43]Homer Croy interview with Dr. and Mrs. Henry Greist.
[44]*Washington Herald*, Aug. 17, 1935.
[45]*Nursing under the North Star* by Mollie Greist, © 1968
[46]Interview with Dr. Henry W. Greist in *Our Will Rogers* by Homer Croy, © 1953

coast, no caskets to be had, and we did all we could under the circumstances."[47]

During the hours of surgery, some sixty or seventy men who had returned with the bodies were fed and warmed at the hospital. Most of them sat patiently, like mourners at a wake, in the hall of the hospital, where they talked among themselves in low voices. There was a reverence, a respect, among the Eskimos, as if Wiley Post and Will Rogers had been honored citizens of the community.

After the surgery, Mollie's squad of four Eskimo-girl helpers and the janitor at the hospital took hours to clean up the two operating rooms and the halls, laundry, and kitchen.

A year later, Henry and Mollie Greist were entertained at luncheon by Betty Rogers in her beautiful ranch home in Pacific Palisades, California. Will, Jr., Mary, and Jimmy Rogers were also present. Then, after the meal, the boys put on a polo game for family and guests. As they watched from high above the field, Betty suddenly leaned forward, and changing the topic of conversation abruptly, she broached a subject obviously close to her thoughts. She said that viewing Will's body before the funeral service, she had been unable to see anything that could have caused his death, then she asked outright: "I wish you'd tell me the condition Will's body was in— do not spare me."[48] Dr. Greist, a most sensitive man, did not know how to reply. Should he really tell her? Would Betty be better off by knowing? At last he said, "He was badly broken." He never told her more.

At Barrow, neither embalming nor an autopsy could be performed. In the Alaskan Territory doctors were not allowed to embalm; and as for an autopsy, the U.S. Commissioner, owing to the excessive zeal with which the authorities make a show of economy, deemed it unnecessary. Short of an autopsy, it was impossible to determine whether the two victims had died instantly from their injuries, or from drowning. In any event, Post's abdominal wound and Rogers's crushed chest together with his fractured skull, "would in the aggregate as to each have likely proved fatal sooner or later, and possibly at once. Certain it is that both men lost consciousness instantly with

[47] Interview with Dr. Henry W. Greist in *Our Will Rogers* by Homer Croy © 1953.
[48]Homer Croy's interview with Dr. and Mrs. Greist

the accident and suffered no pain, that death was sure and certain and quickly had, in the position of the bodies when found."[49]

Perhaps Charles Brower, the "U.S. Commissioner" who denied Greist the autopsy, felt certain that death was due to the crash, and that any further mutilation of the already badly mangled bodies would be insensitive. The question of whether the actual causes of death were the injuries or, possibly, drowning, could have been settled forever by an autopsy. To this day there is no consensus in the matter. The faces of both men were found below the water level, so the crash could have left the two men only seriously injured, and they might have drowned while unconscious. Both Dr. Greist and undertaker Hosea H. Ross in Fairbanks confirmed the fact that the faces of both men had been submerged for considerable time. Mr. Ross also is noted to have claimed that all indications pointed to Will Rogers definitely having drowned; however, as Dr. Greist stated, little doubt exists that both men would have quickly succumbed to the massive injuries received in the crash.

The hospital was not the only busy place that night in Barrow. Sergeant Stanley Morgan, awake now for almost twenty-four hours, finally received a response to his persistent search for a connection. Day had come to the west coast, and he reached his WAMCATS relay contacts. The account of the crash raced through Fairbanks, Anchorage, and Palmer. Men, women, and children, who only a day ago had seen both Post and Rogers walking in their towns, could not believe the tragedy. Was there no mistake? Maybe an error in transmission? Nothing like that could happen to men like Will Rogers and Wiley Post!

In Fairbanks, without a doubt, the man most affected by the news was Joe Crosson. Only hours ago he and Wiley, an old, dear friend, a hunting companion, and a fellow flier had been making plans for the future. Perhaps, Joe accused himself, he had not been insistent enough about Wiley not flying to Barrow; perhaps if had he been more assertive—but how could anyone keep Wiley from flying? Nonetheless, Joe Crosson must have blamed himself for failing to say or do or suggest something that would have saved those two lives.

---

[49]From the mimeographed newspaper, published by Henry W. Greist in Point Barrow, 'just across the ice from the North Pole.'

Now all he could do was to see that their bodies were promptly returned to their families. Without waiting for PAA's approval, he made up his mind to fly to Barrow and bring back the bodies of his friends.

Joe hurried home to break the news to his wife, Lillian. She was stunned. How did it happen? she wanted to know. Where? When? It could not be. It was unreal. Will Rogers and Wiley Post had sat right there, at her kitchen table. Here the plan to fly to Barrow had been born; here they had eaten their last home-cooked meal. Here they had escaped the curiosity of the townspeople who asked for autographs or just stood and stared at the celebrities. Here, too, Will Rogers had decided to fly with Wiley across Siberia. Lillian had only to close her eyes to see them all sitting there at her table, eating and laughing; there were Wiley and Joe poring over maps; there was the spot where Will had stood in the kitchen, with Virginia Rothaker and mashed potatoes.

When Joe told Lillian of his decision to fly to Barrow, she became frantic. She could see the anguish in his eyes; she felt his torment over the loss of his friend Wiley. She knew that the flight to Barrow needed a fully alert, clear-minded pilot. It was a hazardous trip even on a clear, sunny day; but this day, the sixteenth of August, weather conditions were identical to those of the day before—and Joe Crosson was shaken and distressed by the tragedy. Only yesterday he had tried assiduously to persuade his friend Wiley Post not to tempt fate by flying into the foul weather of the North Slope; his friend had not listened and now he lay dead at the top of the world. And now, barely twenty-four hours later, Joe Crosson himself was determined to fly into precisely the same weather. No argument she could pose, no entreaty, could alter Joe's stubborn resolve. His sentiment over-ruled logic; his sentiment and a sense of duty to his comrade.[50]

Lillian, the loving, worried wife, finally realized that no words would change her husband's mind. He was resolute. It was the very least—the very last—he could do for his friends Wiley and Will. But Joe would not do it alone. Though an old hand at Arctic flying, he was not about to venture into the dangers of a fog-bound North

---

[50]Sterlings' interview with Robert J. Gleason, November 11, 1986.

Slope without a top-rated radio operator. He selected Robert J. Gleason. Even though Bob was barely twenty-nine years old, he was already Communications Superintendent for Pacific Alaska Airways.

Joe and Bob had met for the first time in 1929, when Gleason was radio operator aboard the three-masted schooner "Nanuk". The small ship, given the Eskimo name for the polar bear, was a mere 261 tons, and though rigged for sails, carried a powerful two hundred-horsepower diesel engine in her hold. Scheduled to pick up furs from Russian Arctic-Ocean villages and return to the United States before winter set in, she left Seattle on June 15, 1929. After many ports of call and heavily laden, the Nanuk became icebound at North Cape in the Arctic Ocean on October 4, 1929.

For the next six months, young Bob Gleason was the icebound schooner's sole voice with the outside world. In touch by Morse code with the WAMCATS operators at Barrow, Teller, and Nome in Alaska, at Barrow he frequently 'talked' with a Sergeant Stanley Morgan. Through Bob Gleason's messages the press in the United States and abroad, kept alive the story of this small ship trapped in the icy vastness of the Arctic Ocean. That same winter when the famous flier Carl Ben Eielson and his Alaskan Airways mechanic became lost somewhere on the frozen Arctic, the Nanuk, being stationary, served as the hub of the rescue operation, which included the PAA pilot Joe Crosson and which introduced him to the invaluable Morse code key operator, Bob Gleason. They became friends and maintained contact even after Gleason returned home to Seattle. The friendship that began on the Siberian ice grew further when Bob, now a graduate electrical engineer from the University of Washington, joined PAA and settled down into domestic life in Fairbanks.

Bob and Joe knew each other's strengths and knew that they could depend completely on each other. Such symbiosis was essential in Arctic flying, where the slightest miscalculation could trigger disaster. Not surprisingly, then, on the mission Joe Crosson planned that Friday morning, August 16, 1935, he wanted the best man for the job, his friend Bob Gleason.

Early that morning, Bob received a call at home from John White, the division accountant at the PAA offices. His message was cryptic: "Joe wants you to go with him to Barrow. He called by telephone.

He'll pick you up in half an hour."[51] Thirty minutes later Joe Crosson pulled up in his car at Gleason's house. Only then did Bob learn about the crash.

If Gleason had any reservations about flying to Barrow under prevailing weather conditions, he did not voice them, and the thought to back out never occurred to him. Bobbing in the water of the Chena Slough were several of PAA's Fairchild 71 cabin monoplanes on floats. Crosson, who was eminently familiar with this type of plane, and felt entirely at ease at its controls, had telephoned ahead to have Number NC 10623 made ready for takeoff. When Joe Crosson and Bob Gleason arrived at Spencer's Float, a small crowd of townspeople had already collected. Like the initial news of the disaster at Walakpa Lagoon, the report of Crosson's projected mercy trip had rapidly spread around Fairbanks.

Among the people waiting for the fliers was Murray Hall, the local inspector for the Department of Commerce, Bureau of Air Commerce. The accident had occurred in his jurisdiction and it was his duty now to investigate. Indeed, earlier that Friday morning, August 16, he had received instructions from Washington, D.C.:

REPORT RECEIVED POST AND ROGERS KILLED THIS MORNING ENROUTE NORTH FROM ANCHORAGE OR FAIRBANKS STOP RADIO AVAILABLE INFORMATION IMMEDIATELY STOP USE ARMY RADIO IN CODE IF THIS DOES NOT CAUSE DELAY OTHERWISE REGULAR CHANNELS.

(SIGNED) J. CARROLL CONE,
ASSISTANT DIRECTOR OF AIR COMMERCE (AIR REGULATIONS)

According to signal corps officers' estimates, it took an average of two hours to transmit and retransmit a message from Point Barrow to Seattle. It took even longer for the following telegrams to reach Mae Post and Betty Rogers:

1935 AUG 16 AM 7 10

REGRETTED THAT I MUST NOTIFY YOU OF RECEIPT FOLLOWING MESSAGE FROM SIGNAL CORPS OPERATOR AT POINT BARROW "POST AND

---

[51]Sterling's Interview with Robert J. Gleason, November 11, 1986.

ROGERS CRASHED FIFTEEN MILES SOUTH HERE FIVE IT IS P.M. LAST
NIGHT. BOTH KILLED. HAVE RECOVERED BODIES AND PLACED CARE
DOCTOR GREIST."

> KUMPKE (SIC), COLONEL
> SIGNAL CORPS

Another, more detailed telegram was sent almost four hours later to
the Rogers ranch in California and to Maysville, Oklahoma:

FOLLOWING FROM POINTBARROW DATE QUOTE TEN PM NATIVE RUN-
NER REPORTED PLANE CRASHED FIFTEEN MILES SOUTH BARROW STOP
IMMEDIATELY HIRED FAST LAUNCH PROCEEDED TO SCENE FOUND
PLANE COMPLETE WRECK PARTLY SUBMERGED TWO FEET WATER STOP
RECOVERED BODY ROGERS THEN NECESSARY TEAR PLANE APART EX-
TRACT BODY POST FROM WATER STOP BROUGHT BODIES BARROW
TURNED OVER DOCTOR GREIST ALSO SALVAGED PERSONAL EFFECTS
WHICH AM HOLDING ADVISE RELATIVES AND INSTRUCT THIS STATION
FULLY AS TO PROCEDURE STOP NATIVES CAMPING SMALL RIVER FIFTEEN
MILES SOUTH HERE CLAIM POST ROGERS LANDED ASKED WAY BARROW
STOP TAKING OFF ENGINE MISFIRED ON RIGHT BANK WHILE ONLY FIFTY
FEET OFF WATER STOP PLANE OUT OF CONTROL CRASHED NOSE ON
TEARING RIGHT WING OFF AND NOSING OVER FORCING ENGINE BACK
THROUGH BODY OF PLANE STOP BOTH APPARENTLY KILLED INSTANTLY
STOP BODIES BADLY BRUISED STOP POST WRISTWATCH BROKEN STOPPED
EIGHT EIGHTEEN PM UNQUOTE

> KUMPE[52]

The telegrams were eventually forwarded, but in this age of radio
and telephone, news, especially bad news, traveled much faster than
a hand-delivered telegram. So it was that the whole Rogers family,
scattered in different cities, and Mae Post in Ponca City, and Wiley's
parents in Maysville learned of the tragedy long before the telegrams
reached them. Rogers's youngest son, Jimmy, and his cousin Jimmy

---

[52]Colonel George E. Kumpe, in charge of the Alaska telegraph system headquarters,
operated by the U.S. Signal Corps, Seattle Washington.

Blake, in their trek across the country, had reached New York City, when they learned the news. On August 15, the oldest son, Will, Jr., had signed on as an engine-room helper aboard the Standard Oil tanker H. M. Storey. Will, Sr., had had to send by wireless his consent for his son's long voyage as a lowly 'wiper.'

> Young Bill was brought the news by a plainly shaken Standard Oil Company official [who] shouldered his way through sailors on the deck of the company's tanker, the SS H. M. Storey, at Los Angeles Harbor. He clambered down the engine room ladder.
>
> "Where's Will Rogers, Jr.?" he asked the grimy men there.
>
> "Here I am, sir," said a smiling lad in oil-stained dungarees.
>
> "Boy," said the official, "change your clothes and come ashore."
>
> On the dock, the young about-to-be-seafarer was met by his cousin, Mary Ireland, who lives in Long Beach. "Billy, your father's dead. He was killed in a crash with Wiley Post."
>
> Stunned as though struck, young Will took the blow dry-eyed and rode silent to his ranch home with his cousin.
>
> The vessel sailed late yesterday, with crew members silently sharing the grief of the boy who was a shipmate for an hour.[53]

In Skowhegan, Maine, the news arrived in the forenoon of August 16. Betty Rogers and her sister Theda Blake were visiting at a neighboring cottage when Betty saw a car coming up the road. It was driven by Grant Mills, the actor. He took Theda Blake aside, and as Mrs. Rogers looked on with growing apprehension, he spoke agitatedly, though too low for Betty to hear him. Quickly her "alarm turned to panic,"[54] her first thought being that her son Jimmy and his cousin Jimmy Blake had had a car accident. "Has something happened to Jimmy?" she asked. Grant Mills did not answer; Theda then broke the news. "No, Betty, it's Will. Will has had an accident."[55]

[53]Los Angeles Examiner, August 17, 1935
[54]Will Rogers by Betty Rogers; ©. 1941; p. 307
[55]Ibid.

For the briefest of moments, Betty Rogers felt relief; Jimmy was all right and nothing could ever happen to Will. She thought that the news, most likely, concerned a forced landing, or some other minor mishap blown out of all proportion by a creative press. The look on Theda's face dispelled any such notion, however. Betty could read the grim facts in her sister's eyes. Grant Mills and Theda Blake then faced the sad task of telling Mary Rogers the tragic news.

The family in Maine went into immediate seclusion, and all incoming telephone calls were screened. There were calls from eager reporters wanting statements; there were condolence calls; there were calls from the curious and the morbid.

Governor W. Troy of Alaska sent messages of condolence to both Mae Post and Betty Rogers. The message to Mae Post read:

> "WE ARE ALL PROFOUNDLY SHOCKED AND GRIEVED AT THE TERRIBLE ACCIDENT WHICH RESULTED IN THE DEATH OF YOUR HUSBAND AND MR. ROGERS. YOU HAVE OUR WHOLEHEARTED SYMPATHY. PLEASE ADVISE IF THERE IS ANYTHING I CAN DO TO HELP."

To Betty Rogers he telegraphed:

> "THE GRIEVED PEOPLE OF ALASKA EXTEND THEIR DEEPEST SYMPATHIES TO YOU. EVERYONE FEELS A PERSONAL LOSS ON ACCOUNT OF THE SHOCKING DEATH OF OUR GUEST. PLEASE ADVISE ME IF THERE IS ANYTHING I CAN DO."

Colonel Charles A. Lindbergh, who was spending the summer with his family on North Haven Island, off the coast of Maine, spoke with Betty Rogers several times. He was an old friend of the family and offered his services. As a director of Pan American Airways, Lindbergh assured the Rogerses that Pacific Alaska Airways, a Pan Am subsidiary company, would attend to all matters. Unaware that Joe Crosson, on his own, was already on his way to Barrow, Lindbergh sent the following telegram:

> PACIFIC ALASKA AIRWAYS IS SENDING PLANE TO BARROW AND WILL ARRANGE ALL ALASKAN TRANSPORTATION STOP FOR YOUR CONFIDENTIAL INFORMATION THE PRESENT PLANS ARE FOR THE ALASKAN PLANE

TO CONTINUE THROUGH DIRECTLY TO LOS ANGELES STOP WILL KEEP
YOU INFORMED.

CHARLES LINDBERGH

The Associated Press reported the reactions of Mae and of the Post
family to the news of Wiley's fatal accident.

Mae Post, was in Ponca City, Oklahoma, since Monday, August
12, visiting with old friends, the L. E. Grays. It was at their house
that she learned the news. "I wish to God I had been with him
when he crashed!" she cried out. She was prostrated by the tragic
news and went to bed for several hours. When she rose, she left
Ponca City by plane for Maysville, Okla. Mrs. Ceney Post, Wiley's 95-year old grandmother, sat in calm meditation for almost
thirty minutes after being informed of her grandson's death.
Then, as she wept, she slowly talked of Wiley's youth. "I am
sorry Mae didn't get to fall with him, instead of Mr. Rogers,"
she said. "She's always told us she wanted to die with him when
he crashed. And I know she hates to be left like this." Mrs. Post
had come to Ponca City from Oakland, Cal., by plane.[56]

William Francis Post, Wiley's father, found inner composure
first. Sitting in a rocker on the porch of their modest home he
said: "This is the thing we have been dreading for years and
years." Wiley's favorite quail dog, Tailspin, bayed and crawled
away on its belly under the porch, refusing to eat.[57]

Mae went to Maysville to confer with Wiley's parents about funeral arrangements. She told them that she would agree with their
decision. At first the elder Posts considered holding funeral services
for their son in a small grove in front of their home so that local
folks could gather to pay their last respects. "I think the best place
would be right here at home. We could have the services out in the
yard where it is shady." Later Wiley's gray-haired father changed his
mind: "We may not be here always. We would like to know our

[56]Associated Press; August 17, 1935.
[57]Associated Press, August 16, 1935.

son's grave never would go unattended." Great consolation came to Mae Post when Betty Rogers called and the two women had a telephone conversation. "Mrs. Rogers was so brave, her conversation gave me courage," Mae told relatives.

Responses to the tragedy arrived from most major capitals. In England, newspapers carried banner headlines on the tragedy in Alaska. Associated Press reported from London: "It was the greatest display of interest in British journals since Reichsführer Hitler announced the rearmament of Germany."[58]

French Air Minister Denain presented condolences to the United States Embassy on behalf of French aviation.

Ireland's newspapers recalled for their readers Will Rogers's benefit performance in 1926, to assist the relatives of those who had perished in the Limerick County theatre fire.

Norway's newspapers honored Rogers's memory by publishing the words he had written into the Golden Book at Copenhagen, Denmark, the previous summer, after he had taken a flying visit to Norway's high mountains:

> Denmark is beautiful but I can't forgive the Danes who stole Greenland from my Norwegian friends.

O Globo, Rio de Janeiro's great newspaper wrote: "The disaster in Alaska deprives America of two of the highest expressions of her civilization."

Most revealing was the Soviet reaction. In Moscow, an official Russian spokesman expressed deep regret at the deaths of Wiley Post and Will Rogers: "Both victims were very popular in the Soviet Union. We were looking forward to their arrival in Russia with the greatest interest. The news of the disaster naturally came as a profound shock to us." The Soviet Union's declaration of interest in Post and Rogers's expected "arrival" indicates the Russian knowledge of a flight plan that the rest of the world could only guess at. Through Soviet Ambassador A. A. Troyanovsky the Soviet government also transmitted official condolences. In a message to Secretary of State

---

[58]*Los Angeles Times* and *New York Herald Tribune*, August 17, 1935

Cordell Hull, he extended "sincere condolences to their families and to the nation for the loss of these famous and brave Americans."

President Franklin D. Roosevelt, who was weekending at the summer White House in Hyde Park, New York, expressed his deep regret at the deaths of Will Rogers and Wiley Post. Informed of the tragedy when he returned from a motor trip through his estate, President Roosevelt further authorized this statement:

> I was shocked to hear of the tragedy which has taken Will Rogers and Wiley Post from us. Will was an old friend of mine, a humorist and philosopher beloved by all.
>
> "I had the pleasure of greeting Mr. Post on his return from his round-the-world flight. He leaves behind a splendid contribution to the science of aviation. Both were outstanding Americans and will be greatly missed."[59]

From Honolulu, in the Territory of Hawaii, Shirley Temple was reported to have burst into tears when she learned of Will Rogers's death. The child star was a favorite of Rogers and frequently the two 'cut-up' together. Crying bitterly, Shirley was reported to have said: "I hate airplanes!"

Also in Honolulu, John Ford, the famous Hollywood film director and Rogers's friend, recalled how he had wanted Will to accompany him to Hawaii. Learning of Will's death, he was too shocked to utter more than a grief-stricken exclamation: "God, that's terrible!"

Postmaster James A. Farley, too, was vacationing in Hawaii. When the news reached him: "I am inexpressibly shocked at word of Will's death. We were close personal friends," was all he could say.

In Washington, D.C., the governmental agency responsible for civil aviation issued this statement:

> Eugene L. Vidal, Director of Air Commerce in the Bureau of Air Commerce, Department of Commerce, upon being informed of the accident in which Will Rogers and Wiley Post were killed, made the following statement:
>
> "Will Rogers has been regarded for years as the country's

---

[59] *Los Angeles Daily News*, August 17, 1935.

Number One air passenger. Wiley Post's exploits in round-the-world flying and in stratosphere tests are known wherever people know about airplanes.

"The news of their accident shocked and stunned all of us in the Bureau of Air Commerce. The loss of these able men cannot be measured.

"We have already set in motion the machinery for investigating the accident, to determine the cause, if possible.

"The Bureau of Air Commerce inspector in Alaska will proceed to the scene immediately and report to us when he has learned the facts.

"Wiley Post was flying a three-place Lockheed Orion Special which bore a Department of Commerce restricted license authorizing its operation on long cross country flights and special test work only.

"The plane was a special job, made up of an assembled Orion fuselage and Sirius wing. It was originally built in May 1933 and was licensed as a commercial plane, but was relicensed under a restricted license August 8, 1935 after being rebuilt. Its license number is NR 12283.

"Equipped with a controllable pitch metal propeller and 550 horsepower engine, it had a rated speed of approximately 180 miles."

The statement shows how little this agency actually knew about Post's plane and flight plan, and that what few facts it did offer contained basic errors, some of which would never be corrected; but Washington was a long way from Alaska.

Leaving Fairbanks at 11:15 in the forenoon, Alaska time, Crosson set his course for Barrow. The plane carried twelve five-gallon cans of gasoline that just sat on the floor of the cabin. They were not lashed down, as their own weight kept them in place. The crew had removed all the seats, except two in the very front, one for Crosson, the other directly behind the pilot's left shoulder, for Bob Gleason. It was advantageous to have the radio operator close to the pilot because the roar of the engine made ordinary conversation difficult and Gleason could yell in Crosson's ear if he had to, or hand him a hastily scribbled note. Bob Gleason sat with earphones clamped against his head, and a clipboard with a hand key in his lap. Communication with ground was, of course, via radio telegraph, not by voice. The cabin's vacant floor space served constantly to remind the two men of the purpose of their mission. Gleason got weather readings from Wiseman and Barrow; neither report was encouraging. The weather north of the Endicott Mountains had not changed since the day before: fog and cloud cover. Arrangements had been requested to have the Signal Corps observe a special broadcast schedule with Wiseman and Barrow so that updated weather summaries could be relayed to the plane in flight; the Signal Corps had complied. As Crosson and Gleason were headed toward the Endicott Mountains and the solid weather beyond, they first had to negotiate the White Range and then cross the Yukon River. They had to attempt several passes in order to find one that was not closed in by fog and clouds. Once they managed to get through the mountains they flew out over the flats, the tundra. By this time they had flown close to five hours. Crosson set the plane down on the first lake that looked long enough to allow a comfortable landing and subsequent takeoff.

As soon as the plane stopped its forward motion, the two men began the job of refueling. Gleason, the younger, climbed out of the plane and up onto the high wing and engine. Crosson, standing on one of the pontoons handed him the funnel with a chamois skin in it; the chamois skin acted as a filter, straining the gasoline of minute impurities and absorbing any water. Joe would hand the full can up above his head, and Bob would grab it, set it down as level as possible and chop a hole into one corner with a small hand axe. Then he would chop a hole in the corner opposite, to allow air to enter the can, and carefully pour gasoline through the filter into the tank. The two men emptied all twelve cans of gas. Because gasoline fumes inside the cabin would have constituted a grave danger. Bob simply dropped the emptied cans into the lake, where they filled with water and sank.

After gassing up, the engine was started with an inertial starter. In this two-man operation, Gleason stood outside the plane and rapidly hand-cranked the heavy flywheel until it reached speed. Inside the plane, Crosson adjusted the throttle and engaged gears, which turned over the engine and started the motor.

Crosson now set course directly for Barrow—against his own advice, for weather conditions were identical to those Wiley had encountered the day before, with dense fog and low clouds allowing very little visibility. But Crosson knew the North Slope well, and he "hit Barrow just a little bit west of it—not much—we were very close to it and landed on Barrow's lagoon."[60] The time was 5:15 in the afternoon. There was no ice on the lagoon, or on the Chukchi Sea; indeed, the ice floes, which only yesterday had threatened a coast guard cutter, had completely disappeared in less than twenty-four hours. Heavy currents may have carried them farther out to sea.

Securing the plane just a few feet from the lagoon's shore, the two men briefly discussed plans for their return trip. They decided to wait until shortly after midnight, when it would get light, before starting back. While there was no hurry to return to Fairbanks, it was Joe's axiom that it was "never wise to hang around Barrow too long, or the weather would shut you in." The time of departure set, Crosson made his way toward the village, to call on Dr. Greist and catch a few hours' rest. The manse, a modest shingled house, built in 1930, was the most modern structure in Barrow.

Bob Gleason stayed with the airplane. Even though he was now on the ground, he remained in good communication with Fairbanks via short wave, which is much more subject to ionospheric storms in high latitudes than in lower latitudes. Sometimes, in fact, short waves are useless in the far North, but on August 16, 1935, propagation via the ionosphere's reflecting layers was good and stable enough that Gleason used only 5692.5 KHz on the entire trip, which was PAA's regular daytime frequency. Through contact with Chuck Huntley, the PAA key operator in Fairbanks, he received news and weather updates from Fairbanks and Wiseman. He did not go into the village because he felt that he ought to stay at his post at the key. He stretched his legs, and he took some photographs of the plane, and he ate the hot meal brought to him from the village. But he did not sleep.

While Joe Crosson stole a few hours sleep, some other visitors to Barrow, were resting too. For another plane had also arrived at Barrow that day. It had reached Barrow along the upcoast from Nome, via Kotzebue and Wainwright on the west side of Alaska, and be-

---

[60]Sterlings' interview with Robert J. Gleason, November 11, 1986.

cause it was equipped with wheels, it had landed away from the lagoon, on the hard beach.

Its occupants had come north on a mission to bring out the first photographs of the crash site and the wrecked plane. In the next few hours a race would develop, but neither Crosson nor Gleason would be aware of it.

The four-man crew of the other plane kept a wary eye on Joe Crosson; they knew he would be taking rolls of film back to Fairbanks. They knew that Sergeant Morgan had sent his reports to the Signal Corps, and Frank Daugherty had relayed his version of events to United Press through Morgan's wireless, but the photographs taken by Morgan, Daugherty, and David Brower would have to be taken south by Crosson's plane. As long as Crosson was asleep, they had no competition, but once he took off in his Fairchild 71, a faster plane than theirs, they had only one advantage: the secrecy of their mission.

The Fairchild 71's gas tanks having been topped with fuel, Crosson and Gleason took twelve additional five-gallon cans of gasoline aboard. Toward evening a silent crew of Eskimos carefully carried the bodies of Wiley Post and Will Rogers to the lagoon and placed them in the cabin of the waiting PAA plane. They were not lashed down. Close to midnight Crosson and Gleason started the engine. It took some time to heat the engine oil to its prescribed minimum temperature of 40 degrees Centigrade [100 degrees Fahrenheit], and the persistent roar of the motor alerted the crew of the other plane that the great photo race was on—even though Crosson and Gleason did not know it. As far as they were concerned, they had simply flown north for the bodies of Wiley Post and Will Rogers. The fact that they were also transporting a few rolls of film from Barrow meant little to them. So far, Crosson and Gleason's trip had no sense of urgency.

Once the Fairchild's engine had warmed up, the tether was released. Crosson had maneuvered the plane into position for takeoff when one float ran aground on a barely submerged sandbank. Joe Crosson tried to gun the engine, to get the pontoon over the sandbar, but the plane refused to budge. Gleason put on a pair of hip boots, then stepped out into the water of the lagoon. He tied a fifty-foot rope, a standard piece of equipment, to the tail of the airplane and walked along the shore as far as the rope would reach. While Crosson gunned the airplane engine, Gleason pulled at the tail section. Still, the plane did not move. Bob walked repeatedly from one side to the other, pulling first this way then the other, as Joe gunned at full throttle, until finally the plane slid off the bar. Gleason detached the rope from the tail and got back aboard. The cabin door closed; Bob struggled out of the hip boots and took his seat. At last they were ready to go. Taxiing to one end of Barrow's lagoon, Crosson headed into the wind and took off. A small group of Eskimos stood watching, and as the plane rose, they waved a silent farewell. The time was 12:45 a.m., August 17, 1935.

Stanley Morgan would sit at his key for still one more hour, tapping out messages to the world before he would get his first sleep in almost forty-eight hours.

While the world slowly learned more details of the tragedy, Crosson and Gleason faced the most dangerous part of their entire trip. "The ceiling was a hundred feet, visibility perhaps a half mile, the weather was almost unflyable.[61] With the prevailing ceiling it made no sense to fly southwest to the crash site to get a view of the shattered plane. They had other more important concerns. In the flight back to Fairbanks, they would have to cross the Endicott Range, this time approaching from the shrouded side. Because it was impossible to recognize, or even see, the passes from any distance, Crosson's first task was to find the Colville River. Though one of Alaska's large rivers, it was not easy to locate with visibility a mere half mile. If Crosson took the plane up too high, he was enveloped in fog and clouds, and if he flew low he could not see far enough ahead. Once he did locate the river—which runs out of the Endicott Mountains and then parallels the range, gathering tributaries rushing down the mountainside as it flows east then north toward the Beaufort Sea— Crosson followed it. He stayed close to the surface with the pontoons almost skimming over the low water.

Now that nights had returned to northern Alaska, the shorter daylight hours no longer supplied melted snow and ice as freely as during the earlier twenty-four-hour summer days, so the water in the streams was noticeably lower. When a tributary from the south

[61]Sterlings' interview with Robert J. Gleason, January 3, 1987.

seemed wide enough, Joe would follow it upstream into the mountains, in the hope that it would lead him to a pass, but the rising terrain would soon force the small plane into solid overcast. The fog was almost impenetrable. Unable to make out any landmarks, Crosson would have had to fly still closer to the water's surface, his sole guide. The banks of these streams were:

> . . . about 20 feet high and we flew up the river and sometimes I couldn't see over the banks. I couldn't see the land, we were right down on the river. So we went on up there, of course there are a lot of tributaries into the Colville and Joe looked at two or three of those, but turned around and came back every time and finally we got through on one of them, I don't know which one it was. But all at once something wonderful happened. We broke out into clear weather. Sunshine! Sure did. Joe then picked out a lake, which was Wild River Lake. And there we started to gas up again; put the extra 60 gallons in."[62]

Again the Fairchild 71 took off, but it soon ran out of good weather. Once Joe had crossed the Yukon River he ran into heavy rain, and he still had one more range to fly over before he would get to the Tanana River and then Fairbanks. The rain clouds grew ever darker and more menacing, but Joe had flown this area many times and he knew every stump.

At 7:35 a.m., Crosson swooped low over the center of Fairbanks. On instruction from PAA, he set the plane down on the Chena Slough, just above the bridge at the foot of Cushman Street. Once on the water, a small crowd gathered almost immediately. Several volunteers, among them Lloyd Jarman, helped transfer the bodies which were then taken to the Hosea H. Ross Mortuary.

Crosson brought back from Barrow the personal items belonging to Wiley and Will. The Greists had dried some of them; others were still soaking wet from drifting in the brackish water of the lagoon. Joe took them home and Lillian dried them out in her kitchen stove. In the same oven a few days earlier, she had prepared Post and Rog-

---

[62]Sterlings' interview with Robert J. Gleason, November 11, 1986.

ers's last home-cooked meal. The Crossons would later return the items to the next of kin.

For now, all Joe Crosson and Robert Gleason wanted was to shower, shave, get a meal, and grab a few hours of undisturbed sleep. They had fought the elements in the most inhospitable areas of Alaska, and they had won. They deserved some rest.

The two men did not know that another plane, too, was on its way to Fairbanks or that its sole purpose was to get to Seattle first. The great photo race was on its initial lap, and while Pacific Alaska Airways still knew nothing about the contest, it had won the first round.

CHAPTER XII

THE GREAT PHOTO RACE

T HE NEWS OF the crash of Wiley Post and Will Rogers broke too late in the morning of August 15, 1935 for most American morning newspapers, but not for the midday, afternoon, and evening papers. Then, too, there were the Extras! Those Extras, hawked by newsboys as they ran along the streets, were really the same editions sold earlier, but with the latest developments replacing some other story on the front page. The new tidbits could be major or minor, it mattered little. If a story held great momentary interest for the public, every scrap of new information was disseminated as an Extra! Thus readers would buy the same newspaper several times during the day, simply to learn whatever minute bits of new information had been added, often in red ink. News services would compete fiercely for morsels of minutiae on any major break, just to send those lucrative Extra editions into the streets.

The deaths of Wiley Post and Will Rogers affected most Americans. Post was the aviation hero, a pioneer whose exploits the public followed anxiously, whose pictures had appeared on the front pages of every newspaper and magazine in the country. Rogers was the film star, the humorist, the political analyst, the uncle everyone wanted. He had come into American homes on the pages of 650 newspapers, or over the radio; and if you could afford the movies, chances are that his persona had smiled at you from the silver screen. Even if you did not read newspapers, listen to the radio, or go to movies, your friends would probably be quoting to you what Will Rogers had written that morning.

Few were the Americans who did not personally feel the loss of either man. Thus the familiar cry of "Extry! Extry! Read all about it!" brought out buyers eager to learn the latest developments in the unfolding story of the crash. The paper covered every detail of their lives—from youth to their departure for Point Barrow—and carried innumerable photographs of the two men, in every imaginable pose, with or without their wives, leaving here, arriving there, their homes, Rogers's children, the Posts' parents. Only one major part of the story was missing: there were no photographs of the final act—yet. But in Alaska, a few entrepreneurial men were already challenging the elements to bring back the first photographs of the crash.

In Nome, on the western edge of Alaska, the weather had been bad for several days. By the middle of August every year, fog shrouded the coast, and rain, the expected norm, often turned to snow. A local old-timer, Sam Anderson, had a shortwave radio and early every morning he would listen to news broadcasts from the States. What he heard one particular morning was that Wiley Post and Will Rogers had crashed the evening before, August 15, near Point Barrow, and that both men had been killed. It gave him an idea; there was money to be made.

Anderson roused Chester Brown, an experienced bush pilot for the newly formed Wien Alaska Airways, Inc., one of the numerous small freight lines operating in Alaska. Chet, as he was called, immediately saw financial merit in Anderson's suggestion and went to see Alfred J. Lomen, of the Lomen Reindeer Corporation. Lomen, a well-connected businessman, also saw the monetary possibilities, and being a man of action, he contacted the *Post-Intelligencer,* Seattle's foremost newspaper, with an unusual proposal: He would charter a plane with pilot and mechanic, hire a local photographer and bring to Seattle the first, exclusive pictures of the crash site and the wrecked plane. The *Post-Intelligencer* agreed at once, with only one stipula-

tion: Lomen would have to deliver the first photographs, or the deal
was off. The Seattle newspaper was not about to pay for exclusive
photos if others had already been published elsewhere. Lomen
agreed, though he knew the risk. If Pacific Alaska Airways was carrying films, too, it could easily beat him, as the Wien Alaska Airways
planes available to Lomen were all slower than those used by PAA.
To succeed, Lomen would have to keep his deal with the Seattle
newspaper a secret. He could make money only if PAA remained
unaware that they had a competitor.

Hank Miller agreed to be Chet Brown's mechanic and copilot in
the venture. They would fly a six-place, single-engine wheel-equipped
Bellanca, since no pontoon planes were available. Floats would have
afforded them a certain degree of safety in an emergency by enabling
them to land on any of a million summer lakes, but wheels would
have to do—wheels and a prayer that there be no emergency. The
Bellanca did not need a radio operator, because it carried no radio.
It was a simple plane, with a basic turn and bank indicator, tachom-
eter, compass, altimeter, and oil-pressure gauge its only instruments.
A homemade type of heater, which was little more than a cover over
the exhaust pipe, allowed some heat and almost as much deadly
carbon monoxide to enter the cockpit.

Why supposedly rational men would entrust their lives to such an
ill-equipped plane is astounding. Here was a minimally equipped
plane, without floats or radio, flying into the same weather in which
Wiley Post had just crashed. Even worse, this plane would be carrying four people. Alfred J. Lomen, not about to leave this mission to
others, was himself planning to make the trip, going along to Barrow
and then all the way to Seattle. Now that he had a pilot and a mechanic, he still needed a photographer. He chose Curtis Jacobs, a
local photographer. Most of the other photographers in town
worked as stringers for various news services, but had not yet learned
of the crash near Point Barrow, and Lomen wanted to keep it just
that way. There was no sense in creating even more competition.

On the morning of August 16, a blanket of fog and clouds still
covered Nome, and it was not until 11 a.m. that weather conditions
would permit a takeoff. Even then, Chet Brown had difficulty keeping the landmarks in sight as he headed across the fog-shrouded Sew-
ard Peninsula.

Visibility continued to be a great problem. Flying due north, Chet had to cross the Kigluaik and Bendeleben Mountains, with peaks as high as four thousand seven hundred feet. He could not fly at an altitude high enough to clear all of them because he would lose visual contact with the ground. Furthermore, if he flew above the clouds, it would be extraordinarily hazardous to descend through the cloud cover without knowing the altitude of the mountains below.

By one o'clock Chet had reached Kotzebue. As no other plane had yet come up from Nome, Alfred Lomen believed that so far he was ahead in the race to get photographs. As soon as the fuel tanks were topped, the four men again took off, their next stop Barrow. Flying almost due north from Kotzebue, they had more mountain ranges to cross. In the Endicott Range, the Noatak Mountains forced the tiny plane high above seven thousand feet. Exactly as Wiley Post had searched only a day earlier, Chet Brown now looked for a break in the thick cloud and fog carpet. Two hours had already elapsed, and with almost half their fuel gone, they had nearly reached the point of no return. Now what? Should they turn around and backtrack to safety, or continue and risk not finding an opening through which to descend? The consensus was to continue on. Chet turned westward, hoping that he might be flying along the coast.

Chet found a break over Cape Lisburne. Flying low, he followed the coastline right into Barrow. Just minutes out of Barrow, the four men spotted Walakpa lagoon below. There lay, in a shallow pool of water, the pile of wreckage that had once been a plane, now smashed, like a toy dropped by a giant. This was what they had come to photograph.

Now all Chet had to do was find a place to land. As his wheels were of little use on the lagoon, he circled several times, until he spotted an unbroken length of beach that looked like it would support their weight. A veteran pilot, he set the plane down as gently as if he were landing on a concrete runway. Lomen and his photographer, Curtis Jacobs, walked back to the crash site. Several Eskimos in a skin boat were still there. Jacobs asked them to row him closer, for close-ups. It took but a few minutes for Jacobs to circle the debris and take several photographs.

Trying not to sound anxious or arouse any suspicions, Lomen began to question the Eskimos. What he wanted to know was whether a plane had brought anyone else to take photographs; the natives assured him that no plane had come all day. Lomen was still not fully satisfied that he held the only film of the wreck. He knew that the bodies of Rogers and Post had been recovered the night before, and it had occurred to him that some members of the rescue team might have taken photographs. If that was the case, then the films would still be in Barrow, unless—but, no, who could have flown them south? Lomen could be almost certain that he held the film that was most likely to reach the States first.

At about 8 p.m., Friday, August 16, just twenty-four hours since the accident had occurred, Lomen was thinking ahead to the return trip. First they had to get to Barrow in order to refuel and rest. Chet had difficulty getting the Bellanca out of the soft sand at the crash site, but Chet managed to lift her off, and minutes later landed her on the beach at Barrow. There was no way they could miss seeing the PAA float plane bobbing in the lagoon. Inquiring about it, they learned not only that the Fairchild 71 had come to pick up the bodies of Post and Rogers, but also that it would carry some undeveloped rolls of film back to Fairbanks.

Naturally none of the four men would discuss their own mission, and no one asked them to. By this time at least one other Nome-based team was trying to get to Walakpa lagoon. Frank H. Whaley had been chartered by Universal News to fly a cameraman from Nome to the crash site, but the same heavy fog that had troubled Wiley Post a day earlier, and Chet Brown that same day, had now thickened and became impenetrable. Despite the fact that Whaley was an excellent pilot—or perhaps because of it—he turned back after getting to within a hundred miles of Walakpa lagoon.[1]

Brown needed gasoline for his trip to Fairbanks, but aviation fuel was not exactly a standard staple in Barrow, and the one possible supplier, Pacific Alaska Airways, was not in the business of selling aviation gasoline to competitors, no matter how small. All Brown was able to buy was twenty-five gallons of automobile gasoline from Brower's store. That was not enough to reach Fairbanks, so they would have to fly via Kotzebue and get aviation fuel there.

They ate dinner with their host Charles Brower and then decided

---

[1] Sterlings' correspondence with Frank H. Whaley, September 17, 1980.

to turn in. On the move since six o'clock that morning, they had had a full day with enough excitement and worry to last a full week; and there was still more to come. Lomen wanted to keep an eye on his investment, so he and photographer Jacobs made arrangements to sleep at Brower's, where Crosson was resting. Chet Brown and Hank Miller went to bed down on the other side of the village with Frank Daugherty, the schoolteacher.

Lomen had not yet fallen asleep when he heard Crosson's plane being warmed up. The time was close to midnight. Tired as he was, he could not afford to allow Crosson and Gleason to get too far ahead, especially since his crew had to fly out of their way, via Kotzebue. Without any prearrangement, all four men, having heard Crosson's engine start, met at their plane. They all had had the same thought. Using the last remaining aviation gasoline for takeoff, Brown switched to the automobile gas once the plane had reached altitude. Thus they flew into the new day, August 17. Only some thirty hours had elapsed since the crash.

Arriving in Kotzebue at 4:30 a.m., Brown filled his tanks with aviation gasoline. There, too, a message awaited Alfred Lomen from the office of Wien Alaska Airways; it informed him that on his arrival in Fairbanks, another plane would be standing by, ready for an all-night flight to Seattle. Its tanks topped and the engine checked, the Bellanca was back in the air by 6:20 a.m. Lomen constantly urged greater speed. With a long way to go and a lot of money at stake, he had no time to lose. Three hours later, Brown had to make a refueling stop at Ruby, on the Yukon River.

The Bellanca landed at Weeks Field in Fairbanks almost twenty-four hours after leaving Nome. Chet Brown and Hank Miller had completed their jobs perfectly, as had Jacobs. A new crew took over: pilot, Noel Wien; mechanic, Victor Ross. Noel held a reputation as one of the most steady and reliable pilots in the Territory. He would not take unnecessary chances and every one of his maneuvers showed careful planning and thorough attention to detail.

Wien could have taken Chet Brown's wheel-equipped plane and flown it to Whitehorse, then on to Juneau, and finally into Seattle, though that was usually the route taken by floatplanes. Noel, however, did not trust Brown's plane without a thorough overhaul. He chose, instead, to fly a Bellanca with a Wasp Jr. engine. This plane, too, was equipped with wheels, and thus almost useless in an emergency flying mostly over water. So Noel pored over maps and decided on a different course into Seattle, namely via Whitehorse in Canada's Yukon Territory, Prince George, British Columbia, and then nonstop into Seattle. It was an eighteen-hundred mile trip: six-hundred miles to Whitehorse, then some seven-hundred miles to Prince George, and finally almost five-hundred miles into Seattle. It was longer than the coastal route, but he would be traveling entirely over land and thus gain a small margin of safety, even though his flight plan took him over the inhospitable granite spikes of the Canadian Rockies.

Lomen tried to learn whether Crosson and his plane were still in Fairbanks. When he heard that Crosson and Gleason were at their homes, asleep, he must have heaved a sigh of relief. So far his secret seemed safe, and he would be taking off immediately for Seattle. All seemed right with the world.

But Wien's Bellanca was not quite ready. To make the long night flight to Seattle, the plane would have to carry additional fuel tanks and gas cans. Nor would it, on a night flight, be able to land and empty the cans directly into the tanks. The way commonly used to make such a transfer from inside the plane was a wobble pump. This horizontal siphon-pump was simply worked by pushing and pulling a lever back and forth; the pulling motion would suck the fuel through a hose from the can, a valve would close, and the pushing action would then force the fuel through another hose into the fuel tank. Installation of the pump lost the impatient Lomen almost three hours in Fairbanks. Though the work was going on in secrecy inside a closed hangar away from the eyes of any competitor, Lomen was only too keenly aware that every minute on the ground increased the danger of being scooped. Some other photographer could also fly to Barrow and bring back pictures. Crosson, himself, could wake refreshed and fly to Seattle with the film entrusted to him in Barrow; PAA's Fairchild 71s and Lockheed Electra 105s flew faster than the Bellanca. Any number of other things could go wrong if too much time was lost. With a lot of money already at risk and no payoff if he was late, Lomen was prodding everyone on. Noel Wien, however, was not so eager to be on the move so soon, since had just come back on a night flight from Dawson.

Not until 1:15 in the afternoon was the single-engine Bellanca ready to leave.[2] The plane was carrying a capacity 112 gallons in its tanks and 12 five-gallon drums of aviation gasoline in the cabin. Six hours and forty-five minutes later, Wien's Bellanca landed at White-horse, Yukon Territory. After they cleared customs, Noel consulted the latest weather information and refueled the empty wing tanks. He also replenished his cache of gasoline cans, because they would be crossing the mountains in the upcoming hours, and the last thing Wien needed was the added worry of running out of fuel. As a matter of record, to carefully nurture his fuel supply and out of respect for his equipment, Noel cruised at 1650 rpm, so as to consume only fourteen gallons an hour.

As the plane was ready to go, so was the increasingly anxious Lomen. When Noel sat down, stretched his legs out, and relaxed, Lomen, not surprisingly, became irritated. He, after all, was paying the bill, time was of the essence and did not Wien realize how much every minute counted? They might just as well return to Fairbanks as sit here doing nothing!

Wien remained undisturbed and composed. Patiently he explained that if they left Whitehorse now, they would arrive over Prince George in total darkness, and since the airfield there was not equipped with lights, they would be unable to land. What they had to do, Noel made clear, was leave Whitehorse at a time that would bring them to Prince George at the coming of light. Having given one of the longest speeches of his life, Noel Wien continued to rest.

In Fairbanks, a PAA twin-engine Lockheed Electra 10, Construc-tion number 1006, Registration NC 14259, a cabin monoplane, was being checked by mechanics. Warren Tilman, Rogers's new friend from Juneau and Fairbanks, and Ron and Vaughn Taylor removed the seats and in their place welded a platform with fasteners. This plane, which would bear the bodies of Wiley Post and Will Rogers to Seattle via Whitehorse, was to be crewed by Joe Crosson, pilot, William Knox, copilot, and Bob Gleason as radio communicator. The much smaller Fairchild 71, which had brought the bodies and rolls of film from Barrow, was also checked and refueled. It had been

---

[2]Times quoted are those in Alfred J. Lomen's account in the *Seattle Post-Intelligencer*, August 19, 1935.

chartered by Associated Press. When Joe Crosson had flown to Barrow, Pacific Alaska Airways operation in Fairbanks had found itself one plane short, as pilot Al Monson needed a Fairchild 71 to deliver the U.S. mail down along the Yukon River. To cover the temporary shortage, pilot Alex Holden and mechanic Lloyd Jarman, stationed in Juneau, had been ordered to bring a replacement Fairchild 71 to Fairbanks. By an odd coincidence, so Lloyd Jarman remembered, the plane transferred from Juneau was the same one that had damaged the pontoons that eventually ended up on Wiley's plane.

Now that Crosson had returned from Barrow, Alex and Lloyd would take that extra plane back to its home base, along with a special cargo: the rolls of film containing photos of the crash site, the films that Crosson had received from David Brower and Frank Daugherty. Both United Press and Associated Press were clamoring for those photographs, and PAA was fully intent on delivering them as quickly as possible. But no one outside the Lomen group had any knowledge that another plane was already racing photos to Seattle for the rival International News Service.

Holden and Jarman in their fast Fairchild 71 left Fairbanks about 2 p.m., a half hour ahead of Noel Wien's departure from Whitehorse. After the Burwash Landing on Kluane Lake, Yukon Territory, they planned to fly at night to Juneau, where a fresh pilot would take pick up the cargo and fly it by another plane to Seattle. As Lloyd Jarman reported, it was not a pleasant flight. Balking and rearing, refusing to fly in a straight line, the plane handled like a "truck." Johnny felt certain that Crosson's brush with the sand bank in Barrow lagoon changed the alignment of the pontoons, although Crosson himself had not experienced such turbulance or quirks. It seems odd that Holden would have flown Crosson's plane back to Juneau, instead of the one he had brought to Fairbanks, and odder, as well as most unlikely, that the careful Crosson would ever have allowed anyone to fly a plane he did not think airworthy.

Holden and Jarman reached Burwash Landing, where their plane was immediately refueled. They took off for Juneau in the semidarkness, with Jarman striking matches for light to read compass headings for Holden. Not long out of Burwash Landing they ran headlong into a howling storm, and rather than risk flying into it's face in their night trip through Chilkoot Pass, they returned to Kluane Lake, and waited it out. They managed to land safely and after securing the plane decided to catch some sleep and set the alarm clock for 3 a.m. They also reported their new plan to the resident radio operator, a PAA employee but also a member of the Royal Canadian Air Force, as Canadian authorities did not allow Americans to operate radios in Yukon.[3] As standard procedure, the radio operator at Burwash Landing reported the new flight plan to other PAA radio facilities up and down the line. With no plane now due to move until after 3 a.m., the various stations shut down until then.

Alfred Lomen, Noel Wien, and Victor Ross awaited their departure time at the Whitehorse Inn. The arrival of strangers in a small town always brought out residents eager to hear the latest first-hand news from the outside world, and quite a number of men had assembled around the visitors when Ronny Greenslide, one of PAA's radio operators, walked into the inn. He had just come off duty. Not aware that his company, Pacific Alaska Airways, was involved in a big race, he innocently announced that "Alex Holden and Lloyd Jarman are staying in Burwash until morning. We're going back to work at 3 a.m." Lomen must have shot quick, knowing glances at Wien and Ross when he heard that their only rivals were bedded down for the night. This was good news. Not only was their competitor a hundred miles northwest behind them, but its crew was fast asleep until at least 3 a.m.

Still another PAA employee unwittingly helped his company's competitors. The station manager at Whitehorse made it possible for Wien to take off in darkness. He offered to light the runway with the headlights from his old Ford automobile. At 11 p.m., aiming his plane at the two lighted spots from the car at the far end of the field, Noel raced over ground he could not see. Finally the heavily laden plane lifted off. He set the compass course for Prince George and flew through the moonless night over some of the craggiest, hostile mountains in the world. The night was absolutely clear, but the faint starlight only silhouetted the mountain ridges that surrounded the plane. The slightest miscalculation, the sudden malfunction of the engine, the wrong compass setting, an inaccurate reading of the maps—any one of them could mean death. In an emergency, lakes

---

[3]Sterlings' interview with Robert Gleason, November 11, 1986.

or rivers, even had they been visible, would have been useless to a plane equipped with wheels. There were no landing fields amid the cliffs of steep mountains; and if by chance some level ground had appeared, and if Noel Wien could have seen enough to set the plane down, search teams could never have found them in the vast northen wilderness. Further, without a radio aboard, they could neither learn of the weather ahead nor ascertain or confirm their position. They were blind and deaf to the world.

Promptly at 3 a.m. Holden and Jarman arose at Burwash Landing. The storm had cleared, but the wind was still brisk. As Jarman walked to the lake, to warm up the engine, he could hear the hungry wolves howling nearby. By 4 a.m. Holden and Jarman were ready to take off. The waves were running pretty high on Kluane Lake, and Alex could not get the plane on the float step for takeoff. He raced along the surface for over a mile and still the plane would not rise. He turned back to the landing and tied up. Jarman loosened the propeller blades, which had been set for sea level pitch, and reduced the pitch by three degrees, since Kluane Lake lies at an altitude of over six thousand feet. In the darkness he tried to adjust them evenly, by checking his settings with light from matches that blew out as fast as he struck them.

On their next attempt, Holden was at last able to lift the plane off the water and the two men headed for Juneau. It was now 4:30 a.m. on Sunday, August 18. Three hours and forty-five minutes later, Alex Holden landed at Juneau. Bob Ellis, a seasoned pilot, and Paul Brewer, his mechanic, had been waiting for them. Their plane, Alaska's fastest single-engine plane, a Lockheed Vega on floats, was warmed up. Extra cans of gasoline had been put aboard, to make it possible to fly the more than nine hundred miles nonstop to Seattle. They, too, would have to use a wobble pump. Ellis and Brewer took off five minutes after Holden's Fairchild 71 touched the water of Gastineau Channel. It was now up to them to fly the films into Seattle. They headed south along the coastline.

By this time PAA had become fully aware that Noel Wien was also carrying films and was racing to Seattle. PAA had communicated to Juneau that they had no report of Noel Wien's flight. Since none of the regular airfields in Alaska had reported Wien's Bellanca, PAA assumed that the storm which had forced Holden and Jarman back to Kluane Lake, had also forced Wien, known to be a cautious flier, to set down and stay down. That Wien might have left Alaska and at that moment might be flying across Canadian territory apparently never occurred to anyone at PAA. Bob Ellis, therefore, left Juneau at 7:20 a.m., with Pacific Alaska Airlines convinced that their plane was flying ahead of Wien in his slower Bellanca. Nor did Bob Ellis doubt that in his much speedier Vega he would win. Even though it was slowed by floats, he knew that the Vega could out-cruise Wien's Bellanca by 30 miles an hour. The flight to Seattle had developed into a race.

By the time Bob Ellis and Paul Brewer took off from Juneau, Joe Crosson, Bill Knox, and Bob Gleason had already left Fairbanks. Hosea Ross, the local undertaker, had driven to Weeks Field with the bodies of Wiley Post and Will Rogers. Ross had a startling opinion: "Post died instantly," he told Warren Tilman, "but Rogers, you can tell by the blood in the face, he probably didn't know it, but he probably lived a little bit. . . ."[4].

Tilman, along with Ron and Vaughn Taylor, helped carry the bodies into the plane and lash them down. When both bodies had been securely fastened, Tilman satisfied a strange urge. He had long wanted to know just how tall, or short, Wiley Post and Will Rogers had been. He found out:

> Post was a short guy, but Rogers was a pretty big guy. Boy, cause I laid down on the side of each one of 'em, you know, wrapped, and Ron said: "God, he says, don't do that, you make me sick."
>
> Warren Tilman tried to calm his co-worker: "they're just bodies now." But Ron Taylor did not quite see it that way.[5]

The men also placed salvaged belongings, some still soaked from Walakpa Lagoon, into the plane. A few of them seriously considered taking souvenirs. One man offered Tilman Rogers's knife and watch, or at least the soggy copy of *Arctic Village*, but Warren wanted none of it. He did finally take a waterlogged sheet of paper. It was the bill from Seattle's Northwest Air Service, for the plane's structural con-

---

[4]Sterlings' Interview with Warren Tilman, July 21, 1986
[5]ibid

version to pontoons, which Rogers had paid. Tilman kept it for years. Then one day it was gone or taken by another souvenir hunter.

The trio of Lomen, Wien, and Ross had, meanwhile, landed at Prince George, British Columbia, at six o'clock in the morning after a flight of seven hours and fifteen minutes. They were now sixteen and three-quarter hours out of Fairbanks and had covered thirteen hundred miles. Noel Wien had not slept for almost two days. Everything so far had gone according to his plan. The question was just how much longer his good fortune could last.

Time-wasting trouble developed almost at once. Having landed in British Columbia, the trio was informed by officious airport management, that they would have to go through customs. The fact that they had gone through customs at Whitehorse, in the Yukon—which, after all, was Canadian territory too—and had not left the country since then, was not acceptable. Still, since they were carrying only rolls of film, customs should have presented no problem—but it did. There was no Canadian customs inspector on duty at that time of day.

An hour went by before an inspector was located, but he refused to come to the airport until his tour of duty was scheduled to start. In fact, the inspector was quite irritated at having been disturbed at home.

Promptly at eight o'clock, two hours after they had landed, the Canadian customs officer did at last appear—and saw no need whatever for the fliers to clear customs, since they were leaving the country, not entering it. Alfred Lomen's response has gone unrecorded. He did, however, have the vocabulary and the temperament to have been quite articulate about the priceless two hours he'd lost.

Noel Wien had another five hundred miles to go. He was tired, and the trio became dispirited. They had little doubt at that moment that they had lost the race. Still, they went through the motions. It was daylight, and the rest of the flight was easy. Noel followed the Fraser River west, then cut south below Vancouver. The usual morning fog along the coast had burned off. Seattle was sparkling in the early afternoon sun when Noel put the Bellanca down at Boeing Field at 1:45 p.m. local time. Before Wien could even cut the Wasp engine, the cabin door was jerked open, identifications were hurriedly exchanged and the film was snatched from Lomen's hands.

Bob Ellis and Paul Brewer, coming south from Juneau, had an easy nine hundred-mile flight:

> The weather was beautiful. The weather bureau reported "not a cloud in the sky from Fairbanks to San Diego." I read magazines all the way to Seattle. Another airplane in the sky was a rare sight in those days. Really, a hum-drum trip."[6]

At 3:35 p.m. Ellis landed at Seattle's Boeing Field. He shut off the engine, grabbed the precious films and walked into the administration building. The first thing he saw was someone reading a copy of the Seattle *Post-Intelligencer*, with pictures of the wrecked plane splashed across the front page. Noel Wien had beaten PAA by almost two hours.

All was not lost for Associated Press, however. Having come in second in the race to Seattle, they had only lost a single market; they still had the rest of the country, indeed the whole world. AP split the number of negatives right in Seattle, retained some for immediate service there, and dispatched the remainder to San Francisco.

Edison Mouton, an outstanding pilot, had flown a special plane north to make the final relay. He took off at 4:30 p.m., stopped at Eugene, Oregon, from 6:05 to 6:15 p.m., and then completed the 716-mile hop to San Francisco's airport at 9 p.m. The packages of negatives were rushed to the Associated Press office by motorcycle, and the first prints were soon being distributed by wire-photo throughout the country.

Wien Alaska Airways, Inc., received $3,500 for the flight, based on a fee of fifty dollars per flying hour of a round trip. Noel, being in Seattle, immediately used the money for a down-payment on a Ford Tri-motor previously owned by North-West Airline.

On his return trip, Noel Wien carried several passengers, among them Alfred Lomen. Both men arrived back in Fairbanks more than two weeks after they had left that Saturday, August 17, 1935.

---

[6]Sterlings' interview with Robert E. Ellis, October 14, 1986

CHAPTER XIII

LAST RITES

Betty Rogers, with her sister, Theda Blake, and daughter, Mary, left Skowhegan, Maine, for New York City on Friday night, August 16, by train. Will, Jr., flew from Los Angeles aboard an eastbound United Airlines' plane to join his family. Questioned by a reporter at the airport whether he now feared flying, Will, Jr. said: "The accident was just unfortunate. It will not keep me from flying." Younger son Jimmy, was already in New York City, so the newspapers stated.

So the Rogers family gathered in New York and the Posts in Oklahoma. The deaths of two singular Americans were prompting expressions of grief and tribute in countless parts of the United States.

News of the crash had stunned the U. S. Capital. As soon as a quorum was assembled, Senator Joseph T. Robinson of Arkansas, majority floor leader, arose from his seat directly in front of the vice-president. He spoke in a composed voice:

> Probably the most widely known citizen of the United States
> and certainly the best beloved, met his death some hours ago

in a lonely and far-away place. We pause for a moment in the
midst of our duties to pay brief tribute to his memory and that
of his gallant companion. I do not think of Will Rogers as
dead. I shall remember him always as a sensible, courageous
and loyal friend, possessed of unusual and notable talent. He
made fun of all mankind. In nothing he ever said was there an
intentional sting. He was kind, generous and patriotic. His
companion was a courageous representative of a gallant group
who on the wings of adventure sought remote places and conquered long distances. All the nation mourns these great citizens. They were both representatives of the highest type of
manhood. Peace to them.

Senator Charles L. McNary, the Republican floor leader, rose immediately from his place on the Republican side of the aisle to
state that every Republican Senator shared the same feeling. He
concluded by adding that Will Rogers had "brought joy and good
feeling to America and would be missed by everyone." In the
House of Representatives, Jed Johnson from Oklahoma, and a
friend of both men, was selected by Speaker Byrns to announce the
deaths to the House.

Preparations were made for the funerals of Wiley Post and Will
Rogers in Oklahoma City and Los Angeles, respectively, each city
assuming the role of a hometown, though neither was. Not only
throughout Oklahoma and California communities, but in leading
cities of the nation, flags hung at half staff in honor of Wiley Post
and Will Rogers.

In Washington, D.C., the Department of Commerce, through its
Bureau of Air Commerce, announced that it had dispatched Inspector
Murray Hall from Anchorage, Alaska, to the scene of the Rogers-
Post accident to gather all possible data. Obviously the Department
was unaware that Inspector Hall was in Fairbanks, not Anchorage;
that he never went anywhere near the site of the accident to examine
the wreckage and engine; or that he had interviewed neither any
mechanic who had worked on the plane in Fairbanks, nor anyone
who had witnessed its fall. Congress, too, announced an investigation, although nothing ever came of it.

"No inspector will be sent from here, the Bureau said," declared the *Los Angeles Times* in its August 18, 1935 edition—and that was the truth.

What readers of the nation's newspapers also learned was that in the first Session of the Seventy-fourth Congress, the U.S. Senate had passed Senate Resolution S.3436, introduced by Senator William Gibbs McAdoo, (Democrat of California). It was "A BILL TO AUTHORIZE THE INTERMENT IN THE ARLINGTON NATIONAL CEMETERY OF THE REMAINS OF THE LATE WILL ROGERS AND WILEY POST." On August 19, 1935, the bill had been read twice, considered, read the third time, and passed.

In the House of Representatives, Republican leader Bertrand H. Snell rose to block the resolution. He said that it "hurt and embarrassed" him to object to the resolution. "I was a friend of Will Rogers," he continued, "but as far as I can find such a thing has never been done before. It is true that Lincoln's little boy was buried there, but that was during the time Lincoln was commander in chief of the United States Army. If we make an exception now, there will be other requests later as other great men die. The soil of Arlington is hallowed ground reserved exclusively for those who have served in the nation's armed forces. I am forced to object." Democrats joined Republicans in applauding Snell when he concluded."[1]

Elsewhere mourning was shown openly. In Bartlesville, Oklahoma, heavy folds of black crepe hung around the *Winnie Mae*, the plane that had taken Wiley Post to world fame. Colonel Art C. Goebel, eminent pilot and Post's friend, supervised the draping of the plane. By a strange twist in the path of events, years earlier the same Art Goebel had refused to accept delivery of the Lockheed Explorer that Roy Ammel had subsequently wrecked in the Canal Zone. Wiley later bought that Explorer's wing from Charley Babb and had it joined to the Orion fuselage of the plane that carried him to his death.

In Seattle, Washington, the local Elks Club lowered its flag to half-staff, saluting the two men who only recently had been guests in their city.

In Ventura, California, so the Associated Press reported, the *Ven-*

---

[1] U.P. report, *Seattle Daily Times*, August 22, 1935.

tura Free Press, in an editorial, urged President Roosevelt to declare
a national day of mourning in tribute to Will Rogers and Wiley Post.

Arkansas, Betty Rogers's home state, observed a day of mourning,
as decreed by the governor.

Nome, Alaska, sorrowfully canceled arrangements for a grand reception. Will Rogers had been quoted in an Associated Press story
as saying that he wanted to rope a reindeer, and the Nome citizens
had had the deer all picked out for him to lasso.[2]

The National Broadcasting Company over KFI and the Columbia
Broadcasting System over KHJ from Los Angeles canceled two thirty-
minute national programs to allow for special coast-to-coast broadcasts. Political leaders, fliers and motion picture celebrities, speaking
from Washington, New York, Chicago, and Los Angeles, expressed
their admiration and affection for the two men. Captain Edward V.
Rickenbacker, the World War's number one American flying ace,
opening a special program of the National Broadcasting Company
from its studios in Washington, New York, and Los Angeles, told
his audience that "They were both men whom aviation can ill afford
to lose."

In Chicago, in the studios of the Columbia Broadcasting System,
former President Herbert Hoover, en route to his California home,
joined former Vice-President General Charles G. Dawes, round-the-
world flier Jimmy Mattern, and veteran airline pilot Jack Knight in
a radio tribute. Mr. Hoover had earlier expressed his personal sorrow over the deaths of Rogers and Post. Breaking their practice of
never speaking out of character on the air, Freeman F. Gosden and
Charles J. Correll interrupted their regular "Amos 'n' Andy" broadcast over WEAF to express their grief.

Mayor F. H. LaGuardia, a wartime pilot, speaking from New
York's own municipal broadcasting station WNYC, shared the personal sadness he felt at the death of two men who were his friends:

> How often, Will Rogers has given each of us something to smile
> about or something to reflect upon. His wise and humorous phi-
> losophy developed into a distinct school of thought. Every day,

---

[2]*Seattle Daily Times*, August 17, 1935.

"Will Rogers Says" started conversation at the breakfast tables of millions of American families. Wiley Post is another martyr to the progress of aviation development. He was another pioneer, a great and courageous flyer. Both men typified to the world, although each in a different way, all that is finest and best in the fiber and soul of American manhood.

A memorial program presented by WOR in New York City, was directed by Bide Dudley, newspaper man and drama critic, who had introduced Will Rogers to newspapers in the 1920s. Others taking part in the program were Jimmy Durante, Victor Moore, Dorothy Stone, and Frank M. Hawks.

A program broadcast from Columbia Broadcasting System station in Los Angeles was devoted to the tributes of leading figures in the motion picture world, who had been friends of both men, while another program broadcast over the Columbia system, through WABC in New York, included eulogies by Senators Warren B. Austin of Vermont, Jesse H. Metcalf of Rhode Island, W. Warren Barbour of New Jersey, James F. Byrnes of South Carolina, William E. Borah of Idaho, Daniel O. Hastings of Delaware, Henry F. Ashurst of Arizona, and Tom Connally of Texas.[3]

At the conclusion of the program in the East, the NBC studios in Los Angeles continued the tribute. Darrell Zanuck, vice-president of Twentieth Century-Fox, Rogers's home studio, paid tribute, as did Col. Roscoe Turner, aviator, and Fred Stone, Will's closest friend. Ruth Etting concluded the program by singing "Just a 'Wearyin' For You."

A number of crusades started at once. The most immediate one was filmdom's ban on actors and actresses flying. New contracts contained a strict clause against travel by airplane, while established stars with longtime contracts were persuaded to take the train.

Francis Lederer, Czechoslovakian-born stage and film star, announced his plan to build a memorial for Rogers and Post as 'Leaders for Peace.' Lederer, himself, was a prime leader in the world peace movement.[4] Postmaster General James A. Farley was requested

---

[3]*New York Herald Tribune*, Aug. 17, 1935.
[4]*Los Angeles News*, August 17, 1935.

through the Denver Rocky Mountain News to issue a special air-mail stamp in tribute to Will Rogers and Wiley Post.[5] A Will Rogers stamp was issued in 1938, and a second one in 1979, both at the then current first class mail value. In 1979 two stamps were issued in memory of Wiley Post. Their value was twenty-five cents, a postage then rarely used.

Newspapers all over the country carried banner headlines of the tragedy and featured the story daily. Some consulted public and self-anointed experts for their analyses of the crash near Barrow. Magazines devoted pages upon pages to recreate the accident. All aspects of the lives of the two men were told and retold. The press asked famous men and women for their evaluations of Rogers and Post. It conducted interviews with friends, acquaintances, co-workers, competitors, and anyone else who ever had come within a mile of either man in order to capitalize on the hot news story.

Without a shred of first-hand information, news writers pointed to the cause for the crash. The most common reason they offered was the most simplistic: "carburetor icing." They argued their finding on grounds that temperature and moisture conditions were right for the formation of tiny ice crystals, which temporarily blocked the free flow of fuel in the carburetor. The engine stalled, they claimed, and the plane fell. An easy conclusion, it placed the blame on an inanimate object, the engine; and it persuaded many.

In Seattle, Washington, Dr. James Whitcomb Brougher, Sr., pastor of the Hinson Memorial Baptist Church, was preparing to leave for Glendale, California. Betty Rogers had specifically requested that Dr. Brougher, an old friend of the Rogers family, be asked to officiate. Her wish was relayed on the telephone by Oscar Lawler.[6]

Though all arrangements concerning the funeral were strictly Betty's, she left the decision regarding transport of the bodies and transportation of the family to the man who had offered to attend to it, her and Will's loyal, dependable friend Charles Lindbergh.

At Lindbergh's instructions, Pacific Alaska Airways had arranged the air transportation for the bodies of both Rogers and Post to Los

[5]Ex: Associated Press dispatch, August 17, 1935.
[6]*Seattle Post-Intelligencer*, August 20, 1935

Angeles and Oklahoma, respectively. The expected day of arrival in California was to be Monday, August 19, weather permitting.

The friendship between Will Rogers and Charles Lindbergh began in 1927 in Mexico, when U.S. Ambassador Dwight Morrow had invited the two of them to help close a rift with the United States' southern neighbor. Morrow's plan not only had worked well, but he also ended up gaining a son-in-law when his daughter, Anne Spencer Morrow, married the famous transatlantic flier in May 1929. After the 1932 kidnapping and death of the Lindberghs' infant, Charles, Jr., perhaps the most sensational crime of the 1930s, Anne and Charles found themselves constantly trying to elude the press. On a visit to Los Angeles in 1934, they did so successfully in the solitude and privacy of the Rogers ranch in Pacific Palisades, California.

Over the years the interest in aviation that Rogers shared with Lindbergh had grown into lasting friendship between the two families. So it was only natural that Lindbergh would contact Betty and offer his services immediately upon hearing of the crash, even though his own family was in the midst of celebrating son Jon's birthday.

Air transportation via TWA had been arranged for the entire family to travel back to California from New York, but the Rogerses decided instead to go by train—not because of aversion to flying, but for the sake of convenience. For a large group of people traveling with substantial baggage, it would simply be easier to use ground transportation. Perhaps, too, they felt that the longer journey on the train would allow the family time to recover enough composure to face the ordeal ahead in Los Angeles.

When the family emerged from their hotel in New York, the Waldorf Astoria, Betty Rogers looked drawn, but composed. Newspapers felt it necessary to point out that the strain of the tragedy showed plainly on the faces of the family. Mary, her golden curls mostly hidden under a small dark blue hat, wore no makeup and, close to tears, stood beside her mother. When the flashbulbs of press cameras exploded, she leaned heavily on her brother's arm. Betty greeted the crowd of reporters and photographers. With a tremor in her voice, she said, "Don't forget to tell the boys that Mr. Rogers was always your friend and he always will be your friend. He was one of you and I know he would want me to give you this message."[7]

A large party drove to Pennsylvania Station that Sunday, August 18. Betty Rogers was accompanied by her daughter, Mary; her two sons, Will, Jr. and Jim; her sister, Theda Blake; her nephew, Jim Blake; Dorothy Stone; and Frank Phillips, the oil millionaire from Bartlesville, Oklahoma and Will's long-time friend, and sponsor of Wiley Post's last four stratosphere flights. They would share the private coach put at their disposal.

That same Sunday, Pacific Alaska Airways' twin-engine Lockheed Electra 10 cabin monoplane, license number NC 14259, bearing the bodies of Wiley Post and Will Rogers, left Fairbanks at 6:05 a.m., local time[8] with Joe Crosson at the controls, Bill Knox as copilot, and Bob Gleason as radio operator. The weather was good in Fairbanks. The flight plan called for a refueling stop at Whitehorse, Yukon, a hop of close to five hundred miles; from there they would fly on to Prince George, British Columbia, and then on to Seattle, Washington.[9]

Ordinarily, crossing the Canadian border was a routine procedure easily resolved at the time of landing. This time protocol was strictly observed. Whether it was the fact that corpses were being taken across an international boundary, or whether it was the fame attached to Post and Rogers, is not known, but in any case the United States Department of State sought authorization from the Government of Canada for the plane to fly over its territory. The State Department acted at the request of Mrs. Wiley Post and Mrs. Will Rogers as well as on representations of Pan-American Airways, Pacific Alaska Airways' parent company. Ottawa immediately granted permission.

After refueling at Whitehorse, the flight proceeded smoothly in the trouble-free weather, and the three men realized that with the fuel reserve aboard, they could reach Seattle without any further stop, provided the atmospheric conditions remained good. Crosson's route took them over more than a thousand miles of rugged, towering

---

[7]*Los Angeles Examiner*, Universal Service, August 19, 1935.
[8]*Fairbanks News-Miner*, August 19, 1935
[9]Sterlings' Conversation with Robert J. Gleason, March 12, 1988

peaks and mountainous plateaus, but the trip seemed almost monotonous. Few of the trappers and prospectors who saw the plane racing through the skies across Alaska, the Yukon, and British Columbia knew its cargo, nor did the advance of Crosson's plane prompt any publicity. Bob Gleason made the flight practically without any radio contacts except for the several required position checks and mandated reports.

Betty Rogers and her party were traveling in a special car attached to the exclusive Pennsylvania Limited that Sunday afternoon. It was the private coach of General W. W. Atterbury, former president of the Pennsylvania Railroad. Scheduled to arrive in Chicago at 7:35 a.m. on Monday, they would then change terminals and continue their journey aboard the Santa Fe Railroad's crack train, the Chief, which was scheduled to reach Los Angeles on Wednesday afternoon, August 21. Plans called for Will's sister Sallie, Mrs. Thomas McSpadden, of Chelsea, Oklahoma, to meet the train at the Kansas City station.[10] Some sixteen years Will's senior, Sallie had raised her ten-year-old brother after their mother's death. Now she would attend his burial.

In Chicago, while changing trains, reporters badgered the family. Will, Jr. provided a buffer by acting as the family's spokesman. With remarkable composure he repeatedly parried the same questions with the same answers. He had also told the press that his father's funeral would be held in Los Angeles on Thursday, August 22, with a private service in the afternoon. The body, he said, would be placed in a vault in Los Angeles and would later be interred in the family's plot at Claremore, Oklahoma.[11]

Even though she was in transit, Charles Lindbergh kept Betty informed of developments. When the Rogers party reached Chicago, they learned that the plane carrying the two bodies would arrive in Los Angeles Monday night. A second telegram informed them that the plane from Fairbanks would spend the night in Vancouver. This second message might have puzzled the Rogers family since they had been expecting the plane to land in Seattle, as planned.

The Lockheed Electra 10 had indeed landed in Vancouver at 4:11

---

[10]*Los Angeles Times*, August 18, 1935
[11]*The Evening Star*, Washington, D.C., August 20, 1935.

p.m., Fairbanks time.[12] A few minutes earlier, over Squamish, thirty miles to the north, the funeral plane's radio operator, Robert J. Gleason, had tapped out: "PLEASE NOTIFY VANCOUVER AUTHORITIES WE ARE ARRIVING. THANKS."

Pilots in Vancouver were impressed, as Crosson's flight from Fairbanks to Vancouver, completed in ten hours and six minutes, was equivalent a transatlantic flight from Newfoundland to Ireland. The reason for the landing in Vancouver lay in a minor complication:

> Well, we flew on down [to Seattle] and the weather was good the whole trip. I had good communications with our station at Fairbanks and Juneau and the PAN-AM station at San Francisco. From them we would get our instructions and Joe [Crosson] headed for Seattle and all at once we got our message from Mr. Prep: 'Land at Vancouver's Sea Island Airport. We actually queried that message to be sure that that was what they wanted us to do—why they wanted us to land at Vancouver. We did land at Vancouver after being told that all arrangements had been made and I had no voice transmitter there so the message was being relayed to Vancouver that we were arriving at such and such a time, and so on. We landed there and they put the airplane in a hangar and they took us out to this I'd say mansion— somewhere—and they put us up for the night—meantime Joe's on the phone with the Pan-American people and—the problem was that the Pan-American airplane which was coming up from Texas to meet us at Seattle wasn't there yet. So we stayed overnight and they told us to arrange to arrive in Seattle at—I don't know whether it was 9 a.m. or 10 a.m."[13]

At Vancouver the airport was almost deserted, its Sunday activity minimal. Crosson was directed toward an empty hangar and he taxied into it. Once Crosson, Knox, and Gleason had assured themselves that their plane was in proper hands, they entered the administration building, where all three refused to be drawn into interviews. Crosson, the captain, made several long-distance telephone calls to New

---

[12]*Fairbanks News-Miner*, August 19, 1935.
[13]Sterlings' interview with Robert J. Gleason, November 11, 1985.

York City and San Francisco, in order to report his whereabouts to
Pan-American Airways officials and to receive new instructions. Ha-
rassed by one persistent reporter, Crosson said only that northern
Alaska was grief stricken and that he knew no more about the crash
than what had already been told—that the motor had misfired as the
plane took off from the small lagoon, and then fell into the shallow
water.

The next morning, Monday, August 19, after Canadian officials
had placed a wreath aboard the ship as Vancouver's tribute to the
dead men, Joe Crosson took off from Sea Island Municipal Airport.
The time was 8:22 a.m. Pacific time. Flying through the early morning haze, forty-seven minutes later he reached Seattle, where he was
met by an army plane and escorted to the airport. Three navy planes,
which had joined him midway between Seattle and Vancouver, followed him to Boeing Field in the southern part of the city; they
circled over the airport, but did not land.

The funeral ship, the curtains of the passenger cabin closely drawn,
was awaited at the field by a large group of civic representatives,
among them W. W. Connor, governor for Washington State of the
National Aeronautics Association and Rudolph Block, secretary for
Mayor Charles L. Smith. Mayor Smith was expected at the field later.
A police detail under Captain L. L. Norton held back from the hangar apron a crowd of some fifteen thousand, some of whom had
remained at the airport all night. More than twenty thousand had
arrived at the airport the day before, to see a plane that did not come.

Without stopping the motors, Crosson taxied the plane into a
United Airlines hangar at the side of the field. The huge doors were
locked, and the hangar was then completely surrounded by the honor
guard of twenty Marine Corps reserves from service Squadron No.
3 and Observation Squadron No. 9, and by the state patrol.[14]

Waiting inside the hangar were thin, dark-haired Colonel Clarence
M. Young, former assistant secretary of commerce for aeronautics,
now Pacific Coast manager of Pan American Airways, and *Fort
Worths Star-Telegram* publisher Amon Carter, who had flown north
from Texas. Parked inside the hangar was a Douglas DC-2 transport
plane, license number NC 14295, with a crew of five men, piloted

---

[14]*Seattle Post-Intelligencer*, August 20, 1935.

by William A. Winston. Pan Am had dispatched the plane from Alameda, California.

With the huge doors of the hangar locked and its security assured, the crew under the direction of three undertakers, transferred the bodies into the after-cabin of the waiting transport. They then strapped down the bodies of the two famous men, still wrapped in their plain white sheeting. Between them were placed a dozen floral pieces. Blue curtains, drawn over the windows, darkened the interior. Somewhere in the emptiness of the cargo plane, Will Roger's long-time friend Amon Carter found a place to sit down; he spent the next hours in private mourning.

At 11:53 a.m., the large DC-2 air transport plane rolled out of the hangar and took off for Los Angeles, California. Pilot Winston charted his course southward mostly along the Pacific coastline. The plane made a single stop, a brief pause at Alameda, where the plane was checked and refueled.

Because the DC-2 was flying along a populated path, it was difficult to keep the plane's progress a secret. News had already been leaked that funeral services for both Rogers and Post would take place at the same time, Thursday, August 22. Will's rites would be held in the Wee Kirk o' the Heather, at Forest Lawn cemetery in Glendale, California, whereas Wiley's service would take place in Oklahoma City, Oklahoma. That much was known, but the press had been unable to discover where in the Los Angeles area the plane would land.

Nor had the newspapers managed to learn the plans for transporting Wiley Post's body to Oklahoma City, although it was assumed that efforts would be made to fly clear of large cities and well known airports in order to prevent the gathering of large crowds.

Monday evening, August 19, at 10:20 p.m., the gray funeral plane bearing the bodies of Wiley Post and Will Rogers landed at Union Air Terminal, Burbank, California. Hours before, crowds had begun to gather at the Terminal. In an effort to reduce the throng to a manageable crowd, the port authorities started the rumor that the funeral plane would land at the Grand Central Air Terminal, in Glendale. The ruse drew only several hundred to the other field, and even those returned quickly to Burbank. Somehow, the crowd knew where the bodies would arrive.

Once on the ground, the plane was wheeled into a hangar where funeral cars waited to take Will's body to Forest Lawn Cemetery. A scuffle broke out when police discovered a photographer hidden in the rafters of the hangar, high above the plane. The intruding photographer was dragged down by police, who smashed his camera and then placed him under arrest. Outside the hangar, police engaged in hand-to-hand skirmishes with photographers and curious spectators who pressed in a body against the doors. Removal of Will Rogers's body was delayed for almost half an hour. Then, preceded by twenty motorcycle policemen, a hearse and two limousines sped out of the hangar and headed for the cemetery. Wiley Post's body was to be taken directly to Oklahoma City, where Oklahoma's Governor Ernest W. Marland had proclaimed Thursday, August 22, a day of public mourning.

> The schedule for Oklahoma's day of mourning was short:
> 12 noon—Memorial service on the south steps of the Capitol, following a period when the body would lie in state in the marble rotunda, and coinciding with the hour of Rogers's funeral in Los Angeles.
> 2 p.m.—Funeral service in First Baptist Church, followed by burial in Memorial Park.

Governor Marland was scheduled to direct public memorial services. Frank Phillips, who had backed the Post stratosphere flights, acted as chairman of a delegation of 150 honorary pallbearers, including Harold Gatty, copilot of Post's first globe-circling flight; Jimmy Mattern, the pilot lost for some time in Siberia in his attempt to break Post's around-the-world record, and Art Goebel, winner of the Dole-Hawaii race. Joe Crosson, Wiley's closest friend, was to be one of the active pallbearers.

The Rogers family wanted to express their gratitude personally to Joe Crosson for his effort to recover the bodies. Charles Lindbergh provided them with the necessary information:

AUG 21, 1935 BILL ROGERS, CARE SANTAFE CHIEF CAR 319 DUE 1 10 PM CROSSON PROCEEDED WITH ALASKAN PLANE FROM LOSANGELES TO OKLAHOMACITY STOP PLANE WILL GO FROM OKLAHOMA CITY TO

TEXAS STOP CROSSON WILL RETURN FROM OKLAHOMACITY TO JUNEAU
ALASKA STOP ADVISE YOU CONTACT HIM IMMEDIATELY CARE MRS POST
OKLAHOMACITY AND ARRANGE FOR MEETING AT MUTUALLY CONVEN-
IENT TIME AND PLACE=

LINDBERGH

Even before the Rogers family arrived back in Los Angeles, the
funeral arrangements for Thursday, August 22, were made public:

7 a.m. to 12 noon—Body lies in state at Forest Lawn Memorial
Park.
2 p.m.—Private funeral rites at Forest Lawn Memorial Park, restricted to the family and friends with cards.
2 p.m.—Memorial services in Hollywood Bowl, open to the public.
2 p.m.—Memorial service, Beverly Hills Community Church.
2 p.m.—Services at motion picture studios.

Governor Marland had telegraphed Mrs. Will Rogers, offering the
use of Oklahoma's State Capitol for the body of her husband to lie
in state:

"If you are going to bury Will in Oklahoma, the people of
Oklahoma would appreciate the privilege of showing their respect, and I tender the use of the State Capitol at whatever day
and hour you choose for the body to lie in state," the wire read.
"The flag on the State Capitol is now flying at half-mast, with
deepest sympathy."[15]

Mrs. Rogers had seriously considered the offer but decided to bury
Will in Los Angeles instead of Oklahoma because she simply did not
feel equal to another long trip after the transcontinental journey from
Maine.[16]

In Los Angeles, several proposals were made to erect a monument

[15]*Los Angeles Times*, August 17, 1935.
[16]*Los Angeles Examiner*, August 18, 1935.

to the memory of Will Rogers, among them one by Joseph Mesmer, a pioneer civic leader and president of the Los Angeles Historical Society. He suggested that the public be invited to participate and that he would contribute $100 to start the fund.[17]

In separate efforts, numerous independent committees and commissions were formed to "crystallize the nationwide sentiment which calls for some tangible expression of the regard in which Will Rogers was held by people in all walks of life." One such commission, headed by Vice-President Nance Garner comprised 230 members, who might have been drawn from *Who's Who in America* and who included many of Will's personal friends: Herbert Hoover, Alfred E. Smith, Marion Davies, Thomas Gore, Billie Burke, Clarence Darrow, James A. Farley, Edsel Ford, Evangeline C. Booth, Patrick J. Hurley, Mountain K. Landis, Louis B. Mayer, William S. Paley, Mary Pickford, Elliott Roosevelt, Igor Sikorsky, Henry Ford, Amelia Earhart, Eddie Cantor, Mrs. Woodrow Wilson, Bernard M. Baruch, William E. Boeing, Richard E. Byrd, James Doolittle, Harry F. Guggenheim, Joseph P. Kennedy, Alice Roosevelt Longworth, Joseph Pershing, Mrs. Adolph S. Ochs, Eddie Rickenbacker, Nelson Rockefeller.[18] While this commission raised a huge sum of money, it never built a memorial. Instead, the money collected went to establish a Will Rogers Memorial Scholarship Fund for handicapped students in three states. UCLA, the University of California at Los Angeles, received a check for $125,000. Another $125,000 established a scholarship fund at the University of Oklahoma, and $60,000 set up a fund at the University of Texas. The first scholarships were to be awarded from proceeds in February 1940.

The State of Oklahoma raised its own memorial to Will Rogers in 1938, though none to Wiley Post. Later efforts to remedy the unequal treatment accorded the two men progressed slowly, to no effect.

As is so often the case, a fraudulent element saw a splendid opportunity to benefit from a nation in grief. Nonexistent committees pretended to collect for memorials, for statues, for plaques, for shrines—and unfortunately preyed upon the trusting public. Some

---

[17]*Los Angeles Examiner*, August 18, 1935.
[18]*Tulsa World*, September 23, 1935

were arrested and tried, most were not. For some time afterward, Betty Rogers was called upon to testify in court that specific sham organizations had not been empowered by her to collect funds for a Will Rogers memorial.

Acting on Betty Rogers's telegraphed instructions from the east coast, Sallie and Tom McSpadden, Will's sister and brother-in-law, had selected the casket in which Will Rogers would be buried. It was an inexpensive bronze coffin of plain design. Mrs. Rogers stressed specifically that no undue expense or display should mar the funeral or burial. Her husband, she said, must go to his final resting place in a manner conforming to the simplicity of his life and with proper regard to the dislike he held for any form of ostentation.

It was announced that Rogers's body would be removed to the gold room of the Forest Lawn chapel. There he would lie in a blue serge suit—the one he called his dress-up suit—a plain garment of the commonest cut and design, and with it wear a soft-collared shirt and his familiar black bow tie. A dozen or more of those ties still hung in his wardrobe. (Even though Will had, with difficulty, finally mastered the art of tying his bows, he had avoided it whenever he could, and he could whenever Mary was there to do it for him.) That the casket would remain closed disappointed the thousands who had hoped to look one more time on the face of Will Rogers as he lay in state. A spokesman for the family stated it had been Will's own wish—expressed more than once in his life—that the casket not be open at his own funeral.[19]

Five times during 1935, Wiley Post had taken off from Union Air Terminal in Burbank. On four of those flights he had attempted to set transcontinental speed records by flying in the stratosphere. On those occasions he always took off at dawn, when few were around to see it, other than a small number of newspapermen. One interested spectator, though, was Will Rogers, who would drive over from his ranch home in Santa Monica Canyon "just to blather," he always said. But it would be Will's hand that was the last to shake Wiley's and Will's voice the last to wish him success. The fifth time Post had left Union Air Terminal in 1935 was the start of the Alaskan trip on which Will Rogers joined him in Seattle. Now, for the last time Wiley

---

[19] *Los Angeles Herald*, August 20, 1935.

would leave from Union Air Terminal to return to Oklahoma. No longer the pilot, Wiley lay in a darkened cabin with silken shades drawn tightly to bar the morbidly curious.[20]

The same crew that had brought Will Rogers and Wiley Post to Los Angeles only hours earlier, again manned the eastbound airliner. Bill Winston was at the controls; J. L. Fleming, junior pilot; T. W. Dowling at the radio; Tom Ward, mechanic. Col. Clarence M. Young, Pacific Coast manager of Pan American Airways, represented the company, and Joe Crosson accompanied the body of his friend to its final resting place. The twin-engined DC-2 landed at Albuquerque, New Mexico, shortly after 11 a.m. (mountain standard time) for refueling. It took off shortly thereafter to continue its flight to Oklahoma City.

Wednesday afternoon, August 21, Santa Fe's super train, the Chief, stopped at Victorville, California, less than a hundred miles from Los Angeles. Here, far from the crowd waiting in downtown Los Angeles, Betty Rogers and her daughter, Mary, left the train to continue the journey home by automobile. At Azusa, some twenty-five miles from Los Angeles, most of the remaining relatives and friends of the family detrained and proceeded to waiting automobiles. "They were met by Fred Stone, the actor, who embraced his daughter, Dorothy, and the Rogers boys with tears in his eyes," Associated Press reported on August 21, 1935. Eventually the family gathered again in the rambling ranch house in Santa Monica canyon. It was the eve of the funeral, and though they made a rather large group, each was alone with her or his thoughts of the morrow.

The nation's newspapers ran banner headlines on the eve of the two funerals. America paid heed to little else. Many cities lowered their flags to half-staff. Letters and telegrams offering condolences to the Rogers family flooded the post office and telegraph office in Beverly Hills. Hollywood's film colony announced that it would participate in the greatest funeral demonstration ever given one of its number. Fox Studios, where Rogers worked, would close at 1 p.m.

"HOMAGE WILL BE GREATEST EVER ACCORDED TO PRIVATE CITIZENS" shouted a Los Angeles daily. "FAMILY OF ROGERS RETURNS HOME ON EVE OF MEMORIAL" blared the

---

[20]*Los Angeles Herald-Express*, August 20, 1935.

Tulsa World. Reporting on preparations in Oklahoma City, Associated Press announced "WILEY POST'S HOME TOWN PAYS LAST TRIBUTE TO NOTED FLYER." Referring to the scheduled radio broadcast another screamed "NATION WILL HEAR SERVICES IN HOLLYWOOD BOWL."

Radio indeed planned its tribute to the man whose own broadcasts had rallied his countrymen in the depth of the Depression and had, as President Roosevelt said, "brought hope where there had been despair." Now radio, which had brought Will's voice into the nation's remotest villages, would broadcast across a transcontinental network of stations the services held for him at the Hollywood Bowl. Los Angeles station KNX would carry it on the West Coast. The Yankee network and Mutual network would carry the broadcast to the East and Middle West, through their local stations. For the first time ever, other radio stations planned to observe thirty minutes of silence, starting at two o'clock, the time of the funeral services. Furthermore, motion picture houses across the country would interrupt performances with a two-minute break; screens would remain dark.

California's Governor Merriam issued a proclamation asking that all flags within the state be lowered to half-mast: "We cannot let death take Will Rogers and Wiley Post from us, without giving expression to our sense of personal loss." The governor further proclaimed that a moment of reverent silence be observed at precisely 2 p.m. in every town and hamlet of the state. In his proclamation, Mayor Edward Spence of Beverly Hills urged that all business activity in that city be suspended from 2 until 4 p.m. out of respect for Will Rogers. And in the records of Los Angeles' Municipal Court the following order was transcribed: "In memory of the late Will Rogers and Wiley Post, it is hereby requested that everyone rise and stand for one minute in silent tribute to these two great men who have passed on." At the Hall of Justice a bugler would sound taps and at 2 p.m. there would be a minute of silence to honor Will Rogers and Wiley Post.

Maysville, Oklahoma, the home of Wiley Post's parents, was a small town some forty miles south of Oklahoma City. For two hot, sweltering days its citizens had prepared their tiny community for the arrival of the body of their world-famous townsman. Streets in the business section had been swept and washed pristine. Flags were liberally displayed, most of them at half mast along the main thoroughfare. The Landmark Baptist Church, which Wiley's father had helped to build, had been beautifully decorated with homegrown flowers and hothouse bouquets. Unpaved streets within a radius of one or two blocks of the line of procession were periodically sprinkled to settle the dust that thousands of feet would quickly stir into clouds again.

In Oklahoma City, Wiley Post's body lay in state in the rotunda of the State Capitol for two hours. The open coffin, a beautiful bronze casket guarded by a National Guard detail, was seen by 15,000 people, many of them Post's friends. Hundreds of floral displays had arrived and stood around the coffin. Even A. A. Troyanovsky, ambassador of the Union of Soviet Socialist Republics, had sent a wreath, in which five hundred pink carnations were decorated with lilies of the valley and roses; his note expressed deepest sympathy for the family.The display sent by Joe and Lillian Crosson was a large propeller made of flowers which bore in lavender the letters "Q.B." signifying "Quiet Birdmen," aviation's most exclusive organization. The widowed Mrs. Post, appreciative of the outpouring indicated by the thousands of flower displays and bouquets, asked that the flowers be distributed to Oklahoma City hospitals.

At noon, while thousands of mourners still awaited an opportunity for a last look at the flier's face, the state's official observance began. President Roosevelt had ordered that he be represented at the funerals of Post and Rogers, through the War and Navy Departments, by men with the rank of general or admiral. These officers were to lay wreaths on behalf of the president and the government. Brig. Gen. H. W. Butner of Fort Sill, representing President Roosevelt and accompanied by Governor Marland, walked through a lane forced open by guardsmen to the second floor of the Capitol, where the body lay. Overhead, airplanes dipped their wings in salute. Governor Marland, in a short address, said:

> Wiley Post flew around the earth. Wiley Post ascended above the earth to heights unattained by man. Today Wiley Post precedes us, his friends, on that greater journey we all must take some day.
>
> Happy landing, Wiley Post in that heaven of all brave souls.

The body of Oklahoma's son begins the sleep eternal beneath the sod he loves. Nothing we poor mortals can do or say will add to the lasting glory or prestige of these two Oklahoma sons. Fare thee well, Will Rogers, fare thee well, Wiley Post. Happy Landing.

There followed a brief invocation by the Rev. William Slack, former naval airman and now minister of the Methodist Church at Lawton, Oklahoma; then the casket was moved toward the south steps of the Capitol and to a hearse. Because of the crowds, progress toward the church was difficult.

Final rites at Oklahoma City's First Baptist Church began at 2 p.m. Services in the small church were conducted by the Rev. W. R. White, pastor of the church and the Rev. J. H. Gardner of Sentinel, Oklahoma. In a steady line, two abreast, plain men and women, neighbors, friends and admirers walked between guardsmen at arms and through the church to get a fleeting glimpse at the famous flier's face. The number who viewed the remains here was conservatively estimated at near 5,000. The Baptist Church was filled to overflowing and hundreds gathered outside.

When the news made the rounds that Joe Crosson, the heroic flier who had brought the bodies back from the top of the world, was with the funeral party, everyone craned to see him and many pressed in to touch him, or to get his autograph.

The service was simple, as simple as Wiley, the man, had been. Following a prayer, a quartet sang "Lead Kindly Light," and then the Rev. W. R. White delivered a brief sermon. He read from Isaiah: "Who are these that fly as a cloud, and as the doves to their windows?"

As soon as services were concluded, the church was cleared of everyone except immediate relatives. For a few moments more the members of the family remained alone with their dead. Then, on a signal, the national guardsmen and police officers cleared a path to the waiting hearse. Borne aloft by Wiley's friends, the coffin was placed in the hearse and taken along crowded streets to the mausoleum.

Thousands rushed forward toward the hearse as it started on its way to Fairlawn Cemetery. Planes swooped low to scatter roses over

Wiley's coffin and in its path. The thin police line was easily broken and several women fainted in the crush to catch some of the flowers strewn from the sky, but the crowd stayed orderly. Slowly the procession made its way to Fairlawn's Mausoleum, where Wiley Post's body was to rest that night in the company of members of the State Militia standing guard.

Wiley's body was interred in Edmond, Oklahoma, his grave marked by a small, flat stone that easily escapes the eye. It would be six decades before an appropriate sign of admiration for a heroic pioneer would mark Wiley Post's last resting place.

At the very hour of the funeral procession in Oklahoma City, New York City fliers paid their own tribute to Wiley Post and Will Rogers in a massive flight over the city. The display had been mounted by the executive committee of the Gascraft Club, which was composed of representatives of the aviation, motorboat, and automobile industries; Wiley Post had been one of its founders. Led by five navy planes, a squadron of twenty-four planes followed a carefully mapped course from Floyd Bennett Field on Long Island, up New York Bay to the Hudson River, then north over Manhattan and finally back to the field over Brooklyn. The flotilla, trailing black streamers from rudders, was led by Captain William C. Allison and included Clyde Pangborn, famous round-the-world flier as well as one woman pilot, Miss Viola Gentry. More than a million people upturned their faces to witness the spectacular farewell to two great Americans.

Philadelphia, too, bade good-bye to Will Rogers and Wiley Post. Numerous state, city, and naval officials as well as civic leaders delivered eulogies. Airplanes flew over the assembled crowd and dipped their wings in tribute to the great proponents of aviation. Hundreds attended the memorial services at Mustin Field in Philadelphia's Navy Yard. City Hall flags had been lowered to half-mast.

In San Diego, California, sorrow stopped the California Pacific International Exposition in Balboa Park. A crowd of ten thousand, at the behest of a loudspeaker announcement, stood with bared heads as the American flag at the Plaza del Pacifico fluttered slowly down the pole to half-mast and a bugler from the Thirtieth U.S. Infantry rifle company sounded taps in farewell to Will Rogers and Wiley Post. A contingent of soldiers conducted modified military funeral services. After marching down the Avenue of Palaces to the measured strains of Chopin's funeral march, the solemn procession halted as the band took its stance in front of the Palace of Science. The soldiers stood at parade rest. Dr. Roy Campbell, Congregational minister, delivered a short and simple eulogy. Even concession barkers and musicians were silent, and the fair fell to a hush for the tribute.[21]

In Alaska, 22 WAMCATS stations of the U.S. Signal Corps, remained silent for five minutes from noon to 12:05 out of respect for Wiley Post and Will Rogers.

The eyes of the country may have been on Oklahoma City, Los Angeles, or even little Maysville. But Claremore, Oklahoma, the county seat of Rogers County and Will's claimed hometown, conducted its own service. By 2 p.m. the thermometer had topped 100 degrees hours ago and a sweltering crowd broiled under the searing August sun. Women fainted. The restless crowd at the single brownstone hangar of modest Will Rogers Airport fidgeted in the almost unbearable heat through the speeches and songs. Among the mourners were some of Will's relatives by blood and marriage; neighbors and boyhood friends, and his fellow Shriners from the Akdar Temple in Tulsa, who had come in twenty motor cars escorted by six motorcycle policemen. Friends of Will and the Rogers family had come from nearby Chelsea and Muskogee, from Tahlequah and Pryor. Though not the most remarkable ceremony held that day, it was the most heartfelt. An entire small hometown had turned out for its beloved favorite son. Many of the people here had known Willie as a boy, had seen him grow into a man. He had been one of them, he had gone out into the world and had made a happy difference in it. He had put their little town along Route 66 on the way to Tulsa, the town called Claremore, on the map. Now, Uncle Clem Rogers's boy, Willie, was gone, and all of them there that day felt they had lost part of themselves.

The ceremony ended with the Spartan Dawn Patrol, three privately owned small planes, flying over the dusty field. Perhaps fittingly, one of those planes was a Lockheed Orion. At the same moment, an American Air Express plane, en route from Los Angeles to New

---

[21]*Los Angeles Herald Express*, August 16, 1935.

York, circled the airport once and dipped its wing to honor Clare-more's most famous citizen. Indeed, American Air Express had given orders that all their planes flying over Claremore during the next ten days pay similar tribute.

And then it was over. The friends and neighbors of the extended family had met. They had prayed and they had remembered. They would remember to the end of their days.

During the early hours of Thursday, August 22, 1935, a multitude gathered outside Forest Lawn Memorial Park in Glendale, California. The gates did not open until 7 a.m., but already at 1 a.m. men and women had begun arriving to stand in line. The automobiles of mourners were soon jamming highways for miles, and on the San Fernando Road, the main artery leading directly to the cemetery from surrounding communities in the Los Angeles area, the traffic slowed to a snail's pace as early as 5 a.m. Cars looking for parking spaces choked the side streets, and "snack joints" for miles around did brisk business.

Glendale and Los Angeles police, deputy sheriffs and other law-enforcement officers had held several meetings to draw up rules de-signed to preserve decorum, to direct the flow of people in line, and to avoid general confusion. Final plans called for every road and highway leading to Forest Lawn to be posted with four hundred members of the traffic squad of the Los Angeles police department assigned to special duty at the cemetery. In addition, soldiers and marines were detailed to assist the city's law-enforcement officers. The strategies worked perfectly, and at the end of the service, the police would report that they had never worked a more orderly throng.[22]

The honor guard was in place by 7 a.m. It included forty non-commissioned officers, four commissioned officers, and four flying cadets from March Field, under Lieut. Jesse Auton, First Wing U.S. Army, with Major Gen. H. H. "Hap" Arnold of March Field in com-mand of the detail. For five hours, eight at a time for half-hour in-tervals, the honor guard would stand watch at Will Rogers's casket, its drape a floral cover in the shape of a huge American flag. The brisk changing of the guard every thirty minutes was commanded by

---

[22]Los Angeles Times, August 23, 1935.

Lieutenant Auton, who had known Will Rogers personally, and for thirty minutes the eight non-commissioned fliers stood smartly at attention, "their eyes never wavering from their straight gaze toward the heights of the Hollywood Hills."[23] The family had decided that the active pallbearers should be chosen from this honor guard of March Field pilots. There would be no honorary pallbearers because "Rogers had so many friends that we wouldn't know where to start or leave off if we began selecting pallbearers," stated Oscar Lawler, the family's lawyer.

When the gates of Forest Lawn swung open precisely at 7 a.m., the line of mourners extended for more than a mile and the crowd increased at the rate of a block every fifteen minutes. The crowd approached the main gate in three roped lanes, and spectators filed by the flower-banked casket at the rate of ninety a minute, although police soon had to increase that rate dramatically. In the first hour ten thousand men, women and children walked past the catafalque.

Behind the casket, in the middle of the semi-circle along which the public passed, a number of newsreel cameramen recorded the hushed, somber procession; many were deeply affected. Nobody spoke, nobody stepped out of line; many cried openly.

One young boy placed his token near the coffin: a small coil of rope decorated with a single sprig of fern and one rose. The card read, "Just my lariat."[24]

The hours passed and still they came. Thousands upon thousands. Police reports varied in the numerous newspaper accounts, the actual figure lying somewhere between the two extremes cited at one-hundred to one-hundred and fifty thousand. As the closing hour of twelve noon approached, the officers in charge realized that the thousands still lining up would never get to see the coffin. To avoid disappointment, the police officers first doubled, then quadrupled the lines and mourners were "rushed through past the casket in droves, though good order was still maintained," the wire services reported. The police barred the entrance promptly at noon, but they could claim that all those who had come to say their farewell to Will Rogers had been able to do so.

---

[23]*Los Angeles Times*, August 23, 1935.
[24]Ibid.

Only four hundred relatives and friends of the family had been invited to attend the strictly private ceremony in The Wee Kirk o' the Heather in Forest Lawn Memorial Park. Since the small chapel could only seat 125 persons, chairs had been set up immediately outside the stone building. Among the guests were generals and ranch hands, movie stars and unknowns, family and hired help; but all of them were either family or close friends. The onlookers outside the guarded gates witnessed among the arriving mourners a procession of some of Hollywood's most glamorous and the nation's most notable personalities: Billie Burke, Mr. And Mrs. Eddie Cantor, Mr. And Mrs. Harry Carey, Leo Carillo, Charles Chaplin, Walt Disney, Amelia Earhart Putnam, Mr. And Mrs. James A. Farley, Stepin Fetchit, Clark Gable, James Gleason, Mr. And Mrs. Samuel Goldwyn, Sid Grauman, William S. Hart. William R. Hearst, Howard Hughes, Rabbi Magnin, Mr. And Mrs. Louis B. Mayer, Mary Pickford, Spencer Tracy, Col. And Mrs. Roscoe Turner, Cornelius Vanderbilt, Jr., Darryl Zanuck, Patricia Ziegfeld. Rear Admiral W. T. Tarrant, U.S.N. of San Diego, Commandant of the Eleventh Naval District was designated to represent his Commander in Chief, President Franklin D. Roosevelt. Brigadier General H. H. "Hap" Arnold represented the army. The United States Department of Commerce was represented by Gene Vidal, chief of the aeronautics division.

Flowers blanketed the entire slope of the hill outside the Wee Kirk. Wreaths, arrangements, bouquets and funeral pieces had arrived from friends and kin, from cities and states, from organizations and societies, aviation groups and the Baseball Writers Association of America, the Grand British Veterans, the government of the Soviet Union, the Chuck Wagon Trailers, and "the boys from the stables." On Betty Rogers's instructions, the flowers were later distributed among hospital wards in Los Angeles and Glendale.

To the plaintive strains of "Old Faithful," one of Will's favorite hymns, the body was borne into the chapel. Softly the pipe organ then played "Old Rugged Cross," and other airs that had been familiar to Will since boyhood—"In the Cross of Christ I Glory," "Beautiful Isle of Somewhere," "Saved by Grace," and "I Love to Tell the Story." The service began promptly after the family arrived. Betty and the closest relatives were seated in an alcove from where they could view the casket but were themselves out of the view of the congregation.

The Reverend Dr. James Whitcomb Brougher, Sr., delivered the eulogy. For the better part of an hour, he mixed poetry and simple words to paint a picture of Will as the world—and he—knew him. Dr. Brougher and Will Rogers had been friends for years. Once, in the early twenties, they had staged a mock debate: 'Resolved, that the movies have been more beneficial to humanity than preachers.' "It's the most uneven question I suppose ever debated," wrote Will. "I have the movie side, and he is such a nice fellow that I really feel ashamed to see him try and bring preaching up to the level of one of the arts."[25] Often close to tears himself, Dr. Brougher profoundly moved his listeners. Clark Gable sobbed almost continually. Billie Burke, one of the few wearing black, nearly collapsed with grief and almost had to be carried from the chapel at the conclusion of the service.

In his tribute, Dr. Brougher put into words what most of the men and women in the nation were feeling that sad summer day in August 1935:

> ... There are many streams, but only here and there a great Mississippi; there are many echoes, but only now and then an original voice; there are many musicians, but only now and then a Mendelssohn or a Mozart; There are many people, but only now and then an outstanding individual; When a great personality suddenly appears, the world stops in its busy rush to look and listen. The monotony of life is broken for a moment. A man who is "different" has attracted the attention of all. Such has been the unique and commanding position of Will Rogers during the last quarter of a century. He has been the one figure in the life of our nation who had drawn to himself the admiration and the love of all classes of people . . . he had a genius for love. He loved people . . .

While rites were being held at Forest Lawn the life of America virtually stopped. Business paused; public offices closed; masses hud-

---

[25]Will Rogers's Weekly Article, December 16, 1923

dled around their radios; more than a dozen Hollywood film studios were silent. "Never," so Associated Press claimed, "in the history of this country has a private citizen been handed over to eternity amid such a demonstration of public love and admiration as the homage paid to Will Rogers." New York's *Herald Tribune* stated it even more passionately: "Will Rogers hadn't a living peer in the affection of America's millions. Wiley Post ranked next to Lindbergh as their hero of the air."

CHAPTER XIV

THE INVESTIGATION

Wiley was a fatalist, totally unafraid, totally unaware that death might some day catch up with him. Post never used the words 'killed' or 'death' or 'cracked up.' People to him 'popped off.' And there was always a human cause, airplanes just did not kill people because they were airplanes, someone was always to blame.

> According to Bennie Turner, reporter for the *Daily Okla-homan*, a close friend.

THE GOVERNMENT'S INVESTIGATION into the crash killing Will Rogers and Wiley Post was a travesty. It started with an obligation to candor but ended with the much older obligation to protect the status quo.

The Air Commerce Act of 1926 charged the Secretary of Commerce not only with regulating air commerce, but also with certificating aircraft for airworthiness, and with investigating and determining the causes of accidents in civil air navigation. It was an entirely new area of responsibility for a long-established government department. Aviation by the 1930s was a in a state of rapid evolution; what had begun as a precarious novelty was emerging into a respectable necessity. Its growth from infancy toward maturity was temporarily stunted, though, by America's Great Depression, and President Franklin D. Roosevelt's need for economy created a special hardship on aviation. Congress wielded a merciless ax in cutting the department's appropriation to $7.7 million—a stunning blow in itself, but the president then impounded an additional one-third of that already inadequate amount. By 1934, the Air Commerce section had been cut to about half the budget it had had in 1933, when Roosevelt took office. The force in the aviation section of the Air Commerce department was reduced by exactly one-third. All associate and junior airway engineers, all junior civil engineers, and all but six assistant airways engineers were fired. Moreover, the travel allowance for aeronautical and airplane inspectors was cut by 50 percent. And the Aeronautics Research Division in the Bureau of Standards was abolished. Despite declining morale and fear of cutbacks, the Bureau of Air Commerce retained an enviable imperial position. Not only did the Bureau continue to make laws to regulate air traffic and safety, but it also maintained the responsibility of enforcing those laws and—in case of accidents—of acting as judge, jury, and hangman, all conveniently wrapped into one. The Bureau held an ideal vantage point from which to close one or even both eyes to its own complicity or culpability, whenever or wherever found, in matters under its own aegis or investigation.

In 1935, the Secretary of Commerce was Daniel Calhoun Roper. He was well qualified for the position; for two decades he had served his apprenticeship in various elected and appointed positions connected with Commerce, Trade, and Tariff. He had started in the House of Representatives of his native South Carolina at age twenty-seven and had reached the position of first assistant postmaster general before becoming U.S. commissioner of internal revenue in 1917. In 1921, with the Democrats no longer in control of the White House, Roper headed the law firm of Roper, Hagerman, Hurrey, Parks & Dudley until 1933, when Franklin D. Roosevelt called him into his cabinet.

The Bureau of Air Commerce fell under the umbrella of the Commerce Department, but with its own chief executives, including, in 1935, Eugene Vidal, Director of Air Commerce; Col. J. Carroll Cone, Assistant Director; and Denis Mulligan, Chief of the Enforcement Section, Air Regulations Division, and Vidal's assistant. All of them highly competent, honorable men, they worked with vision and integrity in a field then only 32 years old; perforce, they also worked within governmental bureaucracy. To keep their Bureau viable they had to allow—and follow—higher governmental dictates and at the same time retain the public's confidence in governmental aviation supervision. In the matter of Wiley Post's fatal airplane accident, they also had to act with extraordinary discretion because he was not just an ordinary pilot; he was a hero who had conquered the air and the stratosphere. They could not create misgivings in the public's mind by tarnishing the reputation of a man heroized by practically all of America.

The investigation of Post's case turned up instances of irresponsibility and guilt enough to destroy a number of reputations and careers. While these culpable agents could be protected from the public, they did not entirely escape from internal scrutiny. Thanks to that commendable flicker of departmental honesty, documents have survived—scattered though they may be—which reveal a massive web of guilt and responsibility that contributed to the accident. Laws were broken, duties shirked, common sense disregarded, established procedure ignored, and advice scorned. Two lives were lost, and for at least a half dozen reasons. As in almost all such investigations, someone's head would have to roll—as long as it did not belong to anyone of importance.

Announcing investigations, the *Los Angeles Times* on August 18 wrote: "SENATE GROUP OPENS PROBE OF DISASTER." The article explained that Senator Copeland, Democrat of New York, had convened his special committee for investigation of fatal air accidents—a committee appointed just three months earlier, following the crash that had killed—among others—Senator Bronson Cutting of New Mexico. The committee had also proved to be ineffectual in Cutting's case, as had the aeronautical section of the Department of Commerce.

The Cutting accident occurred on May 6, 1935. A scheduled TWA

DC-2 crashed in bad weather near Kansas City. It killed the pilot and four passengers and injured eight others. Learning that earlier weather reports had substantially changed, the pilot had tried to reach an alternate, unfamiliar airport under adverse atmospheric conditions. Here, as in Wiley Post's case, the weather played a significant part in the crash. On the occasion of the Cutting crash, however, immediately after the accident, Vidal dispatched to the scene two Bureau of Air Commerce officials—Denis Mulligan, and R. W. "Shorty" Schroeder, Chief of the Air Line Inspection Service, Air Regulation Division. They were joined there by airline inspectors Dr. R. E. Whitehead, Richard C. Gazley, and Jesse L. Lankford. They made up the Bureau of Air Commerce Accident Board,[1] and in six days of hearings, they questioned fifty-nine witnesses and recorded more than nine hundred pages of testimony. The findings were nonetheless bewildering. On June 14, almost six weeks after the accident, the board made their determinations public. In what must be the most ridiculous of board findings on record, the Bureau of Air Commerce announced with a perfectly straight face:

"THE PROBABLE DIRECT CAUSE OF THIS ACCIDENT WAS AN UNINTENTIONAL COLLISION WITH THE GROUND WHILE THE AIRPLANE WAS BEING MANEUVERED AT A VERY LOW ALTITUDE IN FOG AND DARKNESS."

The conclusion that Senator Cutting's death occurred because the plane hit the ground was a revelation of only the obvious. It hardly required five men's trips to Kansas City, a board, or the interrogation of a single witness.

And that, in essence, is what did happen in the investigation of the Post-Rogers crash. The Bureau arrived at its determination without flights to Alaska, members of a board, hearings, or the systematic interrogation of witnesses. Mostly the bureau strove to escape departmental involvement. When that appeared impossible, it hunted some minor culprit. The entire investigation, conducted, largely via long distance by mail or by telegram, amounted to little more than hearsay and rumor.

For example, on August 27, three days prior to the issuance of the

---

[1]"THE CUTTING AIR CRASH" by Nick A. Komons, Dept. of Transport, FAA, Agency Historical Staff. © 1973.

first and most important governmental statement on the crash, Eugene Vidal, the Director of Air Commerce, was still seeking answers:

> JUAN TRIPPE, PRESIDENT, PAN AMERICAN AIRWAYS INC,
> CHRYSLER BUILDING, NEW YORK
> CHECKING FACTORS LEADING UP TO POST ROGERS CRASH WOULD LIKE
> TO KNOW WHETHER OR NOT PAN AMERICAN WAS IN ANY WAY IN-
> VOLVED WITH POSTS FLIGHT OR PROPOSED FLIGHTS.
>
>   VIDAL

One wonders what would Wiley's involvement with PAN-AM or its knowledge of Wiley's current or future plans have to do with the crash.

That same date, the director sent out other telegrams:

> DAYLETTER, ALFRED LOWMAN (SIC), COLMAN BUILDING, SEATTLE
> WASHINGTON:
> DISCUSSED POST ROGERS ACCIDENT WITH YOUR BROTHER TODAY AND
> WOULD APPRECIATE YOUR WIRING US WHAT CONCLUSIONS YOU MIGHT
> HAVE REACHED OR SPECULATIONS AS TO CAUSE OF ACCIDENT AFTER
> VISITING WRECK STOP ALSO IT WOULD ASSIST US IF YOU MAILED SKETCH
> OF LAGOON AND PATH OF PLANE.
>
>   VIDAL, DIRECTOR OF AIR COMMERCE.

How would the Reindeer Corporation owner, Mr. Lomen, who was neither an aviator nor an engineer, have any idea what might have caused an accident? Not having been there at the time, how could he possiby know what had happened? If Vidal wanted to know what had taken place, why did he not interview Stella and Clair Okpeaha instead of asking a man who had been a thousand miles away for his "speculations"?

The following telegram, too, only raises questions about Vidal's reasoning:

DAYLETTER, EDO FLOAT COMPANY, COLLEGE POINT, LONG ISLAND, NY
WOULD APPRECIATE YOUR MAILING IMMEDIATELY ALL INFORMATION
AND DRAWINGS FOR ARRANGEMENT OF FLOATS ON WILEY POST PLANE

EUGENE L. VIDAL, DIRECTOR OF AIR COMMERCE

What could EDO, a company on Long Island, New York, know about the attachment of floats to Wiley's plane in Renton, in the state of Washington? EDO did not even know whether the floats they had sent had arrived, or even if there were other floats that had been attached. It is astonishing to think that the government's statement concerning the Wiley Post-Will Rogers crash was formulated without having from actual eyewitnesses and participants the full answers to any of these and other, even more essential questions.

Director Eugene Vidal did fly to Los Angeles, ostensibly to attend Will Rogers's funeral as a representative of the Department. In reality he wanted to meet with Joe Crosson and talk to Inspector James E. Reed in person.

Inspector Reed had crossed Wiley's path many times and he was very important to this investigation. It was he who had licensed Post for operation of an aircraft radio and he had observed the daily progress of the work done on Wiley's plane at Pacific Airmotive Corporation in Burbank. Reed, too, had approved the issuance of the restricted license, although he himself had never flown in the plane, either as pilot or passenger. He therefore knew nothing firsthand about the actual airworthiness of that plane, and yet he had issued a certificate under which Wiley could not only fly it but also carry people in it.

Point # 10 of Wiley's license application asked: "State most convenient flying field and nearest town where aircraft may be inspected for airworthiness?" Post had answered " 'Burbank, Calif." The government's inspector, James E. Reed, worked at that airport every day, but somehow did not find the opportunity to test for airworthiness. Why? It seems implausible that an experienced employee of the Bureau of Air Commerce with the rank of an inspector, did not distrust such a haphazardly assembled plane and suspect that it was nose-heavy. It is nonetheless indisputable that Inspector Reed did not test Wiley's plane. He admitted it, though he proffered a strange excuse:

He had, he said, issued a "restricted" airworthiness certificate, which limited the use of the aircraft only to those personnel needed to perform the duties assigned to the experimental plane; no passengers were to be transported. If the nation's foremost pilot, Wiley Post, thought that he would like to fly this plane, the inspector seemed to have reasoned, who was he, James E. Reed, to say that it was not airworthy?

Later, in Seattle, the plane underwent still further alterations. Should not the plane have then been tested, or retested, for airworthiness? "Good Lord," Secretary of Commerce Roper must have wondered, "had anybody, anywhere, at any time ever tested this plane?"

Eugene Vidal's foremost thought seems to have been to protect the Bureau of Air Commerce and to prove absence of any contributory responsibility. In a not uncommon bureaucratic response in Washington, D.C., Vidal ordered an internal search to determine the limits of his Department's obligations: Did an inspector really have to test for airworthiness? What about a restricted license? Did a plane already granted a restricted license have to be retested?

On August 27, 1935, Eugene L. Vidal sent an interoffice memo to Denis Mulligan, Chief of the Enforcement Section, Air Regulations Division:

> Following discussion with Colonel Johnson, [Colonel J. Monroe Johnson, Assistant Secretary of Commerce], it was decided to check into the authority of the Department regarding the 'R' license in the case of the Wiley Post plane. We are anxious to find out whether or not an inspector should have checked over the plane in Seattle after Post had changed from wheels to floats, which change, by the way, resulted in a very nose-heavy characteristic.

Denis Mulligan's detailed reply was distressing, as it slammed shut every possible escape hatch by which the Bureau of Air Commerce might have tried to slough off responsibility. Mulligan filed his response eight days after he received the memo, on September 4, 1935. The date is significant, as it is precisely the same date on which the U.S. Department of Commerce, Bureau of Air Commerce, presented

its first official findings on the causes of the crash in a report that
had in fact been prepared several days earlier, but bearing the restriction: "For Release Morning papers Wednesday, September 4,
1935." Thus it is quite obvious that an official conclusion had already been reached and was published when the actual investigation
had barely even begun.

In his extremely thorough report to Director Vidal, Mr. Mulligan
indicated that "This information has been obtained through consul-
tation with members of the Registration, Engineering, and General
Inspection Sections." Mulligan then quoted pertinent points from the
Air Commerce Act of 1926, as amended; the Regulations made
thereunder, contained in Aeronautics Bulletin No. 7; Application for
Aircraft License, Form AB-9; the Inspector's Handbook of Instructions; and Aircraft Folder, NC-12283 "Inspector's Handbook of Instructions, IV.—AIRCRAFT INSPECTION FOR LICENSE Section
A.—Field Inspection of Airplanes # 3. Inspection Procedure, and he
presented the consensus: "Since you are responsible for the airworthy
condition of every airplane which you approve for license, an investigation into the operation and a thorough inspection of each airplane should be made to satisfy yourself that it is eligible for license
and airworthy."

Point # 4. When Airplane is Approved for License
a) IN CASE OF RESTRICTED LICENSE, show the definite
purpose for which the airplane is to be used in the space provided
above the name of owner and write on card:
*NO PASSENGER OTHER THAN BONA FIDE MEMBERS
OF THE CREW MAY BE CARRIED. [Emphasis added]*
Point # 8. RESTRICTED AIRPLANE "airworthy" airplanes
which are being used for some special class of operation, Crop
dusting, Skywriting, Photography, (when the cameras are a permanent installation), Sign-carrying airplanes, Endurance types,
with big fuel tankage, "Special long range planes. . . ."
*RESTRICTED LICENSES WILL NOT BE ISSUED TO
AIRCRAFT USED FOR PLEASURE FLYING.* [Emphasis
added]
Point # 10. *ALTERATIONS IN GENERAL*, airplanes which

have been altered from the approved design as shown in the licensing specifications are not eligible for license and *SHOULD, THEREFORE, NOT BE APPROVED BY INSPECTORS IN THE FIELD WITHOUT WRITTEN OR TELEGRAPHIC AUTHORITY FROM THE WASHINGTON OFFICE.* [Emphasis added]

From the Air Commerce Act of 1926, as amended: Sec. 11. It shall be unlawful, . . .

3)to navigate any aircraft registered as an aircraft of the United States, in violation of the terms of any such certificate.

Class A.—The following changes are examples of alterations from the approved design, which will necessitate submission of technical data and possible flight test. *Planes so altered may not be licensed until approval of the changes has been issued by the Washington office* (Emphasis added):

X   Increase in fuel and oil capacity;
X   Increase in seating capacity;
X   Structural changes of any part or component;
X   Changes in control surfaces or systems; Changes in seating arrangement where load distribution is altered in such a manner that it may affect the stability;
X   Installation of pontoons;
     Installation of skis;
     Installation of wheel pants.

[Those identified with '**X**' apply to Wiley Post's plane, the aircraft described, NR-12283.] "The last operations inspection report was approved and signed by Inspector James E. Reed. Against the question of "Total Air Time?" Inspector Reed wrote: *NONE* The craft is denominated "land plane", and "restricted to long cross-country flights and special test work". Opposite the question "crew" appear the words, *'Pilot, mechanic, and observer.'* [Not in the Mulligan report but noted when the original report was located, was Inspector Reed's hand-written "NONE" against the question of TOTAL AIRCRAFT AIR TIME: This clearly indicates that Inspector Reed did not fly in the plane.

This summary by Denis Mulligan clearly shows that several significant violations of departmental rules and laws had taken place. The fact was that aboard an 'R' rated, restricted aircraft, "No passenger other than bona fide members of the crew may be carried," as Point 4 (a) above states. Yet Inspector Reed took it upon himself to amend the regulations by adding: "Observer." The Restricted Aircraft License No: NR 12283, issued August 8, 1935, specifically states under the item Passengers (less crew): "NONE". In order to qualify as a bona fide member of the crew, and be an observer, that observer would have to be technically qualified to 'observe' something, say, the performance of the plane, or its engine, or some other equipment aboard. Surely an 'observer' looking out the window at the landscape below, would not qualify as an 'observing' crew member. It could conceivably be argued—however feebly—that Rogers was aboard as a special crew member; his function being to tie up, or release, the plane upon landings and departures, so Post could remain at the controls. No similar argument, however, could ever be advanced to warrant Mae Post's presence since she never flew on the plane when it was equipped with floats. Wiley Post had certainly violated restrictions and laws when he flew his wife and Will Rogers to New Mexico, Utah, Colorado, and back to Los Angeles earlier that summer of 1935. On that flight, as the plane was still equipped with wheels, no 'tie-up' or 'release' was needed. Post again breached the conditions of his restricted license when he flew Mae to Seattle.

Denis Mulligan's conclusion to Director Vidal read:

"The answer to the question asked in your memo is that when Post changed his plane from wheels to floats at Seattle, he should have requested an inspection, and an inspection would have been in order by one of our inspectors."

Washington realized that there had been a serious omission on Inspector Reed's part; however, he might rationalize that in awe of Wiley Post's accomplishments he would not have questioned Post's judgment as to the plane's airworthiness, if he, Reed, had taken the plane up; or, that the plane's authorized "experimental" purpose may perhaps have simply been to see whether this odd assemblage of unrelated parts could fly at all?

With Inspector James Reed's dereliction of duty firmly established—

according to the Inspector's Handbook of Instructions—Washington had found one likely culprit. It now went after another, who could possibly be made to share the blame—the inspector in Seattle.

> WESTERN UNION TELEGRAM DAY LETTER, PAID. WASHINGTON D.C. AU-GUST 30, 1935.
>
> W.S. MOORE, SCHOOL INSPECTOR, BOEING FIELD, SEATTLE, WASH. "AD-VISE WIRE WHETHER YOU INSPECTED INSTALLATION PONTOONS WILEY POST LOCKHEED NR ONE TWO TWO EIGHT THREE ALSO GIVE NUMBER LOCATION CAPACITY GAS TANKS STOP FORWARD AIRMAIL ALL INFOR-MATION COVERING ALTERATIONS MADE SUBJECT AIRCRAFT AT SEATTLE AND REPORT COVERING INSPECTION IF MADE.

But Inspector Moore was not to be reached. Western Union Tele-graph Company notified Washington that the telegram sent to W. D. (sic) Moore "is undelivered for the following reason: "ADDRESSEE LEFT CITY WILL RETURN SEPT. 3, SIGNED: SHUMATE."

Shumate, sitting in Seattle, had only to pick up the telephone to call suburban Renton, the location of Northwest Air Service, to get answers to the questions asked in the telegram. But Shumate did not do that. Instead he sent a telegram to Oakland, California:

> SUPERVISING AERONAUTICAL INSPECTOR, OAKLAND AIRPORT, OAKLAND CALIF FOLLOWING WIRE TO MOORE RETURNED UNDELIVERED STOP FORWARD TO HIM QUOTE ADVISE WIRE WHETHER YOU INSPECTED IN-STALLATION PONTOONS WILEY POSTS LOCKHEED NR ONE TWO TWO EIGHT THREE ALSO GIVE NUMBER LOCATION CAPACITY GAS TANKS IF KNOWN STOP FORWARD AIRMAIL ALL INFORMATION COVERING ALTER-ATIONS MADE SUBJECT AIRCRAFT AT SEATTLE AND REPORT COVERING INSPECTION IF MADE
>
> SIGNED SHUMATE

At Oakland, California, apparently, a Bureau of Air Commerce officer named Bedinger did show initiative. He evidently knew that Northwest Air Service in Renton was the only company in that part of the country that converted land planes to floatplanes and so had checked with the company and had come up with all the answers. He then notified his superiors:

CHIEF, GENERAL INSPECTION SERVICE, BUREAU OF AIR COMMERCE, WASH. DC, (COLLECT, DAYLETTER) RETEL MOORE ON SEVERAL DAYS LEAVE STOP NORTHWEST AIR SERVICES ADVISE QUOTE FOUR WING TANKS FIFTYSIX EACH ONE HEAD REST TANK SIXTEEN ONE PILOT SEAT TANK THIRTY WE INSTALLED PONTOONS AND RUDDERS REPAIRED GENERATOR AND STARTER MOTOR NO ALTERATIONS NO INSPECTION REPORT THROUGH HERE AND AM SURE MOORE MADE NO INSPECTION STOP WILL HAVE MOORE AIR MAIL FURTHER DETAILS IF ANY UPON HIS RETURN SEPTEMBER SECOND

SIGNED BEDINGER

The missing Inspector Moore, who had at first been unreachable by Western Union because he was supposedly away on leave until early September, suddenly reappeared. The Washington Bureau was informed on August 31 that the telegram addressed to W. S. Moore had been telephoned to him "OK." There is no indication where or how he had been reached, but he obviously received the message, for that very day, as instructed, he filed his written report:

August 31, 1935.

[Letter from William S. Moore, Boeing Field, Seattle, Washington;
    Aeronautical Inspector of the U.S. Department of Commerce, Bureau of Air Commerce;)

To Chief, General Inspection Service, Bureau of Air Commerce, Dept. of Commerce, Washington,

The following information is forwarded in accordance with your wire of August 30, and regarding Wiley Post's Lockheed NR 12283. There was no inspection made of the airplane after the installation of pontoons at Seattle.

The installation and other work on the airplane was completed the evening of August 5, and Mr. Post departed Renton airport at 9:20 a.m. August 6. All work done on the airplane while at Renton airport consisted of installation of Edo 5300 floats, rebuilding of generator, and installation of new starter motor, and was done by the Northwest Air Service Inc., approved repair station number 90. Floats, struts and water rudders were approved. Gas tanks installed in the airplane consisted of 4 wing tanks of 56 gallons capacity each installed 2 in each wing stub, 1-30 gallon tank installed under and to the rear of pilot's seat and 1-16 gallon tank installed in the headrest fairing behind the pilot's head on on (sic) outside of fuselage.

Respectfully,
sign. Wm.S.Moore

This letter was stamped as having been received in Washington, D.C., on September 4, 1935, 2:01 p.m. It should be noted first of all that despite repeated official licensing of a plane ostensibly capable of holding 260 gallons, the above capacity totals 270 gallons, the latter being correct.

Far more important is the apparent cover-up for the absence of an inspection. Questioned whether he had performed an inspection, Inspector Moore replied that the floats attachment had been completed in the evening of August 5, and that Post left at "9:20 AM August 6." The implication, of course, is that Post and Rogers left town before he, Moore, had an opportunity to make the necessary inspection and that had the plane stayed longer, he, Moore, would surely have performed his duty. Moore's excuse seems to have satisfied the U.S. Department of Commerce.

The facts are that Northwest Air Service did indeed finish work on Post's plane on the evening of August 5, but the plane with Post and Rogers aboard did not leave Seattle until 9:15 a.m. on August 7, a full twenty-four hours later than the time misstated by Inspector Moore. Wiley took the plane up that August 6, but only for a test flight, and he invited two teenagers to join him because he needed "ballast." It was on that occasion that young Gordon Williams from nearby Clyde Hill, and his friend Bob McLarren, visiting from Los Angeles, had the ride of their lives. It was also on August 6 that Will Rogers played Polo at the Olympic Riding and Driving Club's new polo field. Newspaper articles and photographs exist to substantiate that date and game.

Perhaps, as the regulations read, Wiley Post was at fault. Maybe he should have requested a new local inspection; or should North-west Air Service, having made those alterations by replacing the wheels with pontoons, have applied for an inspection? It would seem not! As far as they were concerned, no inspection was needed, as any work performed by Northwest Air Service, a government-licensed, accredited station was considered officially accepted. So the request for an inspection for airworthiness, it would therefore seem, fell upon Wiley Post. Still, whoever should or should not have submitted the request, nagging questions remain: was the plane, once it had been equipped with floats, safe to be flown? Or was it, instead, less safe to be flown than it had been before the floats were attached? Was this plane ever safe enough to be flown? As the investigation progressed it became quite obvious that neither Inspector Reed in Glendale, nor Inspector Moore in Seattle, nor Director Vidal, nor his Bureau of Air Commerce proceeded by the book, nor indeed did any of them seem even to know the regulations in that book.

The Department now had two government inspectors guilty of failing to inspect the plane. A third inspector, Murray Hall, was about to join their ranks. Though not at all culpable on the charge of failing to inspect a plane, he would end up being the most censured of all. His would be the head that would roll.

Inspector Murray Hall was stationed in Anchorage, but mid-August 1935, found him in Fairbanks, which was part of his territory. The Bureau of Air Commerce had telegraphed instructions for him to go to Point Barrow and investigate all factors involved in the airplane accident that had killed Wiley Post and Will Rogers. Three days later, August 19, the Bureau of Air Commerce had still received no word from Hall. "Transportation is pretty slow up there," an official explained, "Hall has to travel by dog sled sometimes, or any other way he can. He has one land plane, but I doubt if he is using

it now.[2] Whoever the spokesman was, he revealed a singular ignorance of procedures and conditions in Alaska.

In fact, on August 17, Murray Hall did file the following account
of that day, much of it based on second- and third-hand information.
He also fabricated several details, which would haunt him in the days
to come:

JOE CROSSON AND RADIO OPERATOR GLEASON LEFT FAIRBANKS CHENA
SLOUGH AT ELEVEN FIFTEEN AM THE SIXTEENTH FOR POINT BARROW
STOP THE AIRPLANE USED WAS FAIRCHILD-SEVENTY ONE WITH FUEL
TANK CAPACITY OF ONE HUNDRED FORTY EIGHT GALLONS STOP THE
PAY LOAD OF THIS AIRPLANE ON FLOATS IS APPROXIMATELY FOUR HUN-
DRED SIXTY POUNDS STOP BECAUSE OF WEATHER UNCERTAINTIES IT
WAS DESIRABLE TO LOAD THE AIRPLANE CABIN WITH FIVE GALLON
CANS OF GASOLINE TO THE LIMIT OF THE SHIPS PERFORMANCE STOP
THIS ALSO DESIRABLE BECAUSE NO INTERMEDIATE FUELING-POINTS EX-
IST STOP ABOUT TEN CASES OR ONE HUNDRED GALLONS OF FUEL WAS
IN THE SHIPS CABIN STOP WITH THIS LOAD THE SHIP WAS UNABLE TO
TAKE OFF THE WATER STOP TAKE OFF WAS MADE ON THE THIRD AT-
TEMPT AFTER THIRTY GALLONS OF GASOLINE HAD BEEN REMOVED
FROM THE CABIN STOP I WAS PRESENT DURING THESE ATTEMPTS AND
INDICATED TO JOE THE DESIRE TO ACCOMPANY HIM STOP HE SAID TO
ME THAT HE WOULD BE GLAD TO TAKE ME BUT DID NOT KNOW
WHETHER HE COULD GET OFF WITH THE LOAD ALREADY ON BOARD
STOP IN VIEW OF THE NECESSITY OF CARRYING EXTRA FUEL FOR HIS
OWN SAFETY AND THE FACT THAT THE RETURN TRIP WOULD HAVE TO
BE MADE WITH THE ADDITIONAL WEIGHT OF THE BODIES AND EFFECTS
OF THE UNFORTUNATE MEN IT DID NOT APPEAR THAT GOOD JUDG-
MENT WOULD PERMIT ME TO ACCOMPANY HIM STOP IT WAS THEN
THAT I HAD PREPARED NS NINE FOR THE FLIGHT WHICH I PLANNED TO
MAKE BY WAY OF KOTZBUE (SIC) AND WAINWRIGHT STOP ALSO AR-
RANGED WITH JOE CROSSON TO OBTAIN ALL POSSIBLE INFORMATION
FOR ME AND SUPPLIED HIM WITH AB EIGHTY SEVEN (ACCIDENT REPORT
FORM—ED.) WHICH REPORT HE RETURNED TO ME AND HAS BEEN
MAILED YOUR OFFICE STOP BY GOING TO BARROW WITH JOE I DO NOT
BELIEVE ANY ADDITIONAL KNOWLEDGE COULD HAVE BEEN OBTAINED

[2]*Los Angeles Times*, August 19, 1935, dateline: Washington, D.C.

AS ONLY ONE PERSON A NATIVE ACTUALLY SAW THE ACCIDENT AND
JOE DID NOT TAKE TIME TO GO TO THE SCENE OF THE ACCIDENT SINCE
THE BODIES WERE REMOVED TO POINTBARROW (SIC)

The inaccuracies in Hall's report are glaring. How an Inspector of the Bureau of Air Commerce could have made some of these statements and expected not to be challenged, cannot be explained. As a Fairchild 71 is a seven-place airplane designed to accommodate the pilot and six passengers, how could an experienced inspector claim that "THE PAY LOAD OF THIS AIRPLANE ON FLOATS IS AP-PROXIMATELY FOUR HUNDRED SIXTY POUNDS?" Plainly seven people would weigh more than a total of 460 pounds, or 65.7 pounds each. Specifications state that as a landplane, the Fairchild 71 was allowed a maximum payload of 1500 pounds, but equipped with pontoons, as this plane was, the payload was cut back to 1160 pounds.[3]

Errors in mathematics are evident, too, in Inspector Hall's claim that Crosson had the cabin filled "WITH FIVE GALLON CANS OF GASOLINE TO THE LIMIT OF THE SHIPS PERFORMANCE STOP . . . ABOUT TEN CASES OR ONE HUNDRED GALLONS OF FUEL WAS IN THE SHIPS CABIN." Of course, ten cases of 5 gallons each would be a total of only 50 gallons. Since each U.S. gallon of gasoline weighs 6 pounds, the payload was only 300 pounds. But assuming that Crosson had carried 100 gallons, as Hall's faulty multiplication claimed, that would have weighed 600 pounds, far in excess of the limits asserted by the inspector. In actuality, the plane carried neither 100 gallons, nor 50 gallons.

Inspector Hall also stated: "TAKE OFF WAS MADE ON THE THIRD ATTEMPT AFTER THIRTY GALLONS OF GASOLINE HAD BEEN REMOVED FROM THE CABIN STOP I WAS PRES-ENT DURING THESE ATTEMPTS. . . ." Robert J. Gleason, who was aboard the flight, remembers no difficulties with the takeoff: "As I recall, we had twelve five-gallon cans of Red Crown gasoline, 60 gallons." There would thus be no reason in the world for Crosson to experience difficulties taking off from Chena Slough. Furthermore, the weather was perfect. Also, with the plane way below cargo limit,

---

[3]Juptner, U.S. Civil Aircraft, Vol. I, p. 223.

there was enough weight allowance and space available to accommodate Murray Hall, had he seriously wished to fly to Barrow. Events will show that he was not too anxious to leave Fairbanks, especially on a day when even birds on the North Slope walked.

On August 17, Murray Hall sent a handwritten report that relayed in essence some of the same facts already transmitted:

Col. J. Carroll Cone Fairbanks
Asst. Director of Air Commerce August 17, 1935.
Washington, D.C.

Dear Sir:

Wiley Post took off from Harding Lake, forty miles from Fairbanks for Point Barrow between 1:30 and 2:30, August 15. The motor had been serviced by mechanics of Pacific Alaska Airways and everything was in apparent good working order except generator. Replacement was suggested but was declined by Wiley. The ship was partially fueled at sea-plane dock owned by P.A.A. and located in slough 2 miles from city of Fairbanks, and flown then to Harding Lake where the tanks were filled, making total of 260 (sic) gallons fuel. Since the slough at Fairbanks is narrow and winding, take offs with heavy loads are not generally possible and are not generally attempted, accounting for final fueling at Harding Lake where about 2 miles of good water is available.

Before departing from Harding Lake, it had been arranged that Point Barrow weather be obtained by phoning to Fairbanks from the lake. The weather was available at 1:30 p.m. but no phone call was made for it. The report was very poor and the exact report will be obtained and attached to this report. However Post and Rogers had previously decided that wheather (sic) it was poor or not they would proceed and land if desirable on some lake or river enroute, the weather being excellent in Fairbanks. Joe Crosson informed me that at Point Barrow the people informed him that the weather at the time of the accident was a approximately the same as it was when he arrived a day later, which was unlimited visibility solid overcast 4 or 5 hundred feet ceiling. Therefore it is certain that the weather was not a cause for the accident. Wiley having arrived at the Artic (sic) coast to the left of Point Barrow, and Barrow is easy to miss either way according to Joe Crosson, spotted a couple of huts on the Lagoon over which the accident happened, no doubt decided to land and inquire direction to Barrow. It is reported that landing was made and the shiped (sic) taxied to the beach in front of native huts and the motor stopped. One native, a fairly old man, was there and directed the fliers to their destination. The ship was turned around without delay, the motor started and take off made. Soon after take off, the native reported that the ship rose to heighth (sic) of 50 feet and was turning right when motor missed, the ship dived into water. The native then, I understand ran down the shore nearest plane and seeing that it was badly wrecked and resting in shallow water, 2 feet, ran to Point Barrow, 15 or 20 miles away and reported that an Airplane had blown up. A party was formed immediately and returned to scene extracted the bodies and personal equipment and returned to Point Barrow, where they were held until returned to Fairbanks by Pilot Joe Crosson of Pacific Alaska Airways, arriving at Fairbanks about 8 am August 17, 1935. Joe Crosson expects to leave Fairbanks tomorrow, Sunday morning August 18, 35. for Seattle in Lockheed Electra, transporting the bodies and effects. At Seattle he will be met by Douglas Airplane, which will proceed from there Joe Crosson reported to me that the ship must have been very nose heavy, for he had heard Wiley say so, and that he had heard Wiley direct Mr. Rogers to sit to the rear of Cabin and keep the heavy baggage to the rear especially when taking off and landing.

This factor may be the real reason that the ship went out of control, when motor missed, quit or stopped.

The ship would climb very fast and at a steep angle after leaving the water. A take off of this nature was made upon leaving the slough at Fairbanks for Harding Lake preliminary to departing for Barrow. The ship was equipped with a three ways constant speed, controllable propeller, Hamilton Standard and appeared large for size of ship. The engine, I understand was the latest type Wasp 550 horse power, geared. When I viewed the plane Monday of this week, everything appeared to be in excellent order and condition.

Attached is copy of weather report and telegram recieved (sic) by Local U.S. Weather Bureau. I am enclosing also the local papers.

Yours very truly.
(signed) Murray Hall, Inspector

Two reports by meteorologists were discovered during this investigation. One, dated August 18, was signed by R. L. Frost, Assistant Meteorologist. Whether this is the one mentioned by Murray Hall, cannot be established; the date would be right. A similar report was filed by G. L. Prucha, Assistant Meteorologist, but dated August 29, 1935, which date would make it too late to be the enclosure with Inspector Hall's handwritten report. R. L. Frost's report contains the now familiar weather data, but also offers some interesting additional information:

During the time Post was in Fairbanks he never came in contact with the Weather Bureau Officials or telephoned for weather information.

In fact the Weather Bureau Officials did not see either Post or Rogers. There seemed to have been considerable secrecy regarding Post's plans and all dealings with the Weather Bureau were made through the Pacific Alaska Airways, a subsidiary of the Pan American Airways.

Shortly after noon on the 14th the Pacific Alaska Airways requested information regarding the landing conditions at Point Barrow and also requested an Airway Weather reports for the following morning on the regular 10:00 a.m. radio schedule. It was not stated that this information was desired for Post and it was not known at the time that Post and Rogers intended to fly to Point Barrow. The information regarding the landing conditions at Point Barrow was received at the regular 2:00 a.m. Weather schedule but the 10:00 Airway Weather report was not sent.

As a more favorable take off with a full load of gasoline could be made from Harding Lake the plane was flown from the Chena River to the lake on the morning of the 15th. People who witnessed the takeoff from the river stated that Post made a very steep and unnecessary climb after leaving the water and it is the general impression that this was his usual method of taking off. Harding Lake is located about 50 miles south of Fairbanks and due to the poor condition of the trail at least one hour and a half is required to drive the distance in an auto. There is a telephone at the lake and communication with Fairbanks is possible at all times. However it is not possible to telephone to the lake from town as the telephone office cannot ring the telephone there. At 1:30 p.m. the following report was received from Point Barrow; "BARROW ONE THIRTY PM DENSE FOG ZERO ZERO FORTY FIVE SOUTH NINE."

This report was promptly telephoned to the Pacific Alaska Airways hangar and the officials there said they would try to deliver it to Post. Apparently no effort was made to telephone in from the lake for the report, and Post took off before it could reach him by auto. Pilot Joe Crosson is Chief Pilot for the Pacific Alaska Airways. He is a veteran Alaskan pilot and has made many trips from Fairbanks to Point Barrow. No one knows this country better than Crosson. Post disregarded this advice and made known that he would land on some lake if he could not get through to Barrow. Before reaching Point Barrow the plane evidently ran into low clouds and fog as Eskimos reported having heard the motor but were not able to see the ship. At Walakpi, an Eskimo settlement fifteen miles south of Barrow the plane landed in shallow water. Post waded ashore in rubber boots and inquired the way to Point Barrow, from the Eskimos. Upon receiving the information he went back to the plane and took off. The water was only two deep (sic) and the pontoons plowed trenches in the muddy bottom. There is some question as to what occurred after the take off as the Eskimos have evidently told several versions of the accident. It is said that after leaving the water the plane rose "in a very steep climb". The motor stopped and the plane came down and landed up-side-down. It is also said that after leaving the water the plane banked sharply to the right at an elevation of fifty or sixty feet.

The motor stalled and as the plane came down the right wing and pontoons struck the water. The country in the vicinity is reported to be very low and flat. It is difficult to understand why the pilot found it necessary to rise in an unusually steep climb or to make a sharp bank to the right. There were no obstructions to be avoided.

The weather at Point Barrow at the time of the crash was reported as: 1000 OVC 10 42 SW 13" This reads: Ceiling 1,000 feet, Overcast, visibility 10 miles, Temperature 42 degrees, Wind Southwest, 13 miles per hour.

Eskimos report practically the same conditions at the place of the accident. Pilot Crosson was at Barrow the next day and was told that the weather then was about the same as the previous day. He reported; 300 OVC UNL" [good visibility beneath a heavy layer of clouds] Ceiling 300 feet, Overcast, Visibility Un-limited.

"It would seem that the crash was due solely to motor failure, the state of the weather being only a minor contributing factor. Before leaving Fairbanks, Post was advised by the mechanics that serviced the plane, that the generator needed adjusting. This ad-vice was not followed. There is also a possibility that the motor might have cooled off after the plane landed. The temperature was around 40 and a 13 mph wind was reported at Point Bar-row. The sea between here and Barrow contained considerable ice. It would seem that Post took unnecessary chances in at-tempting this flight, particularly so when considering the fact that he was not familiar with the country. Pilots with years of flying experience in Alaska would not think of making a flight from Fairbanks to Point Barrow with no weather reports and Post was advised against it by the best pilot in the Territory.

Respectfully
(signed) R. L. FrostAsst. Meteorologist.

This report, which far exceeds the limits of a meteorological sum-mary, provided the Bureau of Air Commerce with significant facts and data that it failed to use in the official statement prepared on August 30, 1935.

Perhaps the Bureau of Air Commerce in Washington was too busy laying the foundation of its case against Inspector Murray Hall to concern itself with Frost's investigation. No less an official than J. Carroll Cone, Assistant Director of Air Commerce (Air Regulations), prepared the memorandum that was sent to Colonel J. Monroe Johnson, Assistant Secretary of Commerce. It was not intended to become public knowledge, but merely to prepare an excuse for not divulging all that was known. The Bureau could not come forward and say, for example, that the cause of the accident was the fact that the plane was not airworthy and that Inspector Reed had disregarded his duty by not flying in it before issuing it a license. Nor could the Bureau blame Inspector Moore for not testing the float-equipped plane for airworthiness. The last thing the Bureau of Air Commerce could do was implicate itself through its inspectors in any part of the blame. On the other hand, shifting all the blame to Wiley Post would have seemed a cowardly thing to do, as the man was dead and could not defend himself. Besides, the Department of Commerce would not blemish the name of a national hero, and how would it have looked to the millions of Will Rogers fans, had the Bureau admitted that a trusting Will Rogers had been killed because both government and a national hero had dodged their full obligations?

The simplest solution was to blame some inanimate object, like an engine, or attribute the crash to carburetor icing, and claim that further investigations could not be carried on because Inspector Murray Hall failed to go to Barrow when ordered. This was exactly the kind of solution bureaucrats loved—a nice, tight case of CYA, bureaucracy's famous acronym for "Cover Your Ass." With Inspector Hall way north in far away Alaska, who would hear his cries of 'FOUL!' if the Bureau shrouded him in blame? Who would care that he in fact had no reason whatever to inspect Wiley's plane, nor could he have tested it if he had wanted to. He simply happened to be in Fairbanks at the same time as Will Rogers and Wiley Post. There is nothing he was supposed to be doing, nor anything he could have done to prevent Post from taking off. The only serious matter against him was the fact that he did not fly to Barrow with Joe Crosson and Bob Gleason, and that he had fabricated apparently invalid excuses. He was the perfect fall guy. But first it was necessary to get Hall to stick his head in the noose:

Mr. Murray Hall,   August 27, 1935.
Supervising Aeronautical Inspector,
Bureau of Air Commerce,
Anchorage, Alaska.

Dear Murray:

I am enclosing copy of a letter I have written to Crosson, which is self-explanatory to a certain extent.

There have been several slightly conflicting statements made to various officials as to what actually happened in connection with Crosson's flight to Point Barrow and the reasons why you did not accompany him, and in order that the matter may be completely cleared up once and for all, I think it would be beneficial to all parties concerned to have a first-hand statement from Crosson, which statement I am sure will eliminate any vestige of doubt as to the proper functioning of the Regulation Division, particularly your own activities.

I understand, among other things, that Crosson has stated that he invited you to go with him to Point Barrow but at the same time advised you that you would have to arrange for some other transportation on your return trip.

We in the Regulation Division are fully satisfied that we know the reasons for the accident and that a trip on your part to the scene of the accident would not have developed any new information.

We feel that the accident was caused primarily by motor failure while the ship was in a steep climb, which resulted in the stalling condition of the aircraft. We have rather complete information as to the flying characteristics of the aircraft.

Of course the reason for the unusual interest on the part of the officials of the Department of Commerce in this accident is occasioned by the prominence of the pilot and passenger.

                Kindest personal regards.
                Sincerely yours,
                J. Carroll Cone,
                Assistant Director of Air Commerce (Air Regulations).

The following letter on official stationery addressed one of those "resons for the accident:

DEPARTMENT OF COMMERCE BUREAU OF AIR COMMERCE WASHINGTON D.C.

August 31, 1935.

Memorandum to the Director:
    Subject: Balance data on Post's Lockheed Seaplane
    1. Pursuant to your request of yesterday, I have obtained information from the Lockheed Company through our Western Office, which indicates that the center of gravity of Post's Special Lockheed as a landplane was approximately 4°, or 5% of the mean aerodynamic chord of the wing, further forward than the same airplane as approved before alterations.
    2. Drawings of the seaplane float installation, for which we do not have definite weight specifications, indicate that the change-over from land gear moved the center of gravity forward still further.
    3. The much higher drag of the pontoons, acting below the center of gravity, induces a considerable diving moment which is the equivalent of a still further forward movement of the center of gravity.
    4. It can reasonably be concluded that the balance of the seaplane was such that, in the event of loss of propeller blast over the tail due to engine failure, an uncontrolled dive would ensue, from which recovery could not be expected under an altitude of 300 to 400 feet.

(signed) L. V. Kerber
Chief, Manufacturing Inspection Service.

Obviously, the important facts in the memorandum were not known on August 30, when Eugene Vidal submitted his statement to Secretary of Commerce Roper. Secretary Roper may have approved the release to the press of the Eugene Vidal account, but men in and out of the department knew that it was far too incomplete and that it contained too many errors.

In Fairbanks, Jim Hutchison shook his head. Jim, a savvy, experienced mechanic, wise to ways of the north, had had a good chance to study Wiley's plane. "I didn't think much of it. I don't think anyone else did, either. Wooden airplane, low wing, had Fairchild 71 floats on it—I don't know—the thing was built up from different models, big prop—big three-bladed propeller—but the engine is the thing that worried me on account of the size of the thing, great big cowling and he couldn't see too good over it . . . I looked at that airplane sitting out there and I could tell that it looked funnier than the Dickens . . . I don't think I would have flown in that plane, I didn't like the looks of it. . . . We do know what happened—I do in my own mind. When he took off from this lagoon, he had flown all the way from here, I bet you he was short of gas—not too short, but when he took off he made this steep climb and bank and he tips his wing up, there was no gas in this tank on the upper side of the wing, or anyway near dry . . . when he banked like that—even though the lower tanks may have a lot of gas, if that wasn't enough to get into the outlet and fill the pump, you know, the pump sucked air, it only took one instant and the engine quit."[4] Jim Hutchison paused; he usually didn't talk this much, but he had given this matter a lot of thought. "If he would have listened to old Crosson, he would be alive today, too. Crosson would have taken him up there with his own—one of the Pan American airplanes . . . in a Fairchild 71 on floats . . . Sure Crosson wanted to, he tried every which way to talk him out of taking that thing up there. . . ."

Jim had mentioned a most important point, though he had not realized it. Indeed, he had probably come up with the only correct reason for the crash, but had failed to make his point stronger. For the major part of his flying career, Wiley Post had piloted Vegas, high-wing planes that supplied fuel to the carburetor via gravity feed. The tanks were in the wing above the engine and the fuel flowed downward into the carburetor. On his hybrid 'bastard', which was a low-wing plane, fuel had to be pumped via suction from the tanks in the wings below the fuselage up to the carburetor. Most pilots

---

[4]Sterlings' interview with Jim Hutchison, Fairbanks, Alaska, July 22, 1986.

flying a low-wing plane would try to keep one tank strictly for take-offs, then switch to another one; that way, with the plane in an inclined position when taking off, the fuel intake line would always be in a full tank, rather than in one that could be near empty. Wiley was not used to low-wing planes and their idiosyncrasies. The takeoff at Walakpa lagoon was the only one on which Post had taken off when all the tanks had not just been filled. When Post left from Chena Slough to fly to Harding Lake, the tanks were quite full, although they had not been topped; but when Post took off from Walakpa lagoon, he was—most likely—on the same tank he had used when landing, and no one will ever know how much—or rather how little—fuel there was left in that tank. Not even Wiley would have known, for he had no fuel gauges on five of his six tanks. Nor did the plane have a warning system to alert the pilot that fuel in the tank was too low for a steep ascent. With Wiley's habit of draining each last drop of fuel from a tank before switching to a fresh one, it is reasonable to assume that he followed that same pattern on this flight, too. With the plane cllimbing steeply, as was reported by eye-witnesses, and banking to the right, all six tanks would be in a tipped position. The residue of fuel in each tank would seek the lowest point and it is not only likely, but almost definite that the fuel pump sucked air—instead of fuel—into the carburetor and caused the engine to stall. The conclusion of the Bureau of Air Commerce never considered human error. It should have.

Warren Tilman, too, had worked on Wiley's plane and had inspected it closely. Tilman asked Wiley how he rated the strange-looking aircraft, and the round-the-world traveler admitted: "Screwiest damn plane I ever flew." Tilman would never forget Post's words, and no amount of money could have induced him to fly in that plane.[5] Although both Hutchison and Tilman had worked closely on the plane, nobody from Washington came to Alaska to interview either man—not even the government's inspector, Murray Hall, who was in Fairbanks at the time and had been ordered to investigate the crash.

Roscoe Turner, one of America's foremost fliers, shared Jim Hutchison's reasoning behind the crash. "Roscoe Turner tells me he

[5]Sterlings' interview with Warren Tilman, July 21, 1986

is convinced the accident was due to using a fuel-feed from an almost empty tank. This would easily account for the engine stopping just after takeoff.[6]

In a copyrighted story from Seattle, Universal Service[7] quoted the dean of Alaskan fliers, Noel Wien. Like so many men thoroughly familiar with the north country, he did not even consider carburetor icing, but blamed "Impossible weather and fuel supply failure" as the probable causes of the crash.

> Noel Wien declared that it was his belief that Post emptied one of the gasoline tanks of his monoplane, and then failed to switch to the other. He said Post probably had no warning of the fuel shortage until he attempted to bank sharply when only a few feet above the lagoon in which he and Rogers had landed to ask the way to Point Barrow . . .
>
> A climbing turn, such as Post tried to make, according to the descriptions of native witnesses to the tragedy, would have put the entire strain of carrying the plane on the motor, then, if the motor failed, it would be too bad—as it was.

The United States Senate sat in safe, sweltering Washington, D.C. and no senator felt inclined to launch a dangerous investigating junket to . . . to . . . what was the name of that out-of-the-way place? Oh, yes, Barrow, Alaska. Let somebody else do the investigating. Didn't the Air Commerce Bureau order its investigator stationed up there to investigate? Wasn't that what we paid those boys for?

Of course, the senate investigating committee did not know that Inspector Hall had already filed a hearsay report. He, like the senators, had not been too anxious to take the perilous trip. Vidal had relied on Joe Crosson's first-hand knowledge of what took place in Juneau and Fairbanks and of what Post had told him. As to the crash itself, everybody relied on someone else's hearsay and rumors, for no one had reliable information.

Reliable as Joe Crosson was on many matters, he himself had not investigated the wreck. He had not even seen it from the air. Yet it

---

[6]From *Challenge to the Poles* by John Grierson, © 1964, Foulis & Co., London.
[7]August 18, 1935.

was his account that had most heavily influenced Eugene Vidal's report. And then, there had been Inspector Salzman's letter. It was typed on official Department of Commerce stationery, Office headquarters, Sixth Inspection District, Kansas City Airport, K.C. Missouri.

August 23, 1935.

WILEY POST-WILL ROGERS ACCIDENT, PT. BARROWS (sic) ALASKA.

Chief, Airline Inspection Service,
Bureau of Air Commerce
Department of Commerce
Washington, D. C.

Dear Sir:

Flying from Chicago to Kansas City yesterday, I was a fellow passenger with Mr. Joe Crosson, whom I have known for many years. During our conversation he told me of his trip to Point Barrows (sic) and what he found on his arrival, and I would like to submit a summary of his conversation, which is as follows:

The aircraft was a Lockheed Orion equipped with a Wasp S1H1 engine and a three (3) blade controllable propeller. This plane, according to Mr. Post, was so nose heavy that he had to load everything possible in the rear of the cabin and after the pontoons were installed it was still more nose heavy, and Mr. Rogers was required to sit on the baggage in the back of the cabin. On the flight to Fairbanks, Mr. Rogers had moved some of the baggage forward in the cabin to make himself more comfortable, and Mr. Post had requested him to refrain from doing this as it made the airplane very nose heavy.

Mr. Crosson said he had no idea what caused the engine to quit, but that he was inclined to suspect ice in the carburetor, as the temperature at the time of the accident was about 38 degrees F. He did not, however, have any idea what the dew point was. From all indications, the airplane had gone in on it's (sic) nose, and then over on it's (sic) back. The wing, which was nearly torn from the fuselage, was broken off on one side. He said that he believed had Post been flying a Vega and not an Orion seaplane, with which he was not too familiar, he would have gotten away with it and would have made a safe landing.

Post had requested Crosson to fly the airplane, as he did not like the characteristics, and Crosson said he wished he had done so as he probably would know more about what happened.

Post and Rogers had flown through the fog and storm and landed on a lagoon near Point Barrows (sic) to ask some Eskimos their direction.

They were on the ground about twelve (12) minutes. When they took off the weather was clear and no fog existed. The Eskimos said that the engine quit and the ship made a slight turn and dove into the water. Crosson said he believed that Post was making a climbing turn and that it was impossible for him to hold the nose up with the power off.

Mr. Crosson said that the engine had gone through the cockpit and into the cabin, and that he did not make any attempt to check the gas valves or switches because the wreckage of the cockpit was such that he doubted if anything could have been learned from such an inspection.

This information represents Mr. Crosson's personal opinion of what happened and is not an official statement from him, however, it is submitted for whatever good may come from it.

Very truly yours,
(signed) Phil C. Salzman,
Airline Maintenance Inspector.

This statement by Joe Crosson, the only one apparently on record, supports the judgment made by men less close to Wiley than Crosson. Wiley and Joe talked as friends and fellow pilots. They would freely exchange the straightforward facts. With Joe, Wiley had no reason to cover up the shortcomings of his plane, nor did he have to exaggerate. Therefore, when Joe Crosson disclosed to Inspector Salzman that Wiley Post did "not like its characteristics" we have a confirmation of Wiley's reported statement to Warren Tilman "Screwiest damn plane I ever flew." When Crosson offered the opinion that

Wiley would "have gotten away with it" if he had been flying a Vega and not an Orion seaplane, "with which he was not too familiar," we have the opinion of an expert that Wiley was not adept at handling this type of plane—an opinion also widely held throughout the flying community. After the accident Crosson had not only not attempted to check "the gas valves or switches," he had not even visited the accident site. All his knowledge as to what happened after Wiley and Will left Fairbanks, was, therefore, second-hand and hearsay.

The Department of Air Commerce was relegated to fending for itself as best it could. It would have to render a decision on an accident about which it knew relatively little. It could not declare once again that the cause for the crash was the fact that the plane hit the lagoon; it would have to satisfy 130 million Americans, and half the world. It would have to sound knowledgeable, sincere, logical, and authoritative without injuring anyone's reputation. It seemed an almost impossible task.

It was perhaps the easiest and most diplomatic way out for all concerned to lay the cause in carburetor icing. It had a certain ring of logic that could not be entirely refuted nor disproved. Nor would a little hint that the engine had stalled hurt—that is, it would not hurt the Department, though it could do enormous damage to Pratt & Whitney, the manufacturers of the engine. Still, it is always convenient and not uncommon to claim engine malfunction. After all, did not the engine stop in mid-air? It could have stalled for a number of other reasons, however. There could have been an aerodynamic stall, caused by too steep an angle of climb on Post's part; or the stall could have been due to Post's sharp right turn and the intake pipe sucking air instead of fuel into the carburetor. Then, too, tiny ice particles could have blocked the finely adjusted needle valves and caused the engine to stall. None of these occurrences could be even remotely considered a malfunction of the engine. But because of this initial blame on a carburetor blockage—which in most minds translated into a fault of the Pratt & Whitney engine, the company kept very quiet. An internal memorandum, dated August 28, 1935 and signed by H. M. Horner, Pratt & Whitney's Assistant Corporate Secretary, later Chairman of the Board, suggests that "this engine be

written off immediately. It is now in the consignment account at
$3500." The following day, a response to this memo signed D. L.
Brown, President of Pratt & Whitney, agrees and suggests: "Personally, I feel that we should drop the matter and write the engine off
in our year-end adjustment." Even though Pratt & Whitney felt quite
certain that its engine was not responsible for the crash, the company
believed that it was cheaper to write the engine off as a total loss,
than to invite additional adverse publicity by arguing the finding in
public. Efforts to recover the engine would surely make new headlines. Only immeasurable harm could come from being closely associated with an engine tied to the number one tragedy in the
country.

Matters soon became known, however, that began to shed a different light on the crash. In New York, Wiley's 'flying acquaintances'
offered an entirely new image:

> ... he [Post] was flying a type of craft with which he was almost
> wholly unfamiliar when he and Will Rogers crashed in Alaska.
> It was a hybrid machine, pieced together under Post's direction
> from the parts of several airplanes, but his flying acquaintances
> in New York attached far less significance to this than to the fact
> that it was a seaplane equipped with heavy pontoons rather than
> the light wheels to which Post was accustomed.
>
> No pilot in New York who knew the globe-girdling flyer in-
> timately could recall that he ever had flown a marine type plane,
> other than a casual local trip, until he started this vacation flight
> to Siberia. The ship was transferred from wheels to pontoons at
> Seattle and veteran seaplane pilots said that the unaccustomed
> bulk of these floats might be disastrous even to a pilot of Post's
> ability, if he found himself in a sudden jam.[8]

This article caused quite a flurry since for the first time it cast some
guilt on America's hero, Wiley Post. But Wiley himself had contributed to the opinion expressed by the fliers. "I don't know much
about Alaska," Post had been quoted as saying, "I haven't had much

---

[8]*New York Herald Tribune*, August 17, 1935, p. 5

experience flying planes with pontoons. I wonder how it's going to work out."[9]

This beginning of open doubt in Wiley Post's hitherto unquestioned mastery of the air caused a change of heart at Pratt & Whitney. No longer did the company want to be disassociated from any involvement with the crash; it now considered reclaiming the engine—a plan that may have been triggered by another developing news item. For newspapers were reporting that Sergeant Stanley R. Morgan had answered an inquiry about the salvage of Wiley Post's plane:

> I believe salvage with crew of 15 or 20 men, loaded on small boats and brought to Barrow would cost approximately $500 to hire men and boats. I doubt if pontoons and other small parts worth salvage unless for particular purpose other than repair. Last few days strong onshore wind brought in loose scattered ice but no large fields pack ice yet in sight. General weather conditions are foggy with freezing temperatures during night.[10]

Before action was taken by any Washington agency, Charles Brower, as the Commissioner in charge, took it upon himself to send "twenty-five men with a couple of lighters and a launch to try and save what was left of the wrecked plane." Winter was coming fast, and with it he expected serious damage to any part of the plane immersed in water. It turned out to be a two-day job. Lashed to two whale boats, pontoon-like, and towed by the motor boat, the men brought back what was left of the fuselage, the engine and propeller. Brower stashed the fuselage out in the open where the early snow soon spread a blanket over it. He took the engine and the propeller into his warehouse. Then, on September 9, 1935, he wired Pratt & Whitney:

ON ACCOUNT OF WEATHER CONDITIONS WITHOUT AUTHORITY HAVE
SALVAGED ENGINE AND BROUGHT SAME TO BARROW STOP. . . .

---

[9]*Seattle Post-Intelligencer*, August 17, 1935
[10]*Washington Post*, United Press, August 19, 1935

Brower suggested that if Pratt & Whitney were interested, he would clean and inspect the engine for a small additional charge. Pratt & Whitney ordered him to go ahead. Three weeks later, September 30, 1935, Charles D. Brower wrote:

> "At your request I have taken to pieces and cleaned your engine. Reassembled the same and crated it for shipment the coming summer. I found that the main part of the engine was allmost (sic) perfect in its working parts. The engine had evidently stoped (sic) dead before the crash as the principal parts were in perfect working order after cleaning. allthough (sic) every place in the inside was full of sand even the cylinders and timing gear were full. but (sic) after cleansing and oiling they worked perfectly.
>
> Of Course (sic) all the outside parts were smashed beyoud (sic) repair. (sic) and the Alloy parts that had been under water so long were all eaten away and turned to a grey clay which rapidly dissolved in gasolene (sic) . . . [11]

It was of course perfectly normal for crankcases made of magnesium alloy to corrode when immersed for a time in salt water. In late December when newspapers carried Brower's surprising deduction: "Charles D. Brower, veteran of half a century as an Arctic trader, whaler and trapper, said today the motor of the Wiley Post—Will Rogers plane stored in his warehouse here is in perfect condition despite the crash which cost the lives of the two fliers last August. Brower's knowledge of gas engines is extensive."[12]

The engine may have been found to be in fine working order, but by that time the governmental investigations had long ended and the official conclusion had been published. Case closed! A lengthy telegraphic exchange ensued between Charles Brower and Pratt & Whitney about the return of the engine. Though a whole year would pass before the engine finally reached East Hartford, the company was glad to have the engine back. Charley Brower charged four hundred dollars for salvage; it was only forty dollars more than its cost.

At the factory, the engine was thoroughly checked and found to

---

[11]From United Technologies archive.
[12]*Los Angeles Times*, December 22, 1935, dateline: Barrow (Alaska) Dec. 21 (AP)

be in perfect working condition, just as Charley Brower had stated. Pratt & Whitney saw no reason not to use the engine in other aircraft. It was rebuilt and sent out. Nonetheless, a certain aura of failure clung to this engine. It was never installed in a contract-winning model.

On February 9, 1937, the engine went to Northrop in Inglewood, California, for use in the Gamma 2J, a plane that was entered as a demonstrator in the competition for the U.S. Army contract for basic and advanced trainers. Some ignition problems developed, along with installation mount complications in this particular aircraft, and the engine was returned to the plant sometime later that year.

On April 6, 1937, the engine went back out on consignment to Seversky Aircraft, Farmingdale, L.I., N.Y. for their XBC, Experimental Basic Combat trainer. Again the engine was used for demonstration purposes in competition for the U.S. Army trainer contract, which North American eventually won.

After the engine came back from Seversky, it was finally sold on December 21, 1938, to Compania de Aviacion Faucett, in Lima, Peru, for domestic flight use. As far as it is known, the engine that carried Wiley Post and Will Rogers to their deaths may still be in use today.[13]

The fuselage of the plane belonged to Mrs. Post, and Charles Brower notified her that he had it and asked her wishes for its disposition. Mae Post replied that she was most anxious to have the instrument panel returned. She needed the instruments to consummate the sale of the *Winnie Mae* to the Smithsonian Institution, which had required that the plane be restored to its exact condition at the time of the solo round-the-world flight in 1933. Without the completed instrument panel, the deal would have fallen through. The *Winnie Mae* today is on display at the Air and Space Museum of the Smithsonian Institution in Washington, D.C. By the time Brower received Mae Post's request, winter had come and closed Barrow to the outside world. The instruments did not leave until April 1936.

As far as the rest of the plane was concerned, Mae Post wanted it destroyed so that it could not be used by souvenir hunters or sellers. Her instructions came too late. Many of the Eskimos, including Clair

---

[13]Information gathered from United Technologies, August 20, 1985.

Okpeaha, had already made rings of some of the metal parts. Some of those were worn by the Eskimos themselves, but they sold many more to visitors and tourists in the Arctic spring. Tom Brower, in accordance with Mae Post's wishes, towed the rest of the plane out to sea and sank it, except for one of the pontoons, which looked so much like a kayak:

> . . . looking at it, it wasn't damaged. I used it—I took it out to the ranch. And I was going to use it for a little skiff, you know, towed behind the boat in case I had to come ashore, but we got in a storm and I lost it. One of the big lakes, you know, it went right down, never came out—I just cut the rope—it got swamped . . .[14]

Commissioner Brower kept two items from the plane for himself: the Lockheed trademark, and the official license number, both of which he cut from the tail section of the plane. Both now hang in Mattie's Cafe in Browerville, a section of Barrow, Alaska. Once called Brower's Cafe, it is owned today by Tom Brower's daughter and carries her name. Like all buildings on the North Slope, it stands on stilts above the permafrost, just a few feet from the edge of the Beaufort Sea, between the Brower home and Brower's Trading Post. If Post and Rogers had reached Barrow safely, they would have been guests at Charley Brower's home. Outside, they would have walked the gravel surfaces and no doubt stopped by the Trading Post to buy some staples and then drunk the strong, hot coffee while munching crispy, thin Eskimo doughnuts at the Cafe. There is very little to add to the government's 'investigation.' The Bureau of Air Commerce received a number of inquiries from insurance companies and lawyers, their concerns almost identical. To settle insurance claims on the life of Will Rogers they all requested to know whether Wiley Post was a licensed pilot, and whether they could have abstracts of his and the plane's licenses.

The final official word about the accident came exactly two months after the crash. It appeared in the AIR COMMERCE BULLETIN, VOL.7, NO.4, OCTOBER 15, 1935, P.94:

---

[14]Sterllngs' Interview with Tom Brower, July 25, 1986

LOCKHEED ORION POST-ROGERS CRASH 1935 Seaplane Conv.

Statement of probable cause concerning an aircraft accident which occurred to a privately owned plane on August 15th, 1935, at Walakpi,(sic) Alaska.

On August 15, 1935, at about 6 P.M. at Walakpi, Alaska, about 15 miles south of Point Barrow, Alaska, an airplane, owned and piloted by Wiley Post and carrying Will Rogers, fell out of control while taking off, with resultant death to both men and the complete destruction of the aircraft.

The airplane, at the time of purchase by Mr. Post, was a Lockheed Orion, model 9E, and bore Dept. of Commerce license. Prior to the flight, however, the airplane was completely rebuilt and several major changes incorporated which changed it from the original model. The engine, propeller, wings and fuel tanks were changed entirely. This remodeling was inspected and approved for workmanship by the Dept. of Commerce and the remodeled airplane was issued Dept. of Commerce restricted license number NR-12283, which limited its use to long-distance and special test flights. The pilot, Wiley Post, held a Dept. of Commerce transport pilot's license.

At Seattle, Washington, pontoons were substituted for the wheel landing gear. No inspection of the airplane was requested after this change. Mr. Rogers joined the flight at this point. At Fairbanks, Alaska, the airplane was partially refueled and flown to Lake Harding, about 40 miles away, to be completely refueled for the Point Barrow flight.

The takeoff for Point Barrow was accomplished at some time between 1:30 and 2:30 P.M. When next heard of, the airplane had landed on a small lagoon about 15 miles south of Point Barrow where Mr. Post inquired the direction of Point Barrow. Having obtained this information, he proceeded to take off from the lagoon and when an altitude of about 50 feet had been reached, the engine was heard to stop and the airplane fell to the water out of control. Both occupants were killed instantly.

A study of the effect of the various changes made on the airplane indicated that it was decidedly nose-heavy and must have been extremely difficult, if not impossible, to properly control

without the aid of the engine. A statement made by the pilot
after the change to pontoons confirms this conclusion. The exact
cause of the engine failure cannot be determined. The temperature at the time was about 40° and the failure could have been
due to the engine having become cool while standing on the
lagoon or to ice or water condensate forming in the carburetor.
It is the opinion of the accident board that the probable cause
of this accident was loss of control of the aircraft at a low altitude after sudden engine failure, due to the extreme nose-
heaviness of the aircraft.

> Signed for the Accident Board,
> Jesse W. Lankford,
> Secretary

The findings were naive. Ten minutes on the water could not possibly have cooled the engine. And as for claiming that the "probable"
cause for the accident was "loss of control at a low altitude after
sudden engine failure, due to the extreme nose-heaviness of the aircraft," that is what stage magicians call "misdirection." The document introduces the words "ENGINE FAILURE," but no such
"failure" was ever proven. In fact, more assiduous inquiry and investigation have established just the opposite. Any engine will stop
if no fuel sustains it, but still the human failures of Inspectors Reed
and Moore and Post cannot be overlooked. Reed closed his eyes to
what must have been obvious to him; for if a mechanic can see nose-
heaviness from afar, would one not expect at least the same acuity
from an inspector who is close up? Inspector Moore resorted to dis-
torting facts to cover his negligence. Then, too, Wiley Post himself
deceived Inspector Reed and failed to request an examination of his
hybrid plane at Seattle. While it may have been excusable for Post
to stake his own life on a project and a dream, it was inexcusable
for him both to take Rogers's money and risk Will's life. It was, as
mechanics would say "an accident in waiting." This unbalanced aircraft was doomed from the moment it was conceived.

Jesse W. Lankford's report was the final word. It fulfilled bureaucratic expectations. No one was to blame, no one had erred, no one
had either by commission, or by omission, contributed to the acci-

dent. It was all conveniently blamed on carburetor icing, some tiny ice crystals which would in reality have immediately melted in the sun, and disappeared without a trace. Two men had died, and the government's men in their flawed wisdom had determined that it was no one's fault.

It was wise Will Rogers who really had seen it before:

> So you see you can't believe a thing you read in regard to official statements. The minute anything happens connected with official life, why it's just like a cold night, everybody is trying to cover up.[15]

---

[15]Will Rogers's weekly article, October 4, 1925.

ACKNOWLEDGMENTS

D URING THE PAST half century we have researched the lives
and deaths of Will Rogers and Wiley Post. We have interviewed the few principal players who could still share their recollec-
tions with us. We visited numerous depositories of information and
memorabilia. No single one knew the whole story, but each held vital
pieces of the huge jigsaw puzzle. Each was essential; each contributed
towards completing the entire picture. These pages were made possible only through their gifts to us.

We are grateful to them all for their memories and their information, but most of all, for their courteous willingness to share
them with us.

—Frances and Bryan Sterling

AUTHORS AND WRITERS:

Jim Bedford, Fairbanks, AK.
Jerry Belcher, Los Angeles Times, Los Angeles, CA.;
Ben Lucian Berman, ("Steamboat Round the Bend, 1935)
Homer Croy, ("They Had to See Paris", 1929; "Down to Earth", 1932;
"Our Will Rogers", 1953);
Jean Devlin, Editor, Oklahoma Today, Oklahoma City, Ok.;
Mollie Greist, ("Nursing Under the North Star," 1968);
Kay Kennedy, Fairbanks, AK.;
Paula McSpadden Love, Curator, Will Rogers Memorial, Claremore,
OK.;
Charles V. McAdam, McNaught Syndicate, Bal Harbour, FL.;

Tricia Olsen, features editor, News-Miner, Fairbanks, AK.;
Arthur Houston Post, author, Texas
Dr. Richard K. Smith, Washington, DC.;
Patricia Ziegfeld Stephenson, CA.;
Kent Sturgis, editor, News-Miner, Fairbanks, AK.;
Walt Woodward, radio and newspaper reporter, Juneau AK.;

AVIATION

Mr. and Mrs. Randy Accord, Air Museum, Fairbanks, AK.;
Richard Sanders Allen, foremost Lockheed authority, Idaho.;
Robert E. Ames, mechanic, Fairbanks, AK.;
Mrs. Charles H. Babb, Los Angeles, CA.;
Emerson Bassett, Shelton, WA.;
Alan Blum, Northwest Air Service, Seattle, WA.;
Ashley (Ash) Bridgham, Northwest Air Service, Renton, WA.;
Sid Brustin, pilot, Los Angeles, CA.;
Max Christman, mechanic, Mercer Island, WA.;
Lionel B. Clark, veteran master mechanic, E. Hartford, CT.;
Randall S. Crosby, Dir., Operations, Search & Rescue, Barrow, AK;
Lillian (Mrs. Joe) Crosson Frizell, Seattle, WA.;
Gen. James (Jimmy) Doolittle, Carmel, CA.;
John W. Dudley, wireless authority, Seattle, WA.;
Robert Ellis, pilot, author, Ketchikan, AK.;
Lt. Col. Robert J. Gleason, Communications Superintendent with Pacific
    Alaska Airways, Fairbanks, AK.;
Wes Gordeuk, United Technologies, E. Hartford, CT.;
Capt. John E. Grimmett, Tucson, AZ.;
Jesse Hendershot, United Technologies, E. Hartford, CT.;
Jim Hutchison, master mechanic, Fairbanks, AK.;
Lloyd Jarman, mechanic, author, Bellevue, WA.;
Dr. Nickolas Komons, FAA Historian, author, Washington, D.C.;
Harvey H. Lippincott, Corp. Archivist, United Technologies, (Pratt &
    Whitney), East Hartford, CT.;
Everett Long, Air museum, Fairbanks, AK.;
Dr. Anne Millbrooke, Corp. Archivist, United Technologies, AK.;
Dr. Stanley R. Mohler, Dayton, OH.;

Denis J. Mulligan, Investigator, FAA, Upper Montclair, NJ.;

Anne C. Rutledge, Archivist, Museum of Flight, Seattle, WA.;

Duncan Shand, pilot, Tacoma, WA.;

Ted M. Spencer, director, Alaskan Historical Aircraft Society, Anchorage, AK.;

Capt. Robert W. Stevens, pilot, author, Seattle, WA.;

Warren Tillman, mechanic, Fairbanks, AK.;

Orville Tosch, Tosch Aircraft Industries, Tacoma, WA.;

Fay Gillis Wells, veteran pilot, writer, reporter, VA.;

Frank Whaley, pilot, Valley Center, CA.;

Anne Whyte, Pan Am Airways, New York, NY.

N. Merrill Wien, pilot, Kent, WA.;

Gordon S. and Marcie Williams, aviation authorities, Bellevue, WA.;

PRIVATE AND PUBLIC CONTRIBUTORS:

Elvis Allen, historian, Fruitvale, TX.;

Jesse (Mrs. Karl) Anderson, Fairbanks, AK.;

Forbes Baker, Redmond, WA.;

Renee Blahuta, University of Alaska, Fairbanks, AK.;

Eileen Bowser, MOMA, NY.,

Lyman Brewster, Reindeer Superintendent, Nome, AK.;

Jeffrey Briley, Curator, State Museum of History, Oklahoma City, OK.,

Jane Brower, Barrow, AK.;

Thomas Brower, Barrow, AK.;

Joseph H. Carter, President, Will Rogers Heritage, Inc. Claremore, OK.,

Michelle Lefebvre Carter, Director, Will Rogers Memorial and Museum, Claremore, OK.,

Mable Cook, Historian, Van, Texas

Chester Cowen, Photographic Archivist, Oklahoma Historical Society, Oklahoma City, OK

Alma (Mrs. Peter) Despot, Medina, WA.;

William Dugovich, public relations, Seattle, WA.;

Robert H. Fowler, National Archives, Washington, DC.;

John M. Gerard, Seattle, WA.;

Thomas (Butch) Girvin, Barrow, AK.;

Dr. and Mrs. Elwood Greist, Livermore, CA.;

Carol Jordan, historian

Lynn Kitchens, Historian, Grand Salkine, TX

Robert W. Love, Manager, Will Rogers Memorial, Claremore, OK.;

Patricia Lowe, Librarian, Will Rogers Memorial and Museum, Claremore, OK.,

Gregory N. Malak, Curator, Will Rogers Memorial and Museum, Claremore, OK.,

Barrow and Donna Morgan, Nome, AK.;

Prof. Claus Naske, Univ of Alaska, Fairbanks, AK.;

R. Ann Ogle, Oklahoma Historical Society, Oklakoma City, OK.,

Rose Okpeaha Leavitt, Barrow, AK.;

Fred Okpeaha, Barrow, AK.;

Patrick Okpeaha, Barrow, AK.;

Robert Okpeaha, Barrow, AK

Earlene Paddock, Seattle, WA.;

Don and Donna Raymond, Pacific Palisades, CA.;

James B. Rogers, CA;

Mary Rogers, CA;

Will Rogers, Jr., AZ;

Gene Rogge, Fairbanks, AK.;

Emil and Trudy Sandmeier, Pacific Palisades, CA.;

Max and Dorothy Sherrod, Palmer, AK.;

Charles Silver, MOMA, NY.,

Inez Snell (Mrs. Don Gustafson), Fairbanks, AK.;

William Welge, Oklahoma Historical Society

Charles Banks Wilson, artist, historian

Charles L. Wilson, author

PUBLICATIONS, NEWS MEDIA

Alaskan Empire, Anchorage, AK.;

Anchorage Times, Anchorage, AK.;

Associated Press; New York, NY.;

Houston Chronicle, Houston, TX.;

Kansas City Star, Kansas City, KS.;

London Daily Mail, London, England;

London Times, London, England;

Los Angeles Chronicle, Los Angeles, CA.;
Los Angeles Examiner, Los Angeles, CA.;
Los Angeles Herald-Express, Los Angeles, CA.;
Los Angeles News, Los Angeles, CA.;
Los Angeles Times, Los Angeles, CA.;
News Miner, Fairbanks, AK.;
Newsweek, New York, NY.;
New York American, New York, NY.;
New York Evening Post, New York, NY.;
New York Herald Tribune, New York, NY.;
New York Journal, New York, NY.;
New York Mirror, New York, NY.;
New York News, New York, NY.;
New York Post, New York, NY.;
New York Sun, New York, NY.;
New York Times, New York, NY.;
New York World Telegram, New York, NY.;
Oklahoma Today, Oklahoma City, OK.;
Seattle Post-Intelligencer, Seattle, WA.;
Seattle Times, Seattle, WA.;
TIME, Inc., New York, NY.;
Tulsa World, Tulsa, OK.;
United Press, New York, NY.;
Washington Evening Star, Washington, D.C.;
Washington Herald, Washington, D.C.;
Washington Post, Washington, D.C.;

RESEARCH CENTERS

Alaska Historical Aircraft Society, Anchorage, AK.;
Federal Aviation Administration, Oklahoma City, OK.;
Federal Aviation Administration, (FAA), Washington, D.C.
George Eastman House, Rochester, NY.;
Grand Saline Historical Society, TX
Library of Congress, Washington, D.C.;
Library, Public, Los Angeles, CA
Library, Public, New York City, NY

Library, Public, Seattle, WA.;
Museum of Flight, Seattle, WA.;
Museum of History and Industry, Seattle, WA.;
Museum of Modern Art, New York, NY.;
National Air & Space Museum Library, Washington, D.C.;
National Archives, Washington, D.C.;
National Cowboy Hall of Fame and Western Heritage Center, Oklahoma
    City, OK.;
National Museum of American History, Washington, D.C.;
National Press Club, Washington, D.C.;
New York City Public Library, New York, NY.
New York State Public Records, New York, NY
Northridge University, Los Angeles, CA.;
Oklahoma Historical Society, Oklahoma City, OK.,
Smithsonian Institution Library, Washington, D.C.;
Toronto Public Libraries, Canada;
University of Alaska, Anchorage, AK.
University of Alaska, Fairbanks, AK.
University of California, Berkeley, CA.;
University of California, Los Angeles, CA.;
University of Michigan, Ann Arbor, MI.;
University of Southern California, Los Angeles, CA.;
University of Washington, Seattle, WA.;
Westminster Research Library, London, England;
Will Rogers Memorial and Museum, Claremore, OK.;
Will Rogers Ranch, Pacific Palisades, CA.;

Show Business:

Academy of Motion Picture Arts and Sciences, L.A., CA.;
American Film Institute, Washington, DC.,
American Film Institute, Los Angeles, CA.,
Lew Ayres, actor, ("State Fair", 1933);
Hermione Baddeley, actress, (Charles Cochran Revue, 1926);
Clarence Badger, director, ("Almost A Husband", 1919, "Jubilo", 1919;
    "Water, Water Everywhere", 1919; "The Strange Boarder", 1920;

"Jes' Call Me Jim", 1920; "Cupid, The Cowpuncher"; 1920; "Honest Hutch", 1920; "Guile Of Women", 1920; "Boys Will Be Boys", 1921; "An Unwilling Hero", 1921; "Doubling For Romeo", 1921; "A Poor Relation", 1921; "The Ropin' Fool", 1922; "Fruits Of Faith", 1922; "One Day in 365", 1922;"

British Film Institute, London, England;

Tom Brown, actor ("Judge Priest", 1934);

David Butler, director, ("A Connecticut Yankee", 1931; "Business And Pleasure", 1931; "Down To Earth", 1932; "Handy Andy", 1934; "Doubting Thomas", 1935);

Harry (Dobe) Carey, Jr. actor;

Olive Carey, actress;

Charles Collins, actor/dancer;

Dorothy Stone Collins, musical comedy star, ("Three Cheers" 1928/29;

Fifi D'Orsay, actress, ("They Had To See Paris", 1929; "Young As You Feel", 1931);

John Ford, director, ("Doctor Bull" 1933; "Judge Priest" 1934; "Steamboat Round the Bend" 1935);

Janet Gaynor, actress ("State Fair", 1933);

Ira Gershwin, lyricist;

Jetta Goudall, actress, "(Business And Pleasure", 1931);

Sterling Holloway, actor, ("Life Begins At Forty", 1935; "Doubting Thomas", 1935);

Rochelle, Hudson, actress, ("Doctor Bull", 1933; "Mr. Skitch", 1933; "Judge Priest", 1934; "Life Begins At Forty, 1935");

Maria Jeritza, opera star;

Henry King, director, ("Lightnin' " 1930; "State Fair," 1933);

Myrna Loy, actress, ("A Connecticut Yankee", 1931);

Joel McCrea, ("Lightnin' " 1930; "Business and Pleasure," 1931);

George Marshall, director, ("Life Begins At Forty", 1935; "In Old Kentucky", 1935);

Evelyn Venable Mohr, actress, ("David Harum" 1933; "The County Chairman", 1935);

Hal Mohr, director of photography, ("David Harum", 1933; "State Fair", 1933; "The County Chairman," 1935);

Irene Rich, actress ("Water, Water Everywhere", 1919; "The Strange Boarder" 1920;" Jes' Call Me Jim", 1920; "Boys Will Be Boys", 1921;

"The Ropin' Fool", 1922; "Fruits Of Faith", 1922; "They Had To See Paris", 1929; "So This Is London", 1930; "Down To Earth", 1932);

Hal E. Roach, Sr., producer/author; "Hustling Hank", 1923; "Two Wagons, Both Covered", 1923; "Jus' Passin' Through", 1923; "Uncensored Movies", 1923; "The Cake Eater", 1924; "The Cowboy Sheik", 1924; "Big Moments From Little Pictures", 1924; "High Brow Stuff", 1924; "Going To Congress", 1924; "Don't Park There", 1924; "Jubilo, Jr.", 1924; "Our Congressman", 1924; "A Truthful Liar", 1924; "Gee Whiz, Genevieve", 1924;

Anne Shoemaker, actress; ("Ah! Wilderness," 1934);

Twentieth Century Fox library, Los Angeles, CA.,

Peggy Wood, actress, singer, authoress, ("Almost A Husband", 1919; "Handy Andy', 1934);

Keenan Wynn, actor.

INDEX